PORTRAIT OF PRISCILLA

Marie K Dickens.

PORTRAIT OF PRISCILLA

A Biography Tracing the Ancestry, Life and Times of Miss Priscilla Hannah Johnston (1842–1912)

Marie K. Dickens

Book Guild Publishing
Sussex, England

First published in Great Britain in 2006 by
The Book Guild Ltd
Pavilion View
19 New Road
Brighton, BN1 1UF

Copyright © Marie K. Dickens 2006

The right of Marie K. Dickens to be identified as the author of
this work has been asserted by her in accordance with the
Copyright, Designs and Patents Act 1988.

All rights reserved. No part of this publication may be
reproduced, transmitted, or stored in a retrieval system, in any form or by
any means, without permission in writing from the publisher, nor be
otherwise circulated in any form of binding or cover other than that in which
it is published and without a similar condition being imposed on the
subsequent purchaser.

Typesetting in Garamond by
Keyboard Services, Luton, Bedfordshire

Printed in Great Britain by
Antony Rowe Ltd, Chippenham, Wiltshire

A catalogue record for this book is
available from the British Library

ISBN 1 84624 028 X

Contents

Acknowledgements ix
Illustrations and their Sources xiii
Introduction 1

Part 1 The Ancestry of Priscilla Hannah Johnston

1 The pedigree of Priscilla Hannah Johnston 11
2 Introducing 'Lame' Anna Gurney 14
3 Introducing Elizabeth Fry (née Gurney) 17
4 The Ancient de Gurneys and their Faith 21
5 The Fowell-Buxtons 25
6 The Gurney Children 31
7 Extracts from the Journals of her Grandmother, Hannah Gurney (1805–1808) 38
8 A Brief Portrait of T. Fowell Buxton (1807–1818) 44
9 An account of Priscilla Buxton's Early Childhood by her Mother (1808–1822) 46
10 From the Cradle to the grave an account of the 'Hampstead Catastrophe' (1820) 51
11 Extracts from Priscilla Buxton's Journals (1822–1834) 62
12 The 'Great Anti-Slavery Interest' 79
13 Introducing Mr Andrew Johnston MP 84

Part 2 The Johnstons. The Early Life and Times of Priscilla Hannah Johnston

14	The Events of the 1st August 1834 and Afterwards	91
15	Arrival and Early Family Life at Rennyhill, Anstruther (1834–1839)	94
16	Removal to Bank House, Halesworth, Suffolk (1839)	109
17	The First Years in the Life of 'Dearest Priscilla Hannah' (1842–1845)	114
18	A Grandchild's Early Recollections of Life at Northrepps	129
19	Her Mother's Failing Health (1848–1852)	138
20	A Grandchild's Further Recollections of Life at Northrepps	148
21	The Marriage of Euphemia 'Effie' Johnston to Miles MacInnes	155
22	Extracts from the Journals of Hannah Lady Buxton (1860–1862)	162
23	Her Father's Death (1862)	166
24	Extracts from the Diaries and Sketchbooks of Ellen Buxton (1862–1866)	170
25	Northrepps Through the Eyes of Priscilla Hannah: From her own Collection of Photographs and Paintings (c.1860s)	199
26	An End and a Beginning (1867–1872)	200

Part 3 The 'Unspeakable Turk' and the 'Angels of Mercy'

26	Introducing Paulina Irby and her Work	209
27	The Eastern Question	212
28	Priscilla Hannah, 'Angel of Mercy' (1872–1884)	216

Part 4 'Aunt Pris' of The Beeches, Rickerby Village, Carlisle (1885–1912)

29	Introduction	279
30	Introducing her Friends and Fellow Philanthropists Miss Amy Beevor and Miss Mary Ellen 'Polly' Creighton	300
31	The Origins of Some of Priscilla Hannah Johnston's Philanthropic Work in Carlisle	306
32	The Death of Miss Priscilla Hannah Johnston in 1912	341
33	The Opening of the Miss Johnston Memorial Watering Trough (1913)	349

Epilogue	355
Appendix	375
Select Bibliography	383
Notes	387
Index	397

Acknowledgements

Previous research has shown that the local historian cannot create his or her own data, but has to use what time and chance have allowed to survive. Filling in the gaps in the lives of people who lived in former times can be somewhat daunting and complex. I therefore have relied to a large extent on surviving material produced or preserved by others gone before.

All the information contained in this book has been collated with references (see 'Notes') and acknowledgements. Ultimately the copyrights belong to these original sources and every effort has been made to contact copyright holders, but in some cases this has not been possible owing to the great lapse of time, deaths of individuals and closure of publishers. However, I would be pleased to hear from anyone concerning these un-traced copyrights, so that the matter can be cleared up in the future.

One of the highlights of this project has been the opportunity of encountering so many people and meeting with such generosity of spirit in doing so.

I would like to express my gratitude to the family descendants of Miss Johnston who, by granting me access to, and allowing me to reproduce, family archive material, journals, portraits and sketches, have made this publication possible. They are Mrs E.J. MacInnes and her son Mr Miles MacInnes of Cumbria; Mrs Verily Anderson Paget, of Northrepps, Norfolk; Mrs Ellen R.C. Creighton, of Stanford-in-the-Vale, Gloucestershire, the grand-daughter of Ellen Buxton (Priscilla Hannah's cousin); Angela and Simon Kendall, of Liss, Hampshire, Angela being a direct descendant of Miss Johnston's grandparents; Mrs Anna Mary Devereux, of Kent and her brother Mr Robert Vale, of Denbigh, who are the great-great niece and nephew respectively of Miss Johnston's maternal grandparents.

Thanks are due to Mr Jim Addison from the 'Kingdom of Fife' for his research and help; to David Blyth and Hugh Hales, the present owners of Bank House, Halesworth, for allowing me to view the lovingly restored former home of the Johnstons.

I am greatly indebted to all the authors named in the bibliography, in particular to Verily Anderson Paget and Dorothy Anderson. As it was not in Miss Johnston's unassuming character to 'blow her own trumpet' she left no account of her life's works, except for her letters published in *The British Friend* and *The Friend*. Had these ladies not had the foresight to keep written accounts of their childhoods at Northrepps Hall, the people, places, events, and her works, which at the time were still within living memory, then a large proportion of Miss Johnston's life and works might have been lost to future generations and forgotten forever.

I must also thank Verily for showing me many of Priscilla Hannah's pretty watercolours and family photographs, and for taking me to visit Northrepps Hall; Mrs Ellen R.C. Creighton for inviting me into her home to view Ellen Buxton's unpublished diaries and sketches and Mrs Rachel Major for her permission to include these in this publication.

Thank you also to Dr Prue Barron, the great niece of Miss Mary Ellen 'Polly' Creighton, for allowing me to visit her Edinburgh home in order to photograph the 'Mourning Brooch' to the memory of Priscilla Hannah, which had belonged to her Great Aunt Polly.

Among the many others whose assistance has been invaluable in the preparation of this biography: Mrs Caroline Gurney and her son Simon of Northrepps Hall; Pamela Gurney of Northrepps; Miss Hannah Buxton of Lymington, Hampshire; Mrs Pauline M. Barclay, formerly of High Leigh House, Hoddeston; the staff of Public Services and the Humanities Reference Section of the British Library, London; the staff of the Norfolk & Norwich Millennium Library; the staff of 'Answers Direct', Chelmsford Library; Brenda Gower of the Suffolk Records Office, Lowestoft; Gary Thorn of the British Museum, London; Dennis Yardley, senior library and information officer of Newcastle City Library; The Library Cultural Services of Fife Council; Mrs Masry Prince of the Kilrenny and Anstruther Burgh Collection; Richard Harris, Archive Service Manager for Essex County Council; the Staff of the Essex Records Office; Jennifer Milligan of the Religious Society of Friends in Britain; Chris Reed, Records and Information Officer for the RSPCA, West Sussex; Luci Gosling, picture Library Manager of the *Illustrated London News*; Olivia Flaxman, Managing Editors Office, the *Daily Mail*, London; Sir Thomas Beevor of Hargham, Norwich and Anne Carter, *The Beevor Story*; Christopher Jakes, senior Librarian Local Studies, Cambridgeshire collection, Central Library and Mr Tudor Allen, Archivist, Central Library, Clements Road, Ilford, Essex; The National Portrait Gallery, St Martin's Place, London; Wordsworth

Editions Ltd; *Country Life* Magazine; The Victoria and Albert Museum, London; Mr David Hall, Deputy Librarian Cambridge University Library; Nina Mackay of Ditchling, East Sussex; Mr John K.H. Cook, of Heswall, Wirral, Merseyside; All Nations Christian College, Easneye, Ware, Hertfordshire; 'Collectors World of Eric St John Foti', Hermitage Hall, Downham Market, Norfolk; Michael and Sheila Gooch of Halesworth; Nerine and Tony Halton, Lincolnshire.

Thanks are also due to those who have provided assistance in my home city of Carlisle, where Miss Johnston resided for the last twenty-seven years of her life: the staff of Cumbria Heritage Services, Alma House, Carlisle Castle; Stephen White and the staff of Carlisle Library, The Lanes; Mr Chris Robinson, Chairman and Managing Director of Charles Thurnam & Sons, Lonsdale Street; Mr John Martin of NorWest Books (UK), Nelson Street; Denis Perriam, local historian; Mr William McCrone, Family History Department, The Church of the Latterday Saints, Lanrigg Road; the staff of Dalston Road Cemetery Bereavement Services/Records; the staff, Cumberland Infirmary Education Department Library/Records; Mr Paul Wiggins, Head of Information Management & Technology, Cumberland Infirmary; Heather MacLean, Director of The Animal Refuge, Wetheral Shields; Mr J.P. Templeton; local historical photograph collector; Dr W.P. Honeyman; Mrs A.M. Armstrong, Hon. Branch Secretary, RSPCA, Cumbria North and East Branch; The Religious Society of Friends, Fisher Street; Mr Grahame Winter, Parish Administrator for St Michael's & St Mark's, Stanwix; Lord Ballyedmond, Corby Castle, Great Corby; Carlisle Council for Voluntary Service, 27 Spencer Street; Cumbrian Newspapers, Dalston Road; the staff of Print Out, Denton Holme Industrial Estate, for the reproduction of photographs.

Finally, I wish, as always, to thank my parents, Kathleen and Geoff Dickens, who have travelled the country with me in pursuit of my research. They hear all about and read my books before anyone else and offer such wise counsel. However after reading the account of Priscilla's life in Bosnia, and given today's present volatile political situation around the World, they chose not to accompany me on a trip to Sarajevo.

Illustrations and their Sources

Part One

Joseph John Gurney, from an engraving after the portrait by George Richmond. John Kent, *Elizabeth Fry* (London: B.T. Batsford, 1962), p. 48. By permission of Mrs Caroline Gurney of Northrepps.

Sir Thomas Fowell Buxton. Sir Thomas Fowell Buxton, *Memoirs*, 2nd Edn, ed. Charles Buxton (London: John Murray, 1849), inside cover.

'Lame' Anna Gurney in her chair. Copied by Pamela Gurney from the original sketch by Anna Curtis. *The Northrepps Grandchildren* (London: Hodder & Stoughton, 1968) p. 145.

Elizabeth Fry in 1823. By permission of Miss A. Isabel Fry.

Bust of George Fox. Library of the Society of Friends, London.

Earlham Hall. John Kent, *Elizabeth Fry*, p. 15.

Map of Cromer, Norfolk. *The Northrepps Grandchildren,* inside cover.

Anonymous painting of three of the Gurneys of Earlham (1798). *ibid,* p. 64.

The Family at Earlham. Janet P. Whitney, *Elizabeth Fry, Quaker Heroine* (London: George G. Harrap, 1937).

Earlham Hall, 1808 by Richenda Gurney. *The Northrepps Grandchildren,* p. 81.

Bellfield, from a sketch by Priscilla Buxton. *Memoirs of Sir Thomas Fowell Buxton,* p. 209.

'The Silent Cradle', by Dudley Hardy. *The Sketch,* April 25th 1894.

Betsey. A pencil sketch by one of her family, of Elizabeth Fry when a grandmother. *The Northrepps Grandchildren*, p. 80.

Cromer Hall 1820, from a sketch by Priscilla Gurney. *Memoirs Of Sir Thomas Fowell Buxton*, p. 106.

Hannah Lady Buxton in 1830 with her two youngest sons ... from a tinted drawing by W.C. Ross. *The Northrepps Grandchildren*, p. 144.

The earliest surviving picture of Northrepps Hall, drawn by Priscilla Buxton in 1834, *ibid*, p. 80.

Part Two

Historic map of Anstruther. From the Kilrenny and Anstruther Burgh Collection. By permission of Richard Ellison, Anne Fairburn and Mrs Masry Prince.

Rennyhill, a sketch by Priscilla Johnston.

Bank House, Halesworth, from the garden.

The Baptism Register of St Mary's, Halesworth ... 4th December 1842. From the Suffolk Record Office, Lowestoft Branch.

The Baptismal Font, St Mary's Church, Halesworth.

St Mary's Church, Halesworth, Suffolk.

The Boat at Northrepps Hall from a sketch by E. Ellen Buxton. By permission of Mrs Ellen R.C. Creighton.

Anna Gurney's experiment on the Silver Fir at Northrepps Hall with Captain Manby's gun for saving lives in shipwrecks, copied by Pamela Gurney from the original pencil drawing by Hannah Buxton.

Norfolk's forgotten hero, Captain Manby. By permission of Dickens World, Downham Market.

Andrew Johnston. Priscilla Buxton Johnston, *Extracts from Priscilla Johnston's Journal and Letters, collected by her daughter E. MacInnes* (Carlisle: Charles Thurnam and Sons, 1862).

Brass Memorial Tablet to Andrew Johnston in the north aisle, St Mary's, Halesworth.

Ellen Buxton, from a portrait of her in 1864 when she was 16. In the possession of Mrs Ellen R.C. Creighton.

A family picnic on Runton Hills, west of Cromer. By permission of Mrs Ellen R.C. Creighton.

'The Accidents at the Illuminations', *The Cumberland Paquet*, 17th March 1863.

The Viaduct over the River Eden at Wetheral. Cumbria Heritage Services, Alma House, Carlisle Castle.

Ferry Cottage, Wetheral. Cumbria Heritage Services, Alma House, Carlisle Castle.

Wetheral Church prior to 1882. Cumbria Heritage Services, Alma House, Carlisle Castle.

The Howard Statue by Nollekens, Wetheral Church. Cumbria Heritage Services, Alma House, Carlisle Castle.

Corby Castle. By permission of Dr E. Haughey.

The Statue of Polyphemus in the gardens of Corby Castle. By permission of Dr E. Haughey.

Mumps Hall, 1885. Cumbria Heritage Services, Alma House, Carlisle Castle.

Lanercost Priory. Official Guide Book of Lanercost Priory.

The wedding procession of Sarah Maria and Mr Daniel Wilson. Sketch by Ellen Buxton. By permission of Mrs Ellen R.C. Creighton.

October 1864. Granny and 'Pris' in the Northrepps Hall Drawing Room. Sketch by Ellen Buxton. By permission of Mrs Ellen R.C. Creighton.

October 28th 1864. 'Pris', 'Isa', and 'Lisa' sitting on a gate near Northrepps Hall. Sketch by Ellen Buxton. By permission of Mrs Ellen R.C. Creighton.

1864. An evening at Northrepps... Sketch by Ellen Buxton. By permission of Mrs Ellen R.C. Creighton.

May 28th 1866. 'Lisa', 'Pris' and 'Isa', working at Northrepps. Sketch by Ellen Buxton. By permission of Mrs Ellen R.C. Creighton.

Relations on the Lawn at Northrepps Hall (1866). Sketch by Ellen Buxton. By permission of Mrs Ellen R.C. Creighton.

Easneye. [Ellen Buxton's former home. Today the All Nations Christian College.].

A Buxton / Johnston / MacInnes family photograph. By permission of Verily Anderson Paget.

St Martin's Church, Overstrand.

Part Three

Adeline Paulina Irby. From a portrait in the museum of the Old Orthodox Church, Sarajevo.

Miss Florence Nightingale from Florence Nightingale by Cecil Woodham-Smith.

Brod in Bosnia. Amand von Schweiger-Lerchenfeld, *Bosnien: das Land und seine Bewohner: Geschichtlich, geographische, ethnographisch und socialpolitisch* (Vienna: L. C. Zamarski, 1878).

Sarajevo in the 1860s. *ibid.*

Bashi-Bazouks ravaging a village ... *La guerre d'orients,* 1876.

A Turkish Guard with the heads of captured insurgents. *ibid.*

The Drawing Room of 10 Ovington Gardens. The *Illustrated London News*, 7th October 1876.

Refugees among the mountains of Dalmatia. Mortitz B. Zimmermann, *Illustrirte Geschichte des Orientalischen Krieges von 1876–78* (Vienna, Pest & Leipzig: 1878).

Letter to *The Friend,* September 1877. By permission of The Religious Society of Friends in Britain.

Letter to *The Friend,* November 1877. By permission of The Religious Society of Friends in Britain.

Letter to *The Friend,* December 1877. By permission of The Religious Society of Friends in Britain.

Letter to *The British Friend,* December 1877. By permission of The Religious Society of Friends in Britain.

Letter to *The Friend*, March 1878. By permission of The Religious Society of Friends in Britain.

Letter to *The British Friend*, April 1878. By permission of The Religious Society of Friends in Britain.

Letter to *The Friend*, April 1878. By permission of The Religious Society of Friends in Britain.

The distribution of corn by Miss Irby and Miss Johnston ... From The Florence Nightingale Papers, British Museum.

Refugees on the Austrian Border. Mortitz B. Zimmermann, *Illustrirte Geschichte des Orientalischen Krieges von 1876–78* (Vienna, Pest & Leipzig: 1878).

Letter to *The Friend*, June 1878. By permission of The Religious Society of Friends in Britain.

Letter to *The British Friend*, July 1878. By permission of The Religious Society of Friends in Britain.

Letter to *The Friend*, September 1878. By permission of The Religious Society of Friends in Britain.

Letter to *The Friend*, September 1878. By permission of The Religious Society of Friends in Britain.

Letter to *The Friend*, January 1879. By permission of The Religious Society of Friends in Britain.

Letter to *The Friend*, March 1879. By permission of The Religious Society of Friends in Britain.

Letter to *The British Friend*, July 1879. By permission of The Religious Society of Friends in Britain.

Letter to *The Friend*, July 1879. By permission of The Religious Society of Friends in Britain.

Letter to *The British Friend*, September 1879. By permission of The Religious Society of Friends in Britain.

Letter to *The Friend*, October 1879. By permission of The Religious Society of Friends in Britain.

Letter to *The Friend*, July 1880. By permission of The Religious Society of Friends in Britain.

Letter to *The Friend*, September 1880. By permission of The Religious Society of Friends in Britain.

Letter to *The Friend*, March 1881. By permission of The Religious Society of Friends in Britain.

Letter to *The Friend*, October 1882. By permission of The Religious Society of Friends in Britain.

Letter to *The Friend*, August 1884. By permission of The Religious Society of Friends in Britain.

Part Four

Aunt 'Pris' of Rickerby. By permission of Verily Anderson Paget.

The Beeches, Rickerby. By permission of Mrs June Cawley, the present occupier.

The Memorial Tablet in Overstrand Church...

Rickerby Mansion. Anna Grace MacInnes, *Recollections of the Life of Miles MacInnes* (London: Longmans & Co., 1911).

Miles and Effie MacInnes. *ibid.*

Miles and Effie MacInnes with their grandchildren. *ibid.*

Miss Amy Beevor. Mary Scott-Parker, *Forty Years On: Carlisle and County High School for Girls* (Carlisle: Bookcase, 1995).

The Creighton family c. 1870. By kind permission of Dr Prue Barron, Edinburgh.

Bull Baiting. Edward G. Fairholme and Wellesley Pain, *A Century of Work for Animals: the history of the RSPCA, 1824–1924* (London: John Murray, 1924).

Bear Baiting. *ibid.*

Richard Martin, MP. *ibid.*

Queen Victoria and Princess Beatrice with their favourite dogs. The Queen's Medal. *ibid.*

Letter from the President of The Naples Society for the Protection of Animals to *The Times*, 4th June 1906.

The 1904 CCOS report. By permission of Carlisle Council for Voluntary Service.

The Fusehill Union Workhouse. Carlisle Library.

The Board of Guardians of the Fusehill Workhouse. By permission of Mr Jim Templeton.

The 1897–98 Carlisle Union List of Guardians. Carlisle County Record Office.

The grave of Priscilla Hannah Johnston in Stanwix Cemetery.

The gathering at the opening of the watering trough on Scotland Road. From the *Cumberland News*.

The Watering trough. By permission of Verily Anderson Paget.

Master M. Saul turning on the water. By permission of Mr Jim Templeton.

The Buxton Family Memorial Gravestone in Overstrand churchyard.

Epilogue

The grave of Adeline Paulina Irby. In private possession.

Andrew Johnston and Fowell Buxton Johnston. Priscilla Johnston, *Edward Johnston* (London: Faber & Faber, 1959) p. 49.

'The Chairman' by F. Carruthers Gould. The *Essex Review*, Vol. 12, 1903.

Memorials to Fowell Buxton Johnston and his son, Andrew.

The MacInnes family grave, Stanwix Cemetery. Anna Grace MacInnes, *Recollections of the Life of Miles MacInnes*.

The graves of Priscilla Hannah Johnston, Amy Beevor and Catharine Isabel de Noé Walker.

Note

Anna Sewell. Adrienne E. Gavin, *Dark Horse: a life of Anne Sewell*, (Stroud: Sutton, 2004)

Colour plate section

1. The Watering Trough, now used as a planter dedicated to the memory of Priscilla Hannah Johnston situated in the village of Rickerby near to Carlisle. Author's own.
2. Hannah Lady Buxton from the memorials of Hannah Lady Buxton.
3. Priscilla Johnston (*née* Buxton) by kind permission of Mr Robert Vale, a watercolour originally in the possession of his late sister, Richenda.
4. Miss Creighton's Mourning Brooch, by kind permission of Dr Prue Barron, Edinburgh.
5–16. A selection of photographs and watercolours from Priscilla Hannah Johnston's own collection by kind permission of Verily Anderson Paget.
17. The Illuminated Address for Mary Ellen Creighton as contained in the Dormont Book in the custody of Cumbria Archive Service, Carlisle Castle. One of the most important documents owned by Carlisle City. It can tell us a lot about everyday life in Medieval Carlisle. Carlisle City bought the book in 1561. It was stored in the guildhall in an iron-bound fireproof wooden chest. It contains the Oaths and declarations of all those taking office until 1689, a register of the indentures of apprenticeships of future freeman 1672–1844 and details of those who were given the Freedom of the City.

Introduction

Philanthropist: Lover of mankind, one who exerts himself for the well being of fellow men.

(*Oxford English Dictionary*)

Whilst walking through Rickerby Village, near Carlisle in Cumbria, one day in February 2004, I came across an old watering trough, being used as a planter, bearing the inscription:

> In grateful remembrance of
> Priscilla Hannah Johnston, of The Beeches, Rickerby
> and of her work for animals, here and in distant lands
> erected by friends and neighbours 1913

'I am poor and needy, but the Lord careth for me.'

It brought to my mind the scene from the film of Anna Sewell's, *Black Beauty* depicting the granite fountain of 1891 providing water for people and working horses, which had been donated by Caroline Phelps Stokes, an admirer of *Black Beauty* and was built outside the Public Library in Ansonia, Connecticut, inscribed: 'Blessed are the Merciful – Anna Sewell author of *Black Beauty*'. This fountain is now also used as a planter.

As a horse lover *Black Beauty* has always been one of my favourite books, evoking many a tear at the plight of horses in the 19th century. You can imagine, therefore, how pleasantly surprised I was to find, eight months into my research, that the Sewells had come to know the Buxtons and the Gurneys, the maternal grandparents of Priscilla Hannah Johnston, Anna Sewell having been born into a family that on both sides had been Norfolk and Quaker for many generations.[1]

It is especially as a leading Quaker family of England that the Gurneys of Earlham became celebrated. Through their personal qualities and their devotion they played a more conspicuous part than any other set of brothers and sisters in the religious and philanthropic life of England during the first half of the nineteenth century. The story of several members of the family has been often told before. The public may be familiar with the names of the financial genius Samuel Gurney, Joseph John Gurney, Elizabeth Fry, and their brother-in-law Sir Thomas Fowell Buxton.[2] However, the story of Miss Priscilla Hannah Johnston has not been told so out of curiosity I decided to investigate further.

My quest led me to discover the fascinating path that the life of Miss Priscilla Hannah Johnston had taken and how she must have been influenced by many generations gone before. Having been introduced to the ancestry of Miss Johnston, you too will find that she was well fitted by her birth and background to become the 19th Century Philanthropist who truly 'lived life as to be missed.'

I feel that a 'Portrait of Priscilla' is encapsulated in the pages of a number of personal Gurney, Buxton, MacInnes and Johnston family journals and letters. (Being Quakers they of course used the 'Thee' and 'Thou', 'The Single Language' as it is called.[3]) In places these said journals contain sketches and paintings of the era produced by family members, which I have included. This material has been very kindly loaned to me by Mrs E.J. MacInnes, of Cumbria, to assist in my research into the life of a lady who devoted her life to making the lives of her fellow creatures better.

Part One traces the early ancestry of Miss Johnston, beginning with her pedigree or family tree, which I have extensively scaled down for the purpose of this book. Then, from around the turn of the nineteenth century I outline the lives of her grandparents along with the early life of her mother, also touching on the life and works of her grandfather, Sir T.F. Buxton, and great aunt Elizabeth Fry, amongst other members of the extended family who must also have had a bearing on the philanthropic path that Priscilla Hannah's life followed.

In Part Two I have referred to the journals of her mother, Priscilla, and grandmother, Hannah, giving an insight into the lives of her parents and the early life and times of Priscilla Hannah Johnston, following her life into her teenage years and twenties, through the recollections of Mrs Verily Anderson Paget, whose mother was a Gurney. Also included are extracts from the Journals and sketches of 'Prissy's' cousin, Ellen Buxton, covering the period of the 1860s. At this time Priscilla Hannah also produced many of her own sketches and watercolours, depicting her surroundings, some of which have been reproduced here.

For these first two parts I have collated extracts from the family journals and letters, linked by informative and historical narratives in a manner such as to allow their 'voices from the past' to provide an insight into the atmosphere of a bygone age.

Part Three deals with Miss Johnston's philanthropic efforts to help those victims of the 'Balkan Problem' (perhaps better known as 'The Eastern Question'). Turkey had been supported by Great Britain and France in the 1854–56 Crimean War in the belief that she could be persuaded to set her 'house in order'. But for the following twenty years that proved to be unsustainable.

By the early 1870s Turkey's finances had grown desperate. On the one hand she could not pay or organize properly the administration of her troops. On the other, the ever growing taxes exacted by the authorities acted as an incitement to local revolts.

About midsummer 1875, following a bad harvest in 1874, the Serbs of Herzegovina rose in rebellion against these excessive taxes. Volunteers from Serbia helped them, and soon the uprising spread all over Bosnia. Early in May 1876 uprisings of armed Guerillas, directed by a revolutionary committee occurred in Bulgaria. In retaliation the Turkish government now let loose the armed irregulars known as Bashi-Bazouks, who went on to commit appalling atrocities against the Bulgarian population and is collated from *Miss Irby and her friends*. I have also included extracts from letters which appeared at the time in the *Daily News* and the *Manchester Guardian*. Gladstone's speech (*The Times* 17th July 1877), in compliance with copyright regulations, has been reproduced in full. This part is further illustrated with a selection of Miss Johnston's letters, in which she gives the British public vivid eyewitness accounts of the terrible suffering occurring in the Balkans; letters which appeared at the time in the Quaker Journals, *The British Friend* and *The Friend*, the latter of which Joseph Stickney Sewell (Anna Sewell's cousin) became editor in 1878. Also included are sketches from the *Illustrated London News* and other sources.

In Part Four I have referred to the 'Recollections of Miles MacInnes' and those of his grand-daughter Jean MacInnes to give an insight into the MacInnes family and endeavoured to give an insight into the origins of some of the charitable institutions which Miss Johnston became involved with, in particular the RSPCA, the Society for which Miss Johnston's philanthropic contributions, are commemorated in Carlisle. Latterly I have also included extracts from articles which originally appeared in the 'Carlisle Journal'.

My epilogue takes the form of a 'What became of...?' section, where I bring closure to the 'times' of Miss Priscilla Hannah Johnston.

An Introduction to Miss Priscilla Hannah Johnston

The Victorian age produced some outstanding families, which for both size and talent have never been rivalled since, their lives being permeated by their religion and the philanthropy arising from it.

Here the story of the nineteenth century philanthropist, Miss Priscilla Hannah Johnston, begins with that of her ancestors, in particular her maternal grandparents. Her grandfather was Sir Thomas Fowell Buxton who is remembered for his fight in parliament for the emancipation of the slaves of the British colonies after Wilberforce, through ill health, had handed over parliamentary leadership of the anti-slavery cause to him in 1821[1] and her grandmother, Hannah Lady Buxton (née Gurney), the younger sister of the well-known Quaker prison reformer, Elizabeth Fry. With Mrs Fry as a sister-in-law, Sir Thomas could hardly escape being involved in the reform of the penal code. He helped in the moves to reduce the number of offences which carried the death penalty from 230 to nine.[2]

Hannah Gurney was the fifth daughter of John Gurney of Earlham and Catherine (née Bell). Catherine was the younger sister of the once well known Priscilla Wakefield, author of innumerable volumes, but best remembered for her delightful children's books of the time. The name Priscilla, afterwards so frequent in the Gurney family, was derived from Priscilla Wakefield.[3]

For many years the profession of John Gurney of Earlham was that of a wool-stapler and spinner of worsted yarn. It was not until 1803 that he, together with his brothers Richard and Joseph, were admitted as partners into the Norwich Bank by their cousin, Bartlett Gurney.[4] This bank, which had been established in 1770 by Henry Gurney of Keswick, near Norwich, was the forerunner of today's Barclays Bank.

The Gurneys' summer home was a country cottage at the village of Bramerton, near Norwich. Here the Gurney children were taught from an early age to make acquaintance with all the inhabitants and visit the poor.[5]

Hannah Gurney and Thomas Fowell Buxton married in 1807. They went on to have eleven children, six of whom died; in 1820 losing four in as many weeks to scarlet fever and measles. Following these tragic circumstances the Buxtons then moved to Northrepps Hall, Cromer, Norfolk, which became the family home for many generations to follow. The Buxtons' surviving eldest daughter, also named Priscilla, was destined to become the mother of Priscilla Hannah (names were repeated in almost every generation on both sides of the family).

Priscilla Buxton was a sickly child. However as she got older she became stronger, so from the ages of 20 to 26 she was able to assist her father in his anti-slavery campaign. It was through this work that she met the MP Mr Andrew Johnston, her future husband. He had also identified himself with Buxton's anti-slavery campaign.

Priscilla Buxton and Andrew Johnston were married on 1st August 1834, the same day as the bill for the 'emancipation of the slaves' was passed. Following their honeymoon the happy couple settled at Andrew's ancestral home of Rennyhill, in the Royal Burgh of Kilrenny and Anstruther, the 'Kingdom of Fife' in Scotland. However Priscilla, used to the hustle and bustle of London, could not settle so they moved to Bank House, 35 The Thoroughfare, Halesworth, East Anglia, where Andrew Johnston now took up a position with the Gurneys Bank. It was here at Halesworth that they raised their six children; Andrew (b.1835), Euphemia (b.1837), Fowell (b.1839), Sarah (b.1840), **Priscilla Hannah** (b.1842) and 'Isa', Catharine Isabel (b.1844). The Johnston children also spent many happy times at the Northrepps Hall home of their maternal grandparents.

In 1852 following the early death of Mrs Priscilla Johnston, who it was said died young 'being exhausted by her efforts in assisting her father in his campaign' Priscilla Hannah (Prissy), aged nine years and seven months, and her siblings were now more often than not left in the care of their widowed grandmother, the dowager Hannah Lady Buxton, at her home of Northrepps Hall, Cromer, Norfolk. In 1862 after the death of their father, Andrew, the Johnston children now took up permanent residence at Northrepps Hall. Here the circle about Lady Buxton grew smaller as Priscilla Hannah's siblings married. By 1870 Priscilla Hannah alone was a 'constant companion' to her grandmother.

Following Lady Buxton's death in 1872, Priscilla Hannah, now aged twenty-nine, joined Miss A.P. Irby abroad in her educational and benevolent work among the South Slavs of Bosnia in Sarajevo. In 1876 and 1877 this developed into 'an extended effort on behalf of the refugees from the Turkish reprisals of the Bosnian uprising'. The two women became seasoned relief workers to whom thirty miles in a spring-less cart was nothing of a day's journey. They appealed to friends at home, which included Miss Florence Nightingale, for funds, and such was the public confidence in them, and so great the effect of it being known that they paid all expenses of distribution themselves, that as much as £20,000 was placed at their absolute disposal for their relief work.

Priscilla Hannah, on her own initiative having collected £500 from her friends and relatives, then persuaded and financed Dr Michael Laseron of the Deaconesses Institution at Tottenham, to set out for Belgrade with seven surgeons, where they were to report on conditions in the hospitals there and the needs of the Serbian army medical department. This resulted in the setting up of the Sick and Wounded Fund which aimed 'to provide for the pressing need of surgical and medical assistance for the sufferers of war – irrespective of creed and any political party or object'.[6]

During this harrowing time Priscilla Hannah's correspondence with Sophia May appeared in the Quaker publications of the *British Friend* and the *Friend*; writing in disbelief, 'How can such atrocities be happening in this the nineteenth Century?' resulting in the Society of Friends contributing £6,750. In July 1877 a large meeting was held at Willis's Rooms, London at which Gladstone delivered an eloquent address on their behalf. Thomas Carlyle was also present to show his feelings about the 'Unspeakable Turk'.

At the age of forty-three years old in 1885 Priscilla Hannah finally settled at The Beeches, Rickerby Village, Carlisle, to be closer to the family of her sister Euphemia, who in 1859 had become the wife of the MP Mr Miles MacInnes of Rickerby. Here she now became 'Aunt Pris' to all the Johnstons' and MacInnes' young relatives; 'Aunt Pris' who was a 'bit eccentric and interested in good works'.

In Carlisle she found plenty to keep her busy. Her life in public and private was given up to helping others. As her grandmother had done, so 'Aunt Pris' would visit the poor in their homes. She also became involved with many of the local charitable institutions; the Carlisle Charitable Organisation, the Board of Guardians, the Carlisle District Nursing Association, the local branch of the RSPCA (Cumberland and Westmorland) and the National Society for Prevention of Cruelty to Children. Here we find Aunt Pris' work with children and animals went 'hand in hand', the RSPCA being the founding society for the NSPCC.

For a time Aunt Pris was joined by her good friend and companion, who also shared her interest in charitable work, Miss Amy Beevor, headmistress of the Carlisle and County High School for Girls (1892–1902), who took up residence with her at The Beeches.

Aunt Pris began to withdraw from many activities as her eyesight began to fail and 'rejoiced that her place was filled by others'. But in the hearts of those who mourned her passing at the age of 69 on the 15th January 1912, her place could never be filled. Bosnia had long since been forgotten and no legends grew up of 'Aunt Pris' and the Bosnian children, only one relic remained, a 'Bosnian boy's costume' preserved in an attic, its source and history unknown.

The watering trough for horses, originally erected on the 27th June 1913 at Kingstown on the northern outskirts of Carlisle to the memory of Miss Priscilla Hannah Johnston in recognition for her works for the RSPCA, was bought with the proceeds from fund raising which had been initiated by her friend and companion Miss Amy Beevor.

With the development of housing in the Kingstown area the trough was firstly removed to the area of Stanwix, where it became situated behind the Miles MacInnes Hall in the 1930s, then in the 1980s to Rickerby village, where it still stands today, used as a planter and tended to by the residents of the village.[7]

PART ONE

The Pedigree of Miss Priscilla Hannah Johnston

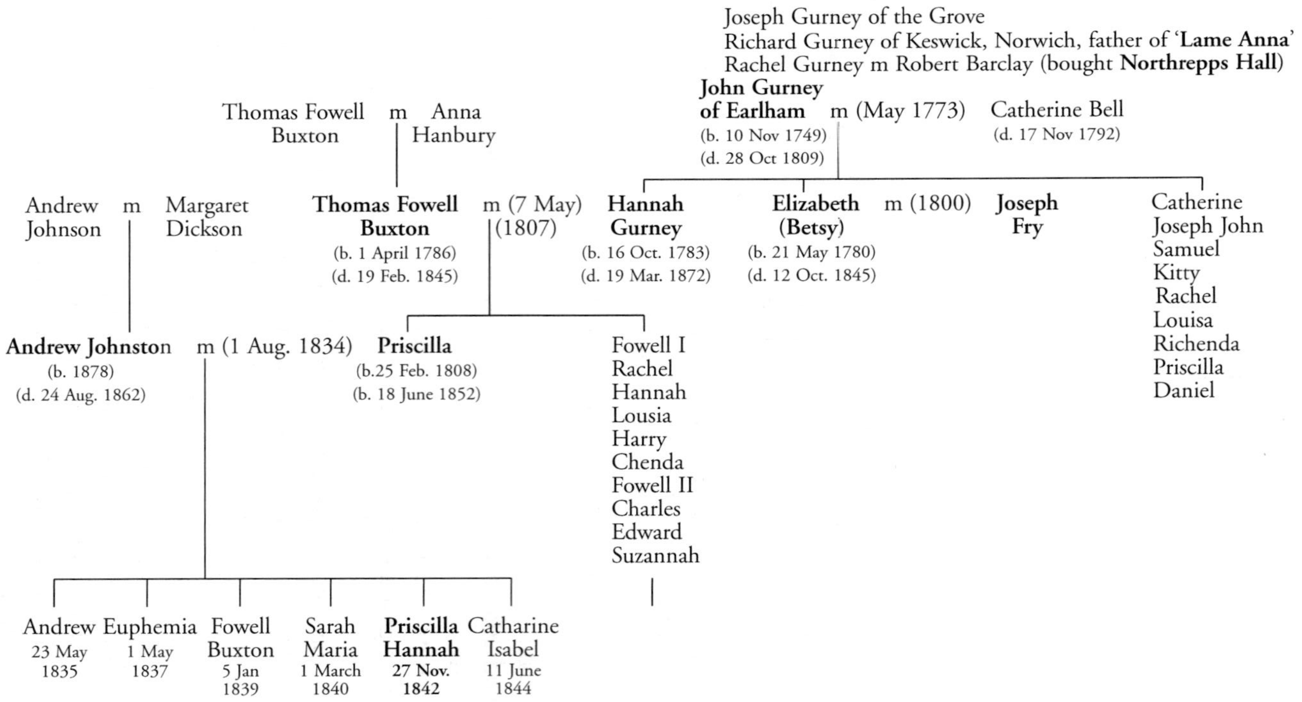

Joseph Gurney of the Grove
Richard Gurney of Keswick, Norwich, father of 'Lame Anna'
Rachel Gurney m Robert Barclay (bought **Northrepps Hall**)

John Gurney of Earltham m (May 1773) Catherine Bell
(b. 10 Nov 1749) (d. 17 Nov 1792)
(d. 28 Oct 1809)

Elizabeth (Betsy) m (1800) **Joseph Fry**
(b. 21 May 1780)
(d. 12 Oct. 1845)

Catherine
Joseph John
Samuel
Kitty
Rachel
Louisa
Richenda
Priscilla
Daniel

Thomas Fowell Buxton m Anna Hanbury

Hannah Gurney m (7 May) (1807) **Thomas Fowell Buxton**
(b. 16 Oct. 1783) (b. 1 April 1786)
(d. 19 Mar. 1872) (d. 19 Feb. 1845)

Fowell I
Rachel
Hannah
Lousia
Harry
Chenda
Fowell II
Charles
Edward
Suzannah

Priscilla
(b.25 Feb. 1808)
(b. 18 June 1852)

Andrew Johnson m Margaret Dickson

Andrew Johnston m (1 Aug. 1834)
(b. 1878)
(d. 24 Aug. 1862)

Andrew	Euphemia	Fowell Buxton	Sarah Maria	**Priscilla Hannah**	Catharine Isabel
23 May 1835	1 May 1837	5 Jan 1839	1 March 1840	27 Nov. 1842	11 June 1844

1

The Ancestry of Priscilla Hannah Johnston

Miss Priscilla Hannah Johnston, born on the 27th November 1842, was the third daughter of Andrew Johnston of Rennyhill, Anstruther, Fifeshire. He was for a time MP for the East of Fife Burghs in the last unreformed Parliament and for the St Andrews Burghs in the first two reformed Parliaments. Her mother, Priscilla Buxton, was the daughter of Hannah (née Gurney) and Sir Thomas Fowell Buxton with whom Mr Johnston had identified himself in the fight in Parliament and the country for the emancipation of the slaves.[1]

Priscilla Hannah Johnston was of Quaker ancestry and of Presbyterian parentage on one side; she was trained in the evangelical school of thought. Priscilla was brought up to have the firm rectitude of purpose which characterises the Presbyterian, whilst retaining much of the simplicity of dress and habits of the Quaker as well as a strong conviction of their great spirituality.

Her grandfather's views on education were wise and progressive and he particularly stressed the importance of teaching children 'habitually to seek for the truth, whether for or against our previous opinions or interests'. Her grandmother believed that 'one should search out and live the truth'.

This mix gave her a great tolerance of view with those who differed. She also developed a wide outlook and a ready sympathy for every effort to raise the conditions of all around her, which she would endeavour to carry out throughout her life. From her mother's family she inherited a passion for freedom and a hatred of oppression, which in her gentle personality was to find practical embodiment in her work for animals – a family tradition, as her maternal grandfather had been chairman at the first meeting of the Society for the Prevention of Cruelty to Animals.

Through her grandmother Hannah, Lady Buxton, she was related with those East Anglian families of Gurneys, Barclays and Hoares, with their background of banking and breweries, strongly evangelical and given to good works and philanthropy. Her great uncles, Samuel and Daniel Gurney, are credited with greatly multiplying the family fortunes by banking and bill broking, and much of what they created still exists as part of Barclays Bank.

'Joseph John Gurney'
From an engraving after the portrait by George Richmond

Another great uncle, Joseph John Gurney, became the spiritual driving force of a revival of English Quakerism until his death in 1847. There was also the background of her maternal grandfather, Sir Thomas Fowell Buxton, and his achievements; her maternal grandmother's cousin, 'Lame' Anna Gurney, who, despite her disability, still managed to assist sailors shipwrecked off Cromer; and the legend of her great Aunt 'Betsey,' Elizabeth Fry, the Quaker philanthropist and reformer.

Sir Thomas Fowell Buxton, country gentleman, several times member of Parliament, was finally made a Baronet. Buxton, before reaching the age of 30, 'rushed into print' giving to the world an inquiry into the question whether crime and misery were produced or prevented by the system of prison discipline then in operation. This composition was illustrated by descriptions of several gaols and some accounts of the proceedings of the ladies of the committee in Newgate Prison. He entered Parliament in 1818 for the Borough of Weymouth. To this constituency he remained constant for nearly 20 years. He bore a prominent part in many debates respecting the state of prisons, the condition of criminal law, the suppression of state lotteries, foreign policy or internal government, the strife of party warfare, finance and diplomacy. He also devoted himself to the exposure of the barbarous practice among Hindu widows of offering themselves as a living sacrifice on the funeral pile of their deceased husbands. However, to the majority he is probably best remembered as 'The emancipator of the slaves', after the passing of the bill in 1834 which gained him so much recognition as 'Buxton The Liberator'.[2]

T. Fowell Buxton

The longer I live, the more I am certain that the great difference between men, between the feeble and the powerful, the great and the insignificant, is energy – invincible determination – a purpose once fixed and then death or victory. That quality will do anything that can be done in this world; and no talents, no circumstances, no opportunities, will make a two-legged creature a man without it.[3]

2

Introducing 'Lame' Anna Gurney

Anna Gurney, was the youngest daughter of Richard Gurney of Keswick, near Norwich. Her father and mother were strict 'Friends' (Quakers), and to her death Anna preserved a simplicity of dress and a certain peculiar kindliness of manner which were among their distinguishing features.

Anna Gurney was born on New Year's Eve 1795. She was a strong vigorous baby but at ten months became crippled – it was said by a fall from her nurse's arms, although later reports suggested that she was more likely to have been a victim of poliomyelitis – and deprived forever of the use of her lower limbs. Her mother took her to a celebrated surgeon in Leicestershire who put her in irons, which were afterwards said to have done more damage than the actual disability. Her tremendous force of character, coupled with her physical energy and intelligence, made her a difficult baby to keep amused. From a small child onwards she refused to accept that she was handicapped and endeavoured to do all that other children could. At the age of eight she insisted on being carried down to the sea to learn to swim with the rest of the smaller cousins her age.

She was always a bulky child yet she had an amazing nimbleness of movement, except when staggering on her heavily clad legs; she spurned chairs, except for transport, preferring the floor on which she could roll freely, reaching up for books and spreading herself out to read them. She read with studious fervour all her life. She was chiefly educated by her elder sister and other near relations, but as her thirst for knowledge displayed itself at an early age her parents procured for her the instructions of a tutor, whose only complaint was that he could not keep pace with her eager desire for, and rapid acquisition of, knowledge. She thus learned successively Latin, Greek and Hebrew, after which she familiarised herself with the Teutonic languages, her proficiency in which was soon marked by her translation of one of the Anglo-Saxon Chronicles, published under the pseudonym of 'A Lady in the Country'.

Anna struggled to become as valuable a person as her lovely sister Elizabeth had been. She could never hope to be as beautiful, but she could be interesting and she could study and do good to others. She could never run, nor ride, nor dance gracefully for she could only walk a few steps at a time and those only awkwardly on two sticks or with the aid of an extra rail, pulling herself upstairs. But she could be active in her own way; she could move about in her self-propelled chair as swiftly as others could move on their feet. She even learned to fire a gun from her chair, which her grandfather taught her to do at an age when most children's arms would not be strong enough to hold a firearm. She also fed and cared for her pet rabbits and puppies from this chair.

In 1825 after her mother's death she went to live at Northrepps Cottage, Cromer, Norfolk – a neighbourhood peopled almost exclusively by the various branches of her family, Northrepps Hall being the country residence of Sir Thomas Fowell Buxton and his family. Sir Thomas's sister Sarah Buxton now went to live with Anna.[4]

Here at Northrepps the two devoted friends became affectionately known as 'The Cottage Ladies'.[5] They were both vigorous supporters of the campaigns of Sir Thomas. The papers Anna prepared for Buxton when he was in Parliament were enough to show the clarity and magnitude of her mind, yet all were introduced with the lightest, simplest and often most humorous touch which made working with her a stimulating delight. The two devoted cousins resided at the cottage in a beautiful abode surrounded by every comfort and dispensing to all around them a profusion of kindness and Christian benevolence. Schools, lifeboats, guns for the preservation of shipwrecked sailors, Bible and missionary societies – in short, all that could benefit others – occupied their well spent hours.

Finding no school of any sort at Overstrand, Cromer, Anna and Sarah started teaching the Overstrand children daily themselves at Northrepps Cottage till they could build a school for them in their own village. Each child paid a penny a week. There was a great emphasis on encouragement with sweets rather than punishment, and the cottage kitchen was used to cook the children's dinners.

They were only half a mile from the sea and whenever there was a storm Anna would demand to be dragged down to the cliffs in her chair by her two men-servants, Spinks and Stephans. She had taken the trouble to learn foreign languages so that she could speak to foreign survivors of shipwrecks, taking them to her home and giving them food and warm dry clothes, then assisting them out of her own pocket to return to their own land.[6]

In 1839, Sarah Buxton died. Anna, to whom this loss was entirely irreparable, continued to live in her beautiful cottage finding consolation in dispensing every kind of benefit and service around her.[7]

'Lame' Anna Gurney in her chair being taken down to the cliffs by Spinks and Stephans

3

Introducing Elizabeth Fry (née Gurney)

Elizabeth Fry (1780–1845) in 1823, C.R. Leslie

My remembrance is of the pleasure of my childhood being almost spoiled through my fear, and my religious impressions, such as I then had, were accompanied by gloom; on this account, I think utmost care needed in representing religious truth to children, that fearful views should be carefully avoided, lest it should give a distaste for that which is most precious. First show them the love and mercy of God in Christ Jesus, and the sweetness and blessedness of his service.[8]

Elizabeth Gurney was born in Norwich on the 21st May 1780. Known affectionately by her family as Betsey, she was the elder sister to Hannah. After losing her mother at a young age Betsey was looked after and taught by the family's eldest daughter Kitty, who worried that Betsey's concentration was appalling, 'Unless it were on the purple laces with which she had gaily fastened her purple boots: and her spelling was most unreliable.'

The other siblings were all rather sorry for her, she was so awkward in her ways and so moody – yet when there was dancing and charades it was Betsey who was the gayest and most bright. This prompted Mr Pritchford, a young friend of the Gurneys of Earlham, staying at Northrepps Cottage in 1798, to write:

> Elizabeth Gurney at fourteen is a most sweet girl, her manners uncommonly elegant, her beautiful hair between flaxen and auburn, her lovely blue eyes beaming with intelligence and full of inexpressible sweetness, her complexion exquisitely fair and her whole countenance full of the glow of youth. If she were two years older I believe I would fall in love with her.[9]

By the time she was fifteen she was in fact engaged to James Lloyd of Bingley Hall, Birmingham, then a charming park-enclosed country house. James, however, rode away and Betsey turned her attentions elsewhere.

Among her younger brother John's school fellows at Wandsworth had been a boy named Joseph Fry, youngest son of William Storrs Fry of the Quaker cocoa and coffee importers. His was an old family, which took its name from Frie in Normandy. He was afterwards placed with Robert Holmes, a 'friend' in Norfolk, to learn farming, but spent his time chiefly in coursing and other country pursuits. The Gurneys' charms both of mind and person, their joyous freedom and general circumstances, delighted the young Londoner, whose heart was soon especially touched by Betsey. Joseph first proposed to Betsey in July 1799, but was unhesitatingly refused. He could not, however, be induced to relinquish her.

Betsey and Joseph Fry, were married on the 19th August 1800 at the Friends Meeting House, Norwich. It had been a stormy courtship, particularly after Betsey had, at seventeen, shocked the family by casting off all dancing and frivolous amusement, along with her gay clothes, and taken to the sombre dress of a plain Quaker. Her thirteen-year-old sister Richenda wrote thus in her journal:

Sunday, March 1798

I have felt extremely uncomfortable about Betsey's Quakerism, which I saw, to my sorrow, increasing every day. She no longer joined in our pleasant dances, and singing she seemed to give up; she dresses as plain as she could, and spoke still more so. We all feel about it alike, and are truly sorry that one of us seven should separate herself in principles, actions and appearance from the rest. But I think we ought to try to make the best of it, and reconcile it as much as possible to our own minds. Betsey's character is certainly, in many respects, extremely improved since she has adopted these principles. She is industrious, charitable to the poor, kind and attentive to all of us; in short, if it was not for that serious manner which Quakerism throws over a person, Betsey would indeed be a most improved character.

However, it was not Joseph who inspired this change but an American preacher named William Savery, whom she had heard speak at the Norwich meeting on the 4th February 1798, after which she was moved to much weeping, such was the great feeling of religion she had experienced. Her sisters' response was to assure Betsey that she was obviously in love with this Mr Savery. Betsey, however, declared that it was an entirely spiritual experience. Believing that marriage would divert Betsey, her father encouraged Joseph Fry's attentions. At last, urged on by her sisters who hid in the bushes to witness Joe's final proposal, Betsey accepted him.[10]

Prison reformer Mrs Fry, a most impressive Quaker minister at the age of 29, was horrified when visiting Newgate Prison in 1813 by the condition under which women prisoners and their children lived. In 1817 she formed an association to improve such conditions and for the rest of her life campaigned for prison reform in Britain and Europe. She travelled widely, becoming friends of kings, queens and princes all over Europe, ceaselessly promoting voluntary efforts and persuading governments to make improvements.

Elizabeth Fry, Prison Visiting, March 4th 1817

I have just returned from a most melancholy visit to Newgate, where I have been at the request of Elizabeth Fricker, previous to her execution [for robbery] tomorrow morning at eight o'clock. I found her much hurried, distressed and tormented in mind. Her hands cold, and covered with something like perspiration preceding death. The women who were with her said she had been so outrageous before our going that they thought a man must be sent for to manage her. However, after a serious time with her, her troubled soul became calmed. But is it for man thus to take the prerogative of the almighty into his own hands? Is it not his place rather to endeavour to reform such; or restrain them from the commission of further evil? At least to afford poor erring mortals, whatever may be their offences, an opportunity of proving their repentance by amendment of life. Besides this poor young woman, there are also six men to be hanged, one of whom has a wife near to her confinement, also condemned, and seven young children. Since the awful report came down, he has become quite mad, from horror of mind. A strait waistcoat could not keep him within bounds: he had just bitten the turnkey; I saw the man come out with his hands bleeding, as I passed the cell.[11]

Elizabeth also succeeded in persuading the government to regulate the appalling conditions under which convicts were shipped to New South Wales. She instituted an order of nursing sisters which helped to raise standards in British hospitals, and she alleviated the miserable state of vagrants, particularly those in London, by founding hostels for the homeless.[12]

4

The Ancient de Gurneys and their Faith

The name Gurney, or Gournay, is of great antiquity in the county of Norfolk, and is derived from the town of Gournay en Brai, in Normandy. The Norman lords of this place held fields in Norfolk, as early as the reign of William Rufus. Two young branches of this Norman race existed for some centuries. The one which was the most distinguished was seated in Somersetshire, the other at Hingham Gurneys, and West Barsham, in Norfolk, where it continued till 1661; thereafter it became extinct in the direct male line, and the estates devolved on the heiresses.

John Gourney of Norwich, merchant, descended from a younger son of the West Barsham branch, was the immediate ancestor of the family of Gurney. He was born in 1665 and in early life embraced the tenets of the Society of Friends on their first appearance under George Fox, their founder. Joseph Gurney, his son, purchased Keswick, which continued to be the residence of the head of the family. John Gurney of Keswick, his son, died in 1770, leaving three sons, of whom John Gurney of Earlham, the father of Hannah Lady Buxton and Elizabeth Fry, was the second son.[13]

George Fox, born in Leicestershire, began travelling to promote his ministry in 1647. He believed in an inner light and 'That of God in every man', a doctrine which was misunderstood and perceived as blasphemy. During his travels he gained much opposition as well as many followers. Those who were convinced became known as 'Children of the Light'. They chose to be known as Friends and became the Society of Friends in 1665, a nonconformist sect, their nick-name of Quakers being derived from the spiritual 'trembling' experienced during meetings.

In the mid 1660s George Fox lived for a time at Swarthmoor Hall, on the edge of the South Lakeland market town of Ulverston. (This residence is still in existence today.) George Fox founded a society whose ideal was absolute religious spontaneity under the direct guidance of the

Spirit of God. For Fox himself this meant rejection of every aspect of the Church of England: its professional priesthood, its fixed liturgy, its sacraments of Baptism and Holy Communion, its system of episcopal government, its acceptance of state control and even its church buildings, since these formalised the whereabouts of God. But Quaker freedom devised its own restrictions: the Friends were obliged to wear a special, sober form of dress; to use a method of dating which substituted, for example, 'First Day' for 'Sunday'; to use 'Thee' and 'Thou' in ordinary speech. The men had also to keep their hats on when custom required them to remove them. This was taken as a sign of disrespect and made them targets of religious persecution. They were tolerated under the Protectorate and, after the Toleration Act in 1689, they became increasingly involved in humanitarian activities, campaigning against Slavery in the nineteenth century.[14] They fully supported the temperance movement. These rules affected the Gurneys sharply in the early nineteenth century. Friends who were unwilling to be pacifist, or who married non-Quakers were expelled from the Society. Many members of the Gurney family had solved the problems presented by the elaborate code of behaviour of the Society by departing to the Church of England throughout the last quarter of the eighteenth century.

The said John Gurney of Earlham was born in 1749 and educated in the principles of the Society of Friends. It was clear that although he was still faithful to the local Quaker Meeting he ceased to live his life entirely within the borders of the sect and allowed his children to mingle freely in Norwich society. 'As he advanced in life his pursuits led to contact with persons of various denominations; this, with his natural disposition, induced unusual liberality of sentiment towards others. He was a man of great talent, of bright discerning mind, singularly warm hearted and affectionate, very benevolent, and in manner courteous and popular.'[15]

His marriage to Catherine, daughter of Daniel Bell, a merchant in London took place in 1775. Catherine's mother was the daughter of David Barclay, a descendant of the Barclays of Ury, in Kincardineshire, and grand-daughter of Robert Barclay, the well known apologist of the Quakers. John and Catherine Gurney first established themselves in a roomy quadrangular house in St Clement's Parish, Norwich, which belonged to that branch of the family, where for some years they passed the winter months, spending summer at Bramerton, a pretty village about four miles from Norwich.

Mrs Gurney was a person of excellent abilities and of considerable attainments, as well as much personal beauty. She was disposed to scientific and intellectual pursuits, and delighted in the charms and beauties of nature, imbuing her children, almost in infancy, with tastes that would remain with them and urging upon them the necessity of prayer and personal piety.[16]

In 1786 the Gurneys removed to Earlham Hall, a seat of the Bacon family, in Norwich. Of the twelve children, nine were born before their removal to Earlham; one of them died in infancy. The three youngest sons were born after their settlement there. The mode of life continued with little alteration at Earlham till November 1792 when 'it pleased god to remove from this large family the kind mistress, the loving wife, devoted mother'. She died after an illness of three weeks, leaving eleven children, the eldest, Catherine, scarcely seventeen, the youngest not two years old.[17]

Bust of George Fox (1624–1691) by Alfred Turner (1900)
From orginal in the Library of the Society of Friends, London

During Fox's travels he preached in Carlisle in 1653, at the Market Cross, and the Cathedral. He was attacked, but protected by soldiers, who were later punished, while Fox himself was imprisoned in the dungeon at Carlisle Castle. Other Quakers were imprisoned in a private house in Castle Street, Carlisle until they embarrassed the authorities by leaning through the windows to address the people going to the 'steeple house', as they called the Cathedral, and had to be moved. In time they gained the right to worship freely and their Meeting House is now in Fisher Street in the City.

5

The Fowell-Buxtons

The Buxtons were Suffolk Squires. Priscilla's grandfather, Thomas Fowell, was the son of the High Sheriff of the county; his mother, Anna Hanbury, who belonged to the Society of Friends, had imbued him with an intense hatred of slavery. As a boy he was 'of a daring and violent, domineering temper', but apparently neither particularly clever nor remarkably devout.

The family from which Sir Thomas Fowell Buxton was descended, about the middle of the 16th Century, resided at Sudbury in Suffolk, and subsequently at Coggeshall in Essex. At the latter place, William Buxton, his lineal ancestor, died in 1624. Thomas, the son of William Buxton, claimed and received from the Heralds' College in 1634, the arms borne by the family of the same name settled before 1478 at Tybenham in Norfolk.

Isaac Buxton, a merchant, and fifth in direct descent from William married Sarah Fowell, of Fowelscombe in Devonshire. From her was derived the name of Fowell, first borne by her eldest son, who married Anna, daughter of Osgood Hanbury Esq., the Quaker Brewer of Holfield Grange in Essex. The first Thomas Fowell Buxton lived at Earl's Colne in Essex, but was residing at Castle Hedingham when his eldest son, Thomas Fowell, was born on the 1st April 1786.

The first Thomas Fowell being appointed High sheriff of the county availed himself of the authority of his office to relieve the miseries of the prisoners under his superintendence, visiting them regularly. He died at Earl's Colne in 1792, leaving his widow with three sons and two daughters.[18]

The eldest boy was at this time six years old. He was a vigorous child, and early showed a bold and determined character. One who knew the boy well in his early days said of him, 'He was never a child; he was a man when in petticoats.' At the age of only four and a half he was sent to school at Kingston, where he suffered from ill-treatment. His health giving way (chiefly from the want of sufficient food) he was removed shortly after his father's death, to the school of Dr Charles Burney, at Greenwich, where his brothers, Charles and Edward, afterwards joined him. Here he did not make much progress in his studies, and his holidays spent at Earl's Colne, where his mother continued to reside, left a deeper impression on his later life than the time spent at school. Thomas described his early life and his mother, Anna, in a letter:[19]

Cromer Hall, August 23 1825

My father died when I was very young, and I became at ten years old almost as much as the master of the family as I am to this family at the present moment. My mother, a women of great talents and energy, perpetually inculcated on my brothers and sisters that they were to obey me, and I was rather encouraged to play the little tyrant. She treated me as an equal, conversed with me, and led me to form and express opinions without reserve. This system had obvious and great disadvantages, but it was followed by some few incidental benefits. Throughout life I have acted and thought for myself; and to this kind of habitual decision I am indebted for all the success I have met with.[20]

At the age of fifteen, after spending eight years at Dr Burney's without making any great advances in learning, he persuaded his mother to allow him to reside at home, where he remained for many months, devoting the chief part of his time to sporting, and the remainder to reading. He would sometimes spend whole days riding about the lanes on his old pony.[21]

Before this period he had become acquainted with John, the eldest son of Mr John Gurney, of Earlham Hall, near Norwich, with whose family his own was distantly connected.[22]

In the autumn of 1801, the whole course of his life was changed by a visit he paid to Earlham. He was then aged sixteen. This was the home of the Quaker family of Gurney and they exerted an immediate and most powerful influence upon him. It was as though he fell in love with the whole family.

The two families – The Fowell Buxtons and the Gurneys – had much in common, including an ardent love of animals and birds; very tame kangaroos, peacocks and cockatoos were at large in the gardens and parks of both homes. The parents of both families were strong supporters of the Anti-Cruelty Society for the Protection of Animals.

John Gurney had for several years been a widower. His family consisted of eleven children, which included seven of the gayest Quaker daughters imaginable. 'A set of dashing young people, dressing in gay riding habits and scarlet boots, riding about the country to balls and gaieties of all sorts, they were also accomplished and charming young ladies.' In the summer they would lie on the lawn of Earlham and sing together or read poetry aloud to spell-bound young men. One such young man was Thomas Fowell. He was charmed by the lively and kindly spirit which pervaded the whole party while he was surprised at finding them all zealously occupied in self-education and full of energy at every pursuit, whether of amusement or of knowledge.[23]

[The Buxtons were not Quakers, though Fowell's great-great grandfather narrowly escaped prison as a Nonconformist at the time that the Gurney and Barclay great-great grandfathers were in prison for their Quaker faith.][24]

Earlham Hall itself was large, old, and irregular; placed in the centre of a well wooded park. The river Wensum, a clear winding stream, flowed by it, its banks overhung by an avenue of ancient timber trees which formed a favourite resort of the young people. They are described at the time of his visit as spending fine autumn afternoons in sketching and reading under old trees in the park; or taking excursions, some on foot, some on horseback. The roomy old hall was also well fitted for the cheerful though simple hospitalities which Mr Gurney delighted to exercise especially towards the literary society, for which Norwich was at that time distinguished.[25]

Although Mr John Gurney belonged to the Society of Friends his family was not brought up with any strict regard to its peculiarities. He put little restraint on their domestic amusements, and music and dancing were among their favourite recreations. The third daughter, Elizabeth, afterwards the well known Mrs Fry, had indeed united herself more closely to the Society of Friends.[26]

In 1800 Elizabeth Gurney married Joseph Fry. In the beginning of 1802 Mr Gurney and his six unmarried daughters took a journey through the Lake District. Hannah Gurney writes: 'Our party consisted of my father, us six, Fowell Buxton, Mr John Crome [their drawing master, afterwards became distinguished as the landscape painter 'Old Crome'], nurse, William and Peter Witten, the coachmen, in two chariots and a postchaise.'

At the end of summer of 1803 the party took a trip to Cromer, Norfolk.

Cromer Sept 20 1803

My dear Betsey,

Our party is now complete, as John continues with us, and the Buxton's arrived yesterday; it was extremely pleasant to us, seeing them both again, particularly Fowell; their being here will add very much to our pleasure, as there is suitability between us and the Buxtons, which always makes it pleasant being together. Our time is spent here in a way that exactly suits the place and the party. Each is left in perfect liberty to do as they like all day, to form any engagement, &c, &c. Yet the party is so connected that hardly a day passes but some plan is fixed for all to meet. When they are all met it is an uncommonly pretty sight, such a number of young women and so many, if not pretty, very nice looking. I wish thee could have seen us the other afternoon; Sally gave grand entertainment at the hall, where everybody met. The ladies almost all dressed in white gowns, blue sashes and nothing on the head; after dinner we all stood on a wall eighteen of us, and it was one of the prettiest sights I ever saw. To give thee an idea how we are going on, I will tell thee how we generally pass the day. The weather since we came has on the whole been very fine, so imagine us before breakfast with our troutbecks [hats] on and coloured gowns, running in all directions on the sands, jetty, &c. After breakfast we receive callers from other houses, and fix with them the plans for the day; after this we now and then get an hour's quiet for reading, writing, &c, though my mind has been so much taken up with other things that I have found it almost impossible to apply to anything seriously. At eleven we go down in numbers to bathe, and enjoy the sands, which about that time look beautiful; most of our party and the rest of Cromer company come down, and bring a number of different carriages which have a very pretty effect. After bathing, we either ride on horseback or take some pleasant excursion or other; I never remember enjoying the sea so much and never liked Cromer a quarter so well. We continually dine out, and others stay and receive company at home; we always dine in the kitchen; nurse is our cook, and makes a very good one. Molly Witton is here besides, and seems thoroughly to enjoy herself. We have short afternoons and

Earlham Hall, Norfolk
From a lithograph after a drawing by Mrs F. Cunningham

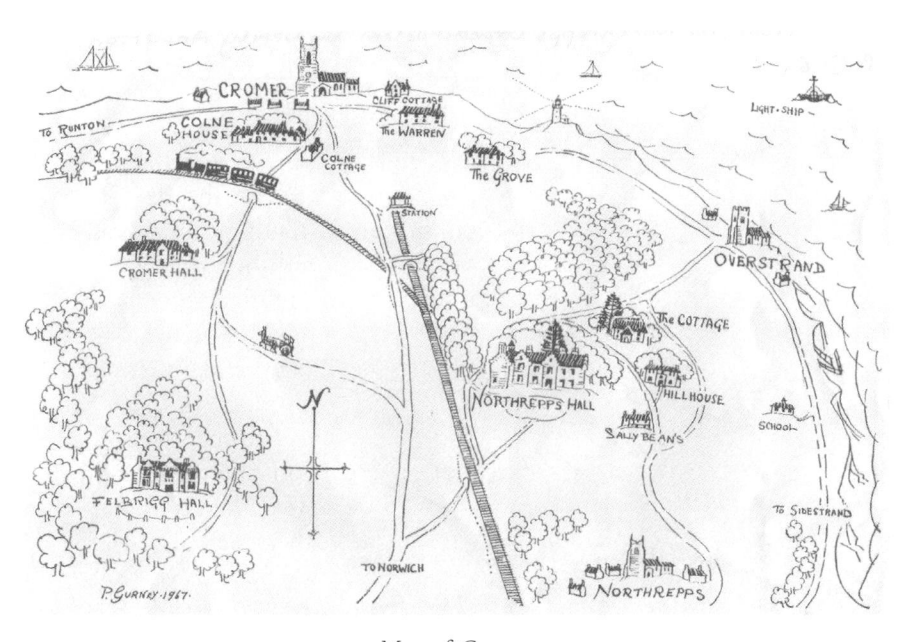

Map of Cromer

spend the evening with music, or something of that sort; with all these most pleasant amusements, and this pleasant party it would be very odd if we did not enjoy ourselves.

John Crome has been a great addition to our party. I hope he has enjoyed himself; we have had two or three most merry days since he came. The day before yesterday we spent at Sherringham wandering about the woods all morning sketching, &c; everybody met at a beautiful spot to dinner – three knives and forks between twenty six people and two or three plates. All manner of games took place after dinner, which John completely entered into and seemed to enjoy as much as any of the party. We completed our day by a delightful musical evening; Miss Gordon our old Cromer friend came to tea. She played and sang to us all evening in a wonderful style; it was the greatest treat to us all. John goes away on Sunday; he stays over tonight to be at a dance which some very agreeable people who are at Cromer Mr and Mrs Windham are going to give jointly.

It seems a long time since we have heard anything of thee. I have often and often thought of thee and thy darlings, and longed to hear more of their proceedings. I hope thee will write as soon as thee possibly can.

Thy Affectionate sister, Richenda Gurney.[27]

6

The Gurney Children

In the Fry family are preserved seven letters by the seven Gurney sisters of Earlham, containing long tresses of their hair, for the most part bright glistening auburn.

All the Gurneys adored each other and used up all possible superlatives in describing not only their brothers and sisters but all their innumerable relatives and connections. Fowell Buxton joined in wholeheartedly. He too adored the whole family, saying of one sister, Louisa, 'She came as near to perfection as any human being I ever knew', and of another, Priscilla, that 'She was a saint of God'. It was Hannah whom he married, having fallen in love with her at first sight when they were both sixteen.[28]

Hannah Gurney was born on the 16th October 1783 at Bramerton, near Norwich, where her early childhood passed. In 1783 the family moved to Earlham and there her mother, Catherine Gurney died in 1792. Catherine Gurney (Kitty), the eldest sister, describes the family at that time:

> In November 1792, my mother's death took place after an illness of two or three weeks – a most comfortless period indeed it was.
>
> Here then we were left, myself [not seventeen] at the head, quite unprepared for filling an important station, but my father placed me nominally at the head of the family. The continual weight wore my health and spirits, and I had none of the joy and glee of youth.
>
> I must now turn to my chief companions, my two eldest sisters, Rachel and Betsey, and describe them as well as I can. Rachel was fourteen when my mother died, a lovely girl, full of native charm and attraction, very sweet in her person, beautiful dark blue eyes, fair and rosy, and the finest flaxen hair. She has a gifted uncommon talent for humour and drollery. She was fascinating, and became the most attractive of any of the sisters. Her voice and singing had

a compass and expression of the first order. I have never since heard such touching sounds as her and Betsey singing together, for Betsey also had an exquisite voice.

Elizabeth (Betsey) was rather more than a year younger, and was a very uncommon child. She certainly had a genius more than was understood in her early youth. She was of a retiring disposition and reckoned shy, but she was extremely affectionate and tender in her feelings, especially toward her parents.

Next to these sisters came our eldest brother, John, who had been sent to school at Wandsworth a few months before my mother's death, being about twelve years old, a most beautiful boy, of good talents and affectionate nature.

Then 'the four girls' as we used to call them, Richenda, Hannah, Louisa and Priscilla. At the time of my mother's death they were charming, promising children, gifted by nature in various ways, with much diversity of character. Richenda was always the most easy, good tempered, active, happy child imaginable; with as fine a voice as her two elder sisters. She was the leader amongst the four sisters in all their out of door exercises and amusements, of which they had a great variety.

Hannah was a girl of peculiar charm from a certain naivety and playfulness of character, combined with sweetness and sense, which made her attractive. She had also a lovely expression of countenance and real beauty of feature and complexion, and was generally reckoned the handsomest of the four, though they were all very pleasing in person and manner.

Louisa was a noble girl and the most talented of any of them. She had a fine understanding, a great energy, and a turn for excellence which produced a high stimulus in her pursuits; and success, for the most part, in all she undertook.

Priscilla was extremely sweet and pleasing, very clever, complete and accurate in all she did, of an exquisite tact and taste and fine sense, as her character became developed and sanctified by religion.

The three boys, Samuel, Joseph and Daniel, were all very young when my mother died. Samuel was a fine boy of great independence of character, given to out of door, active objects, and resisting the schoolroom and learning. He was sent to school at Wandsworth when he was eight.

Joseph was of a very different turn, and my mother, on her deathbed, called him her 'morning star,' as if presaging the remarkable person he would become with his various gifts and graces. He was a delightful brother to his sisters.

Daniel was only a year and a half old when he lost his mother, and was the great object of motherly care and affection to his attached and excellent nurse, who had his early training chiefly in her hands.[29]

After the death of their mother it now became the young Kitty's duty to teach her siblings. She used as a guide a syllabus drawn up by her remarkably well-educated mother, on the lines of which she had started to teach her children before her untimely death:

> ...To be useful it is necessary and very agreeable to be well informed of our own language, of Latin also, being the most permanent, and of French, as most in general request. The simple beauties of Mathematics appear to be so expert an exercise for the understanding that they ought on no account to be omitted, though perhaps scarcely less essential than a competent knowledge of Ancient and Modern History, Geography, Chronology. To these may be added a knowledge of the most approved branches of Natural History, and a capacity for drawing from nature in order to promote that knowledge, and facilitate the pursuit of it. As a great portion of a woman's life ought to be passed in at least regulating the subordinate affairs of a family, she should work plain neatly herself. Also, she should not be ignorant of the common properties of table, or deficient in the economy of any of the mass of minute affairs of a family. It should be observed that gentleness of manner is indispensably necessary in women, to say nothing of that polished behaviour which adds a charm to every qualification; and to both of these it appears certain that children may be led without vanity or affection by amiable and judicious instruction.[30]

Kitty who was by then still barely twenty-one and whose own education had been cut short, felt herself sadly inadequate as she tried to follow the instruction her mother had set herself. It was not that the children were stupid, but merely hard to keep indoors. In the summer she solved this problem by teaching them, whenever possible, in the garden.[31]

The Gurney children were a lively band, laughing and squabbling and generally brightening up the scene in the scarlet cloaks they always wore in the garden instead of the more usual bonnets and mantles of the time – all of them also avid journal writers.

'I was in a very playing mood today,' wrote Richenda, 'and thoroughly enjoyed being foolish. I tried to be as rude to everybody as I could. We went on the highroad with the purpose of being rude to the folks that passed. I do think being rude is most pleasant sometimes.' In a less playful mood she writes, 'I cannot help just mentioning my dinner, which was particularly delightful to me; I really felt true pleasure while I was eating excellent apple pudding and partridge; how I did enjoy it.'

'We romped most of the morning. In the afternoon we read a novel. In the evening a blind fiddler came and we had a most merry dance and ended in a violent romp,' wrote Louisa. 'We lighted a fire in the field this afternoon and roasted potatoes in the ashes. There was company in the evening and my father would have Chenda and me dance a Scotch minuet.'

How they all loved Kitty. 'When I had a sore throat and was poorly on Friday, Kitty nursed me most kindly. I never saw so kind and sweet a nurse,' wrote Louisa. How they all hated their governesses. Louisa writes, 'Governess, disliked by most of the family, sits in the drawing room almost all day.' And again, 'Governess is going away. I am most glad she is, I dislike her so very much. I think it must do harm to the heart to feel such dislike as I do.' Eventually Kitty, seeing her younger sisters commit their hates and adorations with such fierce glee to their 'penny notebooks' put a temporary brake on it. 'Kitty has forbidden us to now write more than six lines in our journals. I entirely see that it is now her plan to treat us as babies. I am very, very sorry,' writes Louisa.[32]

Cousins would often visit with the Gurneys at Cromer. It was a young cousin aged twelve who prompted the eleven-year-old Louisa to write, 'Young Sam Hoare was most disgusting; we were on most good terms for the first part of the evening but at last he went so far as to give me a kiss; it was most disgusting.' But possibly she had led him on for she had already decided in her journal, 'I am afraid I shall be a flirt when I grow up. I really do think I shall. To be sure I am not a flirt yet, but I think I shall be.'[33] (Louisa Gurney and Sam Hoare would eventually marry.)

Another happy visit by their cousins prompted Louisa to write:

> On Thursday [October 28 1798] we took our famous ass ride. We were all dressed for the occasion, and I never laughed more than when fifteen asses arrived saddled and bridled for us. After a great deal of noise and bustle, we seven, five Barclays, John, Joseph, and Kitty Hanbury, were mounted upon fifteen capital donkeys,

Anonymous painting of three of the Gurney Children (1798);
Richenda (16), Hannah (15) and John (17)

with various sorts of saddles. During our seven miles' ride various changes took place in our cavalcade. Sometimes we went all in a row, so as to form an extremely long string, now and then we went two and two, and then again we were all in a bustle. Three men followed us on foot to pick up those who fell, and indeed we had a bountiful share of falls, which added to the extreme drollery and merriment. We rode up the park with loud halloos and everything that could show the success of our ride, and the surrounding friends and neighbours were assembled to see us arrive.

On a more serious note, 1803 saw the declaration of war with Napoleon's France. With the daily expectation of the descent of Napoleon on the Norfolk coast, a young Priscilla Gurney writes of her concerns:

> I think we shall be in a very unprotected state if the French should land whilst my father is away, without a single man or even boy to take care of us. We had a quite serious conference about it yesterday morning; thee would have been entertained to have heard the various plans that were proposed. It is however finally decided

THE FAMILY AT EARLHAM

	Born	Married	Died
John Gurney	Nov. 10, 1749	May 26, 1775	Oct. 28, 1809
Catherine Bell[1]			Nov. 17, 1792

THEIR CHILDREN

	Born	Married	Died
Catherine	March 28, 1776	—	June 26, 1850
John	Oct. 28, 1777	—	May 24, 1778
Rachel	Nov. 21, 1778	—	Sept. 17, 1827
Elizabeth	May 21, 1780	Joseph Fry (Aug. 19, 1800)	Oct. 12, 1845
John[2]	June 17, 1781	Elizabeth Gurney (Jan. 6, 1807)	Aug. 9, 1814
Richenda	Aug. 5, 1782	Rev. Francis Cunningham (Jan. 1816)	Aug. 12, 1855
Hannah	Sept. 15, 1783	Sir Thomas Fowell Buxton, Bart. (May 7, 1807)	March 20, 1872
Louisa	Sept. 26, 1784	Samuel Hoare III (Dec. 24, 1806)	Aug. 1836
Priscilla	Nov. 27, 1785	—	March 25, 1821
Samuel	Oct. 18, 1786	Elizabeth Sheppard (April 7, 1808)	June 5, 1856
Joseph John	Aug. 2, 1788	1. Jane Birkbeck (Sept. 10, 1817) 2. Mary Fowler (July 18, 1827) 3. Eliza Paul Kirkbride (Oct. 21, 1841)	Jan. 4, 1847
Daniel	March 9, 1791	Lady Harriet Jemima Hay (Dec. 12, 1822)	June 16, 1880

[1] Catherine Bell was a great-granddaughter of Robert Barclay, author of Barclay's *Apology*.
[2] Second of the name.

The Family at Earlham

that as soon as ever we hear the news of their arrival we six sisters, Danny, and if we can manage it, Molly and Ellen (two of the maids) are immediately to set off in the coach-and-four, for Ely where we are to take up our abode, as my father thinks it is a safe place.

Luckily this plan of action proved to be unnecessary and life carried on as ever. Hannah writes of a family party day, 'This afternoon was delightful and the sociables, the horses and walkers on the sands formed quite a beautiful scene. On the sea there were supposed to be 400 vessels in sight and the sea was such a colour.'[34]

The Gurneys, by their example and their powers of fascination transformed the young Thomas Fowell Buxton from a boy whose chief interests were shooting and fishing into a young man who studied like a demon and, by sheer determination, outstripped his fellows at college. He also became, partly through their influence, profoundly devoutly religious.

7

*Extracts from the Journals of her Grandmother
Hannah Gurney (1805–1808)*

Thomas Fowell Buxton's intimacy with the Gurney family since 1801 had ripened into a warm affection for Hannah, and they were engaged to be married in 1805. However, with no mother to engineer suitable occasions for proposals the Gurneys of Earlham fanned love's flame for each other. When Fowell and Hannah were suffering agonies of indecision, Kitty and Rachel shut them up in a room together till Fowell had proposed and Hannah had accepted him.

Earlham, April 1805
Catherine Gurney to her brother Joseph: 'Hannah is in excellent spirits, much happier than before Fowell's visit; they correspond constantly, and he writes charming letters.'

[As there were reasons for expecting that her son would inherit considerable property in Ireland, Mrs Buxton deemed it advisable that Thomas Fowell should complete his education at Dublin; accordingly, in the winter of 1802 he was placed in the family of Mr Moor of Donnybrook, who prepared pupils for the university. Here he found himself inferior to every one of his companions in classical acquirements. He spent the Christmas vacation in such close study, that on the return of the other pupils, he stood as first among them.]

College, Dublin, May 3 1805
Fowell Buxton to Hannah Gurney:

> My dear Hannah,
> The examinations are over, but alas! I cannot describe the disasters that have befallen me.

Think how disagreeable a circumstance must be to me, to have all my hopes disappointed, to lose the certificate, to have my gold medal stopped, and what is worse to know that my Earlham visit, as it was the cause of my idleness, was the cause of my disgrace.

Think of all this and fetch a very, very deep sigh and look very grave and then think how happy I must be, to have to tell you that my utmost examinationary hopes are realized, that I have the certificate, and what is better, that I can ascribe my success to nothing but my Earlham visit. I must thank you, or rather congratulate you on the effects of your influence. I am sure that if I had not thought that I was partly working for you, I never should have been able to read so much during this month. Now I have told you all about the examination, and if I have been the trumpeter of my own praise a little too much, you must remember that one word of approbation from you and my sisters would be more grateful to me than the applause of the whole world.

Yours affectionately,
T. Fowell Buxton

Earlham, Dec 15 1805

From Catherine Gurney to Fowell Buxton:

My dear Fowell

I daresay thee wishes me to tell thee about Hannah. She is, in the first place, quite well and in very good spirit. It seems to me that her attachment to thee is of the strongest, and consequently most durable nature. One of the strongest proofs of this is its effects on her character, which has in my opinion been highly beneficial, so that thee has derived advantages from her influence.

Thee knows without me repeating it here the great satisfaction and pleasure thee has hitherto afforded us all, and how much thee art dear Fowell, after our own heart exactly what pleases both our judgement and taste. I like and love everything thee says and does; however I do not like to give way to this kind of partiality, for after all, how imperfect the best of us are, and how frail are all our virtues, unless they are derived from the only source of true strength, a principal of religion in the conscience. I have no faith in any virtue which arises from natural impulse, because though frequently amiable and excellent in appearance, we are sure to find that it partakes of variability of our present weak and corrupt nature, and on this account can never stand the test of trials, as that virtue will, which has its basis on Christian faith. Now I have sometimes thought from thy natural impulses being remarkably good, there is some danger of thy depending too much on thy self and not sufficiently seeking for assistance and direction in thy conduct from that source of light and strength which can alone insure thy continuance and progress in the best things. I know Hannah's happiness is completely dependent on thee. I know too how strongly she feels the importance of religious principle; therefore, for her sake as well as thy own, I am most anxious that thy mind should be equally impressed by the importance and the necessity of seeking to possess it, as the foundation of all your future comforts. I am quite sure that Hannah with her feelings on the subject, never would be completely happy, unless it were the constantly regulating principal action of thy mind, in preference to any particular affection. Do not suppose, dear Fowell, I mean to lecture thee. I only mean to advise thee not to depend too much on the gifts of nature, but to look to a power, from whom those gifts are derived, and by doing so learn the true means of turning both the one and other to thy own and dear Hannah's advantage.

Our dear friend and favourite Mr Wordsworth has been paying us a visit of two weeks; we have enjoyed his company exceedingly; how beautifully the influence of religious principal united with deep learning, appears in his character. This morning we had some delightful hours sitting with him altogether in the dressing room, talking on different subjects, and then he read to us in Taylor's 'Life of Christ'. What wilt thee say to this long letter? Thee must for once excuse it, and believe me, dearest Fowell,
       Thy Truly affectionate Catherine Gurney

In the summer of 1806, Mr Gurney and his daughters travelled in Scotland. Fowell Buxton and others were also of the party. Hannah's elder sister's letter must have had the desired effect in encouraging the young Fowell to seek religious knowledge for the sake of Hannah's happiness, for on their travels, whilst visiting Perth, he purchased a Bible that they might read it together on their journey.

Fowell Buxton to Hannah Gurney:

Dublin, Sept 19 1806

I must tell thee, dearest, that I have read in our bible with greatest interest and I think I may tell thee, I hope with some benefit; I have devoted a place near my bed side to hold it, and have generally, morning and night, opened it and closed the day with reading something of it. I believe I never felt so earnest desire to correct my faults and to devote myself heartily to endeavouring to improve myself in those things which alone will contribute to our mutual happiness.

Dublin, Nov 2 1806

I am sure that the desire I feel of pleasing Earlham has done me more good than the approbation or censure of all the world beside would have been able to effect. The dreadful accounts of the Continent have led me to reflect a good deal. How has thee felt them?

I often anticipate with the greatest of pleasure our evenings – thee sitting industriously making clothes for the poor people, I sprawling over the chairs (if thee will permit) with a book, well chosen and not sullenly perused in selfish silence. I wish I knew what part of the bible thee will read tonight, that I might be thy companion, however I shall not go to bed without reading some part.

Thursday. – I have just returned from chapel and from receiving the sacrament. I hope thee were with me, for thee were very much in my thoughts.

Dublin, Nov 18 1806

I perfectly agree with thee, love, on the satisfactory effect of thinking on the transactions of the day before we go to sleep. I hope that I have lately confirmed myself in this habit. I intend to pursue a new plan in reading, which is to copy into a book for the purpose, all the passages which strike me in any book. I shall begin this plan tomorrow and I hope I shall be industrious enough to persevere in it. Thee must be pleased with this intention of mine, for I feel earnestness to mark, and I hope I shall write down, because I expect that it will be a pleasure to us both in future.

By the time this arrives at Earlham, not much more than seven weeks of the time for which we parted will remain. I cannot tell thee with what pleasure I look forward to my next visit.

Sketch of Earlham Hall by Richenda 1808

Thomas Fowell Buxton and Hannah Gurney were married at Tasborough meeting, near Norwich, on 7th May 1807. The following account of the day is from her sister, Rachel's journal.

Earlham May 1807

We all rose in good time, the weather mild and summer like; our bride composed and cheerful. Many collected to read as usual, before breakfast and after it we dispersed till it was time to equip ourselves in bridal array. The house was overrun with bridesmaids in muslin cloaks and chip hats. We led our sweet bride to Tasborough. The meeting was to me solemn in its beginning, and striking from such a circle of brothers and sisters, so united in affection, it might well recall a verse in the psalms; Behold how good and how pleasant it is for brethren to dwell together in unity. Our dear couple spoke with much feeling, and Fowell with his usual dignity. Preparing for dinner took up the rest of the morning, and nothing could be prettier than the train of bridesmaids dressed alike in white, with small nosegays; except the bride, who looked lovely, she was still more white and was distinguished by one beautiful rose. She had a sweet colour, was very cheerful, and quite herself. The dining room was full, but nothing could be more orderly than the dinner, or more beautiful than the circle of young people; there were my father's fifteen children, and four grandchildren. We did not go into the drawing room till late, and then the whole party dispersed in different parts of the house. Hannah sat with dear Elizabeth in her room. Everybody had a cheerful face and it was pleasant to reassemble to tea. The company cleared off in good time, but not till we had spent a short but delightful evening in full assembly. Our dearest Fowell was most affectionate and sweet to us all; I think there scarcely ever was such a brother admitted into a family. The next morning we met to a most interesting and even happy breakfast, consisting of our whole family and the Barclays and Buxtons. The love and harmony that prevailed throughout the circle made everything pass off most agreeably.

Hannah had been perhaps of all the Gurney sisters the one who loved Earlham most. To break her parting from home, the bridal pair stayed there a few days after their marriage.

The first few months of married life were passed at a small cottage close to Mr Buxton's grandmother's seat at Bellfield, and in the neighbourhood of his mother, who had contracted a second marriage with Mr Edmund Henning and had left Essex to reside at Weymouth.[35]

Bellfield, the home of Buxton's grandmother, where it was noted that she had more than once entertained George III. On her death Fowell would inherit Bellfield.

8

A Brief Portrait of T. Fowell Buxton (1807–1818)

Buxton's expectations of wealth had been disappointed, and he found that his fortunes must depend upon his own exertions. In later life when referring to this period he said, 'I longed for any employment that would produce me a hundred a year, if I had to work twelve hours a day for it.'

Nearly a year passed away before his anxieties were brought to a conclusion by an unexpected turn in his fortunes, resulting from his friendly interview with his uncles. Within a few days Mr Samson Hanbury of Trueman's Brewery Spitalfields, Middlesex offered him a situation in that establishment, with a prospect of becoming a partner after three years' probation. He joyfully accepted the position and threw himself into the work with such dynamic energy that in 1811 the firm became Trueman, Hanbury and Buxton. At the close of 1808 he had succeeded Mr Hanbury in occupation of a house connected with the brewery, in which he continued to reside for several years. Fowell was, of course, closely bound to his London avocations, but almost every Autumn he spent some weeks at Earlham, enjoying the recreation of shooting. It was here in 1808 that their eldest child, Priscilla Buxton, was born.

From childhood the duty of active benevolence had been impressed on him by his mother, who used to set before him the idea of taking up some great cause by which he might promote the happiness of man. On beginning to live in London he at once sought opportunities of usefulness in this pursuit. The brewery was in Spitalfields, surrounded by some of the worst conditions there, and one of his first speeches was made at a public meeting organized for this purpose. He must have been a born orator for, according to a friend, his descriptions of the sufferings of the poor 'set a whole bench full of turtle fed aldermen whimpering.'

At a subsequent period, he says: 'From the time of my connection with the brewery in 1808 to 1816, I took a part in all the charitable objects of that distressed district, more especially those connected with education, the Bible society and the deep sufferings of the weavers.'

In the summer of 1815, he removed from London to a house at North End, Hampstead, that his children, now four in number, might have the benefit of country air. He went on to study conditions in prisons and discovered there 'a system of folly and wickedness which surpassed all belief' which led to his publishing an enquiry, 'Whether crime be produced or prevented by our present system of discipline', which would eventually result in the passing of the Prison Discipline Bill.

In the same year, 1818, he entered Parliament as member for Weymouth. In May 1821, the evening after hearing Buxton's speech on criminal law and being extremely impressed, Wilberforce, who was growing old, asked him to support and take over his campaign for the abolition of slavery. After a long, mature deliberation he accepted the 'weighty charge' involved in Wilberforce's proposal, arriving at his final decision in autumn 1822, at which time anti-slavery operations commenced with vigour.

9

An Account of Priscilla Buxton's Early Childhood by her Mother (1808–1822)

Priscilla Buxton was born in February 1808 at Earlham. She had several early childhood homes before her parents finally settled at Northrepps Hall, Cromer, Norfolk.

Priscilla was from an early age deeply religious, an attribute which became a great source of comfort to her throughout troubled times in her life. She was a delicate child and for years suffered from trouble with her hip which made her unable to walk, very often being confined to the house for months.

The following extracts are from the journal and letters of Hannah, Lady Buxton.

> My dearest child Priscilla was born at Earlham Hall, near Norwich, February 25th 1808. It was delightful having a child born at Earlham, and much was made of the event and of her – the first child born there since my brother Daniel, in 1791.
>
> When she was about six months old we settled in a house lent to us in Southampton Row, Russell Square. Here Priscilla soon became the most lively, active baby I ever saw. She had a most providential escape from Scarlet Fever. I, in my inexperience, went to see a child who had it, and caught the fever. I had sent Priscilla to spend the day at St Mildred's Court with her Aunt Fry. That day I sickened, and it proved a severe illness. When recovered I thought I might have her home: she came. When the doctors happily called and ordered her away again. That evening when her father returned the fever was upon him and he became dangerously ill. After a while my beloved husband was restored and at last we were allowed to rejoin our child, whose animation and merriment were remarkable.

In January, 1809, we settled at The Brewery, Brick Lane; Priscilla eleven months old. That same day she walked off through several rooms.

In June 1811 Hannah describes her new baby Susannah in a letter to her sister-in-law, Elizabeth.

> I have so enjoyed my baby, and have set my mind on showing thee my darling. Thee cannot think how sweet and dear she is to me. I never felt so proud of a baby before, or so delighted with one. She is so flourishing and good, and I scarcely have to care about her. She takes so much notice I almost fancy she knows me, and is so bright and lovely that she is much admired. She has a sweet colour in her cheeks, and is in my eyes very pretty. Thee will be amused by such a partial account.

In November 1811 the family suffered the great trial of losing baby Susannah. Hannah writes in her journal:

> *Brick Lane Nov 17*
> This has indeed been a week of deep trial. The hand of the Lord has been raised to afflict me, and He has taken to himself my beloved baby. I have found it hard to resign her, but I pray that I may be delivered from a spirit of murmuring. It is the Lord, therefore let me not dare to have a wish for a different dispensation arise in my heart. My dearest child has been dealt with in great and tender mercy; she has been gently removed from a peaceful life to a glorious inheritance through her merciful Lord and Saviour.

Three years later she writes, 'Scarcely a day ever passes that I do not feel the vacancy in my little flock, and picture Susannah filling her place. May I one day be united to this sweet treasure, which was with me but for a short time. I cannot but frequently feel, oh, may I never be tried in this way again.'

At a very early age Priscilla received some religious impression; and, before she could read it, liked to have a bible and take it to bed with her.
One day my sister Cunningham being with us, she saw Prissy in

bed, her countenance looking heavenly. Her Aunt said to her, 'My darling what are you doing?' She replied, simply and sweetly, 'I am thinking about God.'

In March 1815, she wrote in her journal:

Priscilla has been an object of intense interest to me. I am thankful to find the seeds of what I believe to be grace in the heart. Last Sunday she told me she felt particularly comfortable because, she said she trusted in herself that she had been doing the will of God; and now Mamma, the reward seems all ready, everything so pleasant.

In June 1815, we moved to North End, Hampstead, to be near our brother and sister and to bring up our children together. We had eight between us, one sweet little girl had been taken from us, [a reference to death of baby Susannah in 1811] and Priscilla was then the only girl, with seven boy companions – four of the Hoares and three her own brothers. The one girl was very delightful amongst the troop of boys.

In 1816 we were several months at Earlham, in consequence of a trying complaint in Priscilla's hip, for which she was closely confined and kept from all lessons except what I could teach her. She was perfectly sweet and easy, and, as usual, unfailingly industrious throughout this long illness.

Oct 27 1816

I write of her (8 years old). I had some very interesting conversation with Prissy this morning. She told me she had passed a few minutes the night before, during which she had been remarkably happy and felt more subdued than ever she did in her life; that the fear of death had been much removed.

She had no doubt been anxious about her health. Towards the end of that year she became much stronger. Her father was a most congenial, indulgent companion to this precious child; cultivating her mind, exercising her powers and pleasing her by entering into her pursuits. They were both extremely fond of poetry and he enjoyed to exercise her, as she advanced in years, in learning it rapidly.

January 19 1819

In endeavouring to look back on the past year, I do not know if I have stepped forward in my heavenly course. In entering this year I feel very thankful that I can do so without much anxiety on account of my dearest husband. I feel his commencement in the parliamentary career, but one thing I am determined – to make no complaint, but to submit cheerfully to the inconvenience of it.

Our seven darling children are a continual source of pleasure, the elder ones especially; my dearest Fowell most sweet and lovely in his conduct, though sadly idle, and painfully backward in his lessons. Priscilla is most promising. My darling Edward and Harry are much pleasure to me, Edward some care, for I feel that I am deficient in my pains with him. He is very good, and at times sweetly simple in his religion. Harry remarkably generous and noble, truly promising. My two little girls, Rachel and Louisa, are, I fear, too much a source of pride, as well as of particular enjoyment. They are a beautiful, black-eyed pair, fat and healthy, and universally admired. My precious baby, Hannah, a source of tender interest and pleasure, full of smiles and activity, but not very handsome. I do not find my heart so much wrapped up in my babies as it used to be, and yet, when fears arise for any of my tenderly loved treasures, how soon do I become sensible that they are entwined very tight about my heart.

Priscilla was the eldest of their eleven children, of whom six had died in childhood, four of them being lost within a few weeks of each other – Fowell, aged ten, and three sisters: Rachel, aged four, Louisa, aged three, and Hannah, aged eighteen months, to whooping cough and measles.

To a man devoted to his children as Fowell was this must have been an unthinkable blow, but for him and his wife Hannah all things came from God, a belief that was also shared by the young Priscilla. His affection for his children was such that, however urgent the work upon which he was engaged, he could hardly bring himself to turn them out of his study and only did so with great reluctance and presents of sweets and cakes.

The following entry appeared in Lady Buxton's journal in December 1820, after a 'most sorrowful time', which would later be referred to as the 'Hampstead Catastrophe':

Priscilla twelve years old. Through all our sorrowful, overwhelming trials she was our devoted, loving, sympathising child. My expression about her at this time is, 'Prissy greatly upheld'. Truly strong in faith, in knowledge, and in appreciation of the truth, though suffering much in health and acutely afflicted by our bereavements, she strove to be our comforter and diligently searched scriptures to bring consoling and helpful texts and thoughts to me.

We went to Tunbridge Wells and there she was my invaluable companion and friend; and I remember her especially at that time as a girl full of mind and feeling, sweetness and constant love, with great simplicity.

10

From the cradle to the grave, an account of the 'Hampstead Catastrophe' (1820)

At this period of time, *the general probability is about three to one that a new-born infant will not live to complete his fifth year. Of a given number of new born infants, one half, by fault of nature or man is extinguished before the age of puberty and reason – a melancholy consideration.*

Gibbon's Dictum Supplement à l'Histoire Naturelle, vii

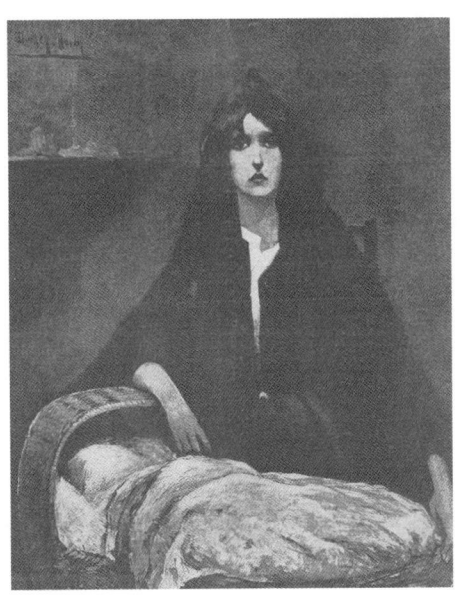

'The Silent Cradle' by Dudley Hardy, *The Sketch*, April 25 1894

At the end of 1819, Mr and Mrs Buxton settled at North End, Hampstead, in a small house near their brother and sister, Samuel and Louisa Hoare.

Thus far Mr Buxton's career had been one of almost un-chequered prosperity. As a member of Parliament, as a man of business, as a husband, as the father of a large and promising family, his heart's desires had been fulfilled. His public undertakings were becoming daily more important and engrossing and his home was a scene of unclouded happiness.

The year 1820 opened in great prosperity, increased by the birth of their ninth child, Richenda, on January 6th. But the bright home life so often described was now to be shattered by death in the short space of five weeks – Thomas Fowell, taken on March 6; Hannah, April 17; Rachel April 27; Louisa, May 1.

Despite every effort being made to prevent the disease spreading, by a constant changing round of beds and cots, and frantic efforts made to get steam kettles and hot compresses to relieve their chests, the last three died of simultaneous whooping cough and measles.

The story of this sorrowful time is best told by extracts from their parents' journals and letters.

Thomas Fowell Buxton writes in his journal:

> On Monday March 20 Mr Ward sent our dear Fowell home with inflammation of the lungs. He looked poorly, but no suspicion of danger crossed our minds. On Wednesday he rode with me; on Saturday he was very unwell; on Sunday grew worse and worse, and breathed his last on Tuesday morning at ten o'clock. Thus has left us our eldest son, the peculiar object of our anxious care, a boy of great life and animation, and of a most beautiful countenance. During the whole illness he was perfectly patient and sweet. The last night he gave me the most endearing kiss, and acceded to my intimation that God was taking care of him. My darling wife having suffered severely from anxiety, has conducted herself with a serenity and cheerfulness which could only come from the Author of every blessing. May God grant her the choicest of blessings. May Christ himself in the fullness of His mercy be consolation of her heart.

From the pages of Hannah Lady Buxton's journal:

March 30 1820

I am now sitting by the corpse of my precious boy, whom the Lord has in tender mercy towards him taken to himself. 'Precious in the sight of the Lord is the death of his saints'. He was an inexpressibly dear child to me, but God has seen, in his wisdom, that it was better for this sweet fellow to be removed from the cares, and pains, and fears of this world, to join the great company of His saints in Heaven, to sing the praises of the Redeemer, and to render him everlasting thanksgiving. Excessively as I loved him, I do not mourn excessively. I feel assured that he was a child of God and that the Lord so loved him. Fowell [her husband] did not conceal his feelings, and rose from his knees with tearful eyes saying 'He is taken away before wickedness should alter his understanding or deceit beguile his soul'.

April 3 1820

My two little ones were in black frocks, Hannah with a black sash. They made no remarks, nor did I, though I felt it deeply affecting to have them mourning for my precious eldest boy. His funeral entirely engaged my mind. Bitterly sorrowing, we sat in the dining room round his coffin, but comforted by Betsey's [Hannah's sister Elizabeth Fry] ministry, though more occupied by natural spiritual feelings. How did the tolling bell strike my heart. The service was a strength to me while I was in church, and my faith and hope were strong as I stood over his grave 'In full and certain hope of his resurrection'.

The young Fowell had died at the home of his Uncle, Mr Charles Buxton, not being allowed to come home because of the other children being ill; already suffering with whooping cough they were seized within a few days with the measles, which 'quickly assumed a serious character'.

From Hannah Lady Buxton's journal.

Thursday, April 13

We have been passing a time of constant anxiety, first with one beloved child, then with another. Many a heartache have I had

Betsey. A pencil sketch by one of her family, of Elizabeth Fry when a grandmother

watching my darling Harry, Louisa, Hannah at the same time; and since my dearest Rachel has pained me by continued high fever. What a gift it would now be to feel as well as know that my most beloved boy has entered into everlasting joy. I thank God that I am not left without faith and hope.

Friday April 14

Stillness and Illness affectingly prevail over our nursery. Edmund and Anna [children of Charles Buxton] and all our own are ill. It was an awful afternoon. Deep trial.

Tuesday April 18

I am this time sitting by the body of my sweet little Hannah, who was taken from me about one o'clock yesterday morning, and entered into fullness of joy through the mercy and merits of our ever blessed redeemer. Though very poorly, she appeared to be recovering the measles, and in my mind being chiefly occupied by Rachel's state,

I did not watch this little darling as I would have done, could I have foreseen which was to be removed hence. I was not particularly anxious till Saturday, when I took her into my arms to nurse her about twelve, and I immediately apprehended inflammation of the wind pipe. We applied remedies, but no abatement appeared in the symptoms. Very overwhelming was it to me to be thus brought to watch a fatal illness. I suffered inexpressible conflict over my sweet girl, and also from a hiding of the face of God from me. Dearest Chenda watched by her, she on Susan's lap [Susan Atterton, their faithful attendant from the beginning of their married life] and on the foot of the nursery bed. She took much notice, her blue eyes following us about, putting out her hand for milk, or else pushing it away, and shaking her head, if she did not like it. We were comforted towards morning, thinking her rather relieved, Oh what a relief it was! But it was not to last, truly affecting was it but mercy compassed her about, smoothing the valley of the shadow of death to this little innocent baby. We were for some hours more hopeful, but when I came from supper I found her much sunk. I took her on my lap, and felt no hope. When death was approaching, I waited in the day nursery till all was over, and then went into the room where my beloved child was sleeping in the Lord. Betsey knelt down; her prayer in thanksgiving that another of our sweet flock was taken to rest. I felt overwhelmed with grief, dwelling on much sorrow of that time three weeks.

I found my dearest Rachel decidedly ill, and had a day of deep sorrow. Fowell gone, Hannah taken, and Rachel so very ill that I had much to look her death; but yet I did feel the Lord to be near with me. I could feel for this darling child [Hannah] that to be absent from the body and present with the Lord was far better, and that to die was gain, and yet I have not had very strongly, the sense of deliverance from the evils of the world, with this little happy cheerful child.

Wednesday, April 19

Sitting by my precious Hannah this morning – it is like having her with me, so completely herself is her sweet little body. The day she was taken was one of deep affliction, from the losses of my darling children, and the acute apprehensions for Rachel's life too, so that yesterday I was comforted by the mercy of having her better.

Friday, April 21

Very hard indeed I find it to obtain resignation. The voids left in my family distressed me. My darling Hannah's absence in the nursery is grievous to me. For this my best remedy is a view of the love of God, in these heavy afflictions towards me and my beloved husband, as well as his love towards his children.

Thursday, April 27

Again has the Lord sent death amongst us, and taken from us our lovely Rachel, in whom no flaw could be found, so complete, so delicious, mind and body, so to be loved – but the Lord delighted in her and loved her more than we did, and has dealt tenderly by her in carrying her through the valley of the shadow of illness and death in great mercy; making her bed in sickness, and sweetening the bitter, with the most innocent and constant enjoyments.

My darling Louisa is now extremely ill. My heart sickens when I turn to her. Her breathing panting, hot and greatly reduced. I hardly hope for her recovery, and indeed feel just now, nearly indifferent to it so marred is my flock – that another gone I see.

May 2

Sitting by all that remains of my darling Louisa, who was seized with convulsions about six, and was translated into everlasting glory at nine last night … This day five weeks – March 28 my most tenderly beloved Fowell put off this mortal and put on immortality. Yesterday fortnight, April 17 my sweet Hannah entered into peace. Last Thursday, April 27, my lovely Rachel, of blessed memory, followed; and last night my tender Louey was delivered from all her conflicts and rejoined her companions, to be to me, I trust, a crown of joy and rejoicing hereafter, and forever more.

After Louisa's death she was carried back to the Hill, Hampstead, where her mother wrote:

May 7

Last evening my two darling and beautiful girls, Rachel and Louisa, after lying one night together in the dining room here, were carried to Hendon, and both put into one grave at the feet of my most sweet and dear Fowell and Hannah. The four buried together in one grave, with the simple inscription, 'Eheu. Eheu [Alas, Alas].'

Deeply do I feel the wonderful truth that they are more than in peace; most thankfully do I confess my strong assurances that they do all partake of unspeakable pleasures, in the presence of the Almighty Father and of the Lamb forever.

Many had gathered round the small coffins which were laid side by side in the dining room ready to be buried together beside the other children's at Hendon. But Hannah could bear no more – to see the graves of her other children was more than she could endure. Instead of going to Hendon she went and played with her sister Louisa's healthy children in whom she found some mild comfort.

That evening Fowell wrote in his Journal:

Oh when one affliction flows upon another, may they burst the bonds by which we are tied to earth, and direct us Heavenwards; may we, having our treasures in Heaven, have our hearts there also. Oh my God, be thou the strong consolation of my beloved, my patient wife.

Immediately after the funeral Mr and Mrs Buxton went to Tunbridge Wells for a few weeks. T. Fowell Buxton wrote:

Tunbridge, May 1820

We came here with the fragments of our family, in hopes that it may recruit strength of my dear wife. She has during the whole time evinced a holy fortitude and a degree of resigned cheerfulness beyond my hopes, knowing how tenderly her heart felt for her children. May God give her every blessing.

His diary from which this last melancholy narrative has been drawn closes at this date. Of the summer, which was chiefly spent at Tunbridge Wells, there are few notices, except that of the before mentioned passing of the Prison Discipline Bill.

On their return to Hampstead, while Hannah busied herself with her remaining children, the four others were never out of her mind – and then, too, she kept remembering little Susannah.

She writes in her journal, 'I have had the most affecting business of clearing out my nursery of every remaining vestige of its late lovely inhabitants. To see their hats in a row bespeaking the departure of such numbers at a stroke was hard. I found my faith tried by it.'

Whenever the other children became poorly she felt, 'Sick at heart lest we should have sorrow still upon sorrow. It makes me live again my grief.'

After this overwhelming experience, in the autumn of 1820 Mr Buxton gave up his house at Hampstead and decided to remove Hannah and his two remaining children to make a completely new life for her, permanently as it proved, in the neighbourhood of her beloved Cromer. Once at Cromer Hannah began to revive and took pleasure in pictures and toys and scenery she had enjoyed in her own childhood.

At first they resided at the picturesque Cromer Hall. It was situated about a quarter of a mile from the sea but sheltered from the north winds by closely surrounding hills and woods. With its old buttresses and porches, its clustering Jessamine, and its formal lawn, where the pheasants came down to feed, it possessed a peculiar character of picturesque simplicity. The interior corresponded with its external appearance, having little of the regularity of modern buildings; one attic chamber was walled up, with no entrance save through the window and, at different times, large pits were discovered under the floor, or in the thickness of the walls, used, it was supposed, in old times by the smugglers of the coast.

It was here at Cromer Hall that their two youngest sons were born: Thomas Fowell, the second in 1821 and Charles in 1822.

Cromer Hall 1820 from a sketch by Priscilla Gurney

From time to time Mr Buxton would attend his duties in London. For a few years he generally resided with his family in the spring and summer near the House of Commons, spending, however, much of his time at Ham House, Mr S. Gurney's seat in Essex, and with Mr S. Hoare, at Hampstead. Amid the turmoil of his parliamentary life, these country visits were of great advantage to him.

In 1825 the Buxton family settled at 54, Devonshire Street as their London home; but as long as Mr Buxton remained in Parliament, a day of leisure generally found him and his family at Ham House or at Hampstead. After a busy summer in London Mr Buxton highly relished the retirement and recreation of an autumn spent at Cromer.

The following extracts are from Hannah's journal:

Cromer Hall, March 3 1822

My dearest Priscilla has been seized with a renewed attack of hip complaint, and we are ordered to remain here for some weeks longer.

March 25

She still has a good deal of pain. She said to me this morning that she had found great help through the night from this verse, 'Thou wilt keep him in perfect peace whose mind is stayed upon thee.'

Sunday, April 1

My dearest Priscilla looked very poorly and languid during my reading with her and the boys. When they were gone I tried to comfort her. She acknowledged with thankfulness the help she had had during last week, and said she thought we ought to pray that this week might be attended with the same blessings.

April 14

My dearest child has been for some days in an unusually cloudy state, and I felt unable to minister to her. Yesterday she told me she was far more comfortable. This evening she talked with great feeling on the pain it was to her to be kept from London, and from the House of Commons during the criminal Law debate...

Oct 27

My beloved girl has been decidedly better the last few weeks, and is now able to walk a little without difficulty.

Dec 22

My dearest Priscilla is wonderfully restored; the complaint apparently gone, though it has left her delicate. Today she told me with tears what her experience of the power and presence of God had been to her. I expressed my desire that we might be deeply thankful for her recovery; she answered, with the deepest feeling, 'Not more so, mamma than for the illness.'

Hannah Lady Buxton in 1830 with her two youngest sons, T. Fowell and Charles

In the beginning of 1828, the Buxtons were obliged, with much regret to leave Cromer Hall, the proprietor Mr Wyndham, having determined to replace it by a new mansion for his own residence. Being much attached to the neighbourhood, they gladly accepted Mr R.H. Gurney's offer of Northrepps Hall which, though smaller than their last abode, possessed many points of attraction, not the least of which being that within a quarter of a mile stood Northrepps Cottage the home of Mr Buxton's sister Sarah Buxton and his cousin Anna Gurney.

They were scarcely settled at Northrepps, which was from this time their home in the country, when he was called to London to resume the parliamentary labours which illness had unfortunately caused him to cut short in the previous year.

11

Extracts from Priscilla Buxton's Journals (1822–1834)

As has been noted, Priscilla was a delicate child and for years suffered from a hip complaint, which made her unable to walk. Priscilla seems to have been just the sort of angelic child who plays so large a part in nineteenth century fiction. She lay there planning how to improve herself and be a greater comfort to her parents, worrying about 'the poor slaves', and, in the true family tradition, recording in her journal the superlative virtues of everyone who came into the house, speaking very highly of her friends, Mary Ann and Catherine Hankinson.

Sunday, Sept 11th 1825

I am considerably, though gradually raised out of my low estate since I last wrote; partly owing I believe to the pleasure I have enjoyed in the company of my beloved friends Mary Ann and Catherine Hankinson. They came the day before I last wrote my journal and we have been constantly together since. Their sweetness and affection, and their cheerful and pious influence has done me good, and I have been a great deal with them bathing, reading, walking, and riding together...

Sunday, October 25th 1828

[On returning from church this day Priscilla had been feeling very unwell, however her friend lifted her spirits] ... darling Catherine Hankinson came home with me ... her company is delicious to my soul. She and I have the most perfect union of mind. We see things and persons in the same light exactly; we understand one another fully with a word or a look, or almost without either ... I feel an ever fresh delight in her... What a precious friend: what a gift from Heaven.

We also learn how the young Priscilla had been affected by the early deaths of her siblings, as she recalls the 'Hampstead catastrophe' at the age of twenty-three in October 1831:

> We all went over the hills to Overstrand: it was to me a very affecting occasion; and I regretted having been exposed to it. The party of the living, healthful, once happy companions of him who sleeps under the sod there, was too striking a contrast, and I could only wonder, as I often do how we remained alive to tell of his early end. The monument put up there to the memory of six brothers and sisters all younger than myself, does indeed speak to my heart in most melancholy tones...

At the age of fourteen Priscilla Buxton began to keep her own journal. In it she records re-occurrences of her health complaints. After one bout of illness Priscilla, having made a full recovery, asks to be sent to boarding school. Life at home was too stimulating to be able to concentrate on the education she felt she lacked. Firstly we learn of a journey that was made at the age of fourteen, during which time we see the 'paving of the way for her future' works: she travelled from Cromer to London by sea. It was at this time that she began to take an interest in the plight of slaves and her father's work for the emancipation of the slaves. She would regularly attend and thoroughly enjoy her father's speeches.

As Priscilla grew older her health improved so that from the age of 20 to 26 she was able to throw herself wholeheartedly into the business of helping her adored father in his campaign. It was through this involvement with his work that she met her future husband and father of Priscilla Hannah, Mr Andrew Johnston, MP for St Andrews. He had also identified himself with her father in the fight in parliament for the emancipation of the slaves.

Hampstead, July 1822

My wishes for my journal are that I should not copy from anybody's journal. Aunt Hoare has let me see great parts of her old journals, when she was a child, and it is from seeing how valuable these old documents are to her now, that makes me wish to keep a journal myself. Perhaps it may end in my only writing on Sundays. I do not wish to write a religious journal or to make any point of writing anything which is not upper most in my mind. I am now fourteen and five months, during which five months I have not walked once, owing to a third attack of pain in my hip. Before we left Cromer Hall this is the way we spent our days:

Directly after breakfast we did a little botany, that is to say, examined a few flowers, found out their classes and orders; then we read a few chapters in the bible; after that we read a chapter in 'Watts on the mind'; by twelve or one we had done this, and then I generally read Italian with Christiana [Miss Glover who lived several years with the family as a valued instructress and friend]. After that, I used sometimes to go out, I was carried down stairs and out on a mattress. Nobody knows how tried I have been during this illness; but through it all I earnestly desire to submit myself to Him who doeth all things well, and to submit cheerfully, remembering that God loveth a cheerful giver.

When Mamma was in London she went to the doctor, who seemed to think that I might safely be moved from Cromer.

Uncle Hoare and Aunt Martha brought Chenda, the boys and me, to London in the steamer. As we began to descend the cliff at Cromer I was terrified. I was lying quite flat so that I could not see except upwards: I saw numbers of people staring at me. When we got to the boat they lifted my mattress in: I was extremely frightened. It was now full half past nine and very dark. Through it all there was indescribable peace granted to me; I looked up to the sky and thought that God was looking at and caring for me, and that he would not suffer any evil to come to me. This was a great mercy, and one to be remembered all my life. We had to go two miles before we got to the ship. Then there was the greatest difficulty to get in; the boat rose and fell so much. I felt the only thing was to be still, and let them do what they would or could with me. As soon as I got on deck, the captain and some other men carried me down instantly into the cabin. During the night we had sad weather, and at one time we went only four miles an hour; and we were all grievously ill. When I could think of anything, I thought how dreadful must be the sufferings of the poor slaves crammed and crowded, and not allowed nor able to stand or lie down. How little do we know the immense quantity of suffering which is going forward in the world! Perhaps it is well for us to taste a little of it now and then.

We landed at Harwich, and next day reached Devonshire Street, where I was carried up into the drawing room, my bedroom being next door; and I never once went out of those two rooms until I was carried down again to come here (to Hampstead). Papa was most affectionate and sweet, and I most thoroughly enjoyed seeing him again. Aunt Fry came, and had a little meeting with us, which was very comfortable; I think Aunt Fry is the person in the world the most comforting to those about her. Mamma said today, when she got me my journal, 'I hope thee will let me see thy journal; I think it will be very interesting.' I do not think I shall, because showing it to anybody would I think take off the pleasure and value of my journal; though if I showed it to anybody, I am sure I should do to that dearest, dearest mamma, whom it has been my habit through life to be so entirely intimate with. What an inexpressible blessing to me to have such parents. How different to mamma herself, whose mother died while she was quite a little child. It is my most earnest desire and prayer, every day and every hour, that I may die before them and not have the killing affliction of losing them. I do not think I ever should have another happy hour except in contributing to the comfort of the beloved surviving parent.

Cromer Hall, Wednesday, August 28, 1822 (still confined to sofa)

I have much enjoyed getting once more to dear old Cromer, having been absent for three months. Yesterday while mamma was asleep, papa and I learnt two hundred and thirty lines of poetry; we took an hour and a half; I enjoyed it very much.

I think the three things which I most wish for now are, first to draw beautifully: I shall not be content until I have aunt Chenda's boldness, mamma's foliage, and dear aunt Priscilla's exquisite softness and clearness: second to write beautifully; and the third is only a help to writing well, but is the greatest convenience through life, and that is to mend pens charmingly. I am determined to accomplish this by my fifteenth birthday; writing, I wish to be done when I shall be sixteen; and drawing when I shall be seventeen, that is to say if I live so long; and so by the time that I am eighteen, my education will be finished. French I consider already very nearly, if not quite conquered, except speaking, which I believe is not to be attained elegantly but by travelling in the continent. As to Italian, I shall never attempt to speak it, but only to be able to read easily the principal books... The chief thing I wish to have accomplished when I am eighteen, is a course of history, beginning with Grecian then Roman, and then English, learning at the same time, the dates as far as I can, and the geography perfectly. In this course I wish to intermingle a little general European history.

September 13th

Mr and Mrs Wilberforce are staying here. All morning they were out. It made me feel very low, I longed so earnestly to be with them. It was such a long time that I was alone. It is quite a loss to lose Mr Wilberforce's company at meals...

Sunday, September 29th

I know it is for the present unavoidable that I should be thrown on myself and my own resources; but then look at what are those which I call my resources! 'Come unto me all ye that are heavy laden and I will give you rest!' There is a noble resource!

October 6th

I walked once across my own room, papa and uncle Hoare supporting me – after not having walked a single step for more than seven months. What a long confinement! ... I am sure I may truly say 'It is good for me to be afflicted' ... Some times those words in Isaiah – 'I have chosen thee in the furnace of affliction' – are applied to my mind ... I go down to dinner everyday. Yesterday, the first thing after breakfast, I began the great business of my life for many years to come, namely, the education of dearest Chenda. She is too young to learn much, but she is not too young to be disciplined ... Darling Chenda born on the 5th January 1820. The first six months of that melancholy year was extremely unsettled ... I first entered Cromer Hall on the 25th August, 1820.

Sunday, December 8th

Aunt Catherine spoke to me about the boys, and I perfectly agree in what she said, namely, that my manner towards them was not nearly gentle enough. She said she could speak from own experience, for when left the head of a large family of brothers and sisters, she had so strikingly found the benefit of always treating them and governing them with the greatest of gentleness, and never exerting authority for the love of it, and only when absolutely necessary ... It is my fullest intention to take warning from her advice and to be far more gentle to the children than I have been.

Tuesday, January 21st 1823 [writing of her father]

With greatest openness and nobility of mind; generous to an excess and considerate to the feelings of everyone, even children; vigorous and energetic in whatever he undertakes; all these invaluable qualities are crowned and cemented together by religion – true, pure, and unadulterated piety ... How I shall enjoy it if I become useful to him in his objects! He told me yesterday that Mr Cobbet's second daughter writes almost all his papers for him, and that he should make me Miss Cobbet the second. I have not heard anything that delighted me so much for a long time. To be his companion in any way is the highest object of my ambition.

Earlham, Monday, March 10th

The other day papa went to the Speaker's Levee with his bag wig all fastened wrong, and all the company laughed at him...

Sunday, March 16th

I feel now more and more the earnest desire to perfect my education. I wish to be nothing less than perfect in all that is to be performed with one's ten fingers...

May 15th

We went to hear the slavery debate. It went off with the greatest interest Mr Brougham did make such a speech. I think altogether it was the most entertaining thing I ever heard ... his squint at the person he is speaking of, is one of the most comical things in the world ... Papa spoke twice, the second time it was the most spirited reply to all that had been said on the other side of the question. Thus ended a most deeply interesting debate, at about half past one in the morning. I shall not attempt to say how I enjoyed it, suffice to say that it was one of the greatest, if not the greatest, treat I ever had, and that I shall look back upon it with feelings of the greatest of pleasure, interest, and I will add pride.

Sunday, November 9th

I shall go over my improvements again I think. I mean, take another survey of my education…

Friday, January 30th, 1824

This week I have been very busy, getting up early, for my father has given me a history of Sierra Leone to write, which is long and difficult.

Sunday, February 1st

Here I am lying on the sofa, staying from church and, as I believe, fairly in for another imprisonment. It is a most thorough exercise for me; I have been lately so much in the full enjoyment of my precious liberty, dancing, walking &c, and now it does seem hard to give it all up again. I endeavour to feel and to say, 'Thy will be done' … I have had to say, 'Thou hast chosen me in the furnace of affliction.'

Sunday, February 7th

My journal of this day week is deeply interesting to me, I feel as if I could not express or even be sufficiently thankful to have had this painful blow averted. On Sunday afternoon I became gradually easier; and on Monday morning so well that we thought it not imprudent for me to go to Earlham.

Sunday, February 29th, Hampstead

On Wednesday I entered my seventeenth year…

Sunday, March 7th

I felt poorly yesterday; I am resigned and ready to die if such be the will of God? … perhaps I shall soon feel better.

The summer of 1824 saw her begin her life at school. She so earnestly longed to improve her education, that she voluntarily decided to leave home for a time, though neither her strength nor her spirits was equal to the effort. She remained at school but for one interrupted year.

Friday night, April 30th, 1824

I have thought seriously how far it would be worth my while to make up my mind to the sacrifice of going to school for a year in order to finish off my very deficient education. I am sure it would not be for pleasure but I think the delight of coming home would be nearly worth the pain of going there…

May 27th

We have fixed that I shall go to school at Mrs Oom's, Halkin St, London. The whole affair is entirely my own doing and my own decision, and I feel now as if I must sink under the effort, as if I had neither strength of mind nor of body to stand alone in a scene of life so totally new to me; indeed I can look for no peace or comfort there, except in full and unshaken confidence in my God and Father … On Friday I shall feel sufficiently miserable, I think.

June 13th, Mrs Oom's, Halkin Street

Well, here I am, actually settled at school; I can hardly realize it to myself, it is so amazingly strange to be actually a school girl. About ten we went up to bed … Some part of the day they all read an hour and a half with Mrs Oom in two classes … I thoroughly enjoy reading with Mrs Oom; she is so intellectual and so very kind.

Sunday, June 27th

I entirely feel that a time in unbroken order, regularity, and industry, is extremely good for me. At Hampstead I was so constantly overdone by one excitement or another, that I had no spirit for settling regularly to lessons … Here everybody is busy and I cannot help it, and slip into it, and enjoy it.

Sunday, September 5th, Cromer Hall

'My sweet brother Fowell is now with me talking and playing. He is the most engaging child possible. I hope I do not love him too much. O what inexpressible anguish it would be to me to lose him...

Sunday evening, September 19th, Halkin Street

Mamma came with me as far as Earlham, and we had some quiet time together ... we had a most interesting little time with dearest papa. I cannot say how very great a privilege it has been to me to be allowed, frequently to join their little meetings of an evening ... In the course of the next day we went to Norwich in the carriage, and at the inn we found the coach nearly ready to start, so I, not without many tears, took leave of my most beloved and precious mother ... It very soon set off, and I was quickly carried away from dear Norfolk.

September 26th

The accounts I receive of the dear autumn party are truly tantalizing to me; however I have throughout all my clouds, the inexpressible comfort of knowing that I am following the path of duty, and entirely believing in following it. I shall be assisted and supported by the same Almighty hand which has been so mercifully stretched out for my assistance and comfort on many former times.

October 6th

How much I have to say since I wrote my journal last. A month ago, in Halkin Street, I felt a slight headache in the morning; it grew rapidly worse and worse; it gave me a great deal of pain to swallow; I was quite unable to hold up my head. Mrs Oom after consultation with the apothecary, sent me to Hampstead. For days I was very ill. My disorder was decidedly scarlet fever, though of a favourable kind. When I found out that it was so, I was much startled. I had an extreme fear of scarlet fever and some of the hours I passed in bed, most wakeful, were awful ones to me. I was deeply struck with a nearness of death, and most powerfully awakened to the sense of my own unfitness for it...

When recovered she set off for Cromer with her mother, and writes thus:

> As we were making our way across Newmarket Heath, all of a sudden we stopped, as one of the front wheels refused to go round, being on fire. The postillion ran for a pail of water, which caused an amazing hissing, but did not put it out. We were obliged to take the wheel off. As we were pacing up and down the Heath a sort of jockey looking gentleman came up to us and offered to take us to his house, which we accepted. Mamma took his arm, and off we set, marching across Newmarket Heath. It was dark, though starlight, and very cold. I should think we walked nearly a mile before we reached the house. I was extremely tired, only having walked with assistance a very little way before. We were ushered into a comfortable parlour. They were extremely hospitable to us; gave us tea, and we sat talking a long time expecting the carriage. After having waited about an hour and a half, word was brought us that they could not get the wheel off, and that therefore the carriage was perfectly immovable; so these kind people immediately offered us their carriage. At length we set off again, but our misfortunes were not to end here. We were happy to reach the Three Cups, at Newmarket, and had got everything out of the carriage, when we found owing to the races there were no beds to be had, or at least none that mamma could sleep in; so tired as we were, we were obliged to pack up again, and once more try our fortune in a post-chaise. We reached Bardon Mills in safety about eleven o'clock.

Tuesday, November 2nd

Before dinner mamma and I had a long conversation about all my employments and plans. All the spirit which I felt at Mrs Oom's seems departed entirely from me; however I cannot say how much I desire to render home as happy as I can this winter...

Sunday, November 28th

Mrs Oom has consented to receive me on the 6th January. Now that that which I have indeed earnestly desired is obtained, I cannot express how much I shrink from the pain of leaving home.

Priscilla returned to the school at Halkin Street on January 16th 1825. However, she found it difficult to settle in. She records how much she misses 'the retirement and comfort of the family' and that she can accept the atmosphere of the school only by 'the guidance and protection of the Lord'.

Friday, February 11th

A day to be always remembered with true gratitude. We went to the riding school, where they put me upon a nasty black horse, which I had not before ridden. I went on prosperously for some time, till at length in the setting off of a canter, it first started, proceeded a little, tripped, kicked and fell; and, accordingly, I found myself flying over his head and under his feet. Mr Stanley, the riding master, who was providentially by my side, saved me extremely well. He was off his horse in an instant, and got me from under my enraged steed, who was plunging and struggling very much. I was thankful mamma was not there: what a mercy my deliverance was to me! I cannot say how strongly I feel the deliverance from such imminent danger: I was perfectly unhurt!

February 25th

This day I have attained the age of seventeen ... It has been a painful feeling to me to be away from all my dear family on my birthday; the first ever I passed away from home ... After eighteen, if I live, I do not expect to have much time for education. I am then to show and give to my parents the fruits of my education ... I am full of good desires, but to realise them is quite another matter...

Thursday, July 7th

And now having come to the end of my time with my dearest Mrs Oom, I must express the lively thankfulness and gratitude which I feel for the tender supporting arm which has constantly been with me throughout the whole. How I have prayed for support and it has been granted me ... It has turned out, I think the happiest time of my life. I do desire that my beloved parents may reap the effects of the sacrifices they made; that they may be satisfied with me, outwardly and inwardly...

Priscilla now returned to life at Cromer and her family. In September 1825 she wrote from Earlham thus: 'All the gentlemen went off to the Slavery meeting: it went off capitally. Papa made one of the best speeches he ever made. There were fifty people at dinner. I must say that I looked very nicely, and papa said he was quite proud of me!...'

Tuesday, January 31st 1826

I have had one thing which has delighted me, that is, papa told mamma that I was the greatest pleasure to him, that I was a delightful companion to him and really added to the comfort of his life. O how can I be thankful enough for this very seasonable help on my way...

From April to November 1826, Priscilla went abroad with her uncle and aunt Cunningham. They travelled through the south of France and Switzerland, and were absent nearly seven months. The fatigue and excitement of this journey were far beyond her strength yet, despite the continuous journeying, a great number of elaborate sketches were achieved, and a minute description of the places visited was recorded in her journal. Whilst she was travelling, her mother kept her informed of her father's work and the highly charged events on the political scene:

June 5th 1826, Bellfield

My dearest Priscilla, everything about papa would interest you, and all the variations of electioneering concerns would interest you were you here; but the state of things is like a web of tangled silk to me. The grand thing to us now is that all sides and factions unite in supporting papa, and there seems no fear of his election...

Weymouth 1826

We are entirely immersed in election concerns ... Papa is considerably at the head of the poll, but our party hitherto beaten by Gordon's, who keeps two above our candidates. The bustles, quarrelling and fightings continue unabated, and yesterday was the worst day we had for riots and tumults, so that the military was obliged to be called in ... In the evening I went with Papa into the mob to see it and the soldiers, and I was quite pleased through the enemy's mob to find the manner in which papa was received – universal shouting and approbation, crowds coming to shake his hands. Indeed, he does not appear to have a person against him in the town...

In November the party returned to England and Priscilla wrote:

Cromer Hall, November 28th 1826

No words can describe how interesting every well-known bush and stone were to me as we approach Cromer, and at length when we drove up the court, I was out in an instant and made but one bound over the hall and up the stairs, till I found myself in the arms of my adored mother, crying for joy...

Cromer Hall, July 3rd 1827 [Writing of her father's alarming illness at Ham House]

On Sunday morning mamma went to meeting, and I stayed with him. He lay on the sofa, as I thought asleep, in a torpid state. I read him a little, but not being able to get an answer from him, I sat perfectly quiet. By the time mamma came home I was frightened indeed. They sent for leeches. We got him upstairs, he every moment becoming more torpid. The awful truth by degrees opened upon us that he was lying in a state of unnatural insensibility. Oh never can I describe what it was; the horrors of the valley we appeared to be entering burst upon us, and despair was on every side. But the scene cannot be described; may it never be forgotten. I can scarcely bear even now to think of my dearest, dearest mother's sufferings. It was pronounced pressure on the brain, and very alarming. Then dear uncle and aunt Hoare arrived. Aunt Fry and uncle Sam were almost the principal nurses. The night was a most awful one, every hour seemed to increase the dreadful suspense. He was totally insensible. We assembled round his bed, and Aunt Fry, who was through all like a ministering angel, burst forth into a song of praise, commending him to God, and beseeching His care for us all ... On the following Thursday he was pronounced out of danger!... I cannot describe the extreme kindness we received from everybody: the enquiries and sympathy expressed by friends and strangers. In the house of commons it produced quite a sensation.

November 22

My dear father, so incomparably sweet ... told me that for the last few months I had been an inconceivable pleasure to him; in short, I may say we do enjoy each others company thoroughly...

Early in 1828 the Buxtons left their beloved home, Cromer Hall and, after spending a few days in Northrepps Cottage, entered their new abode, Northrepps Hall, in February 1828. Just before finally leaving Cromer Hall Priscilla wrote: 'It is a curious and melancholy scene. I cannot help reviewing the time we have spent here; it seems but yesterday since we came here, seven years and a half ago.

> How in a few short moments I retrace
> (as in a map the voyager his course)
> the windings of my way through many years.'

Northrepps Hall, February 4th 1828

Here we are! This day we have entered our new abode; begun this new stage and section of our lives ... God only knows what is most for my good and happiness, and to Him I do altogether, and very solemnly, commit the whole of my future destiny ... Dearest Mamma looked tired and, I thought low when we went to bed ... She is of the most incalculable, unspeakable importance to me every day and hour; I apply to her in every case; in short, no one person can be more dependent on another than I am on her...

Now came a period of tremendous anti-slavery campaign activity for her father. Priscilla worked as his secretary both at Northrepps and in their London house in Devonshire Street. In London Priscilla met Mr Wilberforce and thought that nothing could exceed his kindness. 'He is so extremely affectionate to me – it is quite delightful.' Wilberforce was fairly often at Northrepps. Priscilla writes, 'Overstrand church was rather pleasant, Mr Wilberforce's behaviour quite edifying, nice dinner and evening. Mr Wilberforce most beaming in mind, I have never seen him brighter. He is altogether a glorious sight. The honour that encircles his hoary head, the brilliancy of his genius and the light of his mind contrast with the decrepitude of his body.'

Although Fowell now bought Colne House, he never lived there,

The earliest surviving picture of Northrepps Hall, drawn by Priscilla Buxton in 1834, before extensions were made in all directions

for he was 'entirely delighted' with Northrepps. When he was not shooting, he was organising boys' shoots, cricket matches and excursions with endless children from various families carried in a variety of unconventional vehicles, with many mounted on makeshift horses and donkeys. He was always able to find plenty, other energetic relaxations from the paper-work he brought with him from London. He loved taking Hannah for a drive in his high phaeton if it was fine or the brougham if it was cold, and this is when he would call from the hall when the horses were ready: 'Bustle, bustle Mrs Noah, the ark is at the door.'

Buxton writes warmly of his children at this time:

In my children I have hitherto the greatest cause of thankfulness. Priscilla, her masculine understanding raises her into a companion on equal terms, and her disposition, full of affection, makes her a delightful companion ... Edward, can I wish for a son more full of natural grace ... Harry I delight myself with the promise which he puts forth of vigorous character ... The younger shoots, Richenda, Fowell, Charles, with these I am abundantly contented.

In the beginning of 1829 the family returned to London, and after an interval Priscilla writes of her voluntary work in the hospital:

Monday, May 18th 1829

To the hospital. Read very seriously in St John's Gospel to a poor young woman, who has become wonderfully softened. Several gathered round and I was carried on to address them strongly. I then went to my poor Irish woman, one of my former party following me. She said she had thought continually of what I had said, and that she would have to thank me forever for it. I felt great doubts about her understanding, and feeling most deeply my inability to teach her…

On Thursday I went again to the hospital; I had a very nice reading on the cancer ward, which is indeed an affecting sight and, as it were, the end of the earth. The stillness, cleanliness of it, and the condemned state as to this world of its few melancholy inhabitants are most striking; few if any of them will ever leave their desolate habitation; some have been there for years and have seen many come, and some depart only in their coffins … It is a great effort, but one that always pays to go to them…

Later that year Harry became unwell. He appeared to have rallied round, but then at his sixteenth birthday party he over-exerted himself romping with the younger children, which brought on a violent fit of coughing during which he coughed up blood. His mother writes in her journal, 'A death stroke I knew it to be, our first care was to soothe and cheer him, awful as the moment was, he told me afterwards that he immediately turned to God for help.' They all seem to have possessed this fortitude and mental discipline; it was bred into them by the certainty of their faith. Of such stuff martyrs are made.

His father lay down with him and read to him until he was asleep, leaving 'with an almost broken heart'. Harry was kept in bed for a week or two, only allowed out in good weather. Harry's last entry in his journal was October 25th 1829: 'The thought occurs to me whether I shall ever see October 25th, 1830.' The following spring of 1830 he was well enough to pay a round of visits, for the old cry of 'a change of air' was still prescribed. But by the middle of November Priscilla writes: 'Our dearest Harry is in a most sinking state. I think the step down for the last few days has been decided. His cough has been severe and his consequent exhaustion truly alarming ... Truly might we say, "As the outward man decays the inward man is renewed day by day."'

Friday, November 19th

How can I but write! Our precious beloved one is gone; his dear spirit most gently departed yesterday afternoon...

Thursday, November 24th

The funeral was to me personally a day of almost indescribable affliction ... Never was the loss before me in such colours. I cannot say what it was to leave our beloved brother there; and as I walked with Edward and Chenda, the dear child with us because she had no brother to walk with, I could not but as it were writhe under the idea that I was the eldest and Chenda the youngest of nine, and that there was but our dear Edward between us...

Around this time, inspired by the 'Cottage Ladies', Lame Anna Gurney and Sarah Buxton's Overstrand School, Priscilla started an infant school in the smaller hamlet of Northrepps in the kitchen of a 'Homely woman' who could sing and read and so could replace her when she was helping her father. Later she too had a tiny school-house built in Northrepps.[36]

12

The 'Great Anti-Slavery Interest'

The beginning of February 1831 (until October 1831) found her in London, busily entering into all her father's interests; they were both called to great exertions in the anti-slavery cause. She writes thus to Catherine Hankinson: 'Did I tell you of our large Anti-Slavery party ... it was a fine assembly of fine and interesting gentlemen? Mamma did not appear. Father chose I should; and Aunt Fry was to come to be with me ... My father's mind is turning more and more to immediate emancipation. Slavery, slavery, is more than ever our topic...'; and to her brother Edward she writes, 'The Anti-Slavery meeting went off nobly. There were between three and four thousand people present. Exeter Hall is a noble building. My father spoke first and delightfully I must say. He was amazingly cheered and was in the highest popularity all the meeting ... When someone drew a parallel between the Jews in Egypt and the Negroes in Jamaica, my father got up, and quietly said, "I beg to correct the rev. gentleman ... In the case of the Jews there was compensation, for we hear of the slaves going out with jewels of silver and gold." We were delighted, and made a fine noise. The tone of the meeting was to install my father as leader of the cause.'

In 1832 came the insurrection in Jamaica. The slave holders tried to throw the blame on the missionaries and proceeded with acts of violence and cruelty against them in every possible way, including torture. The Government, for political reasons were unwilling to take up the question. But Mr Buxton was still determined to press his motion for the abolition of slavery, though every effort was used to prevent him from bringing it forward. His own friends said that he would only injure the cause if he persevered and they and other individual members of the government pressed him to withdraw it, receiving over a hundred applications of this kind from different MPs. He often worked himself into a state of utter exhaustion, when he would stretch himself out on the specially long sofa in the drawing room at Northrepps Hall and wait till he recovered. Thanks to a huge female following, however, Mr Buxton was able to present a petition bearing 187,000 signatures from British women in favour of the abolition of slavery, the roll being so enormous that it required four men to lay it on a table in the House of Commons. He had done what he thought right and in May 1833 the bill for the Abolition of Slavery at last received the Royal assent.

On March 5th 1832 Hannah Lady Buxton wrote, 'My dearest husband has been delightful; he is full of grace and truth. The work in which he is engaged is that of God ... To him he looks for guidance, for wisdom, for strength, for ability ... His love towards us is overflowing, abounding in tenderness and indulgence ... For dearest Priscilla he seems ready to lay down his life, or do anything to please and make her happy; for Edward and the children he is only too considerate.'

The following extracts from Priscilla Buxton's journals refer to the 'great Anti-Slavery interest':

London, April 1st 1832

My thoughts have been chiefly occupied about my most beloved father, whose birthday it is. My tenderest love has indeed hovered round him ... oh that we may see his health confirmed, his spirits cheered, his hands strengthened and his cause upheld ... I am entirely employed in his business; sometimes very much pressed. It is a great privilege and enjoyment too, and I am so thankful to be of any use. His tenderness and consideration towards me exceed telling ... Yesterday, the anti slavery meeting most interesting and memorable: my beloved father's speech the best I ever heard. May I never lose the vivid picture of him as I saw him yesterday, the beauty and majesty of his appearance, the perfect grace of his manner. He stood like a living colossus, and I looked at him till I could bear it no longer ... We had a large party afterwards, aunt Fry, Mr O'Connell and others. I sat by Mr Johnston, a young Scotch MP.

December 16th

My dearest father has successfully fought his battle: We heard of his re-election yesterday. He was affectionately supported by the Weymouth people, and he says, 'My only desire is to spend my life in the service of Him who gave it, and of His creatures' ... We have had a great and rare privilege of having aunt Fry settled with us for nearly a fortnight. I have been so impressed with her powers, as well as her extraordinary graces, that I feel as if almost I have never known her before ... She said in our committee that she was morning, noon and night under deep impression of her responsibility towards others ... My dearest mother is the only greater saint in the world, I think.

Friday, February 8th 1833

... Papa was very happy, for the ministers had agreed to undertake the abolition of slavery ... I feel as if I had just attained a platform in life and am looking around me, beholding my inheritance. I have climbed up to full mature life, and have now to take my stand among those who are fully embarked in the business of it.

April 11th

Edward [her brother] is hurrying from place to place, attending committee meetings, and we at home are writing nearly all day and sending off books ... The flame is spreading far and wide. Devonshire is going to send five hundred petitions, the west of Essex three hundred, and fifty from the neighbourhood of Colchester...

April 16th

The delegates meet tomorrow, more than two hundred were expected when we last heard. Edward is gone to speak at a great meeting at the Tower Hamlets.

London, April 19th 1833

Well now for our Anti-Slavery Parliament, which is going to conclude its session and its existence by a grand public dinner at four o'clock this day. Their meeting yesterday was highly successful. There were three hundred and thirty nine delegates assembled in Exeter Hall, from two hundred and twenty seven places to meet the Anti-Slavery Committee...

Evening, half past ten o'clock – I find myself alone, just come back from the dizzy sight of four hundred gentlemen at dinner, lights, speechifying and clapping in proportion. We have indeed had the very great treat of seeing this unique and memorable assembly … they were assembled from all parts of England – clergymen, magistrates, squires, Friends and Methodists. The spirit in which they all have come together has been wonderful … My father's tact and powers of winning have never been more displayed. It is his coronation as leader of the cause! though he, if possible, deserved the crown far more when he was fighting alone than now when he has that army at his back.

April 28th

Yesterday we had a charming party. It consisted of ten MPs all of one mind – ten thoroughly devoted Christians … It was a fine sight, to assemble them in our house was no small privilege.

Here one of the ten MPs Priscilla names is Mr Johnston of Fifeshire, MP for St Andrews, whom Mr Buxton described as 'A dear fellow, who will not bother with such delicacies in the country as a hat.' He in turn found Mr Buxton, 'a delightful chief to work for'.

May 5th

How my heart has been drawn out in desires for our Slavery cause, which comes on next Tuesday week, the 14th. Really the interest of it is become intense; and if the ministers fail on the 14th, what shall we do? What will the poor unhappy sufferers do?

Priscilla, who worked extremely hard as her father's secretary writes of their success from London to her aunt Sarah thus:

May 16th

After this letter I think I must burn my paper and pens and give my poor tired wrist, which is nearly worn out and always aching some rest. I am tired, most utterly tired, of writing and everything connected with work. As for petitions I only wish I might never see the face of another. The fact is, I am exhausted and the almost constant uneasiness in my hip frets my temper … I spent the whole day, till nine o'clock at night, over petitions at Devonshire House, till the great mass became too heavy for us to roll over. Next day a vast number of Slavery petitions were presented. My father's turn came last – he asked leave to take out a deputation of members to bring in our monster. So he, Mr Evans, Mr Andrew Johnston, and someone else disappeared, and returned and heaved it onto the table, amid loud laughter and cheers, it produced a great effect ... We came away at about one. My father was delighted, 'My work in life is done, since I have lived to hear my own doctrines from the Treasury bench. Emancipation is effected. The thing is done' these are the phrases on his lips.

                              Ever Yours (half dead) Priscilla Buxton

The following June, 1834, Priscilla Buxton became engaged to Mr Andrew Johnston of Rennyhill, Fife.

13

Introducing Mr Andrew Johnston, MP

Mr Andrew Johnston was the fourth successive Andrew Johnston of Rennyhill, Fife. The family had originally come from Annandale in Galloway.

> 'In the Vale of Annandale
> The gentle Johnston's ride,
>   They have been there a thousand years.
>   A thousand years they'll bide.'

So says an old rhyme, though the term gentle is said to have been somewhat ironically bestowed upon a family probably as lawless as the rest of the Border Clans whose stories survive in ballads.

Some time in the seventeenth century the son of a certain Sir James Johnston was shipwrecked off the coast of Aberdeen. He was befriended by fishermen and remained among them, marrying a fisherman's daughter. This marriage caused his family to disown him and he found himself penniless, obliged to work for a living and to bring up his son to hawk mussels through the streets. The boy was known as Mussel Andrew.

Mussel Andrew's son, a successful merchant, also named Andrew, restored the family fortunes and bought the house and estate of Rennyhill in Anstruther, some time in the early part of the seventeenth century. For the next hundred years or so Rennyhill was handed down from father to son through four generations of Andrew Johnstons until Mussel Andrew's great-great grandson married Priscilla Buxton and removed to Norfolk.

Andrew Johnston of Rennyhill and afterwards of Holton Hall, Sussex, married first in 1827, Barbara Pearson, daughter of Col Pearson Esq. of Edinburgh, by whom he had two daughters, Charlotte and Margaret. Both died in infancy, and were buried at Kilrenny. Finally Barbara died on 20th January 1830 and was buried in the Rennyhill tomb, where a tablet was erected 'by the only survivor of the marriage'.[37]

After this harrowing experience a dramatic change occurred in Andrew's life. In 1831 he was elected Whig MP for the five burghs of East Fife.[38] On arriving in Parliament he soon made the acquaintance of Thomas Fowell Buxton with whom he now identified himself in the fight in parliament and the country for the emancipation of the slaves, becoming one of his most faithful allies. He became Mr Buxton's companion and assistant on his committees for enquiring into the slave trade, as conducted by foreign nations, between the coast of Africa and the slave states of America and Cuba; the working of the apprenticeship system for the Negro, which resulted soon afterwards in the introduction of a bill enforcing, in Jamaica, certain measures in favour of the Negros. The Aborigine's Committee had likewise been appointed. Mr Johnston took up the position of private secretary to him during Buxton's last three years in Parliament. Andrew Johnston expressed his admiration for Buxton thus:

> I had been well acquainted with Mr Buxton's name, and had watched his proceedings with interest, before I entered Parliament in 1831. Shortly after I took my seat, I introduced myself to him as one who aimed at being enlisted under his Anti-slavery banner, and before long, I was honoured with that friendship which I ever felt I could not sufficiently prize. I was soon impressed by seeing his almost exclusive devotedness to the object he had in hand at any given time; he spared no pains to achieve his purpose, he was constantly on the watch, and by his tact and perseverance frequently succeeded in obtaining documents, which would have otherwise remained in obscurity. Often did he patiently wait to the end of the usually long debates for the small chance of success in a motion for papers; often did one tiresome opponent, in particular, who seemed to make it his peculiar vocation to hinder his progress, succeed in frustrating his endeavours ... He was very often at the Foreign Office, and at the Colonial Office, where he was, during the sitting of Parliament, almost a daily visitor. Though his proceedings called forth bitter opposition from some quarters ... I soon saw that his honesty and singleness of purpose, his manly understanding and the weight of his character, commanded a decided and increasing influence in Downing Street. He was thoroughly liked and respected in the House ... I remember, in particular a debate in May 1832 ... which led to the appointment of a Committee on which I was

one of Mr Buxton's nominees, on the state of the Aborigines connected with our Colonies, and on the working of apprenticeship in the West Indies. These cost him many toilsome hours ... His energy never flagged, nor do I remember his ever losing temper in the fatigues and annoyances of these labours ... Often I urged him to break away from additional strain upon his mind, and leave the heated committee room, but he invariably persevered, until he had dismissed his numerous applicants, satisfied with the manner of their reception, and charmed with his great kindness and consideration.

For some years Mr Buxton and myself were associated with a select band of members of Parliament who, though of varied and even opposite political opinions, met on every 'House night' for a short period, to enjoy confidential intercourse on one subject upon which we all were agreed. Reading for Scripture and prayer, were leading objects for which we assembled. Mr Buxton was one of the most constant attendants, and very often 'the chaplain'. Nor can I doubt that these meetings greatly strengthened and sustained him, under the fierce opposition, with which he was too often assailed.'[39]

The following memorandum, in Mr Buxton's handwriting, appears on the last page of a book of 'Papers on the abolition of Slavery' written in January 1836:

I have finished this collection of papers with a degree of satisfaction and thankfulness which I cannot express. My expectations are surpassed, God's blessing has been on this perilous work of humanity.

Mr Andrew Johnston's career as MP for Scotland saw him represent Anstruther Easter burghs (St Andrews) 1831–32; St Andrews burghs, 1833–34 and 1835–37, before removing to East Anglia where he went into the Gurney's bank at Halesworth, which was later merged into that of their cousins, the Barclays.

The great interest of Andrew Johnston's and Priscilla Buxton's engagement almost immediately followed her return to London. She wrote of it in her journal:

Devonshire Street, Sunday, June 25th 1834

Since I last wrote I have been in doubt and darkness, but now I am in light and clearness, in wonderful peace and happiness, engaged to my beloved friend Mr Johnston, delighted, satisfied, and charmed with my allotment ... To my God I render the praise, and only desire that He would take us under His most gracious and tender protection, lead us gently through our pilgrimage, and bring us in safety to Himself.

Five days before the 1st August 1834 Mr Buxton was able to write in his journal: 'On Friday next, slavery is to cease throughout the British Colonies.' While Priscilla looked forward to the same day in *her* journal:

Thursday, July 31st 1834

Tomorrow there will not be a slave left in any British possession and I am to be married to Mr Johnston. Here is the eve of my wedding day! Everything is done. I am going to lock up my desk and close my single life.

Thomas Fowell Buxton's ten year fight for the abolition of slavery was over. Two of his staunchest supporters, his daughter and the member for St Andrew's drawn together by their mutual devotion to the cause, would not marry until the slaves were freed, on August 1st 1834.[40.] Their wedding reception would also be a celebration of the success of the campaign.

PART TWO

The Johnstons. The Early Life and Times of Priscilla Hannah Johnston

14

The Events of the 1st August 1834 and Afterwards

The marriage of Miss Priscilla Buxton and Mr Andrew Johnston took place in the church at Overstrand on the 1st August 1834, the same day on which the emancipation of the slaves took place throughout the British Empire. Priscilla wrote the following account of the day whilst staying at Henley-on-Thames, which was the happy couple's first 'port of call' on their honeymoon.

Henley-on-Thames, August 2, twelve o'clock

We have decided to stay at this delicious place till Monday, therefore we have a delightfully leisure resting day to-day. It was wonderful what a power of enjoyment is given me.

I have never enjoyed a wedding day half so much … Breakfast was in the drawing room. My dearest father read Psalm 111, and followed it by fervent prayer for the slaves, and then for me. After breakfast I helped to adorn my lovely bridesmaid and sister, and soon Kitty, Elizabeth, and Pris arrived. I was so bright I let them all come into my room, and, in glee I was dressed in my bridal white satin. The girls were a sight one more beautiful than another. They were in fairy white, and all wore natural flowers, mostly in their hair. The scarlet geranium in Kitty's shining locks was one of the most lovely pictures I ever saw … At length I was dressed; my white shoes pinched me dreadfully, but the girls only laughed at my cramp … Soon all drove off, then my parents and I. My bridesmaids were standing about the church door, and others of the party, many caught my hand as I passed and as I walked up the aisle with my father; my mother and Edward next; then Mr Johnston and Chenda. By the altar sat aunt Sarah and Anna Gurney. My father made a great muddle, and would hardly let me get to the rails, and, after all, settled himself on Mr J's side! At length however we were put right – nearly sixty round us. Uncle Cunningham read the service to my heart's content. 'I will', said Mr Johnston, in so sturdy a manner, and so broad an accent, that I (inwardly) laughed. My voice and power were astonishing to myself; but I should leave others to tell of my superior behaviour. How each word seemed to sink into my heart! We proceeded to the vestry, where there was plenty of kissing and signing of names.

She went on to describe the combined wedding reception and celebration for the triumph over the slaves:

We drove home, Bessie and Pris ready to receive us, and I felt quite in glee; we had cake and wine, and talked and laughed. I quite enjoyed greeting everybody ... My mother and I were alone for a few minutes; she was wonderful throughout the whole day, up to everything, attentive to everybody, and looking beautiful. After sufficient loitering the party gathered, and my father took his place by the table in the drawing room. He read several passages; and his prayer was noble, most bold and steadfast, first for the slaves, and, to my comfort, he found words for me, but with a faltering voice. Are they not more to me than silver and gold? I was relieved by tears; he came and sat by me on the sofa while a hymn was sung. I could hardly detain him till Edward Buxton appeared bringing in the silver salver on which is inscribed:

To THOMAS FOWELL BUXTON, Esq, MP.
Presented by his nephews and nieces,
August 1st 1834.
With the humble, but earnest desire that they may be enabled to act through life those high principles which have led him, with undaunted resolution, to pursue the noble object, by the blessing of God this day accomplished, in the
ABOLITION OF SLAVERY
THROUGHOUT THE BRITISH DOMINIONS
'Tu ne cede malis sed contra audentior ito'.[1]

Now it was her father who burst into tears and everyone had to go into the garden for a breath of fresh air to recover for the lunch at which fifty two guests were seated, with Priscilla presiding, flowering myrtle and pomegranate in her hair. There were champagne and toasts. Mr Cunningham, with his usual fertility, began a rigmarole about the descent of the 'Northern Barbarians' ending with 'Mr Johnston'. He could say nothing. I said aloud, 'I think I ought to return thanks for the northern barbarian' which was received with great applause. Afterwards several people took turns to read poetry, some of which was their own, written specially for the occasion. Priscilla then changed into her dove-coloured, silk bonnet, white scarf and veil, took leave of her precious mother upstairs with many tears, and was almost carried downstairs by her father who could speak to no-one else. All the world was gathered at the drawing room door. Priscilla kissed the front row, and off she went with her Scotsman, travelling up the country via Henley-on-Thames, leaving after a few days and going on via Oxford to Matlock, Derbyshire; Halifax; and on up to Glasgow where they were joined by her aunt Elizabeth Fry, going on together to make a tour of the West Highlands for their honeymoon.

Mr Buxton immediately sat down and wrote to Mrs Upcher, a pillar among his workers, who was unable to be there: 'Aug. 1, 4 o'clock. My dear friend, the bride is just off. Everything has passed off to admiration and there is not a slave in the British colonies! Mark the seal "Safe and Satisfactory".'[2]

Priscilla's marriage to Mr Johnston was a severe loss to her father, as that of his helper in all objects; one who fully entered into his mind and feelings. To her he committed the writing of many letters, and with her he would write his important papers.[3] He thus alluded to the circumstance, in a letter to the Revd Dr Philip at Cape-town: 'I surrendered my vocation, and, next to Macaulay, my best human helper in it, on the same day; I am not only well contented, but very happy, and very thankful, that she is so bestowed.'[4]

15

*Arrival and Early Family Life at Rennyhill, Anstruther
(1834–1839)*

Mr Johnston returned with his bride to the home of his forefathers, Rennyhill, situated in the historic Royal Burgh of Kilrenny and Anstruther in the 'Kingdom of Fife.'

The burgh of Kilrenny consists of two villages, Nether Kilrenny or Cellardyke, which is on the sea coast, divided from Anstruther Easter only by a small burn and forming with it Anstruther Wester, apparently one long town; and upper Kilrenny, situated about half a mile inland.

In 1587 it gained its royal charter, which gave the town the right to hold weekly markets and an annual fair. From its monastic beginnings, life in the burgh revolved around the harbour. Over the centuries

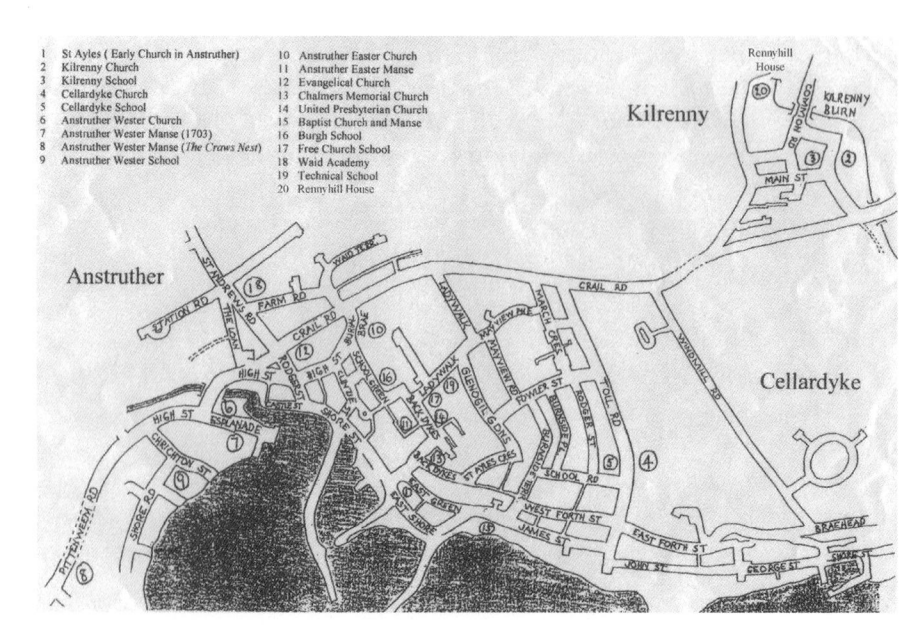

1 St Ayles (Early Church in Anstruther)
2 Kilrenny Church
3 Kilrenny School
4 Cellardyke Church
5 Cellardyke School
6 Anstruther Wester Church
7 Anstruther Wester Manse (1703)
8 Anstruther Wester Manse (*The Craws Nest*)
9 Anstruther Wester School
10 Anstruther Easter Church
11 Anstruther Easter Manse
12 Evangelical Church
13 Chalmers Memorial Church
14 United Presbyterian Church
15 Baptist Church and Manse
16 Burgh School
17 Free Church School
18 Waid Academy
19 Technical School
20 Rennyhill House

Anstruther harbour became one of the busiest ports in Scotland. With Herring fishing being one of the mainstays of the town. Much of Anstruther's sea trade was with Europe. But not all trade was legitimate; wine, tobacco, cloth and sugar were smuggled up the dreel and under the 16th century Smugglers Inn, with white linen and coal being smuggled out. Adjoining the village and the church of Kilrenny, is Rennyhill.[5]

On their arrival at Rennyhill Priscilla wrote to her mother:

Rennyhill, September 24

Well here I am settled and quite entirely happy; I only wish you could peep at me this minute! But I had better begin in order. Very tremulous was I as we drew near, and through Anstruther saw 'nods and winks, and wreathed smiles', bows and curtsies. At last we arrived. First at the gate we saw Marr's pleasant face then Katherine Johnston, dressed in white flew to meet us, and took us to the Laird, who gave me a feeling reception. He is very old but rather

Rennyhill, a sketch by Priscilla Johnston

a fine man, tall and stout. The house looked most comfortable, the drawing room bright with flowers. My room (next to the drawing room) looked as tempting as a room at Earlham or Northrepps could do. We had a grand dinner, and the Laird came into the drawing room to tea, after which we descended, in form, to prayers. You may be sure I went to bed full of pleasure and thankfulness. I cannot stop to describe the 'doocot', the garden, the stables, the ducks, and the dairy. After luncheon today, we three, and two dogs, went for a charming walk oh! so delightful to see the blue sea again, and to be walking in stubble fields and among turnips, a bright autumn day. The Isle of May is a lovely object; and turning one way, you see the Bass Rock and the Firth, the other way, the open German Ocean and the steamers, which you see tomorrow!

The couple now took up residence at Rennyhill with Andrew's aging father. Although Priscilla professed to find the tall old Queen Anne house delightful, it was very quiet after the life she had been used to; hurrying from urgent conferences at the House of Commons and back again. She missed all her friends and, above all, her father and 'the stream of excitement I always drank from him'.[6] She later became downhearted at the prospect of her husband losing his election campaign and his career as an MP. Andrew and Priscilla would spend half the year in Scotland and the other half they would spend in London or Northrepps with her family, to Mr Buxton's 'exceeding comfort'. Mr Johnston became his assistant. When she visited London with her husband she got an intoxicating whiff of the old life, full of action and urgency. She writes thus to her aunt, Mrs C. Gurney:

Rennyhill, Sept. 29

Here I am for the morning in this pleasant drawing room with my large comfortable desk and little table. I sit by the fire so snugly. I do earnestly desire not to make thorns in my nest, it is so peaceful, so resting ... How I can fancy your present seat, probably at your window at Earlham, and see that paradise in the bright autumn sunshine. Altogether, places and people are invested with a peculiar and new charm and interest, they soften in the distance, and everything but their perfection is lost. This is not however, to express any hankering. I was never nearly so happy in my life, the calm waters here are so welcome and like a bed of rest to me.

To Priscilla Scotland was almost a foreign country and in October she writes to her mother: 'I shall make my husband be mistress, for I am sure I can't undertake to regulate this Scotch household with all its plans of porridge, oatcake, broth etc!' She wrote home nostalgically of having 'heard of the success of the waistcoat of the MP for Weymouth', her father. 'Elizabeth Wilkinson says it was lilac satin with purple flowers edged with gold.'

True to type, she started a Sunday school and Dorcas meeting, but 'these wild Scots were independent people and unfamiliar with the proper mode of life for the peasantry, as recognized in Norfolk.'

Rennyhill, 21st Nov

My Dearest Mother, I am oppressed today by my husband having received letters which look very lowering on an election … He means to go to St Andrews and Cupar tomorrow, and then will know more. His undaunted faith and hope are indeed most delightful. It is a matter of the most perfect conviction that, if not for his good and that of others, the way will be made to bring him in. But then he has not the inward heart sinking which the idea of longer separation gives to me.

December 17th

Our chance is now quite gone of being home for Christmas, but really if the election is over, I must rebel, and get my husband to leave the Kirk to its fate.

At the beginning of 1835 Priscilla also expresses her concern for her husband's career as an MP in a letter to her father:

Rennyhill, 7th January

The day of the nomination is fixed for Tuesday the 13th; Poll Thursday and Friday; return Monday 19th. But there may be no poll, so make yourself and the fatted calf ready on any day after the 23rd, because I think we may be very likely amongst you that day.

On 3rd May 1835 Priscilla, having last written in her journal on the eve of her wedding, now returns to it:

> It is almost too much of an effort to re-open my journal book, and yet I cannot help it; I now feel the events of my life too big for my grasp and being unable to cope with them, I can only desire to lie still and passive in the hands of my Maker ... It is well to record such a point in one's life. Here we are just as it were where roads meet – Parliament in the greatest doubt; a business pending for my husband: his father's life in the most critical state; and my confinement. These four great questions and events, all as it were hanging over us. The strong faith of my precious husband is my greatest comfort; and my noble father's exertions, talent, and judgement our greatest earthly help.

Her first child, Andrew, was born on the morning of the 23rd May. When able to move she went to Hampstead, and there on June 21, Andrew Johnston junior was baptized. She continued however very weak and, fever coming on, her strength was still further reduced. About the middle of July 1835 she was taken to Herne Bay, but there grew worse; on the 1st August, she seemed to stand at the very gates of death. By September she was recovered enough to be able to take up her journal again: 'Here I am able to be left a Sunday morning alone. Able to commune with myself and to put down some of my thoughts. What a valley of trial and suffering I have gone through. I am now brought up again, and though in great weakness, am, I trust, treading the upward path of recovery.'

The latter part of the autumn and the following winter and spring of 1836 were spent in and near London. In March 1836 she hears by post of the quiet close of her husband's dear father's life at Rennyhill, he had departed in love and peace at nearly 83 years of age. She recorded her feelings in her journal:

> In this event of his father's death, though there is little personal loss to feel, the whole thing has borne an uncommon tinge of melancholy. The closing of that once well filled house; breaking up the establishment; the dispersion of all; the venerable head laid in the ground; the place left desolate, and all gone. Then there is certainly much to feel in the necessity of giving up the place, of leaving the spot. What a blessing that my dearest is so resolved, so steadfast in faith and submission. My husband is again settled in, as my father's secretary, and in short our abode here in Upton has thus far been uncommonly prospered. There has been on both sides a genuine

preference of it. Our darling baby is a delight to his grand-parents, and in every way I have the amazing comfort of feeling our being here the best thing for us and for them, but there is in me a sort of humility which I cannot describe; a sense of everything being too good for me, everybody so far too kind, of being always in debt and never able to pay. Trying to describe it to my husband, he took me seriously to task for breaking the command be content with such things as ye have.

The next few months Priscilla spent planning a short Highland tour at the end of which they would spend three months at Rennyhill. After a delightful journey they reached Rennyhill on the 31st August. On arrival she busied herself with arrangements as to 'finish off there to some satisfaction' about which she writes to her sister Catherine:

Rennyhill, October 12 1836

I have been much interested lately in 'redding up' as they call it, putting the linen in order that had been spun by Andrew's great grandmother and her maids, making inventories, etc. and spending much time in our curious old garret, where there is lumber of every kind. I am always making some entertaining discoveries, though generally at the expense of being poisoned with dust. I have routed out five swords, a blunderbus, a very fine pistol, golf clubs, fishing rods etc. without end.

We are just come in from a delightful walk, this brilliant wintry afternoon. I did long for you all, the exquisite beauty of the sea, the busy lively scene at Cellardyke of the arrival of the boats, the piles and hundreds of silvery haddocks, the picturesque groups in and around the harbour, the rocks sparkling the waves. We had also some geological sport, every stone and rock on the beach containing some pieces of cactus, or the impression of it on bits of wood. The fossil trees standing straight up out of the rock, full three feet high are most curious. I trudge along well clothed in my bear skins, and with India rubber shoes more curious than beautiful certainly. The poor, the school and the estate find us abundant objects.

On the 8th of November she wrote to her aunt Sarah: 'How long will it be before we shall see another home half or a quarter so much to our taste as this. But I will not allow myself to love it so much. I won't allow myself to plant a flower to give it one hair's more strength over me, for it will not be our lot here to abide, I see.'

On November 13th Priscilla returns to her journal, writing:

> Here we are without a notion what, where, or how we are to be, whether our Scotch affairs are ever to be brought to a favourable settlement, whether any English home is ever to open upon us. Parliament business, everything in the same state of uncertainty. I have indeed been endeavouring to lay one after another before the eye of our good and gracious Father: and oh! that I may indeed find the burden to lie no longer on me ... My time here is spent much like an old mother hen, and who is to call her idle? I do read by myself, and with my husband and Katherine Johnston, keep things amongst the poor a little work and draw, guide the house as much as our regular clockwork routine needs guiding, and play with my bairn. I am very, very happy and remarkably well.
>
> I must tell of our catastrophe. This morning early I heard cries of 'the burn, the burn [brook]'. I sprang up and there was the burn raging along like a little sea, the washhouse entirely surrounded by it. All ran out, but there was nothing to be done but to look on. Soon word came that the pigeon house was an Island too. The next intelligence was, 'the dykes gone'. I covered myself with a cloak, and as soon as we could see through the drifts of snow and sleet, a vast gap, the high thick wall gone! The flood had already abated through this vent, but a great cascade was pouring out of the 'doocot' door, the torrent rushing down in grand style. Poor Mrs Mackill was having a grand wash, and there came all her things, sheets, shirts and table cloths tearing along by us, maids and men screaming after them with rakes and poles. It was very odd, that the little hedge and the apple trees that were nailed upon the wall, did not go too. There were the trees standing alone, stretching out their arms looking most queer and deplorable. About forty yards of the wall are gone. I must say if it was not for the 'bawbees' that it will cost us, I should enjoy the sport. We had a sight of the aurora in the middle of the day a few Sundays since; We thought at first the clouds were very strange, but on looking at them we saw them flickering and shooting up; and sure enough they were the northern lights.

The Johnston's soon after left Scotland, and the next letter is dated:

Upton, Saturday, December 17 1836

Well my dearest mother and all, here we are: you were indeed mistaken in thinking we have been having 'perfect' weather. Alas, alas! We had all the way a very rough passage, and landing at Cromer was utterly impossible and hopeless. It had howled all night before we left Rennyhill and we had almost given up hope of starting, when a lull succeeded the blustering wind, and we found it brightening every hour till we got to Dundee. We were alone in our glory in the noble ship, but, when we reached open sea, found an awful swell; waves as high, they said, as the ship itself. Oh! such a roll; long, sweeping, sickening rolls, more like being in a very high swing than anything. It was not without trouble that we kept in our beds, the things tumbled about in our cabin in every direction. When we passed Cromer, at about twelve or one (AM) every wave washed over the deck; however at last the wind changed, and by a bright moon we arrived in the river the middle of last night; Oh! the blessing of finding the engine at rest this morning. I am wonderfully well.

A month later, on 17th January 1837, the Johnstons were at Northrepps Hall. Andrew was attending to his duties as a member of his father-in-law's committee on the Aborigines. Priscilla observes the very interesting party assembled – Dr Philips, cousin Anna Gurney, her father and Andrew – at the table, each with a copy of the large blue book before them, and pens in hands. 'We all sit round, I say, like Ostrich's eggs scattered outside the nest, to look on and give our valuable assistance from time to time.'

She returns to her journal on Monday 17th April to record 'little Andrew's' illness:

I do earnestly wish for my future good to retain some little record of the illness of my precious little Andrew. One morning I found him heavy, oppressed and fretful. Sunday was a state of sorrow and trial, his state of evident suffering. I spent my time chiefly on the sofa in his room. My desire and plan was to cast up a prayer at every moan; every time he said 'hurt him, hurt him' (which was his incessant cry) I may say I was permitted to see him in the arms of his Heavenly father. I did see and know the tender arm of mercy round about him; we were brought to the point of giving him up, and we did, I believe, most truly and fully relinquish him, in our hearts acknowledging that he had always been a loan – not our own – that our heavenly father had the right to him. When the turn was taken and by degrees he was given to us again. He has indeed been lovely and precious in our eyes beyond what I can say he ever was before, since his recovery.

Her journal is again resumed on Sunday 28th May: 'Tomorrow morning at two o'clock my precious little girl [Euphemia] will be a month old. It has been a favoured time.'

A month later the Johnstons return to Rennyhill where she continues:

My dearest husband retired from the contest for the burghs. I wish to note this corner in our lives, although I have not yet sufficiently digested it to have anything particular to say. His canvas bad, sundry ups and downs, not so his faith and content, yesterday he retired with very great *éclat*. But we do not yet know the changes it will make. May we indeed be directed and blessed in turning into a new path of life. We are now full of the deepest interest, I cannot say, about my father's election.

On Thursday 27th July 1837, bitterly disappointed at his treatment, Mr Andrew Johnston placed the following notice in the *Fifeshire Journal*:

CLACKMANNAN AND KINROSS REGISTER.
TO THE ELECTORS
of the
DISTRICT OF ST ANDREWS

Gentlemen,
When the present contest for the representation of the district commenced, I determined to offer myself as a candidate conceiving that I had some claims upon you, but, at, the same time, resolving not to divide the liberal interest unless I saw a reasonable prospect of my own success.

I do not now see this prospect, and, I therefore beg to intimate my retirement from the contest. To the friends who have so faithfully supported me, I tender warmest thanks. I trust they will never regret their kindness towards one who deserved better treatment than he has met with from many others of the Constituency.

I have represented the Coast Burghs and this district for a period of seven years. I have had the honour of assisting in the passing of the

Reform bill in the abolition of British Colonial Slavery, the opening of free trade to India, the Reform of Municipal Corporations in England and Scotland, the Removal of Disabilities from the dissenters, the settlement of English Tithes, and many other most important measures.

With these I shall always feel it a high honour to have been connected, and I retire into private life with satisfaction, thankfulness and a good conscience.

I have only to add, that my vote and support will be given to Mr Ellice, and I remain,
Gentlemen,
Your faithful and obedient servant, ANDw. JOHNSTON.[7]

The two reformers had been undermined by the great reform act of 1832 and in the first general election of Queen Victoria's reign Johnston lost the Fife Burghs. August 1837 saw Mr T.F. Buxton also turned out of Parliament, following his election defeat at Weymouth after having been thrown into difficulties by the non-appearance of the other Whig candidate. In July, Buxton had foreseen his defeat, saying, 'If Burdon does not stand, I think it all but certain I shall lose the election.'

By now Priscilla and Andrew were celebrating their third wedding anniversary. She addressed letters to her father and brothers thus:

Rennyhill, August 1

My Dearest Father

This day I cannot pass by without one word, though now utterly in vain attempt to put on paper the feelings with which I am filled. Your twenty years labours in Parliament happily and well ended! You, as I believe, most mercifully and lovingly un-harnessed, as it were, and permitted to rest. I find a letter dated December 1834, these words 'The best thing that could happen to Andrew and me would be to use our utmost endeavours to get in and to be kicked out, which fate I think awaits your loving father, T F B.' I cannot condole. I feel nothing but thankful gladness at the blessing of your release.

My dearest brothers

What changes in a fortnight affected! From priding ourselves in having two M.P.s, here are we without one, all our dignities swept off at one blow. I am sorry our men will not have a right to attend the young queen's coronation and get medals.

In October 1837 Priscilla gives us an interesting account of the work of her Sunday classes and Dorcas meetings:

My difficulty is not to fill the hour, but to crowd in it all I have to do. I first begin by hearing them the task I have set them, which is a hymn and two or three verses of the bible. I am very particular that they should say it loudly, distinctly, and slowly and this often requires many repetitions to attain. That done I fix their lesson for next, and read it over with them, make them read it and see that they thoroughly understand it, asking the meaning of every word. We then turn to the bible; and the only difficulty is, to get through eight or ten verses, so many questions arise, and so much conversation. I have been weeks travelling through the first chapter of Genesis – 'God made the Herb'. 'What is an herb?' they ask. I reply, 'In this instance it means all vegetables, tell me what are the uses of vegetables' this rouses them up. 'WE EAT THEM'. Yesterday we had for us a mite of gaiety-nine young ladies to tea! I thought I would try and wake up these half alive damsels, so have got them to form a little Dorcas Society, which is to meet once a month to work for the poor. They came at six. Tea in the dining room, of course shy enough, but melted under the influence of the children and the Laird's sociability – with tea and cake. At seven we adjourned to the drawing-room, all settled round the table, work was prepared. I talked to them, and we formed our Society; then the master came and read the Negro Report, and we expounded and explained, and astonished their weak minds; altogether, our evening was very successful.

The following year, August 1838 saw aunt Elizabeth Fry make a visit to Rennyhill. Priscilla writes of this occasion to her mother:

Great were our preparations; everything we could devise was sent for, orders reiterated, beds, rooms, desks, examined over and over again, dinners, breakfasts, suppers, all arranged; in short, I may say we did our utmost best, and never yet had our house in such order for any of our visitors; often I did think of myself. On Friday we journeyed down to the pier at Anstruther, where, after watching two steamers pass, the third stopped. We got them all up safely on the pier, and we ladies came here in an omnibus. Fires were in their rooms and in the drawing room, fresh flowers so cheerful and gay, all had been brushed up, gates, roads and all. They were very tired, and all went to bed soon after nine.

Next day I was a great deal with aunt Fry in her room; and we had our first Fife dinner party of fourteen, there Lairds and their wives, aunt Fry and her two squires, and others. It all went beautifully, aunt Fry was as charming as herself. When we went upstairs, our tea company (ten more) flocked in. Aunt Fry talked to these ladies before the gentlemen came up, and fascination began to spread. We led her into a speech, after tea and coffee, which soon riveted everybody; and, by a few timely questions and feigned ignorance on our part, we got her to tell all about Edinburgh and Aberdeen, the Newgate Prison, then Paris, till all were quite bewitched, their faces quite droll to look at; and pressing invitations, love, gratitude, and admiration poured in. Next day (Sunday) in the evening, we went to the public meeting, which we found moved from the appointed place to a larger dissenting meeting house, which held about six hundred. Aunt Fry and her companions sat in the reading desk, we on the steps as close as possible. It was crammed, the heat and suffocation extreme. I have been thankful to have a good deal of her company. We took one long walk on the shore yesterday morning. I was with her almost entirely before they went off; she certainly was most delightful all through. I am proud, as you may suppose, of showing off such an aunt; and everybody's admiration of her was extravagant enough to satisfy me. I cannot say how wonderful she is, more wonderful than ever, a perfect genius.

In September Priscilla returns to her journal:

Rennyhill has been to me next to faultless this year; the country is now lovely with harvest, just beginning with great spirit; our garden bright and cheerful, few appearances of autumn yet, though I do see a Virginia creeper just beginning to blush, and as the old gardener said to me, 'the robin is singing of autumn'. About twenty minutes for prayer I find fully short for all my many wants – for husband, children, servants, parents, sisters, aunts, uncles &c &c, self, the slaves, slave trade, our schools and all efforts: may my prayers be made spiritual enough! How wonderful are the scripture's encouragements.

I think it is right to take pains to cultivate the eyes and ears of children for nature – the flowers, clouds, sea birds, all help. I do not so much point out to my children as express my own pleasure and admiration, and it is caught in a moment: also I think if young children are afraid of the dark, the weakness ought to be most tenderly dealt with, by perhaps walking about the house together without a candle, talking and telling stories, and enjoying the quiet dark. Our lessons are very pleasant: we have today finished the second page of three letter words, and I think we shall begin them again. We spell, look at pictures in infantine knowledge, read over the alphabet, and, for a treat, find and mark all the o's or any other letter in a page. The Scripture illustrations: we look at a picture and talk about it – one picture lasts us several days. Sunday is made very much of a treat: the cake, clean clothes, a large picture Bible, walks with papa and mama in the garden – we quite count the days till it will be Sunday.

In October 1838 Priscilla started an infant school. It opened with twenty-four children who came with their parents, and many onlookers. Of this she writes to her good friend Catherine Hankinson:

Rennyhill, October 16

Yesterday, to our great pleasure, our infant school began. We had taken many journeys and bestowed much pains in preparing and fitting up the room and it was very pretty. Armed with a parcel of raisins, I went about. We had some speechifying, singing, &c. Andrew made an excellent address to the parents, wrote down names and took the first pence. Then with care we slipped the parents away; but oh! when the truth broke upon the brats' minds that they were alone with the mistress (Miss Taylor) and me, oh! the unparalleled roaring: I am sure English children could not have yelled with the same perseverance and in the same sort of businesslike way. Raisins being done, in despair I called out of the window to someone to get some sweeties; and at length by coaxing, singing, ringing bells, &c &c they were tolerably quieted except about five little toads who collected round the door, kicked, and stamped, and bellowed, scratching their heads all the time most vehemently, so that I now well know what 'tearing of hair' means. One little fair boy, threw back his head, settled his mouth wide open, and began one continuous and deafening yell. At length being quite afraid and bewildered all the rest joined in chorus, we yielded, and let the rebels out – whether they will ever be brought back, I doubt. My children came in, in the middle; their dear clean faces and wondering stare entertained me not a little.

October 19

We have been down – rather in fear and trembling, to see, as it were 'Daniel in the Lion's den' and to know how poor Miss Taylor was faring. 'Weel, bairns, how's a' wi ye the day?'. 'We're a' greetin thegither' was the reply, in a most blubbering tone.

October 25

We were delighted to hear of some of our infant rebels now crying to go to the school, and the dread of being kept away held out as the worst punishment by their parents. The Sunday school, too, greatly cheered up.

Great preparations were made for Christmas when Priscilla and Andrew Johnston were to return to Northrepps for the birth of their third baby. They sailed from Dundee and after a buffeting thirty-hours passage reached Cromer where, like the coal at that time, they were landed directly on the sands for the usual want of a sound pier. Here they crowded around a blazing wood fire till a carriage was ready, in which they had a 'truly joyful' drive up to Northrepps. But fearing too sudden a surprise, for they had been unable to give any warning of the day of their arrival, decided to stop by the pond. Andrew crept in by the backyard and found the party already reading. In a few moments Chenda and her father came tearing out and, amid acclamations of all kinds, the party were got into the drawing room.

After a tremendous Christmas gathering with all the family, Priscilla retired to the ante-room with the five doors, where she gave birth to a son, Fowell Buxton Johnston, on the 5th January 1839.

Andrew now wondered what was to become of himself and his young family. However, in February Buxton arranged an interview for his son-in-law with the banker, Mr Gurney of the Halesworth Bank. The local director, David Lloyd, had died in 1839, leaving a vacancy which Andrew now filled. Priscilla wrote:

We are to go to Halesworth. Andrew has fixed to begin there on 5th of April. As for poor me and my brood I know not what we shall do but most resolved am I to bear discomforts with cheerfulness and quietness of spirit. The pain and draw back lie almost entirely in breaking away from this most dear home (Northrepps Hall), and in Andrew's giving up his privileged post with my father.

To the onlooker there seems nothing but prosperity in the thing, but I can truly say it is fraught with exercise of faith, patience and submission and the secret tearings of it are not few. We have had lamentable letters from Scotland: there indeed is a thorough pang, yet it is one I am most thankful to feel prepared for; but at Northrepps never again can we hope to be living.

This most lovely spring day, watching my little ones at play under the trees, can my mind be otherwise than peaceful, thankful and joyful. Life is too interesting, too full for this. After reading my father's prayer, such an extraordinary epitome of all our state and interests, family personal, and public; his thanksgivings for our and our children's long stay with them; his prayer for each of his children, for his grandchildren, for our settlement at Halesworth.

The Johnstons now left Rennyhill. After remaining empty for a number of years the property was sold in 1853 and became part of the estate of Kilrenny.

16

Removal to Bank House, Halesworth, Suffolk (1839)

Bank House, Halesworth from the garden

The Johnstons now took up residence at Bank House, 35 The Thoroughfare, Halesworth, where Andrew Johnston became agent for the bank of Gurneys & Co. which was at this time still situated in the Market Place and separate from Bank House. It was not until 1855 that the bank moved to the plot adjoining Bank House, when the *Halesworth Times* on 17th July praised 'the very handsome facade now in process of completion at the Bank of Messrs Gurney.'[8] (The Gurneys bank would later be merged with that of their cousins the Barclays, the forerunners of today's Barclays Bank.)

Halesworth, situated in the picturesque valley of the river Blythe, is a place of considerable antiquity, though little is known of its early history.

Richard de Argentin, who was Lord of the manor in the reign of Henry III obtained a charter for a weekly market (formerly held on Thursday) and an annual fair on the feast of St Luke. From the Argentins, the manor descended to the Allingtons, before passing to the family of Betts who sold it to a William Plumer, Esquire.

In the past great quantities of hemp had been grown in the neighbourhood, with many of the town's inhabitants being employed in the manufacture of Suffolk hempen cloth. This trade was discontinued many years before the Johnstons moved there. However, this is not to say that the town of Halesworth was not a thriving community at the time of their arrival. The Gurneys Bank was one of four in the town: there was also the East of England Bank, with Robert B. Baas as manager; the National Provincial Bank, for which the aptly named Mr J.A. Riches was agent, and the Savings bank at Mr Tippell's Thoroughfare, open on the last Tuesday in every month.

Under an act in 1786 the small river Blythe was made navigable up to the town for barges of from twenty to thirty tons burthen, of which there were about a dozen belonging to merchants employed in carrying out corn and malt and bringing in coal and timber.[9]

Andrew was soon immersed in local affairs, being a regular attender at Vestry meetings, and in 1844 was appointed Rector's Warden to Rector Joseph Badeley. Just after their arrival at their new home Priscilla wrote to her mother:

Halesworth, June 1st 1839

> I must say that in spite of outward confusion and bustle without end, there is a bottom of calmness and peace in my heart of satisfaction and comfort, a sense of rightness and favour in our allotment; may I be thankful for it! The house is very much what I expected, but in some respects decidedly superior. This drawing room is very pleasant and will become a delightful room.
>
> I am quite well and really bright. In yielding to everything, I find wonderful rest and ease. We are really beginning to feel a little homeish, and I can quite conceive that some day I shall love Halesworth.

It was here that they would raise their family. The 1841 census saw the Johnstons installed in Bank House in The Thoroughfare, with Andrew aged 40, Priscilla aged 30, Andrew six, Euphemia four, Fowell Buxton two (also known as 'Buck') and Sarah Maria three months, along with a governess, a nursemaid and five female servants.[10] Over the period of the next three years they would have two more daughters: Priscilla Hannah, born 27th November 1842 and Catharine Isabel born 11th June 1844.

The Johnston children were a delight to their grandparents, regularly spending periods of time at Northrepps Hall, Cromer. Priscilla wrote in her journal of one such visit: 'We went to Northrepps on the 19th of August 1839; they so delighted to see us; and meeting altogether especially bright.'

She continues her journal thus:

Halesworth, Sunday, April 1840

I have sent my maids into the garden instead of reading with them in the kitchen, giving place to the superior teaching of the crocuses and butterflies; and this gives me a minute to record the felicities of this day. Before church I sat on the green house step reading a story to my two darlings, showing them the flowers, the blue sky and seeking gently to draw their young minds upward. They so joyously happy, pointing to the flowers with little shrill screams of joy. I thought what a happy hour is this!

August 2

A delicious summer morning. I am at home from church with a slight head-ache and cold, by which I gain a delightfully long pause. I have been feasting on the sight of my precious little group on the lawn, oh! what gifts, what unspeakable treasures; and this I feel they are, whether permitted to remain with us here, or removed to a better garden above. The sweet garden, cheerful, rural looking house, lovely flowers, &c, have also afresh excited my admiration and gratitude. The coming round of our dear 1st of August we have of course felt, and acknowledged with great comfort how happy we are, how abundantly favoured, more settled and supplied than on any previous one; what may be our experience before next? These are indeed days of prosperity when our children are about us. When the candle of the Lord shineth upon our heads, may we not forget the days of darkness for they are many.

In the summer of 1837 Priscilla's uncle, Joseph John Gurney, had set off for three years to America to preach, with the gospel, anti-slavery and restraint from war. Many admirers had gone to see him off on his journey, including Betsey (Elizabeth Fry) who had gone to his cabin to arrange flowers.[11]

Now in the summer of 1840 there were great family gatherings to welcome Joseph John home. Whilst in America he had attracted an enormous following, the Gurneyite Orthodox Friends sect having formed itself as a result of his visit to New Jersey, and Earlham College for Quaker children, in Richmond, Indiana, having been started at his suggestion.

On the ship on his way to America he had met Eliza Kirkbride, a Philadelphia Quaker Minister and friend of the Grove Gurneys, having been shown over Earlham by Betsey whilst she was in England. Now she became Joseph John's third wife (having been widowed twice). The family now gathered early by the sea that year to make friends with Eliza, who was much liked by everyone; her conversation was 'rich with the ripened fruit of her large experience'.

So great was the family gathering that Aunt Betsey (Fry), Richenda, Priscilla Johnston and her children stayed at Northrepps Cottage with Lame Anna. All went almost daily to Northrepps Hall where 'never was such a welcome seen on any human face' as on Fowell's when he came delightedly out to meet them.[12]

Priscilla wrote to Andrew from the cottage, on August 27th 1840:

> The family and neighbourhood are in commotion this morning about the public meeting which they had fixed to have in the drawing room and hall; but we hear hundreds are coming, and expect to have to adjourn under the silver fir on the lawn. 'All the wisdom' [a reference to Anna Gurney] is gone up to settle arrangements. We went out on a most delicious expedition to Runton yesterday, which dressed itself up to be seen in the most lovely colours, the blue sea, white ships, grey churches, green hills and glowing heather; it did look most beautiful, and we thoroughly enjoyed it. Returned to dinner at the Hall, a busy evening, like thousands before, over uncle Joseph's West India Books.

Aunt Fry wrote in her diary:

I was brought into very near and tender love and unity in my visit with all my dear ones. Indeed it was like days that were past when a large party of us took a beautiful drive and walk on a fine bright day by the sea, over the fine healthy land upon the little hills. Surely the sun shone on us in every way and the next day at Northrepps Hall we had a glorious meeting, and truth flowed.

Joseph John's new wife Eliza was fascinated by it all, and wrote home:

We very much enjoyed our stay at Cromer, especially the daily intercourse which it afforded with our dear sister Elizabeth Fry, who was our near neighbour. She as you know, is always engaged in endeavouring in some way or another to benefit her fellow creatures, and very sweet it is to be able to be co-workers with her for a season in her labour of love.[13]

Eliza attended a revival of the Northrepps Literary Society at which Aunt Fry gave an essay, after which Priscilla wrote home to Andrew:

Oh! my dearest, why were you not here last night? We had such a bright evening over the essays! they were most capital: one or two I shall be able to bring home for you I hope. Oh I did so wish for you...'

In April 1842 Priscilla, now pregnant, once again returns to stay at Northrepps Cottage, spending two days with Anna – 'Truly is her company rich; the breadth and simplicity of her mind, and her great powers, joined with her unfeigned humility, are a spectacle to contemplate.'

17

*The First Years in the Life of 'Dearest Priscilla Hannah'
(1842–1845)*

On 19th November Mrs Priscilla Johnston writes in her journal:

> We went to Northrepps Saturday, October 1. There we stayed, I think, till Wednesday the 24th, three full weeks, four Sundays. A time of uncommon enjoyment, privilege, and prosperity. The Autumn party in its fullest run, enriched by dearest Aunt Fry; my dearest father and mother in health the whole time, and their seven children and eight grand-children also. We were at one time sixteen nephews and nieces assembled; and we managed a present to Aunt Fry of a silver inkstand, which we gave the last evening. She was, as usual, unparalleled, though weak in body.

Three and a half weeks after they returned home the Johnstons' fifth child, a third daughter, 'dearest Priscilla Hannah' ('Prissy') was born at Halesworth on the 27th November 1842. At this time Halesworth was a thriving market town of some 2660 inhabitants consisting of one long street and several short ones extending in a curved line from both banks of the River Blythe which was crossed by Halesworth bridge.

The market was held every Tuesday for the sale of corn, cattle etc. Fairs for pleasure were held on the Tuesdays in Easter and Whitsun weeks, and for the sale of Scotch cattle on the 29th and 30th of October.[14]

It would only be half true to say that Priscilla Hannah and her siblings were raised at Halesworth. For they would often spend the summer months with their mother on the Suffolk coast in the resort of Southwold (about eight miles from Halesworth) also enjoying lengthy visits to their grandmother's wooded estate and home, Northrepps Hall. There was always something of a holiday house about Northrepps, with the sea within walking distance through the woods. Pheasant and partridge shooting to be had, and woods harbouring a greater variety of wild birds than in almost any part of England. For none can the holiday spirit have been stronger than the endlessly recurring families of grand-children who stayed there, many of them regularly several times a year, when there would be numerous and enormous family gatherings.[15]

Here at Northrepps Priscilla Hannah was to grow up in an atmosphere serious, Christian, responsible, yet gay and busy, full of music and outdoor activities, surrounded by the cockatoos on the lawn and numerous dogs, cats and horses. Indeed, all the Johnston children were brought up in the family traditions of love for fellow creatures. With an emphasis on diligence and industry, thoughtfulness for others and a conviction that causes must be fought for, there was a consideration of horizons far removed from the comforts of the Norfolk home. The family might be most actively engaged in philanthropic work in the east of London and in Essex, but their generosity was never restricted to the poor and neglected of England; there was a ready response to all requests for support of missionary endeavours in distant parts.[16]

Of the Johnston children, the eldest, Andrew, was an especial delight to his grandfather who, reluctantly obliged to return to London and the 'House', wrote of a 'poor night in the mail' and 'How much I should prefer hearing little Andrew speak, to Peel'. Sir Thomas Fowell Buxton did not live to see his beloved little Andrew as more than a small boy, but would probably have continued to regard him with the same pride and satisfaction had he seen him grow to manhood. Andrew seems to have come as near to being a model son as any parent could hope for. The younger son, Fowell Buxton (known as Buxton or Buck) was an altogether different proposition, and gave more reasonable cause for anxiety. Andrew was always being adjured to exert a good influence over him and to persuade him to wash his neck. His position in the family, too, may have been somewhat isolated: on the one hand were Andrew and his sister, Effie, devoted friends; on the other the 'three little girls', Sarah Maria, Priscilla Hannah and Catharine Isabel, a group on their own.[17]

The Johnston children were initially educated by their mother and later by a governess, of which Priscilla wrote: 'A nursery reading is a duty which, though somewhat of an effort does, I do believe, bring a present payment more than most.' The eldest son Andrew attended school at Lowestoft.[18] [Although not recorded, young Fowell probably also attended school here, before they both went off to Rugby.] (At this time Halesworth Infant School of around 100 pupils was situated on Pound Street. Older children then attended the commodious National

The Baptismal Register of St Mary's, Halesworth, showing Priscilla Hannah's entry of baptism on the 4th December 1842, by the Revd Joseph Badeley

Schools on the Beccles Road of which pupils numbered 112 boys and 70 girls.[19])

On the subject of education, Mrs Johnston comments in her journal on the running of her school at Northrepps:

> I have a book for marks for the children, which I carefully go over with mistress and pupil every week, and after lessons they bring me 'a character' and the number of marks. The plan answers well; I give a farthing for twenty-five. The hammering part of lessons I am convinced is best and happiest accomplished not by the mother, but I think most differently of the really mental, intellectual, or heart work of teaching. Of course I keep the serious part and scripture history. Today we have begun 'Mary's Grammar', it is a capital book. The child's Arithmetic is very good. I have the pennies they earn for their marks regularly spent on a pencil or a little packet of seeds etc. If it is saved it comes to nothing and is wholly swallowed up; the labour of the weeks proves not to be worth so much as a casual shilling or half-crown from grandpapa; but if it is spent in an immediate pleasure (of a wholesome sort) it gives zest to the system of marks. It is their delight when the gardener prepares little penny packets of mustard and cress, radish etc. and they go in form to buy them.

Christmas 1842 was, as usual, spent with the large family at Northrepps, the reason being made all the more special that year by the first visit of the long-clothed and bonneted baby Priscilla Hannah. As, in her mother's arms, she passed through the front door with its potted plants and pink conches just inside, she became one of the earliest of a long procession of grand-children with their flaxen or apricot hair, clear pink and white skins and blue eyes, who would grow to love Northrepps as long as they could remember.[20]

Christmas over, the Johnstons returned to Halesworth. However, they would be back at Northrepps in April 1843, at which time Mrs Johnston first began to express concern at her father's wandering mind. She writes:

> The pouring out of his mind in prayer this morning (I stayed at home from church with him and my mother) was, even for him, most unusually interesting, only the emphasis and fervour of it almost gave me a nervous turn. He first spoke of his children and grand-children generally, but individually too, 'as we pass them each over in our minds'; but afterwards, as if he could not be satisfied, returned upon

The Baptismal Font, St Mary's Church, Halesworth

The church of St Mary, Halesworth, Suffolk

each. I only wish I could remember the emphatic, beautiful expressions he used respecting me, they were most touching, 'our most dearly and preciously beloved daughter, friend and sister; that I might taste of the richest harvest in my children and their well doing.'

In later life Priscilla Hannah would become a 'much travelled Victorian lady'. The seeds of this lust for travel were sown from a very early age. In July 1843, when she was barely seven months old, Mr and Mrs Johnston took their children from London by sea to holiday at Southwold, a resort at which the family spent many happy summers and of which Mrs Johnston wrote:

Southwold, July 4

I am most comfortably settled in a pleasant drawing-room looking over the sea, though not so near as I should like. The children playing on the green. We have an excellent account to give of ourselves; Our voyage proved faultless and a charming day. We settled ourselves in a nice corner, with broad seats and cushions; they spread an awning, and it hung down to the deck on one side so as to shelter us from wind. We read, and some times walked about, though I chiefly lay still and read. About seven the 'Water Witch' bent her course into Sole Bay, and a boat was descried by that instinct sailors have.

We were soon conveyed in a fishing boat to shore, and found all right and ready for us. We have just now had a delicious morning on the shore in the shade of a boat, reading the bible and wandering about. We are thoroughly enjoying our holiday here; the day is delicious, and the sea most sparkling.

Southwold, July 11

I have just been driving some of my party in our new basket pony-chair all over the grassy sea flats which lie on one side of this place, and which are covered now with horned poppy, the sea pea, yellow stone crop, etc. I more and more enjoy our settlement here. The repose is so delightful, the absence of acquaintance and visitors, and long my days.

To me this season has been a Sabbath; and thankful I am to trust that we have five or six weeks more of it to look forward to.

The complete quiet and retirement, my long sits on the shore, early dinners with the children, long and quiet afternoons, the cheerful and evening walk with husband and bairns are delightful to me.

In the first week of September the Johnstons wound up their near ten weeks sojourn at Southwold with much satisfaction and thankfulness. They had a bustling short time at home at Halesworth, paid a visit to Earlham and arrived once again at Northrepps on September 13th. 'To a dinner on Saturday and a delicious welcome, and finding everything in good measure of prosperity,' writes Mrs Johnston, continuing:

The next day was Sunday; the morning I spent at home with my dearest parents. Before breakfast the lawn, flowers glittering in the dew, the early sunshine in its first freshness between the trees. I have been long sitting by my open window, drinking in the beauty of nature. We then walked in their beautiful garden; how delightful are the pleasures and ornaments now permitted to them after their life of labour, and often sorrow! Northrepps, as usual, is outwardly and inwardly fascinating to me. Love and unity, Liberty and Independence, seem here to reign with native charm, ease and abundance. In the afternoon we all assembled at Northrepps Church. Where Edward Hoare preached such a sermon. His view of this undoubting faith as applied to the work of Christ for our salvation, and then his mention of faith for our children entered my very heart.

After a Christmas spent, as usual, surrounded by relatives at Northrepps, January 1844 finds the Johnstons back home at Halesworth. In March Mrs Johnston returns to her journal to record her thoughts of her children, which she refers to as her 'lambs':

I have been nearly three weeks almost ill with influenza more than a week confined upstairs, and a good deal to bed. I am now getting over it, I hope without much cough. It has been a time of peace and quiet enjoyment, every outwardly luxury so abundantly supplied. Almost above all has been a sense that my indisposition had, rather than not a softening, good effect on my dear lambs. How little does this book convey any idea of the almost ceaseless engrossment of my heart, mind, and time about them! Every day seems marked by care about the body, conduct, or circumstances of one or other of these precious, anxious treasures! I sometimes think if I were taken away, it would be almost a pity they should have no more record of my travail of spirit for and about them.

In order for Mrs Johnston to recuperate and rest, for she was now expecting their sixth child, the whole family spent April at Southwold.

I do wish you could now see and partake of my settlement by this delightful window – the exceeding beauty of the sparkling sea and boats is quite interrupting! I feel already refreshed by the change and the brightness of this house, everything so clean and complete, beds and curtains snowy white – everything trimmed up for the summer season. We went immediately on to the shore with all the children; it was delightfully warm then, and my first proceeding was to buy a cotton parasol. We are tempted to stay on here for another week, there is such a Sabbath in it – 'divine silence' and the rustling waves seem to feed me! The wind is very cold, but it does not signify to me, for I enjoy the climate.

The birth of Priscilla and Andrew's sixth baby, Catharine Isabel ('Isa') took place on 11th June 1844. Catharine too began to travel at an early age. She was just a month old when the Johnstons 'came to Lowestoft on Thursday 18th July with our dearest parents, and settled in a small lodging', Priscilla 'given up to gaining bodily strength, and to enjoy in a passive way, our rich little community – the vicarage, the Parrys, with many attendant friends.'

On 28th August Mrs Johnston became anxious for the health of her 'lambs', after hearing of the sad news that had befallen the Frys, the death from Malignant scarlet fever of William Fry:

This day fortnight they were in complete prosperity; that afternoon their little girl Juliana sickened, and died the next night. William was taken ill in a day or two, and after a fearful struggle of ten days is taken from his large family and most important post. The judgements of the Lord are in the earth. I feel it most awful to see. His hand thus lifted up! One child is very ill, and others threatening; several servants ill. Here is one of ourselves, a contemporary, in the very prime of the career of life, struck down.

On Tuesday 2nd September 1844 two-year-old Priscilla Hannah and her siblings were sent to visit their grandparents at Northrepps. Only her eldest brother, Andrew, remained at home with his parents. Mrs Johnston greatly missed her young family:

> By the open drawing-room window – the garden lovely – waiting for my boy, who is now my only child at home. O what a new world is unlocked, as it were, by having a child ten years old! It seems gradually to engross and occupy so large a portion of one's mind. I cannot say how many more thoughts they take as they grow older. I often think that as children in the charms and fascinations of their first years are like the blossoms, so they go through the state of unripe fruit, their infantine charms are gone, and the full fruit is far from being come; yet this is not true fully, for un-ripeness and hope for the future may predominate, yet how large a measure of enjoyment is there from them in all their stages! I am much impressed with the duty of enjoying them, as well as labouring for them; and I believe this spirit of dwelling with thankful hope on them and cultivating them in love and encouragement would often produce greater fruit than the more careful one which is in my nature. In the absence of all my precious party except Andrew, I have had time to contemplate them; and I have perceived that I have allowed myself to be too much encumbered with cares and labours about them, so that flowers of daily delight, love, and companionship, have been in a measure choked.
>
> *Evening* – How different is the leisure, almost amounting to vacancy, of this evening, compared to my usual allotment! It is rather resting and good for me for once, yet I feel in poverty, and my heart visits Northrepps and the most beloved lovely party there assembled.

Mr and Mrs Johnston and Andrew joined the autumn gathering at Northrepps on Thursday 12th September where they stayed until October. 'We enjoyed the country and drove much about, and the family community was delightful.'

Throughout the year 1844 the health of Priscilla Hannah's grandfather, Sir Thomas Fowell Buxton, and that of her great Aunt Betsey (Elizabeth Fry) was in a failing state.

The following is an account from the journals of Mrs Johnston's father, of this, his last summer:

> Although in a languid feeble state of health, he again spent a tolerably cheerful summer at Northrepps. His spirits were less

depressed, which he said was owing to a greater assurance of being a partaker of the heavenly inheritance. In the fine summer mornings he would often rise at four or five o'clock, and go into his dressing room, where his voice could be heard for an hour or two at a time in fervent prayer.[21]

In the autumn, although he was still able to take a little air and exercise, going out on his pony with his gun, or to visit plantations, his appearance indicated increased languor and oppression, and he described himself as 'Under decayed spirits'.[22]

Both families were now observing that Fowell's and Betsey's hard work was beginning to tell on them. One day, stirred up by news of government activity in Sierra Leone, Fowell started to write a long and urgent appeal to Lord Stanley, but even though dictating he kept sinking back, exhausted, in the middle of a sentence. He finished it and no trace is revealed in it of his debility, but afterwards he was quite overcome by the effort. One evening a well known and most able missionary brought his exciting and adventurous reports straight to Northrepps, but Fowell was unable to take in details which hitherto would have excited and fascinated him. 'His family could not but feel that the blow was struck' and the solemn gravity of Fowell's own manner showed that he too was aware of it.[23]

On the 15th December he was seized with a severe spasm on the chest, the effects of which, in the course of a week or two, became extremely alarming to his family and they all collected around him. His eldest daughter, Mrs Priscilla Johnston, stayed at Northrepps through the remainder of her father's illness.[24] She had taken baby Catharine with her, while Priscilla Hannah and her siblings were being cared for by their great aunt Cunningham.

Towards the end of January 1845, on experiencing some return of strength, he remarked, 'How pleasant is the feeling of rest on recovery from illness, while our worldly occupations are laid aside!' The most cordial welcome was ready for everyone who visited him. On the 6th February he had a painful return of oppression on his breath, but he bore it with entire patience and submission. He was much pleased by the following note from Mrs Fry, who herself was extremely ill:

> I must try to express a little of the love and sympathy I feel with and for thee. How much we have been one in heart, and how much one in our objects. Although our callings may have been

various, and thine more extensive than mine, we have partaken of the sweet unity of the Spirit in the Lord. May we, whilst here, be each other's joy in the Lord! and when the end comes, through a Saviour's love and merits, may we behold our King in his beauty, and rejoice in His presence forever!

My love to you, and your children and children's children is great and earnest; my desire and prayer is, that grace, mercy, and peace may rest upon you in time and to all eternity!

Mrs Johnston wrote a note to her Aunt asking that her little boy (Andrew) should be sent for and told. 'Let him fancy the scene. My mother, Richenda, Edward and Charles on the far side of the bed. My brother Fowell and Rachel Jane and Anna Gurney at the foot; Andrew lying by him on the window side and I kneeling next to him.'

On the 19th February he was very much exhausted, but tranquil in body and mind. Towards the afternoon, symptoms of increasing oppression returned and, as the evening advanced, it was evident that he was dying. He sank into a deep sleep, his family collected round his bed, and, at about 9.45 p.m. he died, aged 58.

The funeral, which was conducted with great simplicity, took place on a mild sunny winter's morning, and was attended by a large train of relatives, friends and neighbours. Long before the appointed hour, crowds of villagers were seen approaching the spot, through the lanes and fields, in every direction. All seemed deeply moved. The assembly was far too large to find room in the church, but great was the solemnity which prevailed in the churchyard while the interment took place. He was buried in the ruined chancel of the little church at Overstrand, the old walls overrun with ivy, the building itself with the sea in full view, and the whole surrounding scenery quite picturesque.[25]

A pencil note survives, sent in the evening from Northrepps Cottage to Hannah: 'I do dearest sister, desire with prayer and supplication that you may be granted peace tonight,' writes her cousin Anna.[26]

Overstrand, is on the coast, one or two miles east south east of Cromer, bounded on the south by a range of hills, and on the north by the lofty sea cliffs. The old church of St Martins had been 'washed down' in the reign of Richard II, at which time it was rebuilt, however only part of the knave was fitted up for divine service and in 1845 the rest was in ruins.[27]

Having been created a baronet in 1840, by the title of Sir T.F. Buxton, Bart, of Bellfield, Dorsetshire, and Runton, Norfolk, his baronetcy now descended to the eldest of his sons, Sir Edward North Buxton, of the firm of Trueman, Hanbury, and Co., the extensive brewers of Spitalfields, London who inherited estates at Runton and Fellbrigg. The estates at Trimingham, Sidestrand, Southrepps and Gimingham were bequeathed to his younger sons, Thomas Fowell and Charles Buxton.[28]

A few weeks after his death, some individuals formed themselves into a committee for erecting a testimonial to his memory. The project was warmly approved. H.R.H. Prince Albert at once gave *50l*. The testimonial, for which *1500l*. was subscribed, was a full length statue, executed by Mr F. Thrupp which was placed near the monument of William Wilberforce in the north transept of Westminister Abbey on the 15th November 1848. Meanwhile the freed slaves erected a bust of him in Sierra Leone.[29]

At Northrepps, when Priscilla and Andrew Johnston had to go home to Priscilla Hannah and their other children, they left baby Catharine Isabel behind to try to cheer up the household. Hannah wrote: 'The whole house, dearest Priscilla, feels thy being gone and the maids too, take it regularly to heart. The baby is a pleasure and occupation to them as well as to us, and I think it thoroughly answers to Chenda to leave her here as consolation.'[30]

Now Betsey felt she too was dying. Several of her grandchildren and her beloved eldest son had recently been fatal victims of scarlet fever and she was in a very low state of mind. Her one earthly wish was that she might see once again the scenes of her childhood, which normally she only visited later in the year. She went back to Earlham for a few weeks and then on for ten days to Northrepps where Hannah was mourning her darling Fowell. And yet it was Hannah who wrote of Betsey: 'I am struck by my sister's heavenly patience and forbearing spirit.'

Betsey saw again the scenery connected with her childhood and 'thoughtful month at Northrepps just before marriage'. She returned to her own home satisfied.[31]

On the 10th October, Mrs Fry appeared rather better than she had been the few preceding days. However, later in the morning, whilst she drove out, she was strangely oppressed, scarcely noticing the lovely views of the sea, which she generally so much enjoyed. That evening she was melancholy and complained of suffering from the light. These many circumstances, each trifling in itself, weighed together, gave so much cause for uneasiness, that her husband and children resolved the next day to send to Broadstairs to learn if Dr Paris was still there, but he was already gone.

Over the course of the weekend Betsey's health deteriorated. On the Saturday morning she awakened suffering severely with her head; she spoke very little. As the morning of Sunday advanced, all hope became extinguished. A messenger was dispatched to summon those of her absent children who might be able to look upon her once again in life. The difficulty of breathing, with convulsive spasm increased, at first occasionally, but after midnight it became almost continuous. At 3.00 p.m. she lost consicousness and died barely an hour later.

Before the evening, the greater number of her children were assembled at Ramsgate. Monday at noon was fixed for her funeral. In the grey of the early morning, the loved, the revered was brought for the last time, for a few short hours, to her home of many years. Vast numbers of persons attended her funeral. The procession passed between the grounds of Plashet House, her once happy home, and those of Plashet Cottage. In the Friends' burying-ground at Barking her grave was prepared, close by that of her little child, whom she had loved and lost, and tenderly mourned so many years before. There is no appointed funeral service amongst Friends. A deep silence prevailed throughout the multitude gathered there. Her brother, Joseph John Gurney, was the first to address the assembly, and by him solemn prayer was offered. Then her immediate family withdrew to the shelter and recollections of Upton Lane.

Afterwards a meeting was held in a tent erected specifically for this solemn occasion. Much was brought forward from the Treasury of Scriptures, of consolation, of warning and encouragement for the listeners assembled there.[32]

Fowell and Betsey were mourned, not only by their own generation, but also by the younger generations who were just coming up to take on responsibility themselves. At the age of three years old Priscilla Hannah had now just lost two close family members whose example would influence her greatly throughout the course of her own life and in her philanthropic works.[33]

Of course, Priscilla Hannah was still too young to have her own memories of her grandfather and great aunt Fry, but over the years she would learn of them and their good works from her mother and grandmother. Later she would read for herself their memoirs. The life of Elizabeth Fry was collated by her daughter, Mrs F. Cresswell, and published in 1856 and the memoirs of Sir Thomas Fowell Buxton were collated by his son, Charles Buxton, and published in 1849.

After the death of her sister, Hannah, on her return to Northrepps, wrote of her circumstances to her daughter:

To Priscilla Johnston

I will leave others letters and send thee some history of ourselves. Our return home has been, more than I could have expected, relieving and helpful to me. The calm and rest, even with all its loss and sorrow, have been just the thing for me. I like being alone, and the retirement of the Grey room has suited me. It has been a pause I needed, and to come back and dwell in the spirit with my beloved and in a way to return to his company has done me good. I love the pictures and the spirit which seems to abide here.
          Most Loving,
          H Buxton.[34]

The bereaved Hannah did not remain alone for long at Northrepps. Here she was consoled in her grief by the frequent visits of the Johnston grandchildren and their many cousins.

January 1849, to Priscilla Johnston

My beloved child, here I am in my room again, Rachel at the window, Prissy begging to play the music, Esther fidgeting after them and the letters. I have felt desolate certainly this morning, but after a time felt it right to stir up and go to the cottage. I met Anna coming up to see after me.

Hannah particularly enjoyed her visits along with the Johnstons to the Buxton family of Leytonstone, then outside London, by Wanstead Flats and just south of Epping Forest. The father of this large family was Hannah's son [Priscilla Hannah's uncle] Thomas Fowell. Ellen Buxton was the second child of this large family of children. From the age of twelve she filled three fat diaries and many sketch books with records of the day to day life of her family at Leytonstone. As we shall see later she also recorded their visits with their numerous cousins – Buxtons, Gurneys, Hoares, Barclays and the Johnstons at Northrepps, where they used to go for several months of the year to stay with their grandmother.

The journals of Ellen Buxton (1860–1868) have been brought to us by her grand-daughter Mrs Ellen R.C. Creighton. From Mrs Creighton's introduction we learn that:

Most days Thomas would go up to the family brewery, Trueman, Hanbury & Buxton at Spitalfields; he was also chairman of a London

Hospital and engaged in other philanthropic concerns. So they lived near London in a tract of country now long built over, but then quite rural. Leytonstone was still a village, though the home of many substantial families whose large Georgian Houses mingled with the shops and cottages along the main road to Epping. In one of these houses, now pulled down, lived the Buxtons.[35]

[In time this family would grow to eleven, six girls; Louisa, Ellen, Emily, Janet, Effie, Ethel and five boys, John Henry, Geoffrey, Arthur, Alfred and Barclay.]

One visit to Leytonstone in particular is recorded in the journals of both Hannah Lady Buxton and Mrs Johnston:

Leytonstone, April 23, 1846

We were a touching party here last evening, I [Hannah] and my eight children. I did so feel it; such a beautiful group, and all as I trust members of one body living, may it be, for an everlasting union – a reunion with the one so wanted amongst us!

While at breakfast this morning a carriage drove up, and who should arrive but the dear Bishop of Calcutta (Daniel Wilson) come to dinner, as we fixed and to lodge, but choosing to begin with breakfast, that he might secure a quiet retired morning, being too much interrupted at home. He met us most affectionately, recognizing Priscilla with the greatest warmth. He sat down and began a full stream of talk from one thing to another, and most exceedingly interesting, bright and amusing.

He spends, he says, the morning here tomorrow for quiet, and goes away before dinner. I dreaded the effort of seeing him, but he is too familiar upon everything to make the communications an effort: nor did he seem to enter into my feelings, so living in 'all being well', cheerful and content with all, speaking very familiarly of my beloved [Sir T.F. Buxton deceased] without any sense or the least expression of the deep sorrow and mourning heart about him.[36]

18

A Grandchild's Early Recollections of Life at Northrepps

At the time Priscilla Hannah and her siblings began to visit, Northrepps was a pleasant scattered village of around 600 inhabitants. Situated nearly three miles south-east of Cromer, picturesquely broken into hill and dale. The village was mostly the property of the Lord of the manor, Lord Suffield. However, R.H. Gurney had a large estate there and two mansions called the Hall and the Cottage. The latter, occupied by Miss Anna Gurney, was a tasteful Gothic structure, sometimes called the Hermitage, situated in a romantic dell, commanding a view of the ocean.[37]

In Cromer there were other family houses, fifteen of them at one time, filled with cousins with a strong Northrepps association who turned up for Sunday tea – or at any other time.[38]

After the death of Sir Thomas Fowell Buxton the Hall remained in the occupancy of the dowager Hannah Lady Buxton, Priscilla Hannah's grandmother, who, as mistress of Northrepps, spent more than half her life there, so that her memories were the most plentiful and far reaching. Her earliest was of Lucy, one of the Barclay twins, being whipped in the 1790s for not drinking her breakfast beer in the new Northrepps dining room, which later became the library, and then being taken into the study and locked in till she drank it.[39]

Priscilla Hannah's great-uncle Joseph John Gurney as a small boy was also imprisoned at Northrepps when Hannah was trying to teach him geography and spelling and had to call Kitty to help her to manage him. Joseph John was shut up in the night nursery. Poor Joseph John! He was also whipped by mistake by his father for moving a lark's nest that turned out to have been placed on the lawn by an artist friend who wanted to draw it.[40]

No amount of punishment had any effect on a young great-uncle Samuel Gurney who, when sent to bed, said cheerfully that there was nothing he liked better. Samuel's independent character and resistance to schoolroom learning caused him to be sent to boarding school when he was only seven. Hannah and his other sisters went with him in the coach on the first stage and put him into the London coach all alone. But it was they who wept, not he, and all of them wrote frequently and sent him cake of their own making.[41]

Let us here return 'back to the future' for a brief moment, and to the recollections of Verily Anderson Paget. Verily has 'memories most plentiful and vivid' of a childhood spent happily at Northrepps Hall, 100 years on from Priscilla Hannah's time, which she has recorded in her book, *The Northrepps Grandchildren*, from which I have here included extracts, which I feel may come close to creating a 'pen Picture' of how life must also have been for the young Priscilla Hannah, so little having changed at Northrepps.

In her introduction Verily writes, 'Over a decade has passed since I came back to write this book. Everything relates back to those earliest memories, either because it has changed or because it has not. Sounds and sights and smells remain ... The garden at Northrepps Hall is unchanged but for a real swimming pool replacing the seashore of our imagination.'

Verily, only one of the long procession of grandchildren and cousins who came to Northrepps, continues:

> My own initial arrival there seems more like my memory than my mother's, so clearly can I see the avenue of Elms forming a tunnel half a mile long up to the gates, where a pair of gentle faced terracotta lions stood, if slightly battered by the weather and over affectionate grandchildren climbing up to fondle them. But as I was only a few weeks old at the time I can hardly have remembered it.[42]
>
> So much must have happened countless times over that many of the memories of one generation must have often become confused with the stories of the last. Some of mine I know to be direct memories from finding evidence years later. There are many more that may well have been reconstructed in my mind after hearing a story told and knowing its environment so intimately.
>
> Just as the trees and gateways have lasted, so have the toys and playthings and secret hiding places in the nursery and garden. Tree houses and huts built by one generation of children have been kept green by the next, to be revived and played in by the grandchildren of the first. Animals and birds have overlapped generations and their

places been taken by others so like the last that changes have been almost unnoticeable. Family servants have outlasted one generation and carried on to the next, taking with them a ready-made affection for the next batch of grandchildren.[43]

Indoors the Sunday tea-parties of relations of all ages and their dogs went on as they always have round the circular table in the hall. The same red leather armchairs bought for the house in 1792 are pulled up and the same stools and drawing room chairs are fetched to make room for children and late comers. Tea is drunk from the same shallow rose gilt-lined cups, and sponge cake is eaten from the recipe, whose main ingredient I always believed as a child to be fine blonde sand from the Cromer shore.[44]

When I recall the tree fringed lawn sweeping down to the library windows, with a Cedar tree on the garden side of the lawn that divided the house from the wood, I remember that on the other side a gigantic silver fir tree rose high above the woods and house. This was called the rescue tree because of 'lame' Anna Gurney's experiment with Captain Manby's 'gun' which would fire a new kind of lifeline out to sea to rescue drowning sailors from shipwrecks.[45]

The path behind the fir tree wound round to a low hooped iron gate, wide enough to admit a pony chaise. Here we would often stand entwining our fingers with the pattern. This was the gateway to the most magical of grandmother's gardens, the kitchen garden itself. Here red and white currants clustered under fisherman's nets on the roseate walls. Gooseberries, whiskered and red and sweet, hung from the lace-curtain-covered bushes, homely protections against the birds. Sticky raspberries, as we called the wine-berries clustering behind their finger pointed leaves, grew at the corner of two crossing paths. And beside a taller hooped gate leading into the meadow, the cherry-plum tree rained delicious little mirabelles onto the path for us to pick up and crush in our mouths. It was always the garden of the greatest promise.

If we had been allowed to wander far we should have been lost. It was the same in Home Wood, where one or two clearings belonged essentially to the nursery. To these we would be wheeled in the mail-cart, without certain knowledge which paths led to these darling places. Here we were set down to creep in and out of the nearby undergrowth.

The mail-cart was an airy conveyance, built on the basic lines of much of the Northrepps furniture, at the time, with wooden handles and legs like a wheelbarrow. Even the pram in which I took my nap was estate carpentered, as were our toys.

So high were we perched on this mail cart as we returned from the woods that we had to put our heads on our knees as we passed under the door way into the backyard through into the courtyard with a dozen or so doors leading off it to the kitchen, scullery, servants hall, game larder, wood shed, oil store, Sunday school room and carpenter's shop.

Into the back door we clattered, sometimes straying into the kitchen where the walls were embossed with copper jelly moulds and silver plated meat covers. There were sizes to fit anything from a cutlet to a brace of peacocks. There were cooking pots too for all occasions. And a kind of chimney went up the side of the range, collecting the steam from each compartment. This way we were told cook could do the different dinners for the dining room, the nursery, the school room and the servants' hall at once. Out of the kitchen, clattering along the flagged corridor, past the log-bin and up the dark back stairs rising steeply between wooden walls. As we passed the dangling bell rope we gave it a push knowing that one real pull would ring the bell under its wooden shelter on the top of the house. A continuous ringing meant that Northrepps Hall was on fire. Then under gardeners, garden boys, farm workers, gamekeeper and estate carpenter would all come flying in to take the scarlet leather buckets of sand down from their pegs all along the back corridor. Terrified by the thought, we panted up to the gate at the top of our stairs to emerge into the safety of our own dear nursery passage with its sunshine and fresh sweet air. This lovely broad alley stretched from the back of the house to the front with two shallow steps midway to jump down. Other passages leading off our alley meant nothing to us then.

Of course we knew every inch of the nurseries themselves. From the sofa below the window we had an intimate view of the front door and forecourt, with all arrivals and departures. Some visitors came in traps or riding horses or very early bicycles with an intricate network of strings to keep their skirts out of the wheels, if they were ladies. [More often than not in Priscilla Hannah's time, they would have been men as the bicycle was still rather frowned upon and thought to be most unsuitable transport for a lady.] The doctor came in a jaunty basket-work gig with yellow wheels and a tall whip standing in its own tubular basket.

The night nurseries looked the other way over the backyard, with sounds that reached up into our dreams and became part of them – the clatter and clank of cans and bins, the mournful sighing of the knife cleaning machine and the voices of the maids coming up through the floor boards. In the walls was the shuffling of mice. Outside was the bellowing of cattle from the farm yard and beyond the pond, where the ducks quacked all night. There was the bray of the donkey and then, just as all was quiet, the sudden passionate scream of a peacock sounding, when half in a dream, like a long drawn out cry of 'Help'.

Merlin and Rhalou [Verily's elder brother and sister] being a little older, slept and ate in a different wing of the house, guarded over by a governess. Our most constant companions were the other tottering, toddling, scrambling grandchildren and their nannies and nursery maids. It is with complete clarity that I recall the eldest of our group, fairer, curlier, pinker and whiter and more dimpled than any of us, as she sat at the nursery table on a cushion with an embroidered bib over a white lace edged frock, licking the white sugar butterfly off her brown biscuit. And so it must have been ever since the mahogany and wickerwork high-chair that could be turned by the twist of a single brass screw into a low nursery chair and table, was first brought into the day nursery with the assortment of semi high-chairs. Baby grandchildren must have been settled round this table by their nurses. Little girl and boy cousins' faces must have been sponged and their flaxen hair combed ready to be taken down to the drawing room.

Enchanted memories of the drawing room after tea remain. Among the toys brought out for us to play with on the floor was the little gaily painted greengrocer's stall that my grandmother set before me. Tiny, glossy oranges could be picked up between finger and thumb and rolled into a miniature barrel. Minute bunches of carrots and crates of cauliflowers could be moved about the stall.

The big wooden letters, hewn by the estate carpenter, were interesting too but in a different way. Grandmother would arrange them on the floor in biblical texts which we learned to recognise in their entirety long before we could read. She would build for us Noah's Ark and the Garden of Eden with wooden bricks, wedges and blocks brought from the timber yard.

On Sundays we came down to tea. It would have been easy enough to tell when it was Sunday even without this, for, though bricks were allowed after tea on account of the texts, certain other toys were not. The market stall was banned, no shopping on Sunday. The papier mâché horse on a wheeled stand was taboo, horses must not work Sundays and a stuffed alligator could be brought out as long as we did not ride on it.[46]

The toy that must have given the greatest pleasure for the most years, must surely be the boat. Shaped like a hump-back bridge when turned upside down (and indeed often used as one) The boat was not designed to be put to sea and would certainly have sunk if it had been, but as a rocking boat none could have rocked higher nor contained more children at once without tipping up. There were two tiers of seats at each end and room in the middle for more. It was mostly kept in the hall, but at times would be moved about the garden, as though drifting on a wayward tide. As soon as we found it we would run to get the best seats, the boys for blood thirsty pirate games and the girls to play at 'willow patterns', chasing lovers across the lake as in the story on the plates. Equally agreeable was merely to rock gently to and fro with a congenial

The Boat at Northrepps Hall from a sketch by E. Ellen Buxton. 'Yoruba Mission' on the wall witnesses the family's interest in the Nigerian missions. Sir T.F. Buxton had been one of the originators of the unsuccessful Niger expedition in 1841

child to balance the other end to the sound of the mowing machine not far off being pulled by the donkey wearing leather boots.[47]

Sometimes the donkey pulled the water cart round the garden with the tank on its pivot clanging as the water lapped its sides, and sometimes, if our grandmother needed a turn round the woods and kitchen garden without exposing herself to the rain, the donkey would be harnessed to the bath chair with its great black leather hood shaped like a poke bonnet. On fine days she preferred the wicker pony chaise, and so did we, for there was room for two beside her and at least two more at her feet. The pony was often in the garden, saddled for the older grandchildren to ride at will. We, however, had to be held on and led.[48]

We were still bathed in a round shallow tub before a coal fire and rubbed dry with warm towels on the knees of our admiring betters, then gradually as our environments began to expand, we were then bathed in the bathroom itself, a large square room lit by a skylight. The bathroom at Northrepps was a cheerful place, smelling attractively of seaweed, which we brought in ourselves.

At Earlham, the Northrepps like home of our great great grand-parents, had been found, we were told, long after it ceased to be used, the earliest bath to be installed by any of the family. It was described rather alarmingly to us as a great black leaden tank under a heavy wooden lid, with the ceiling perforated above for a servant on the next floor to pour pitchers full of water down through the holes on to his master in the tank in a cupboard below.[49]

At about this time I began to be considered fit for family prayers before breakfast. Family prayers were not, of course, before breakfast for us, who had already eaten well round the nursery table, and had our bibs removed, our faces wiped, hands un-stickied and our hair flicked up with the brush. Now we were daily led even further along a new passage and up a short flight of steps along a dark, arched passage and out onto the landing leading to the front stairs. Down the front stairs we went, leaning heavily on the light polished handrail against the wall to see what it felt like to be lame. We were told that they had put this extra rail there for a lame girl to drag herself up by. I liked hearing about this little girl who lived there till she grew up and then moved to a house in the woods on the way to the sea with her rabbits and puppies. At the bottom of the stairs stood her wheel-chair, it had a padded red leather back and arms and to the wooden spokes of its two heavily built wheels other wheels were joined within so that the girl could propel herself about with her own hands. We tried it out ourselves and found it a most satisfactory way to move about. [This little lame girl was Priscilla Hannah's grandmother's cousin Anna Gurney of Northrepps cottage.][50]

Down in the hall the grandfather clock ticked on unhurriedly. A snake skin as long as a man hung beside it. The logs stacked under the stairs gave off a mossy, pithy smell as though the woods had come into the house. Beside them baskets were kept for every conceivable purpose, long flower baskets, round black-berrying baskets, oblong shopping baskets, square picnic baskets and a long tubular basket that I had last seen strapped to the bath-chair to hold grandmother's parasol.[51]

Through an arched doorway we could see grandmother sitting at the round table in the hall with the bible open in front of her. She kissed us in turn as we came in and I would have loved to scramble up on to her silky lap and put my head against the lace on what we called her 'body', but I was quickly drawn away towards the red cushioned window seat on to which the other grandchildren and cousins were climbing and turning round and sitting down to swing their legs, in a flutter of frilly drawers and pantaloons.

It was at family prayers, with so much time to look about, that people began to separate out into individuals. The aunts and uncles and grown up guests were ever changing, and not so easy to sort out. But the single file of maids with their enveloping linen aprons with stiff bibs that stood out well away from their bosoms, filtering in through the swing door from the kitchen passage and seating themselves in two rows with a starchy rustle never varied in their professional places.[52]

Family prayers began with a shuffle that led onto a rousing unaccompanied hymn. Then we had to sit very still while grandmother read from the bible. Her voice rang out like a bell, musically pleasing though I understood not a word. Another lusty hymn and the maids filed out, instantly talking and laughter broke out. It was as if God had withdrawn to the kitchen passage with the maids.[53]

Sometimes on sunny mornings grandmother would take us into the drawing room with her before she had breakfast. How fresh and sweet the roses smelt, arranged in their bowls on the many little tables. This was a golden room with white marble mantle-piece on which stood a clock under a glass dome with all its workings revealed. Beside it flower encrusted candlesticks branched out with china babies clambering about them. Then grandmother would throw open the French windows so that we could run out into the dewy morning, along the pattern of little paths edged with low clipped box hedges, surrounded by a mosaic of brightly filled flower beds. Past the aviary beside them leaning against the high fuchsia covered wall, which, we were told had fallen down in a heavy fall of snow, burying one of the peacocks, which three days later was dug out none the worse. Through the hooped garden doors in the wall to 'The World' in the front courtyard.[54]

In the summer of 1850, though Hannah Lady Buxton and her daughter Chenda gave the usual warm welcome, the now sixteen grandchildren were causing such a crush that drawers had to be pulled out for the smaller ones to sleep in.

The Johnstons had six children. Fowell and Rachel Jane so far had four, and Edward and Catherine had six boys. Now she gave birth to the seventeenth grandchild in the ante-room at Northrepps Hall; to everyone's delight it was a girl.

Edward (Mrs Johnston's brother) decided it was time for his family to have their own house by the sea for holidays, so he bought Colne House [Colne House eventually became a hotel appropriately specialising in families with children] just behind Cromer church, with a huge garden stretching right to the woods. Aunt Catherine then went on to complete their family of eleven with four more girls.

Many joint family picnics were shared by Northrepps Hall and Colne House, of which Hannah recalled:

This is my birthday, sixty eight! The day I was twenty I remember we assembled a very large party to picnic in Sheringham woods. Now how changed, I alone at the head of another party of children and grandchildren at another picnic on the cliff at Trimingham. Everything made it most interesting to me, though now surrounding my life and prosperity rather than sharing it. A lovely sight it was today the bright blue sea, Edward and Fowell with their guns, dogs and keepers. Catherine, Sarah and Richenda, the boy's tutor and six children all congregating for the luncheon under a sheltered hedge. How much I have to be thankful for.'[55]

19

Her Mother's Failing Health (1848–1852)

The next few years brought the dowager Hannah Lady Buxton into anxiety and 'sorrow upon sorrow' (the death of her brother, Joseph John Gurney, in January 1847, after a very short illness; her brother-in-law Charles Buxton of Bellfield followed in the summer of 1848), and yet, as always she remained outwardly calm, showing nothing but love and thoughtfulness for those about her. So far her eldest daughter, Priscilla, had been at hand to support her mother in her many losses ever since, as a little girl, she had called her mother to one of her dying babies during the unforgettable 'Hampstead Catastrophe'. Now Hannah was appalled to see that Priscilla, her beloved 'sister-like child', who had always had such a 'surplus of keen energy' was almost daily, as her father had before her, losing it.[56]

The following extracts are from the journals and letters of Mrs Priscilla Johnston, and deal with her failing health:

February 25 1848

My birthday, forty, pregnant enough with thoughts! Also I have contemplated my past mercies, countless, priceless above all in my mother, what a blessing to have possessed for forty years; how beyond all words to tell. Lord pity those who are deprived of this gift. My dearest husband and children came into my room this morning (I kept in bed with side ache), the darlings carrying vases of sweet flowers, and he with a beautiful present of volume two of 'Lady Willoughby'. He knelt down with them [her children], and in tender precious prayer commended the unworthy mother to mercy. My sense falling short as a mother, oh! it is intense.

July 10

I must say the value of my life looks rather appalling to me; and indeed I feel it my duty to cherish and preserve it. The doctor has frightened me rather about my health.

September 28

How truly touching it is to find in children conduct influenced by health. It shows us how much, and how tender allowance should be made for an irritable or restless state. I truly sometimes pity and compassionate myself for nervous infirmities, which excite strong inward if not outward irritability, while at the same time, I live under a sense of their sin, that it is hard to get from under it, and to feel any sunshine at all within.

Objects of intercession this day, Jan 17 1849

Ellen Buxton, my god-child, her first birthday: Fowell junior, gone off to school this morning; my own dear mother; besides my own regular list, my dearest husband, each child, and governess, servants, my dearest friend, and her brothers and sisters, and many more.

The following letter was written to Priscilla by Hannah Lady Buxton after a melancholy visit to the graves of her loved ones at Overstrand:

February 26 1849

My most beloved child, – I did not much wish to notice your birthday, but yet it looks unmindful not to send my most entire love upon it, and say how thankful I have been to have had such a child, and spared so long, and may I never know its loss! if right for me to be spared; but let us not choose our own portion, only may whatever is appointed, work in us and for us, the purpose of our Lord concerning us. My prayer is often for you, my love, that you may prosper and be in health as your soul prospers, and that everyone connected with you may be brought to the knowledge of the Lord, as you know Him.

Mrs Johnston returns to her journal on 27 May 1849:

In some way I have caught a violent cold, which has laid me low. Great weakness I am brought to, this is clear: death often vividly before me. (The papers I have written of my wishes are in my writing table drawer) and yet awfully does the question return, Am I truly ready? O God cheer, warm, enlighten, refresh, my weak and weary mind. I long and crave for vigour and life; my work seems so great so interesting; and most painfully do I observe the cases of motherless families. This is my grievous want of faith, however: and I often feel may be the punishment I dread; Yet the Lord is pitiful, He knows my weakness. He sees my heart, He knows I would work for him in these precious ones ... I want to write, but time is short, there are such dear ones to be with.

During the summer of 1849 she suffered greatly from ill health, and remained for a long time at Southwold. On 1st March 1850 she returns to her journal:

A word of note this day of two so inexpressibly dear to me, my dearest friend, and my beloved little Sarah Maria. I want to record my sense of the exceeding gift I enjoy in my precious little girl Sarah Maria. I do trust a kind providence may give her a smoother, less exciting and less fatiguing childhood and youth than I had. I would indeed her heart may be spared the deep knowledge of sorrow. I will not say hard work with my father from twenty to twenty six, for surely that is now my best treasure, my patrimony, my honour; yet all tells upon me now, and makes me the worn, the used up person I am. I see that sorrow or eventfulness in mature life brings more experience and less injury than it does earlier; and my strong judgement and earnest desire is, to shield my girls, if it may be so, from undue exertions and excitements.

In August Mr and Mrs Johnston 'went forth with dearest Edward and his boy Gurney, and their son Andrew to the lakes'. She writes, 'I was much better, but my cough never quite left me.' Early in the following winter she passed some weeks at Hastings, where she was very ill. In January 1851 she writes, 'My powers and thoughts are weak and wandering enough now ... I do not see my present allotment to be the very best for me.'

Soon after her return to Halesworth in February 1851, the following was written in her journal-book by her husband:

My own dearest, suffer not doubts of being reconciled to trouble you; we cannot reconcile ourselves to God; it is His Mighty power that effects the reconciliation with us through the precious blood of Christ. That you are reconciled I hold to be a great fact. May God give you a clear sense of it in his own time … Cheer up, then, beloved thou wilt yet say, 'It is good for me that I have been afflicted.' Then as to our young ones, O may the Lord breathe on their souls and renew them in spirit. I desire to be instant with you in prayer for them, dear, dear ones!

In April Priscilla wrote to her mother, 'I am taking great care of my cough, and am resisting every temptation to any good work. I am thoroughly comfortable, and I must say, feel at rest, and in great peace.'

Priscilla said she could not be spared from her children for the prescribed change of air and on 9th November writes thus:

At home alone, truly to my cross and discipline. My chest and cough have been so troublesome, that all seem to agree I must either leave home or shut up in it. The latter is clearly the easiest alternative; and, except for Sunday and church, I do not feel it very difficult to submit.

After spending the whole winter a close prisoner to the house without any improvement in her health, she left home on the 17th March 1851 with her husband, three younger children (Sarah Maria, Priscilla Hannah and Catharine Isabel) and Miss Sendall for the Isle of Wight, where she remained for about two months. It was a time of much bodily suffering, from gradual, though daily increasing, weakness. Her mind was as active as ever but though she entered with spirit and pleasure into her children's occupations and objects when with them, at other times, the thought of giving up life, of parting with them, cost her bitter mental conflicts, subdued only by the grace and patience given her by God.

Again this year was the dowager Hannah Lady Buxton brought into anxiety and sorrow under the failing health of her eldest daughter. Hannah and Priscilla's sister Chenda now joined her and from that time were constantly with her. In March 1852 she writes, 'I do not find any difference yet in my cough, and at times am nervous enough, but my appetite is better, and I am able to bear going out…' and on 14th April, 'I must say the future does seem unusually obscure just now to me. I am certainly discouraged about myself, but we must wait on and trust that light will come...' Then on 30th April, 'I have felt remarkably weak and low the last day or two, almost as if every twelve hours took away some strength ... I shrink from parting from the children under such uncertainties.'

In May a week was spent with Sir Edward and Lady Parry at Haslar and then she moved to her brother Edward's house at 10 Upper Grosvenor Street in London, spending the night before her journey home with her brother Fowell at Leytonstone. During these visits, the tender care and nursing she received soothed days of rapidly increasing illness. She had been much comforted by seeing all her brothers and sisters and many of their children. Her ardent wish was satisfied by her reaching home in safety on 24th of May. In June 1852 she wrote to Lady Parry:

> A great peace is spread over my mind, I have so committed and yielded my soul and body to my God. I feel so sleepy in His arms, I rest there ... I am better this afternoon; but I now almost always feel ill, except just now, it is strange, I feel better than I have done for days ... I suspect the sink is rapid. Now evening – a day of deep illness.

The following note is from Mr Andrew Johnston to his brother-in-law, Thomas Fowell Buxton:

Halesworth, June 13

> My dear Fowell, I grieve to say that Priscilla is very poorly today; there is an uncomfortable drowsiness clinging to her, which if it continues, I fear is the forerunner of a change. We have come down rapidly within the last week, and there is no sign of rally. I would fain hope that Effie may be in time to be recognised by her mother, the mind is still bright; but this drowsiness comes over like a curtain. I have written for the boys, (Andrew and 'Buxton') and hope to have them home on Tuesday. I grieve, dear brother, that we are so far apart at this season of affliction; but it is the will of the Lord ... What a blessing it is, that the spiritual mind of my beloved one is without a cloud.

Halesworth, June 7th finds the dowager Hannah Lady Buxton writing thus of her daughter's declining health:

> It has been a day of deep walks in the valley. The energy of her

mind displayed itself in speaking most seriously and earnestly to many, especially to her children.

About seven o'clock that evening, hearing that Mr R. Hankinson was in the next room, she said, 'Now then, let him administer the sacrament to me and to my elder children. My desire is to unite with them in it, not exclusively, but with all the beloved ones now around me.' It was a heavenly service, her whole soul seemed engaged in prayer during the administration to others; it seemed almost a foretaste of what she was about to fully enjoy. We were so thankful for it; we all needed such food to carry us through.

Mrs Priscilla Johnston now became visibly weaker and more faint as each hour of the weary night passed away, and when morning dawned all knew the end was near.

What a scene was that which opened upon the morning of the 18th June! Being exceedingly sunk the preceding evening, Priscilla was more or less watched all night by Mr Johnston and Chenda (her dear sister and most devoted nurse), and at about one o'clock her mother joined them. Now she was surrounded by the children and her child Effie placed herself at her mother's head, supporting it as far as she was able, while Andrew and Buxton sat at her feet. She became very restless, and despite all Effie's endeavours could find no rest for her head.

Between 4.00 and 5.00 a.m. the sun burst out suddenly, lighting up the garden spread out before them. 'O, look at the beautiful sun!' she exclaimed. 'Yes, my love,' replied her husband, 'and the Sun of Righteousness will soon arise in glory before you.' Her mother sat by her side and saw sweet looks of peace overspreading her countenance, she said to her, 'My darling an abundant entrance shall be ministered unto you into the everlasting kingdom!' Though death overshadowed her she took it in, her face lit up and she repeated again and again 'Abundantly!, Abundantly!' and as the first flood of sunlight poured in through the open window, she turned her face to it exclaiming, 'How glorious, how beautiful' Her husband said to her 'My precious one we shall not be separated long!' She answered eagerly. 'Oh, no!' In a few moments the cough had ceased, and the whole state was one of peaceful quietness. The great oppression became relieved, her head gently fell upon his shoulder before it sank down with ease upon the pillow on one side, her hair, so lovely, falling over her face, and she was gone, not one hard breath or effort.

Her mother wrote, 'It was a lovely sight. Marvellous exchange, from the bed of languishing and suffering to the glories which eye hath not seen, nor ear heard.' However, she also 'felt the darkness thicken' as she had watched her eldest and closest child die at the early age of just 44 years on the 18th June 1852 surrounded by her beloved children, husband and servants.

She was buried in Overstrand church, near Cromer, next to the seat of the Buxtons. Here a tablet records:

> Within the adjoining ruins lie the remains of Priscilla wife of Andrew Johnston of Halesworth Esq. and eldest daughter of Sir Thomas Fowell Buxton Bart. Of a kindred spirit with her father and gifted with like energy of mind, she largely shared his labours and his sympathies in the cause of the Negro. She died the 18th June 1852 in the 45th year of her age.

[The reference to ruins arises from the fact that the church was largely unroofed from the eighteenth century till it was restored in 1914.]

It would later be reported that her untimely death had been due to the fact that she was 'worn out through working too hard in support of her father and his campaigns.'[57] This was an incalculable loss to the children as their father frequently pointed out to them. Moreover, the idea that he was now solely responsible for their moral welfare seems to have weighed heavily upon him. He left the children with their grandmother at Northrepps more often than ever.

Soon after Priscilla's death Andrew began to put together some extracts of her journals and letters, and his wish strengthened that her children, and those who knew and loved her, should possess them in a readable form. He was unable to give much time to the project himself, but his ever ready sympathy and interest never failed, and until three months before his death he continued as sharer in the correction of the proofs.

Hannah resigned herself to what she could only feel was a brief respite, while her youngest daughter Chenda, endeavouring to replace her elder sister, stayed at home and helped to entertain the grandchildren. Chenda wrote of Northrepps during this time: 'Our hay is going on so we sent for the school children to play in it, and an express to Cromer for plenty of strawberries and milk for their supper. This was spread on the lawn and, as usual quickly attracted the parrots, who promptly stole the bread and butter from the children.'

Of Priscilla's children, their Aunt Chenda said: 'In the early morning it was pretty to see the little girls reading on the terrace and the two cockatoos pecking at their feet. The little girls are now crowding round the cistern of water while Francis is eagerly pumping, and a cockatoo is sitting on the edge of the tub drinking.'

The young Priscilla Hannah was a great lover of all animals, and from an early age there came to her squirrels and other wild animals which never seemed to fear her.

Andrew decided to commemorate Priscilla in Halesworth by building and endowing a school in what is now School Lane, and a public subscription was raised in 1853. The subscription list survives in Lowestoft Record Office and, apart from Halesworth people, includes large donations from the extended Buxton family – Barclays, Birbecks, Brightwens, Gurneys and Hoares, and even two pounds from the Buxton family servants.

The school, originally opened for the benefit of 270 scholars, girls and infants, still survives and bears the inscription: 'These schools have been erected by the contributions of neighbours and friends as a tribute of respect and affection to the memory of Priscilla the wife of Andrew Johnston Esq. AD 1853.'

Hannah Lady Buxton did not attend the opening herself but writes of the occasion in a letter to her grand-daughter, dated 7th October, before the opening:

How much I could wish that you might have been at Halesworth. It is such an occasion of lively interest, so gratifying, and yet so affecting. I do deeply feel the love from which this memorial springs; it is love of no common degree, and arises from the high estimation of your most dear mother's distribution of her gifts, not of her gifts only, but for the share given to others from the fullness of her love and kindness. Certainly she was a rare person, and we shall never again see such a pair as she and her father formed, for strong intellect, cultivation, with unbounded generosity, tender sympathy and consideration for others, and this all sanctified by faith and love to Christ and His people. They were, as the tablet says, 'of kindred spirits' and are ever one in Him they loved and served. I do not go to Halesworth, but uncle and aunt Buxton, uncle Fowell and aunt Rachel will go, and uncle and aunt Cunningham will be there also. It is excessively affecting to me to contemplate the whole thing, I confess. Oh the loss she has been to that place!

After the death of their mother we can only examine the evidence and surmise at the path the Johnston children's educations now took.

Certainly, in the cases of Andrew and Fowell, they were removed from school at Rugby. Then aged seventeen, Andrew went on to further education at University College, Oxford. Fowell, thirteen, against his wishes, would be put to work in a solicitor's office by their father.

His daughters, for the periods that they resided at their home in Halesworth with their father, may have continued to be taught by their governess. However, as they appear now to have spent more and more time with their grandmother at Northrepps Hall, their elder sister Effie who was fifteen, may have taken on the task of continuing the education of her younger sisters – Sarah Maria, twelve; Priscilla Hannah, nine years and seven months, and eight-year-old Catharine Isabel – with lessons taking place in the school-room at Northrepps Hall; or perhaps a governess remained for the younger girls, and Effie alone continued her schooling elsewhere.

Often, after the death of a mother, who had been her children's source of education, the responsibility of its continuation would fall to the eldest daughter. We have already seen earlier that this was so in the case of their own grandmother, whose mother died leaving a seventeen-year-old Kitty to educate the young Gurney children of Earlham.

However, the latter development is more plausible given that Mrs Johnston had expressed her views in a letter, written when she was practically on her deathbed, on the advantages of school for girls:

> I have been reflecting on my own experience [she, at the age of sixteen having 'so earnestly longed to improve her education' had chosen to leave home to attend school] and it is this, that I gained greatly. I gained most important advantages in tone of education as well as in actual acquirement; I gained some case of manner, and that sort of undefined enlargement which there is in familiar intercourse with persons of a new sort; but above all, I think I gained religious decision. Having been so carefully trained, and never, as it were, exposed to any doubt what was right, and what was to be done, the fact of being left to keep my own ground, to fight for myself as to religious retirement, etc, and the continual consideration of which course did I choose (something like a youth at college) I believe was made, through grace and mercy, one of the most important processes I ever went through. Everything in nature wants a fillip, a little extra stimulus and help – the egg must break,

the bud must burst. And then returning home is the exact stimulus the bud wants to open widely into the fragrant rose. There is nothing like, in my judgement the regularity, discipline, self denial, and entirely new and educational atmosphere of a school. May you darling, be rightly guided, and see rich fruit either way, and this you will.

We will later learn that Effie, at least, did indeed attend school, for her brother Andrew, in 1858, married Charlotte Anne Trevelyen, described as a 'school friend of Effie's'.

In 1855 Mr Johnston purchased Holton Hall Estate, Sussex, barely two miles from the town of Holton, from the Revd J.B. Wilkinson, and that summer he entertained his children along with the children of the village in its spacious grounds. As we shall learn later from the journals of Ellen Buxton, Holton Hall also saw many happy visits by the Johnstons numerous cousins.

Andrew did not, however, neglect Halesworth, and in 1856 the *Halesworth Times* reported: 'Our institute [Halesworth Institute for Moral and Intellectual Improvement] has been enriched with a hundred volumes of miscellaneous works given by Andrew Johnston.'

20

A Grandchild's Further Recollections of Northrepps

[Apart from royal occasions, historical events do not seem to have intruded much into the family journals. For instance, there is no mention of the Crimean War of 1854–56, though periodicals of the time were filled with news of the heavy losses suffered at the battle of Balaclava on 25th October 1854 and the famous Charge of the Light Brigade, followed by battle of Inkerman on 5th November 1854.]

Once again, in the hope of giving the reader a 'pen picture' of how life may have been for the growing Priscilla Hannah and her siblings, I have quoted from Verily Anderson Paget's, *The Northrepps Grandchildren* – her recollections around the time of World War I:

> The next time we went to Northrepps there was a big change, not in Northrepps but in ourselves. I was no longer a baby. Now, instead of occupying the nursery wing, we abandoned it to the still nannied cousins.[58]
>
> We roamed at will all over the house and garden and into the woods. We went down the steps of the pond and tottered out to the end of a fallen tree that formed a pier. We went into the kitchen garden and helped ourselves to gooseberries and redcurrants.
>
> Another change had come over me. Now I could read. The names painted below the row of bells, hanging high on coils in the kitchen passage, now revealed themselves as belonging to my grandmother, and my mother and her brothers and sisters. We followed the wires upstairs to find out which rooms they had all had before they left home. We followed them up into the attic crawling after them under rafters, testing as we went the triangular springs on which the wires changed direction, so that bells in the kitchen passage set up a continual jangle.

Learning to read certainly opened up the past as nothing else had. That Northrepps was an actual place on the map, independent of the family, came as a shock. When I first read NORTHREPPS 2½ on the signpost, I felt an intense resentment that it was necessary to point it out. Surely anyone needing Northrepps would know where to find it without written directions? As for the thought of Northrepps existing without the family, it had never occurred to us. We took it for granted that it all began and ended with us, till someone let slip the unpalatable truth that others before the immediate family had been returning to our haunts for half a million years.

Old axes made out of stone by prehistoric men 5,000 years ago were still apparently, being found near Cromer. Then there were ape-men here till we came? we wondered aghast.

Apparently all our ancestors found when they came was an open heather and gorse covered heath with an occasional ancient windswept oak and strand of pine trees that were said to be directly descended from the forests that had once covered Europe. Northrepps Hall itself had been little more than a crow-stepped and rectangular farmhouse of cut flint and cobble, sheltering beneath a cluster of tall trees that narrowed into the avenue. Even the sea had not always been there but had crept up over the marshes between us and Germany. Next we learnt to our further dismay that the woods themselves had not existed till the family planted them. Each winding path and broad green ride had been carefully cut. Each mossy glade had been deliberately left open for the sun to reach it. Even the wild daffodils that followed the snowdrops in the spring had been brought by them from Devonshire.'[59]

One can't help but feel that learning to read must also have made a great impact on the young Priscilla Hannah. For one can be sure that her grandmother, Hannah, must have related to her the many facets of the lives of both her grandfather and her great aunt. Priscilla Hannah could now read for herself the family journals which told in great detail of the remarkable good works that her grandfather Fowell and great aunt Fry had achieved during their lifetimes.

At this tender age she could not have imagined the path that her life would follow. Perhaps it was from this early age that she became influenced by those who had gone before. One of Priscilla Hannah's characteristics was that she had a great perseverance in all that she undertook to achieve throughout her life, a family trait that she may have inherited from her grandfather and great aunt.

Verily gives us a fine example of their ancestor's perseverance in the face of adversity:

> When Betsey had first thrown herself forward in an attitude of prayer and made her first public offering in the ministry, it had been to great Uncle Dan's intense embarrassment. From then on she had begun to speak at meetings and to work towards the reform of any social inadequacy with which she came in contact. Regardless of contagious diseases, she had carried her own young babies, into prisons and doss-houses to speak to the inmates in a 'voice that was magical' in the effect it had on them. She had taught them to read and to study the bible and, above all, to love and take pride in their appallingly neglected children.
>
> Her sisters had raised eyebrows over Betsey's own children, of which there were the inevitable eleven, and had helped where they could with the cheerful but obstreperous bunch, which had been referred to affectionately by their aunts as 'Betsey's brats'. Joe Fry had not been an inspired business man and financial crises overtook the Fry family with varying degrees of seriousness. But though Betsey had worried, she had continued with her voluntary work about the family, with her own children dotted about among relations during the crises which had included a sad move to a smaller house that it had been hoped would be less expensive to run. Betsey's married sisters had included the brats with their own children and the unmarried had taken them home or trailed them round with them. However whenever there had been a sickness it had always been great aunt Betsey they had sent for and she had always been first on the scene with soothing words, experienced hands and a variety of remedies. She had trained not only herself but other young ladies in the most up-to-date methods known in nursing.
>
> It was Fowell [Priscilla Hannah's grandfather] who had been first shaken into a fervent desire to better conditions everywhere by the impact of an initial visit to Newgate Prison.'[60]

One can imagine the young Priscilla Hannah's amazement when reading of how her grandfather had even seen Queen Victoria. In a letter, dated July 17th 1837, he had written, 'I this day saw our youthful queen surrounded by all the chief officers of state, herself wearing a crown of diamonds, and arrayed in royal robes, and the House of Lords filled with all the great ones of the country. She delivered an admirable address to the Parliament, with the utmost sweetness of voice and the most exquisite grace of manner.'

Verily continues her childhood recollections:

> We now travelled farther a-field and into the Village. Here at the post office we would mount the two steps and run along the garden path between the pansies. Even we children had to stoop under the honeysuckle that tumbled over the porch. The door handle had hardly to be touched before the bell above it sprang into action. Inside the smells almost overpowered us with their richness, candles and raisins, brandy balls and bacon rinds, sacking and bootlaces made variously of leather, string, and liquorice.[61]
>
> In the afternoons we were taken down to Overstrand for a paddle. It was coming back that made the impression. Would we ever get to the top of the gangway dragging our spades and buckets and wet seaweed, with our yellow oilskin paddlers pinching our thighs where the sand had lodged in its folds? Then we would turn into the lane that curves up through the Cottage Woods. What a relief it was to come to Northrepps Cottage itself and there be regaled with cakes and milk. This was the house in the woods where lame Anna Gurney had lived with her rabbits and dogs, looking after the sailors cast up after wrecks on the shore.
>
> It was a cottage in shape only, with the twisty chimneys, overhanging eaves and small decorated windows of a gingerbread house. We were constantly in and out of the cottage.[62]

From this fairytale image one can imagine how Anna's cottage must have attracted the Johnston children. The young Priscilla Hannah would have gained great pleasure from helping Anna tend her pets and been enthralled with her recollections of past times.

From Verily we learn that Anna had a collection of fossilised bones of pre-ice-age animals which she and her live-in partner Sarah, Thomas Fowell Buxton's sister, had picked up at Overstrand after cliff falls. Anna's collection of stones, arrowheads and fossils was said to be 'the most informative in the country'. She was the first woman member to be elected to the Royal Archaeological Society.[63]

Verily recalls many tales of smuggling at Northrepps and Overstrand, 'which apparently all the villagers had taken part in as a matter of course; they did not see the distinction which more refined moralists would, between this and other breaches of the law. Even lame Anna Gurney seems to have almost turned a "blind eye" to it.'

In her book she also relates the tale of the Buxtons' first December at Northrepps Hall:

> There was a great storm and the sea getting up rapidly. Young Harry was at Cromer, and he mounted his pony and rode up to Northrepps to tell Anna and grandfather Fowell of the ship coming in at a terrible rate.
>
> Cromer lifeboat station had already been equipped with a 'Manby Gun' designed to shoot a life-line to a sinking ship, but it was an early design and besides being heavy was in other ways not entirely satisfactory. Grandfather Fowell had been involved in several attempted rescues with it. When Anna had heard that Captain Manby, the Norfolk inventor of the gun, had produced a lighter and more effective one, she had asked him to bring it for a demonstration at Northrepps Hall, where there would be room in the garden to try it with some of the Overstrand fishermen. Captain Manby had turned up, a small brisk army captain, who began by volunteering the information that he had been at school with Admiral Nelson. The party went on to the back lawn. Captain Manby said that since he was a subaltern in the Gunners he had been trying to find a means of firing a cannon ball into the teeth of a gale for 200 yards. The chief difficulty, after discovering how to arrange the line so that it would pay out evenly and not break under the strain, was to prevent it being burnt by the blast from the mortar that fired the ball. He had got over that by using a couple of feet of plaited hide to attach the rope to the ball. He had now perfected the whole apparatus and mortar, cartridges, balls and line could be carried by one man on horseback. Anna said she had only been interested in whether she could carry it in her wheel chair. This she found, due to the enormous strength in her arms, she could do.
>
> The demonstration had been carried out, using the big silver fir tree in lieu of a ship. This was the fir we called the 'Rescue Tree'. Captain Manby had fired the gun up to the branches, and children and gardeners swarmed up a ladder to play the part of the shipwrecked, riding down to safety in a breeches-buoy slung to a small trolley-wheel on the line, which the fishermen, in their leather souwesters and striped jerseys, held taut on the lawn. Anna had been so

impressed that she had ordered a gun to carry on her knee to Overstrand where she could lead the fishermen in their rescues.

Anna Gurney had also helped to 'tide Captain Manby over' while he expanded his inventions, for such rewards as he received from the government always fell short of his needs. He was then able to go on to invent the first powered lifeboat, a chemical fire extinguisher, and the jumping sheet for rescuing people from blazing buildings.[64]

Towards the end of her life Anna often stayed at her childhood home of Keswick Hall. In the spring of 1857 she went for a visit from which she was destined never to return. She was seized with a strong and rapid attack of bronchitis and died on June 6th. By her express desire she was buried in the chancel of the same ruined church at Overstrand where lay her attached partner, Sarah, Sir Thomas Fowell Buxton and his sons.

Among Anna's bequests were generous legacies to her faithful servants, without whom she could not possibly, as increasing lameness and bulk lessened her mobility, have lived such an amazingly active life. In her will, also, the comfort of all her animals and birds was assured for the rest of their lives.[65]

Anna Gurney's experiment on the Silver Fir at Northrepps Hall with Captain Manby's gun for saving life in shipwrecks, copied by Pamela Gurney from the original pencil drawing by Hannah Buxton

Norfolk's forgotten hero, Captain Manby

Born 1765 at Easthall Manor, Denver, Norfolk. His father who was an officer in the Fusiliers moved his family to a larger house, Woodhall at Hilgay. Here seven more children were born. The young Manby being schooled from the age of five at Mr Chathams School at Downham Market, alongside a young Horatio Nelson. As a young man, due to unfortunate circumstances Manby was put into prison. He was bailed out by his brother, Thomas, a captain in the Navy.

Manby derived his ideas and inventions from personal experiences. This period of his life was considered the most rewarding time. After a colourful life, he felt that he never received the recognition he deserved. Sadly he died a 'pathetic, shrivelled and disillusioned figure at the age of 90'.[66]

21

The Marriage of Euphemia 'Effie' Johnston to Miles MacInnes

Miles MacInnes was an old school friend of Andrew Johnston. It was whilst attending a garden party at Rickerby with her brother that Effie (Euphemia) came to know the banker and MP for Hexam. Miles and Euphemia became engaged on 1st August 1859, a memorable day, as it was both the twenty-fifth anniversary of the marriage of her parents and that of the great day of the Emancipation of the Slaves.

The marriage took place on a very snowy day, at Holton, Suffolk on the 1st December 1859. (The previous year Andrew had married Charlotte Trevelyan, a school friend of Effie's and so the two couples were closely united.)

A 'merry party' had travelled down there the day before, amongst whom were the grandmother and mother of Mr MacInnes, the dowager Hannah Lady Buxton, Uncle Andrew Johnston and 'the three aunts' – Sarah Maria, Priscilla Hannah, and Catharine Isabel – to say nothing of the dog, 'Danny' (probably a Skye Terrier, as this was the breed much favoured by the girls), who walked solemnly up the church, with a white favour on his collar, before the wedding. Euphemia was attended by twelve bridesmaids, who, having all signed their names in the prayer book, gave presents. [Bridesmaids *gave* presents in those days; they did not receive them.]

The happy couple went to Cornwall for their honeymoon, and paid a visit to Miles' uncle, Mr Robert Were Fox, who was distinguished in the scientific world, and his two daughters, Anna Maria and Caroline, at their beautiful home at Penjerrick, the gardens of which were far-famed for having acclimatised more tropical trees and shrubs than almost any other part of England. Here tender camellias flourished and grew large in the open air, sometimes flowering in the snow.

Caroline Fox penned a delightful letter of appreciation of the newly weds in her journal on the 18th December 1859:

We have had a beautiful, really exhilarating little visit from Miles and Effie MacInnes in their Bridal tour; he is beamingly happy, and every fibre of his mobile face tells you so. He has a right to thank God, for He has given him a rare wife, a truly lovely, loving woman, exquisitely conscientious, watching for opportunities to help others, simple, thoughtful, playful, fresh and yet with a depth of experience from which I would fain draw much. She is a thorough Buxton in look and manner; and he, Anna's true son. Of course we collected what we could of the few remnants of the family, and we showed them what we could of our beautiful world. They were delighted with all, and gave pleasure whithersoever they went.

On their return to Carlisle they spent a few months in a house at Stanwix, until a little house on the Scaur fell vacant, which became their cosy, happy little home for three years. There were no houses beyond the bottom of the hill at Etterby Street. The Scaur stood quite alone, and commanded beautiful and uninterrupted views across the river to the lake hills. There was no barrier to the road to protect the steep river bank, and it required some steering to drive the pair of ponies, Pip and Merrimac, out of the little drive into the road.

Mrs Wilson, a faithful and attached servant, writes of life at the Scaur: 'I am sure no one ever saw a hard look or heard a sharp word from Mr MacInnes. The cab men used to say to us servants, "You have such a good master, we will run you up any time free!" Of course we did not let them.'

Their nearest neighbours were Mr and Mrs Wordsworth (he was the eldest son of the poet). They lived at St Ann's Hill, and became very dear friends, as well as neighbours.[67]

The mansion house at Rickerby Village did not become home to the MacInnes' until after the death of the previous owner, the banker, Mr George Head Head in 1876. Born in 1799, George Head Head was the son of Joseph Monkhouse Head.

In 1804 a firm was founded which was to play a prominent part in the financial arrangements of the district of Carlisle. This was the bank formed by Joseph Monkhouse Head, born in 1759, and a member of the Society of Friends.

Joseph was in his early years a grocer at the top of Botchergate, Carlisle, whose careful conduct of his business won the confidence of influential citizens. In the shop Joseph was often asked to advance or take care of money for his customers, so like so many traders all over the country he started a bank as a department of the shop. This was so successful that the shop was given up and Head's Bank became a feature of Carlisle. As bankers the Heads were 'in' on most of the business concerns of the City or indeed of the whole of Cumberland.

The firm was later strengthened by the admission to partnership of his son George Head Head, whose marriage with an heiress added considerably to the resources of the bank. Following the death of the founder in 1841 George became principal of the bank. But his energy was by no means limited to banking, though the original grocers business had long since been abandoned.

George Head Head is chiefly remembered for his kindness. At the time there was no unemployment pay, no insurance, no sick pay and no general education. When times were hard Head opened a soup and rice kitchen in the Caldewgate area of Carlisle, to feed the hungry. He paid an almoner to help deserving people. Finding that there were other needs greater, if not quite as urgent as food he also employed a scripture reader, for very many adults could not read.

In 1834 George Head Head purchased Rickerby House, probably because he wanted to get married. The following year he married an heiress, Miss Woodruffe Smith, the daughter of a merchant who traded with Russia.

Within two years of settling at Rickerby, Head built the village school. He was asked to help with a night school in Caldewgate for boys who were already working, having had no education. He came forward and ran not only the night school but a day school for 400 boys, girls and infants. Then finding the dire need to save boys who were going bad, he started a reformatory in Stanwix. The only rule for admission to this school was that it was for boys who had been to prison. Here they learned shoemaking, tailoring and were trained for agriculture. (The reformatory is now part of Carlisle College of Art and Design.) Mr Head needed his bank's success for he paid the staff and all expenses of these schools out of his own money.

One year Mr Head Head was High Sheriff of Cumberland. He drove through Carlisle in a carriage lined with crimson with two trumpeters on the back. He threw tracts out of the window to any onlookers. (This coach was later sold to Gretna Green where it is shown as typical of the carriages used by runaway couples.)

Sadly the first Mrs Head died in 1855 after a long illness. Three years later Mr Head Head married again, Sarah, a daughter of the famous banker Sam Gurney and, therefore a niece of Elizabeth Fry. Thus becoming 'Uncle Head' to the young Buxtons and Johnstons. Head's record would have made him a very suitable member of the family.

George Head Head's bank was situated at the top of Botchergate in the City of Carlisle (today known as the Griffen). Heads bank, moving with the times, combined with other Carlisle banks to form the Cumberland Union Bank which had connections with Gurney's bank. Mr Head was Chairman of the new Company Bank. When the Gurney's Bank 'broke' in 1865 many Carlisle people would have been seriously affected. But Mr Head Head felt responsible to all who had invested in his old bank and paid most of the rest of his own fortune over to the bank to save people's savings. So he was not rich when he died but he still had the sterling character that the authors of books on banking still praise him. He was paralysed for the last few years of his life but was carried to bank meetings in a chair.[68]

The young Ellen Buxton kept a journal in part of 1859, but did not start it in earnest until 17th January 1860, her twelfth birthday. In the following summer of 1861 she has recorded a visit to her Johnston cousins at Holton Hall.

Tuesday, July 16 Northrepps

This morning till we started for Holton I finished packing my things and then had a walk in the garden on stilts I can manage them very nicely now, and can get up a few steps and jump.

At half past ten Grandmamma, Jay [their maid] and I started in the Northrepps carriage to go to Norwich, we had a very nice drive though it poured with rain the whole day; at Aysham we changed horses, and then went on to Norwich we got there at one, and had to wait 20 minutes for the train; but we had a very nice journey, I sketched every pretty little church there was and saw an old ruined church which looked very pretty from the railway. We reached Halesworth at 1/2 past three; and found Uncle Johnston and his carriage waiting to take us to Holton Hall, he could not come with us as he had to be at the bank at Halesworth; but we went on and came to Holton at about four; Sarah Maria, and Prissy came directly to meet us, and Isabel, and Edith one of her friends who was staying with her came down in a few minutes. Soon we all went a walk and tried the new organ at the church and then came home to 1/2 past six tea...

Wednesday, July 17 1861, Holton Hall

This morning, about eleven, Prissy went to practise at the church, so Edith Fisher and I went with her and while she practised I sketched the church, and then we all sat under the trees for a little while, and then walked into the village to order some buns and pies for some school children, who are coming on Friday. In the afternoon Prissy, Edith Fisher and I went in the carriage to meet Mamma and Papa at the station; first we did some shopping in Halesworth and bought some toys &c. for the children, then we went to the station and found Mamma and Papa just arrived, Mamma and Prissy went in the fly with the luggage, and Papa, Edith and I in the carriage. As we passed the church we all got out and walked home by the fields, and found Sarah Maria sitting under the trees in the garden, and Grandmamma and Isabel walked to meet us…

Thursday, July 18 1861, Holton

This morning we all sat in the drawing room and read Macaulays History of England. In the afternoon Papa, Mamma, Prissy, Edith, Isabel, Grandmamma and I walked to the church; then Prissy stayed to practise there for an hour and Mamma and Grandmamma walked home again, while Isabel, Papa, Edith and I took a nice walk by the side of the river Bligh and found quantities of beautiful sky blue Forget-me-nots, and a great many other flowers…

Friday, July 19 1861, Holton

Today all the little children from the Bulkham Union went for a treat to Dunwich, and we all went to see them there; Prissy, Isabel, Edith and I went early at half past ten in Uncle Johnston's carriage, we got there at about twelve o'clock, and directly went to the 'Ark', a little wooden house on top of the cliffs, where all the children's bread and butter and cake had been put; and we had brought them some bags, dolls, sweetmeats, knives and tops; directly we had arrived at the wooden house we put them all down in the only room, but it was a large one; and then we all went out and found the children, there were twenty-four boys and thirty-five girls.

Soon they all came to the 'Ark' and sat down close by the door, and ate their dinner, while I sketched the ruined church, for we had a beautiful view of it from the 'Ark', also an old priory, close by the church, which was a most beautiful old ruin, and looked so splendid.

When the children had done their dinner Prissy and Isabel played with them till our dinner was ready; and we all came and ate it in the 'Ark'; then we made the boys climb up to the top of the flagstaff, and gave them each a knife and the girls ran races and got a doll each, then it began to rain so we all went into the 'Ark' and the children got under shelter where they could; when it was over we made them scramble for sweatmeats, which lasted for a long time, and then we took them all down to the shore; where they ran some more races, and played more games, and very soon Mamma, Papa and Uncle Johnston came to see them all, they had come in the open carriage from Holton.

Soon after they arrived Papa sent Uncle Johnston's coachman to get four empty beer bottles and he threw them into the sea, and the boys and girls threw stones at them till they were all broken, they then climbed up the cliffs and picked some scarlet poppies to take home with them. The cliffs were all made of sand so the boys got to the top and then came sliding down to the bottom, and Papa offered any boy three-pence who should get to the top but it was so perpendicular that none of them could.

About four o'clock the children all had their tea and then Papa and I walked off and tried to get to see the old priory but it was surrounded with such thick corn that we thought we had better not trample it down so we went and saw the ruined church; it was a very large one and Isabel had told me that it was not the real church but the cathedral, there were most beautiful windows and when we got into the middle of it I found an old vault so old that the stone had been half broken away. The people had been buried there up to 1832 but there were no tombstones later than that.

Papa, Mamma, Uncle Johnston, two of the little Beloes (the Clergyman's daughter's) and I went home in the carriage; left the two little girls at the parsonage and then got home to dinner at seven, Prissy, Isabel and Edith stayed to see the children go away and then came home themselves to tea.

This morning Prissy got up at six o'clock, and went through the pouring rain to practise at the church, because she knew she would have no other time to do it in and came home about a quarter to eight. Tomorrow Mamma, Papa and I are going home to Leytonstone.[69]

22

*Extracts from the Journals of Hannah Lady Buxton
(1860–1862)*

In many respects the lives and interests of the seventy-seven-year-old Hannah and her eighteen-year-old grand-daughter Priscilla Hannah were now so closely associated, living and travelling together, that the memories and story of one describe the other.

> One summer's day in 1860, we had a fine lesson yesterday of the uncertainty of life in such an escape from accident. Catherine came up for us, and persuaded me to drive in her open carriage. As we went through the Avenue lane towards Cromer the powerful horse began to kick, and got its leg over the pole, and with it there he galloped off and for some way, when he extricated himself, kicking the other horse; therefore both, equally frightened, dashed on furiously, Buscall using every effort in his power to check them, trusting that as we came to the gate, a very strong one, they would stop. But no, instead of that they both gave a tremendous leap and leaped over it, the carriage crushing the gate to shrivers, but getting safely through. You may suppose what we felt, and the extreme fear of rushing to the next gate and down the hill. In great mercy it was put into Buscall's mind to turn into the ploughed part of the field through which we were passing, and up the ascent, which baffled them, and they stopped and we were safe. We did thank God for our marvellous preservation. It was terrible danger we were in. Had we gone clean through the gate, what would have become of us? We sat very quietly, and were not terrified as the case called for. We all kept in stillness.

Northrepps, September 26 1860. To E. MacInnes

We are still in a good current of engagements, the arrangements more troublesome to me than the company. There is cricket and riding going on daily nearly, and pleasuring is the order of the day. I drive with Aunt Buxton and see the children on the [Cromer] shore. I doubt if ever I set foot on it again. The groups are lovely.

October 1. To the same

To see and hear the six in merry play is enlivening to life certainly. It is a comfort that I can bear the tumult of my grandchildren. I had six in my room for an hour, before breakfast I go into the nurseries at seven and Emily is then ready to come. I began with my Charlie first before seven, and then they troop in as they are dressed for play and coffee! I shall welcome yours with peculiar love! We have eight new parrots. Two were on the Lighthouse Hills yesterday, I was in the carriage, many walking; but the wind was most boisterous, and I was much overdone, but brightened up again with fifteen to dinner.

November 15. To the same

I quite long to have your baby with me. I am at my usual seat, and the garden still looks very pleasant in the sunshine now come over it. The remnants of the parrots, and some added, are in a large cage in the hall, rather troublesome with their noise, especially at reading in the morning.

Hannah wrote to Leytonstone, after the death of Leonard Fowell Buxton, [one of the Leytonstone Buxton children] of scarlet fever, 3rd February 1861.

February 23 1861. To Ellen Buxton

My dearest Ellen, your letter is really charming, such a picture of you all that it cheers me, trusting you are preserved from further anxiety, and the beloved flock below are mercifully prospering. Sweet Emily being better and able to amuse herself is such an immense comfort, but we miss that precious darling boy, Leonard with his sweet face and dark eyes, a lovely little playfellow for her he was, and a treat for you all. Janet must be quite a help in supplying you all with a delightful object, and the lively baby too. I like much to hear of Louisa teaching the boys to draw. What does John Henry do in the evening, and Geoffrey? I hope my slippers will be ready when I come. What work have you and Louisa been doing? I expect to see some very nice work accomplished. Priscilla Hannah is working a beautiful frock for little Grace.

Your cat is the greatest favourite with Sarah Maria and the girls. They are never happy without her, but I cannot say I admire such love, and such a fuss about a cat. However, I use it when I lie down after luncheon to warm my hands, and I must say she is most comfortable to me. I will not allow her to go up to bed with the girls, or to sleep with them, but I find her in bed with Sarah Maria in the morning.

Your most loving Grandmamma, H. Buxton.

Northrepps, June 25 1861

I have had so very much on my heart that we do not give enough as a family. It is a subject on my mind, and makes me often very low. It is a true anxiety to me. It is fearful to have large sums unused when there is such a cry for help, from the suffering, the sinful and the ignorant. I feel this is a solemn responsibility, and I do most earnestly desire that my sons and grandsons may be led to know that they are but stewards of their Lord and Master, and become afraid to accumulate beyond reasonable and sufficient future for each child. It is very odd with this strong sense of obligation, the duty, the wisdom of giving, yet I do not like to give to too many applications, and hesitate what to give. All this I say today from reading a letter upon the demand, the request for schools in the East by the poor people themselves finding the Turkish Mission cannot grant their request, and even must give up some schools. The same earnest request from the settlers in Canada, and yet more than all the piteous demands for admittance to the refuges in London, and with many vacancies, obliged to be refused because funds are not sufficient. The persecuted Christians in Spain, whose sufferings are grievous, and who may receive alleviations, have affected me, and other objects also

Ought I not to give more money? I long for others to feel these things as well as myself, and it would truly cheer me up if I saw a very liberal feeling, a true generosity and benevolence. I see there is much of generosity to their own objects, but I long for a far more enlarged boundary, and a far more abounding liberally. I have talked to my children upon the subject, and intend to do so with my grandson in time. They will never err in giving. It is fruit that will abound to their own account though there may be now and then objects not deserving; but it is extremely fearful to keep what we ought to give, to lay up largely when there are such cries to be saved, taught, fed, and clothed. This is the point.

This family trait of yearning to help the less fortunate was inherited by Priscilla Hannah, for early in life she found that, 'It is much more blessed to give than to receive.'[70]

In the spring of 1862 Priscilla Hannah grew concerned for the health of her seventy-eight-year-old grandmother after she had a serious attack of illness while on a visit to her son, Edward, and his family at Colne House, Cromer.

Colne House, Cromer, April 10 1862

It is now about two months since I had a sudden and frightening attack in my chest, at Northrepps, which I recovered from in degree and came with Catherine to Colne House, where seven weeks since I was suddenly seized with a fever, which quickly brought me into real and severe illness, and very near did I feel to what in favour and greatest mercy I thought would be blessed termination of my long course here. Truly the saviour was all sufficient for me, and in Him I was in peace and hope, and graciously spared fear, but was rather longing to depart to be with Him and share the heavenly inheritance with my own most beloved ones. But after some days I became better, and though I have had much illness and some conflicts in the flesh and spirit since, yet it has been the will of Him, whose I am, to bring me up again from the brink of the grave, to be, not well again, yet to return to life, to be employed, and probably well enough to return to my post at home next week.

I ought to turn to the cheerful side; and if thee could see Catherine with her five little girls in red cloaks, with four white rabbits, and Francis, now quite a tall boy, on the lawn before me, thee would say, 'What pleasures yet remain.'

23

Her Father's Death (1862)

Andrew Johnston

Early in 1862 Andrew Johnston failed in vigour and spirits, and often remarked upon this himself, saying he could not understand it. In April, when a cloud of sorrow rested upon many hearts, his seemed the most bowed down with grief for his bereaved son, Andrew and his wife, Charlotte at the loss of Beatrice their only child. His already failing strength gave way more rapidly after this heavy trial. In the middle of July he left for the last time his beloved home [now at Holton, Suffolk] and went to London for advice. Then only was alarm first aroused. He became visibly more feeble, and his memory entirely failed. He was moved to Norwood, and on the 9th of August to Sydenham. The disease made rapid progress, but the remembrance of those weeks will be ever stamped with thankfulness; his children were all with him.

He died early in the morning of Sunday, August 24th 1862 at Sydenham, Kent. It was very likely that he was staying with his eldest son Andrew, who reported his death and gave his residence as Wellbeck House, West Hill, Sydenham.

Five days later on the 29th he was laid to rest in the grave with his wife in the ruins of the church at Overstrand. Here a simple tablet beneath his wife's reads, 'In memory of Andrew Johnston of Holton and Halesworth, died August 24th 1862 aged 64'.

[There are two prominent monuments to him in Halesworth. One is the outer north aisle of the church, where a brass tablet proclaims: 'This North Aisle and Chapel were built and enlarged in the year 1863 ... as a memorial to the late Andrew Johnston Esq. of this town and of Holton Hall. Born 1798, died 1862'. The other is the Rifle Hall on Norwich Road, originally a theatre and used as such by the Fisher Company until about 1850. This was remodelled as the Volunteers' Drill Hall at the time of the Napoleon III invasion scares, and a tablet inside used to read: 'This Hall was placed in trust in the year 1862 by the children of Andrew Johnston of Holton in memory of their father for the benefit of the town of Halesworth and especially of the 7th Suffolk Rifles whom for the last two years of his life he commanded'.][71]

Brass Memorial Tablet to Andrew Johnston in the north aisle, St Mary's, Halesworth

The year 1862 was a rather sad year for the Johnston family, the events of which are recorded in the diaries of Ellen Buxton thus:

April 30 1862

I quite forgot to put in my journal the death of little Beatrice Johnston, who was staying here with us in the Autumn, who died last Saturday week, the nineteenth of April. She was Andrew and Charlotte's only child and two years old. They loved her so excessively, and now Charlotte is so ill poor Andrew had nothing else he enjoyed, she was with him always, had her meals with him and all, she died of croup. Poor Charlotte is very ill, she has a very bad knee, which is so bad that she cannot move it, and the doctors say she will have to keep still perhaps for months.

Sunday August 24 1862

This morning just as we were going to church a telegraph arrived to say that Uncle Johnston died at four o'clock this morning – so the consequence was that my Father and Mother went off in the carriage after luncheon to see Sarah Maria, Prissy, Isabel and all, they found them excessively low, but they came home again at 11 in the evening – The funeral will be at Overstrand church on Friday, he always had a wish to be buried there with Aunt Johnston –

On Thursday – my Father went down to Northrepps, to be there for the funeral, he went with Andrew, Sarah Maria, Prissy and Isabel, and the next day, the funeral was at Overstrand church at 11 o'clock...[72]

Andrew Johnston's three unmarried daughters now went to reside with their grandmother, the dowager Hannah Lady Buxton at Northrepps Hall.[73]

At the beginning of 1863 Hannah thus reflects on her grandchildren:

Present circumstances, January 1, 1863. Miles and Effie with Grace at the Scaur, Carlisle. Andrew and Charlotte staying at Malvern. [Fowell 'Buxton' in South America.] Now to begin 1863.

I am thankful to have been spared. May it be for Thy glory, my blessed Lord. Nor did I ask it, but Thou didst will it. Spare my own beloved ones! My cup is still full.

I am very comfortable at home. My three beloved girls, Sarah Maria, Priscilla Hannah and Catharine Isabel, with me as their home. Lord bless us in body and soul.

24

Extracts from the Diaries and Sketchbooks of Ellen Buxton (1862–1866)[74]

Ellen Buxton, from a portrait of her in 1864 when she was 16
In the possession of Mrs R.L. Barclay

Mrs 'Kisty' Ellen R.C. Creighton, the grand-daughter of Ellen Buxton, describes the Johnston's cousin, '...as a most enterprising, bright and precocious girl, who was entrusted with a good deal of the upbringing of her younger siblings. Lessons do not seem to have taken up much of Ellen's time, indeed not much at all after the age of fifteen. This may have been a pity in some respects, but if they had, she would have had less time for her diaries, sketches and for going to see things.

Here by the kind permission of Mrs Creighton I have collated a selection of extracts from Ellen's diaries and sketches, which give an insight into the many delightful events surrounding the lives of the Buxtons and cousin 'Prissy' Johnston and her family during this period in time – a time which was largely spent visiting the extended family of numerous cousins and going on many interesting and educational excursions.

One such excursion recorded in Ellen's diary of 1862, is a visit paid by the family to the Crystal Palace at Sydenham. Open from May to October this housed an exhibition of industrial products from Britain and the continent. Originally built in Hyde Park as an exhibition hall for the 1851 Great Exhibition, which had been planned and opened by Prince Albert, the Crystal Palace, designed by Joseph Paxton, was a huge iron construction with nearly 300,000 panes of glass in the walls and roof. It was dismantled and rebuilt at Sydenham in 1854, where it remained until accidentally burned down in 1936.

Queen Victoria notified her wish that the opening of the 1862 Exhibition should bear as much as possible the character of a national ceremony. Her Majesty therefore was pleased, under the impossibility of herself performing that ceremony, to appoint His Royal Highness the Duke of Cambridge, His Grace the Archbishop of Canterbury, the Lord High Chancellor, the Earl of Derby, the Lord Chamberlain, Viscount Palmerston and the Speaker of the House of Commons to be her representatives to conduct it in her name.

On the day of the opening, 1st May 1862, the invited guests entered at 10 am under the 'Western Dome', the South entrance. Here stood various fine works in marble from the Italian and Roman courts. The effect of these was further heightened by a splendid collection of the finest plants and flowering shrubs from Kew Gardens.

General visitors were later admitted between the hours of 12 and 1.30 pm, through a sufficient number of turnstile entrances to permit upwards of 100,000 visitors to enter in less than one and a half hours. Once inside visitors could not fail to notice that the 1862 exhibition was a third larger than that of 1851. There was a great deal to excite the minds of young and old alike, arranged in lower courts and upper galleries, under splendid domes of glass and iron. With exhibitors being divided into two halves by a central passage, the western half being assigned to foreign nations, the eastern half retained for the British Empire, the house exhibitors being on the South, and the Colonial on the North. To mention all that was on show would be an impossible task, but here we take a glimpse at some of the splendid exhibits which may have excited the Victorian minds of the Buxtons and their Johnston cousins.

There could be seen a tall tower, in which hung a peel of large cast steel bells by Naylor and Vickers of Sheffield; a little museum of cannon, locomotive springs, circular saws, etc made of Bessemer steel; a heroic statue of Oliver Cromwell, and a grand collection of stairs, candelabra, vases and pedestals by the Coalbrookdale Company. Then there was the bright glancing cutlery and showy steel grates of Sheffield; the shining bits, spurs and snaffles of Walsall; the locks, keys and safes of Wolverhampton; the chain cables of Dudley.

Not forgetting the jewellery court, with one diamond worth a 'King's ransom', superb tiaras, necklaces and bracelets of the most precious stones; gorgeous cups, shields, vases and epergnes of gold and silver; the pottery court, where Minton, Copeland, Kerr, Binns and Wedgwood in their branches of useful and ornamental works could be seen to surpass those of Dresden; the glass court, where hung one magnificent chandelier, with pendants six inches long, carafes and decanters so exquisitely cut that the multitude of facets flashed almost with the brilliancy of diamonds. In the naval and military court one could see models of ships showing the gradual progress from the unwieldy 'Harry' of the 16th century to the Warrior Iron Frigate of the 18th; and the civil engineering court where there were plans, sections and models of many bold and successful devices in the great 'art and mystery'.

One could not fail to glance upon the huddled crowd of 'trophies', three lines deep in the British section, remarking the exquisite beauty of the Norwich gates of beaten iron; the elegant contour of a granite pillar from the granite city of Aberdeen; the splendid piles of the rarest skins, furs and leather surmounted by deer, goats, and a Bengal Tiger in a death struggle with a huge Boa constrictor, whose clammy crushing coils enfold the royal animal. Here too there was a display of feathers and hair, where you could see plumes of the most beautiful ostrich feathers and wigs of every shape and colour; the trophy of the small arms makers of Birmingham bristling with swords, bayonets, pistols and guns; the two great organs, the food and raw material trophies. In the opposite aisle could be found a collection of musical instruments from the bagpipe to bassoon; a fine show of furniture and house decorations; and the Colonial courts which were full of blocks of wood, fruit, fishes pickled in brandy, feathers of birds and skins of beasts. In the adjoining transept were some gigantic spars from British Colombia, and a huge pillar of coal from Nova Scotia.

1. The Watering Trough, now used as a planter, dedicated to the memory of Priscilla Hannah Johnston situated in the village of Rickerby near to Carlisle.

2. Hannah Lady Buxton, from the memorials of Hannah Lady Buxton.

3. Priscilla Johnston (née Buxton) by kind permission of Mr Robert Vale, a water colour originally in the possession of his late sister, Richenda.

4. Jet Mourning Brooch, inscribed on the back 'PHJ JANY.15. 1912' containing a lock of Priscilla's hair. The brooch belonged to her fellow philanthropist, Mary Ellen 'Polly' Creighton. It is now in the possession of Polly's great niece, Dr Prue Barron, who remembers her aunt as *'a formidable lady'*.

5. Priscilla Hannah's bedroom at Northrepps Hall.

6. Priscilla Hannah's bedroom at Northrepps Hall, painted by Priscilla Hannah Johnston.

7. Priscilla Hannah's bedroom at Northrepps Hall, painted by Priscilla Hannah Johnston.

8. Water colour of Grandma's (Hannah Lady Buxton) bedroom at Northrepps Hall, painted by Priscilla Hannah Johnston.

9. Grandma's bedroom at Northrepps Hall.

10. Water colour of the drawing room at Northrepps Hall, painted by Priscilla Hannah Johnston.

11. Water colour of the drawing room at Northrepps Hall, painted by Priscilla Hannah Johnston.

12. Water colour of the drawing room at Northrepps Hall, painted by Priscilla Hannah Johnston.

13. Sarah Maria Johnston.

14. Water colour painting of Sarah Maria, 'Pris' and 'Isa' on the lawn at Northrepps Hall with their Skye Terrier, 'Foresce', thought to have been painted by 'Effie'.

15. The carriage awaiting outside Northrepps Hall. Hannah Lady Buxton and 'Isa' seated inside with Sarah Maria in front and Priscilla Hannah behind.

16. The marriage of 'Isa' to Dr Arthur De Noé Walker.

City of Carlisle

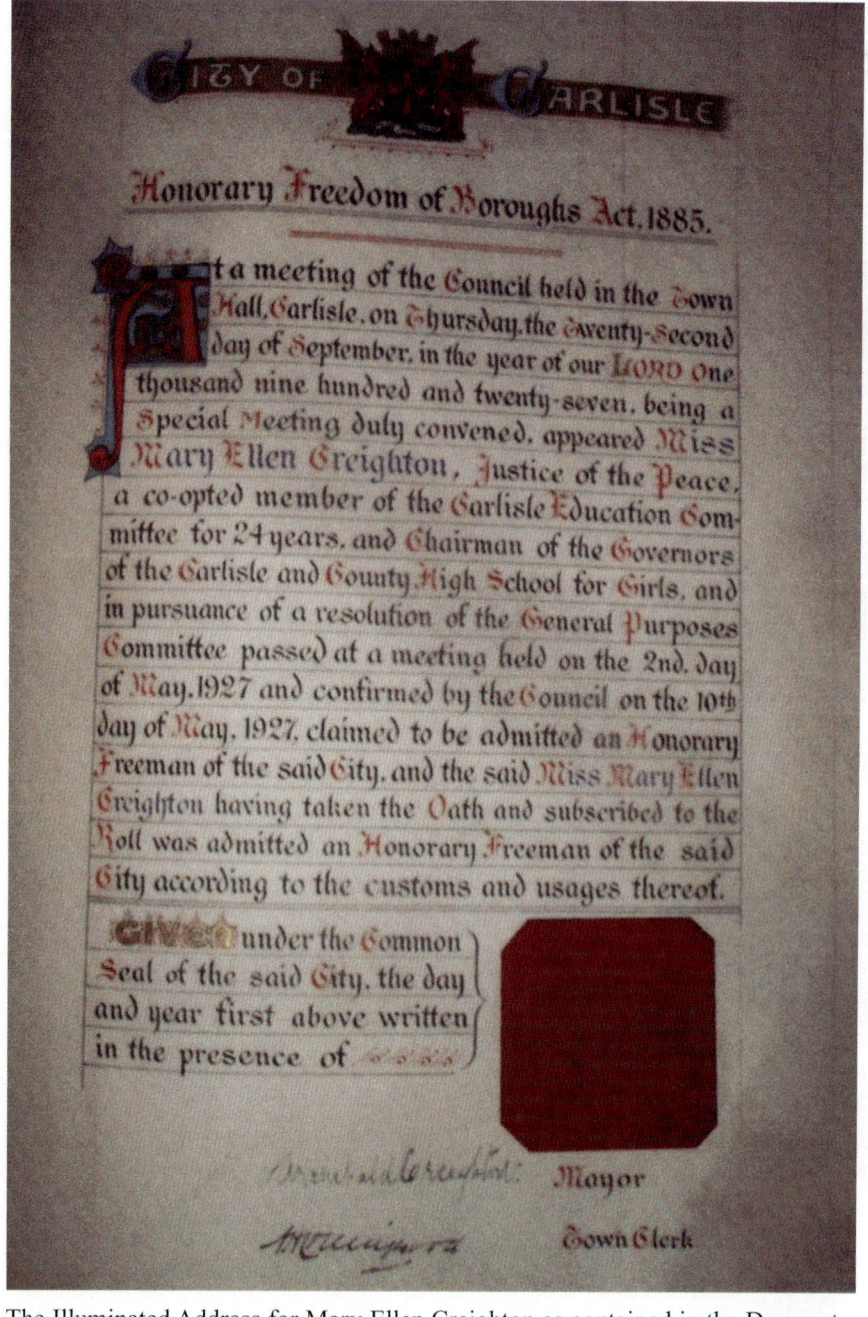

Honorary Freedom of Boroughs Act, 1885.

At a meeting of the Council held in the Town Hall, Carlisle, on Thursday, the twenty-second day of September, in the year of our Lord One thousand nine hundred and twenty-seven, being a Special Meeting duly convened, appeared Miss Mary Ellen Creighton, Justice of the Peace, a co-opted member of the Carlisle Education Committee for 24 years, and Chairman of the Governors of the Carlisle and County High School for Girls, and in pursuance of a resolution of the General Purposes Committee passed at a meeting held on the 2nd. day of May, 1927 and confirmed by the Council on the 10th day of May, 1927, claimed to be admitted an Honorary Freeman of the said City, and the said Miss Mary Ellen Creighton having taken the Oath and subscribed to the Roll was admitted an Honorary Freeman of the said City according to the customs and usages thereof.

GIVEN under the Common Seal of the said City, the day and year first above written in the presence of

_____ Mayor

_____ Town Clerk

17. The Illuminated Address for Mary Ellen Creighton as contained in the Dormont Book in the custody of Cumbria Archive Service, Carlisle Castle. One of the most important documents owned by Carlisle City. It can tell us a lot about everyday life in medieval Carlisle. Carlisle City bought the book in 1561. It was stored in the guildhall in an iron-bound fireproof wooden chest. It contains the oaths and declarations of all those taking office until 1689, a register of the indentures of apprenticeships of future freemen, 1672-1844, and details of those who were given the Freedom of the City.

On crossing the central avenue one found oneself in the Continental division, of which the local newspapers reported, 'with few exceptions these courts are very backward. Although tardy in preparation these courts appear, as a general rule to be got up with great taste, and will have a charming effect. There is a remarkable contrast between the overcrowded, blocked up aspect of the English side of the nave and the sparse, slender line of trophies in the Foreign division.' However in this division there could be observed a group of very showy and luxurious furniture; and some excellent bronze and iron castings; a collection of candles and some huge sheets of glass; a group cast in iron from Norway representing a couple of men grappling in a duel to the death; a magnificent show of the products of the royal pottery of Saxony; and a quantity of metal statuary from ateliers of Belgium and Prussia.

In the upper galleries there could be found a portion given up to the textile manufacturers of Britain; the display of scientific and philosophical instruments was very interesting. Here, one of the most curious instruments which evoked much excitement at the time was a machine exhibited by Mr Peters for micro-copying writing. With this machine Mr Peters could write the words to be written microscopically in pencil in ordinary characters on a sheet of paper at the bottom of the instrument. This pencil was connected by a series of levers with another minute pencil and tablet at the top, to promote the means by which the ordinary writing of the pencil and the writing of the microscopic pencil could both move in unison, resulting in microscopic writing which could only be visible under powerful magnifiers. The object of this machine being chiefly to mark banknotes with certain minute signatures for the prevention of forgery.

In this upper gallery there was also the stained glass section; and of particular interest to the Buxtons and the Johnstons, given their artistic flair, the picture galleries, which lent a powerful charm to the exhibition. Showing art from both the British and foreign schools, these galleries afforded an insight into the qualities of continental art which Britain had never before had the opportunity of procuring.

Stretching out from the eastern and western ends of the main building were a couple of annexes. The western, devoted to machinery in motion and the other to illustrations of mining; and carts and gigs, harrows and ploughs and elegant wheelbarrows.[75]

All in all the Great Exhibition of 1862 was hailed by everyone to be 'a decidedly popular success'.

With the summer of 1862 drawing to a close it was now time for the

Buxtons to visit the family at Northrepps, where they would spend two months with Grandmama, Prissy, Sarah Maria and Catharine Isabel Johnston.

'Kisty' Creighton recalls, 'Their journeys were excitement enough but once settled at Northrepps they always found plenty to occupy themselves. It was uncommon for them to bathe in the sea, but they rode on the shore, met their cousins for huge picnics, picked blackberries which they afterwards made into jam, and drove along the lanes around Northrepps.'

A family picnic on Runton Hills, west of Cromer

During the early months of the following year there was much excitement throughout the country of the forthcoming royal wedding of H.R.H. the Prince of Wales (later Edward VII) and Princess Alexandra of Denmark which took place on the 10th March 1863.

A great historic event like that of the marriage of the Prince of Wales was likely to excite the liveliest interest throughout Her Majesty's dominions. The extent and splendour of the preparations sprung from a deeply rooted feeling of loyalty and affection towards the Sovereign of the day. The newspapers of the time published plans for the proposed celebrations, which would take place not only in London, but all over the country. Firstly there would be an arrival procession to welcome the Princess Alexandra and her family into London. Tuesday 10th March was declared a public holiday, at which the inhabitants of the British Isles gladly availed themselves of the opportunity of testifying their good wishes towards the royal pair by suspending all business and entering heartily into the proceedings of the day. Flags and festoons were in great request.

In London the old chapel of St George's had been specially arranged and decorated for the occasion. In the nave tiers of seats ran the whole length of each aisle from the western entrance to the transept and screen. These seats rose gradually from the floor, and were covered and backed with scarlet cloth and yellow fringe. A gallery for the Queen's servants occupied the northern arm of the transept and a similar structure in the southern for the orchestra. And, at night on the evening of the wedding, the chief towns were to be ablaze with brilliant illuminations and fireworks. After the proceedings had come to a close the Chapel and state rooms at Windsor were to be opened to the public, admission free of charge.

The streets of London filled up with many thousands of people, who had travelled to the capital for the occasion. Needless to say such an event was too important to have been missed, so early March 1863 saw the twenty-one-year-old Priscilla Hannah Johnston travel to Leytonstone, the home of her Buxton cousins, where a young Ellen excitedly records:

Friday, March 6 1863, Leytonstone

Prissy Johnston came last night, to stay with us for a little while. They come up principally to go and see the entry of Princess Alexandra of Denmark who is to come in to London tomorrow from a yacht at Gravesend and is to be married to the Prince of Wales on Tuesday 10th.

The Princess Alexandra, accompanied by her parents and her eldest brother, had left Copenhagen on the afternoon of Thursday 26th February 1863, on her way to England. The city was splendidly decorated and the Danish population made the most cordial demonstration of respect and affection towards the royal lady who was soon to become Princess of Wales.

The royal travellers arrived at Hamburg on the Friday evening where they were greeted by illuminations. The next morning they were at Hanover where they were entertained that evening by the King. Her Royal Highness was then escorted through the Prussian territories by Prince Charles of Prussia arriving at Brussels on Monday afternoon. Then on to Antwerp, from where the royal party embarked for England. The Royal Yacht weighed anchor at Margate shortly after 2.00 pm the following day, to be greeted by a 21 gun salute. The Royal bride to be was then welcomed to her future home with every manifestation of enthusiasm and joy, marked by a Civic Procession.*1

That night there was a brilliant illumination on the beach at Sheerness, the word 'Welcome' being displayed in gigantic letters formed with blue lights which could be seen from the Royal yacht. There was also a torchlight procession, and several large bonfires were lit along the shore.

Throughout the country the local press reported on the preparations being made in London for the forthcoming historical event.

> The aspect of the long line of London Streets from the Bricklayers Arms to Paddington was most remarkable. Crowds of persons, availing themselves of the remarkably mild and fine weather, watched the preparations. Carpenters were at work in front of the majority of houses, erecting seats. Gas fitters were also very busy preparing for a new kind of decoration, the gas illuminations.
>
> The government of the day expended £300 to £400 on the illumination of each public building of importance. The display was most dazzling with Prince of Wales feathers made of hollow tubes fitted with gas jets, which when lit proved very effective. Other displays, also illuminated with gas jets included the initials A A (Albert & Alexandra) and P W (Prince of Wales).*2

Along the whole route which the procession of Princess Alexandra traversed from Gravesend to Windsor, every town, village or railway station was utterly transformed by a profusion of garlands, arches, trophies, banners and emblazonments.

Saturday, March 7 1863

We have just had a grand day in seeing the Princess Alexandra, the whole procession was most grand. Prissy and Isabel helped us to make large favors of white calico for the horses. At 11 o'clock in the morning the fly, and the open carriage came round, and Papa, Mama, Uncle Head, Prissy, Isabel, Louisa, John Henry, Arthur, Geoffrey, Alfred, Emily and myself all got into them to go to London.

As we drove up to London, many houses were adorned with flags, and places for illuminations on Tuesday, which is the Prince's wedding day, and as we got nearer London, the tide began evidently to flow towards London, and when we got into it they increased, till there were thousands and thousands of people all walking towards King William Street to see the sight.

We saw carriages of grand people going to meet the Princess at the Bricklayers Arms Station who were to follow in the procession, and then about 2.45, the procession began to pass…'

Tuesday, March 10 1863

Today is the day of the Prince and Princess's wedding. Of course we shall hear nothing of it till to-morrow. At 6 o'clock a large van came round to take us to see the illuminations and we all got into it, there were 17 of us…

The rejoicings in the metropolis on the wedding day were of the most enthusiastic character, and the show at night surpassed everything which had ever before been exhibited in London.

The time appointed for the commencement of the wedding ceremony was 12.30 p.m.; from 10.00 a.m. till noon train after train arrived at the railway station, all filled with the most elegantly dressed women, noblemen and gentlemen.

At twelve o'clock His Royal Highness, accompanied by his supporters proceeded in carriages from the state entrance of Windsor Castle to the west entrance of St George's Chapel attended by a captain's escort of the First Regiment of Life Guards.

His Royal Highness wore over a full general officer's uniform, with the Stars of the Garter and the Indian Order, the magnificent flowing mantle of the Order of the Garter, and in it looked a model of youthful grace and manliness. His step was full of firmness and dignity, and his whole carriage that of a Prince.

Her Royal Highness Princess Alexandra was looking rather pale, but a most becoming blush frequently tinged her cheek as the procession passed slowly up the nave, and the eyes of all observers were turned anxiously and admiringly upon her. The dress worn by Princess Alexandra consisted of a hand made petticoat of pearl white silk, embroidered with the rose, thistle, and shamrock trimmed with four rows of silver lace at the bottom, robing up the centre, over which was suspended a train of crimson velvet, magnificently embroidered with the same designs in silver as the petticoat. The bodice and sleeves were of the same costly material. The coiffure of her Royal Highness consisted of a wreath of orange blossoms. The eight young ladies who attended her Royal Highness as bridesmaids worthily sustained the reputation of our countrywomen for beauty and grace.

The bouquet was composed of orange blossoms, white rose buds, lilies of the valley, and rare and beautiful orchid flowers, interspersed with sprigs of myrtle, sent specially from Osborne by command of the Queen, the myrtle having been reared from that used in the bridal bouquet of Her Highness and the Princess Royal.

When the bridal procession arrived at the entrance drums and trumpets filed off and as the bride entered the organ and Her Majesty's band played Handel's march, from Joseph.

Reports from various parts of the British Isles tell of one universal outburst of loyalty, in celebration of the Royal Marriage. In tower and town and cottage the enthusiasm was caught up, and everywhere the day was one of general rejoicing and festivity. Cities, towns and villages were gay with banners all day, every disposable bit of bunting being called into requisition, joy bells were rung, bands played, and processions, reviews, dinners and all manner of festivity was general everywhere. At night the chief towns were ablaze with brilliant illuminations, and fireworks hurtling through the air shed their gold and silvery rain in every county and almost every town in the Kingdom. In the rural districts the jubilee was not less universal, and on mountain brows where in days of old the bale fire 'sent up its ruddy signal to the night', blazing bonfires cast their red glare from peak to peak, spreading the tidings of the national joy.

The evening celebrations attended by the young Priscilla and her family threw into the shade all previous efforts in the same line, the decorations and illuminations being of a most lavish character throughout the Country. In London the illuminations were on a scale of unparalleled magnificence.*3

However, for Priscilla the excitement of the occasion may have been somewhat tinged with sadness by the fearfully violent deaths which occurred of several women. For during the time of the illuminations in London, not fewer than twelve fires took place. There was also a great number of accidents which occurred through the pressure of the crowd and the passing along of vehicles, with more than 100 persons injured in the city. The mobs in the streets were so dense that even in some wider parts of the Strand women were carried into shops fainting, whilst in the City the crush was so severe that strong men also became faint and exhausted.

In Mansion House Street a woman named Phoebe Crystal was forced down, and another named Charlotte Donovan, with her husband and a little 12 month old child, fell over her. The three persons and also the child could be seen lying on the ground and struggling violently, but to stop the populace appeared impossible. The child was held up and received by some one in a passing omnibus, and was thereby saved. Just at that moment a cab horse fell at the side of the woman named Crystal, plunged out one of its forelegs and kicked her skull in. The three unfortunate people on the ground were ultimately extricated, but both women were dead.

There was a great rush forward, and another woman was forced down, trodden upon and suffocated. At the same moment another was forced down and trampled upon. After a desperate struggle the poor creature was dragged out and taken to Bartholomew's Hospital where she was pronounced to be dead.*4

The young Ellen recorded that her family and guests spent the night worrying that the wife and baby of one of their servants may have been killed in the crush. As it happened they turned up unharmed the next day.

> DEATHS IN THE CROWD IN LONDON.—The royal marriage festivities in London have been sadly clouded by the serious accidents which took place on the night of the illuminations. No fewer than seven persons were crushed to death, of whom five were women and two children, and about one hundred others were severely injured. In the city the crowd was very great, and the police arrangements are said to have been defective. At the West End, where there is more space, and where there would probably be proportionably fewer people than in the city, the arrangements are said to have been good; but many accidents occurred there, chiefly through the pressure of vehicles. The child of one of the women who perished was thrown into a passing van to save its life. It was an infant of only 12 months old. The death of one of the six women was caused by a kick from a horse after she had been thrown down.

In spite of these tragic occurrences, to have been present at this historic event must have been a marvellous experience for the twenty-one-year-old Priscilla Hannah to look back upon.

In April of 1863 Ellen has recorded in her diary an account of a week's visit to the home of her Aunt and Uncle Head at Rickerby, Carlisle, her family being joined there by the Johnstons. Here it would appear that our visitors have followed, to a certain extent, what was then perhaps considered to be a popular 19th century 'tourist route', as set out in the 1870s *Jenkinson's Practical Guide To Carlisle, Gilsland, Roman Wall and Neighbourhood*. I have included historical narratives from this, along with archive photographs, which give a brief insight into the background behind the sights and scenes of which Ellen has recorded that the Buxtons and the Johnstons found so awe inspiring.

This will be of particular interest to those readers living in the Carlisle district, who will recognise the places visited by the family on their excursions during their visit to the North.

I myself ride my horse along the same banks of the River Eden at Wetheral where Ellen has recorded that the party sat and ate their luncheon. Here at Wetheral the party visited the picturesque church where they gazed upon the beautiful Nollekens statue, before paying 1d. to take the ferry boat across the River Eden to visit Corby Castle and its gardens with its many statues. Recorded in Ellen's diaries are further excursions the party made throughout the week, which included visits to Lanercost Priory, Naworth Castle, Gilsland and the Roman Wall.

From the pages of the Jenkinson's Guidebook:

> Alighting at Wetheral station 5 miles east of Carlisle, the traveller finds himself in one of the most lovely spots in England. Stepping on to a handsome viaduct of five arches, each 80 feet span and 100 feet high, he overlooks that beautiful river appropriately termed the Eden, flowing between thickly wooded banks, past the pretty village of Wetheral, and the renowned grounds of Corby Castle ... From the station, Wetheral may be first visited, and then Corby reached by a ferry-boat over the river, charge 1d. or the viaduct may be crossed from the station by a footway, on payment of 1/2d., and Wetheral reached by ferry-boat after visiting the Corby grounds...
>
> The grounds of the Castle are only open to the public on Wednesdays, and the interior of the house is not generally shown to visitors ... The Castle, the residence of P H Howard, Esq., stands on the edge of a cliff overlooking the Eden ... The interior of the castle is elegantly furnished, and contains many paintings and works of art of great interest and value...
>
> A few yards beyond the village of Corby is the lodge gate where the park is entered (after following paths and reaching the St Constantine's statue) there is a pretty building with steps, pillars

and sculpture in front. It is used as a summer-house, and commands a lovely view through a long avenue to the Castle ... And then having passed a monster statue of Polyphemus in attire of a Grecian warrior by Dunbar, a steep ascent is made to a temple like building containing the figures of two females and two mermaids ... Here is a little picture, exquisitely beautiful, the water descending from the temple above over ledges of rock richly coloured with mosses and lichens of every hue...

Descending to the brink of the river by a pleasant path from the Corby village, the traveller will enjoy a most lovely prospect while being rowed across in the ferry-boat to the Wetheral side of the stream ... Wetheral village is a clean looking, pretty little place. The principal object of attraction for strangers is a small mausoleum attached to the parish church, built over the vault of the Howard family, and which contains a marble monument by Nollekens.[76]

The Viaduct over the Eden at Wetheral
Designed by Mr Francis Giles, Civil Engineer, and built by W.S. Denton, for the Newcastle and Carlisle Railway Co. Length 600ft. Height 100ft. Finished in the year 1835.
The sloping bank on the left is the place where Ellen has recorded that they ate their luncheon. Also note the ferry-boat in which they crossed over the river to Ferry Cottage which was located on the opposite bank at the foot of the cliffs on top of which stands Corby Castle and park.

181

Ferry Cottage, Wetheral, Nr Carlisle

Wetheral Church prior to 1882

The Church, dedicated to the Holy Trinity, is a neat Gothic edifice. Attached to the church is the Howard Chapel or Mausoleum, a handsome structure erected in 1791 by Henry Howard Esq. of Corby, on the foundations of his family place of sepulchre. There are several beautiful and elaborate monuments to various members of the Howard family of Corby Castle including a tribute to the memory of the Hon. Maria, the first wife of Henry Howard Esq. She is represented bearing in her arms the infant to which she has just given birth, and religion in Angel form appears supporting the expiring mother. This exquisite group was from the studio of Nollekens. Speaking of this monument a writer says. 'Mrs Howard died (1789) when she became a mother, and the affecting incident is transferred by the magic chisel to the pure marble. There is the exquisite drapery and the mother and the newborn infant on her lap, looking upward from her couch of pain to the benignant figure of religion, bending over them, T'is surely the sweetest group that genius ever created.[77]

Corby Castle stands on the east bank of the River Eden, 90 feet above the river. The origins of Corby Castle date back to at least the 12th century, for among the deeds of Wetheral Priory, on the opposite bank of the River Eden, is one referring to the sending of a priest to Corby

The Nollekens statue of Maria Howard at Wetheral Church

Corby Castle

on Sundays to say mass, provided the owner was at home. If away, his household must go to Wetheral.

The 14th century building which is incorporated in the house started life as a Pele Tower, erected in order to guard the ford over the river about half a mile north, by Sir Richard de Salkeld, who was granted the manor of Corby by Edward III. This family owned the manors of Great and Little Corby until the early part of the 17th century when they sold the property to Lord William Howard, third son of the fourth Duke of Norfolk, who was executed for his association with Mary Queen of Scots. Thus began the unbroken succession of Howard owners of Corby.

The Howard brothers and their wives were Catholics and had great trouble with Queen Elizabeth, in fact Philip Howard, Earl of Arundel, was imprisoned for eleven years in the 'Tower' for his faith and died there. He was beatified in 1936. Lord William and his wife (they married when they were 15 and 14) eventually escaped from the Queen's clutches after payment of a fine of £10,000, when they were both over 30.

When William Howard became the owner of Corby in 1611 the Pele Tower was all that was standing. He proceeded to build a house on to the back of the Tower which, when finished, was a rather badly shaped letter L, with two storeys and one room thick. This house stood until 1909 when Henry Howard, with the aid of Peter Nicholson, a well-known north country architect, entirely transformed it by converting it into a square Georgian mansion. A portion of the old house was pulled down, a new south front was built, and a new East front was joined on to the Pele Tower. The whole building, except the west side which retained its original 17th century stone work, was encased in red sandstone taken from a quarry in the grounds and surmounted by the Howards' lion crest on the south and east fronts. This rebuilding took about eight years.

In the 18th century Corby became widely known for the naturalised garden laid out by Thomas Howard in the 1720s. He was a grandson of Lord William's and lived there until 1730. These grounds ran along the River Eden for about one mile and were considered very beautiful with fine trees and graced by a number of sphinxes, sea horses, gods and goddesses. (The latter were the subject of a grant by the Historic Buildings Council for England in 1957. The money was principally expended on the restoration of the cascade which lies just below the lawns and takes water from the park down a series of steps to the river.)

The colossal stone figure, which Ellen Buxton describes, on the path leading down to the river from the cascade is Polyphemus, though he is known locally as 'Belted Will' the nickname given to Lord William Howard. It is also referred to as the Corby Giant in a guide book of 1847. Polyphemus was, of course, that giant Cyclops, whose fate was described in the wanderings of Odysseus thus:

> Next, landing on the West coast of Sicily, Odysseus, with twelve companions, entered the cave of a Giant, but the owner, the one eyed Polyphemus, son of Poseidon, came in with his flocks, he blocked the entrance and devoured two of Odysseus' companions. Next evening, by which time only six of his men survived, Odysseus made Polyphemus drunk with his sweet wine and then blinded him with a burning stake as the giant lay in a drunken sleep. At dawn the Greeks escaped by clinging under the bodies of sheep as they went out to graze, and so reached their ship, but henceforth they had to reckon with the vengeful hostility of Poseidon.

In 1831 Mrs Catherine Howard included in her 'Reminiscences for my children': 'Alas! such is the destructive propensity so innate in the English, that, when the pleasure grounds were open to everyone, they left neither a seat nor the smooth bark of a tree un-mutilated with names and low verses; not even a statue or Roman Altar escaped from being broken to atoms and thrown into the river ... Polyphemus alone remains.'

However, when the walks of Corby gardens had been opened daily to the public during the summer months, the statue of Polyphemus was in possession of a golden eye, but one morning the statue was found without its head. Upon searching the missing member was found to have been hurled into the river, and the eye had disappeared for ever. The head was recovered, fastened firmly onto the body again, and another eye of less valuable material was put in its place. The public were henceforth denied admission to the grounds, except on each Wednesday, from the first week in May till the last in October.

Such was the appearance of Polyphemus which Ellen and her family gazed up at in 1863. Sadly he has since suffered more damage. In 1914 he lost an arm after being hit by a falling tree, and after about two and a half centuries of an open air life he is now somewhat weather-beaten.[78]

The Statue of Polyphemus

Gilsland is situated on the Newcastle and Carlisle Railway, 20 miles from Carlisle, and 40 from Newcastle. In 1876 Sir Walter Scott, his brother John and friends fixed their headquarters at the then peaceful and sequestered little watering place of Gilsland. It was here that Scott fell in love with Margaret Charlotte Charpentier, an exile from Revolutionary France. The 'Popping Stone' by the banks of the River Irthing, is allegedly the site of Scott's proposal. There used to be a story current in the locality to the effect that if a piece of the stone were to be placed under the pillow, the features of one's future life partner would emerge during dreams. The couple married a year later.

There are reminiscences of Scott's stay in Gilsland in several of his works: 'Belted Will Howard Naworth' appears in *The Lay of the Last Minstrel*. The most important reminiscences of his visit however are to be found in *The Bridal of Triermain* and *Guy Mannering*, the latter making famous the infamous disreputable inn Mumps Ha'.

Mumps Hall was at Gilsland (a village which straddles the Cumberland–Northumberland county boundary. Most of modern Gilsland is in Northumberland but the bit that included Mumps Hall is actually in Cumbria (formerly Cumberland). Gilsland has been famous for its medicinal waters of sulphur and chalybeate (iron) and spa for at least 300 years, resulting in a succession of hotels and a convalescent home.

All literature and guide books about Gilsland refer to 'Mumps Ha' or 'Beggars Hotel' as an inn of evil repute and mention its infamous trouble-causing inhabitants, the Carricks and the Teasdales. One Meg Teasdale glares as the horrid fictional character of Tib Mumps, the evil landlady rendered so famous by Sir Walter Scott in his book *Guy Mannering*.

Mumps Hall, 1885

Meg Teasdale was notorious for drugging to death such of her guests as had money.

Mumps Ha' was the last house of entertainment for travellers across the waste which there divides England and Scotland – a lone house, tenanted by an Amazonian such as Meg Teasdale is traditionally reputed to have been, stood in a glen by the side of the brawling river: a place to challenge suspicion and inspire terror, the hostelry had a fearful reputation for travellers who could be prevailed to stay over night were seldom heard of more. Such tales of 'dark midnight deeds' are not wanting, and, no doubt, on them Scott founded the incident of his tale. Meg is said to have been in secret league with the thieves and freebooters who at that time of transition represented the former generations of moss-troopers.

She acquired property, and managed to keep clear of charge; and though universally looked upon as a woman of dark and mysterious ways, her stern and masculine spirit carried her unharmed amongst the reckless characters with whom the Borders then abounded through a long, long lifetime until she died on 5th May 1877 at the ripe old age of 98 years. She lies buried in the quiet little church yard of Over Denton, a mile and a quarter away. Her tomb bears the inscription:

> 'What I was once some may relate;
> What I am now is each one's fate;
> What I shall be none can explain;
> Till He that called calls again.'

In Scott's book *Guy Mannering*, Brown or to give him his proper name, Harry Bertram, of Ellangowan, the hero of the tale, is described as on his route from the English Lake District to Scotland through the eastern wilds of Cumberland (probably the very route Scott and his friends took) and as coming to a small public house, at which he proposed to get some refreshment.

> The ale house, for it was no better, was situated in the bottom of a little dell, through which trilled a small rivulet. It was shaded by a large ash tree, against which the clay-built shed that served the purpose of a stable was erected, and upon which it seemed partly to recline. The outside of the house promised little for the interior, not withstanding the vaunt of a sign, where a tankard of ale voluntarily decanted itself into a tumbler, and a hieroglyphical scrawl

below attempted to express a promise of 'good entertainment for man and horse'.

This is an exact description of Mumps Ha' as it existed till the year 1831. In that year a viaduct was thrown over the rivulet, and the road raised upon it to such a height as almost to hide from view the old alehouse in the dell. Yet with knowledge of the alteration, it is easy on the spot to recognise the place as described by Scott as the house by the burn later called Merrilles Cottage.

Of course the infamous Mumps Ha' has long since been demolished, or has it? Printed sources are at variance as to whether the original inn building still exists. The first Ordnance Survey map of 1863 marks Mumps Hall as an area containing several buildings rather than one house but by the time of the second edition in 1900 the name is not used. In a guide book of 1995 it is described thus: 'If you cross the Poltross Burn, into Cumbria and bear left you will see a terrace of houses, Hall Terrace. At the left of the terrace is the famous Mumps Hall...' An earlier guide book of 1962 says that 'Mumps Ha' house has undergone much renovation and now contains two flats, but the old window places can still be seen in the wall.' However, a centenary history of the Gilsland Spa Convalescent Home published in 2001 claims that *The Hexham Herald* reported the demolition in 1877 as follows:

> Gilsland – Another of those landmarks connecting the present with the past is about to be swept away by the inexorable monster progress. Gilsland has lost one of its chief attractions, Meg o' Mumps domicile, over which the wizard of the north (Sir Walter Scott) waved his magic wand making every stone in the low sheiling an object of worldwide interest. The debris is now in course of removal in order to make way for a modern villa. This classic spot had other tenants of ill repute besides the redoubtable Meg. According to tradition the cottage was occupied by the notorious Mendham a name well known on the borders. Here this worthy for many years carried on his nefarious practise. Mumps Ha' was the place where he manufactured spurious notes known as 'Mendham pictures' some of which are in existence yet, preserved as curiosities'.

The same publication tells us that 'the district gradually became less hazardous and people were able to visit a welcoming countryside. The Newcastle to Carlisle railway was completed in 1836 and the building of a station in 1838 made the area much more accessible than previously.'

The station at Gilsland, from which Ellen tells us that they took the train to Carlisle, was unusually named Rose Hill. However the 'Rose' was a corruption of the word 'raise' – a mound. The chosen site was one on which there was a Cairn. On removing the top of the hill to make way for the station several human bones were found which were thought to be of Danish origin.[79]

Referring once again to the Jenkinson's Guidebook we learn that,

> One of the favourite short excursions from Gilsland is to the Roman station of Birdoswald $2\frac{1}{2}$ miles ... A few yards below Orchard House enter the road which branches to the right. It leads over a little dell through which trills Red Beck, and then gradually ascends and commands a view of the river winding through a miniature vale at the foot of the Birdoswald cliffs ... As the ground is rather hilly it is advisable for all who can do so to leave the conveyance and walk through fields by a footpath which is entered at the first gate on the left after passing Hill House ... Another way of reaching Birdoswald, but one suitable only for those who are not afraid of a little rough work, and only practicable when the water is low, is that of strolling along the banks of the river, commencing at Mumps Hall bridge.

Lanercost Priory

Lanercost Priory was founded around 1169 by Robert de Vaux for Augustinian canons. The long since abandoned Hadrian's Wall, conveniently situated on the Priory's northern boundary, was plundered for some of this massive building project. St Mary of Magdalene was chosen as patron saint. Her statue can be seen high above the great west door through which you enter.

Lying close to the Scottish border, the Priory was vulnerable to attack during the Anglo-Scottish wars of the 14th century, and was constantly under threat from marauding Scots. Robert Bruce himself raided it. The canons hosted several royal visits, Edward I and his retinue stayed there for five months in 1306–7, shortly before the King's death.

After Henry VIII's Dissolution of the Monasteries in 1536 the Priory passed to the Dacre family, who converted a part of the monastic buildings into a comfortable residence. Part of the nave continued as the parish church. It was re-roofed and restored around 1740 and is still in use today. The rest of it was allowed to fall into decay. Today the ruined choir and transepts, which stand almost to their full height, form a dramatic silhouette.[80]

On Tuesday, 14th October 1863 Ellen records the fact that an earthquake had been felt all over England the previous Wednesday [7th]. On Friday 9th October local papers around the country reported on the phenomenon, which occurred between 3 and 4 a.m., depending on your location.

> Of course at that hour nearly everybody was in bed. Many persons were awakened by the sound of a loud rumbling noise, resembling distant thunder, this gradually increased and a trembling of the earth followed. The shock was continuous and not consisting of a series of undulations; and the general impression is that it came from a southerly or westerly direction.
>
> Several correspondents stated that they observed a violent agitation of the curtains, and a swaying to and fro of the bed. In some instances the beds were perceptibly raised from the floor and replaced with rattling noises. Doors were shaken and in some cases violently closed. The prevalent idea of the disturbed sleepers was that midnight marauders were abroad and in many instances the household turned out in full strength to seek for the unseemly visitors. From cellar to garret the search was carefully conducted, but necessarily without any result.

As 1863 drew to a close the Johnstons and the Buxtons were filled with excitement at the announcement of Prissy's sister's, Sarah Maria's, forthcoming wedding, which Ellen records thus:

January 25 1864, Monday

And now I have not written my journal for a very long time, no, not since that very important day when Sarah Maria was engaged, which was on Sunday, Dec. 13 1863. Never shall I forget how when she came to Leytonstone that morning she told me that 'Someone had made her an offer and it was Mr Daniel Wilson and he had four children'. That was all she said but that was quite enough to make me spend that Sunday in the greatest excitement, certainly it was the most exciting Sunday I ever spent, and especially as I did not go to church that day, and therefore had all the more time to think about it. She looked so pretty, more pretty than I ever saw her look before, in a black velvet mantle trimmed with grebe and purple bonnet. Well since that time I have enjoyed myself very much it has been so pleasant to see them together evidently enjoying to be in one another's company, we were turned out of our little school room upstairs, and they came and sat there in the afternoon, with a bright fire and no candle and since then it has gone by the name of 'The Lovers Bower'. But now comes the all important wedding day, it is to be next Thursday, the 28th of January 1864…

Thursday, Jan. 28

On the 28th inst., at Wanstead, Daniel Frederic Wilson, vicar of Mitcham, to Sarah Maria, second daughter of the late Andrew Johnston, of Holton, Halesworth, Esq.

So the wedding is over and gone, and a very happy day of excitement is passed. It all went off very well indeed, it could not have gone off better. I got up early and wrote off to the boys [at school] just to tell them that the wedding day had really come, and at 7.30 went downstairs to begin to make our wreaths and bouquets. Louisa, Janet and I are to be the bridesmaids from this house. I made Janet a lovely wreath of snowdrops and dark green pointed ivy leaves, which was very pretty. Lisa made herself a bouquet and Miss Smith made me a very pretty one principally of white flowers. Mr Wilson (the Bridegroom) slept here last night, and after prayers he asked me for a white flower, so I picked out a most lovely Camellia, much the most beautiful we had, and before we went to church pinned it into his button hole. At 9.30 I went up to dress (as dressing to be a bridesmaid takes a long time), and was dressed first. Lucy did my hair beautifully and when I was ready the effect was like the picture I have here drawn with a long tulle veil nearly down to my feet. All the other bridesmaids [including Priscilla Hannah] were exactly alike except the two little girls who had white Llama frocks trimmed with swans down...

The wedding procession of Sarah Maria and Mr Daniel Wilson

Soon we heard that the bride was coming so we all ran to the door, and there she was just getting out of the carriage. She was lovely, with a beautiful white Moree antique silk ... Then we all got into the carriages and drove off to Ham House, where we arranged the wedding breakfast. The green house was in its most exquisite beauty, large trees of Camellias quite white with blossoms and the whole place smelling deliciously. It was a most handsome luncheon with quantities of cold pheasants, partridges and chickens besides beautifully raised pies etc. Then came the jellies creams and all sorts of ices. There were two delicious pineapples grown at Rickerby ... When the Bride came down she was attired in a very handsome purple silk dress, and seal skin jacket and pretty white bonnet. Before they went away we had a few words of prayer and then in perfect silence, the bride began to take leave of us all round, gradually the noise increased till she drove away from the door with tears in her eyes ... I was not the least tired, I only wish another wedding were coming off tomorrow. Weddings are so charming.

Tuesday, Feb. 2nd

We have heard several times from the bride, they spent the first night at Dover, and went onto Paris for the Sunday, and now I suppose they are on the road to Rome, where they mean to stay a long time and not come home till the beginning of April...

July 1864 saw Prissy and her sister, Isa, travel to Kissengen in Germany, along with their brother Andrew and his wife Charlotte. On their return from Germany, Prissy and her sister would have begun to prepare the celebrations for their grandmother's eighty-first birthday on 15th September, when their extended family would once again descend upon Northrepps Hall.

On 2nd September 1864, after a day of packing books and seeing to 'hosts of things', such as Ellen's bullfinch, who travelled too, the Buxton family set off for Northrepps.
Ellen records:

We settled down at Northrepps, out of doors and in. The boat in the hall at Northrepps, they never get tired of rocking in it. We were so happy, we had such nice walks and rides and such happy family parties in the evening, reading and working. There was a good party when we arrived there.

September 15th. 1864

...We kept Granny's 81st birthday by having a picnic on Trimingham cliffs, it was the largest party we had at all, and most pleasant it was...

That evening of 15th September, Grandmamma Hannah was able to write on her eighty-first birthday:

Surely goodness and mercy have followed me since I was born at Bramerton, 1783! What a course have I run, and what blessings have I enjoyed. Today I go to a picnic with children, but far more grandchildren; with these I am encompassed, but do not mind the numbers for myself; I rather feel the immense work for the servants, often more than sixty to feed in the day. I like having Daniel Wilson as a minister, and entirely desire good may attend our meeting together. He is doing something in the village, which is a satisfaction to me. Pleasures seem to be allowed and Given.

Here follow a selection of Ellen's family sketches:

October 1864. Granny and 'Pris' in the Northrepps Hall Drawing room

28th October 1864. 'Pris', 'Isa', and Ellen herself sitting on a gate near to Northrepps

1864
An evening at Northrepps – Granny, Ellen's Father, Effie and Miles MacInnes,
Sarah Maria, 'Pris', 'Isa' and Ellen's sister, 'Lisa'

The birthday celebrations over, and Ellen Buxton and her family returned to their home at Leytonstone in November. However, they would return again in December, for at Christmas in 1864 there were fifty six people gathered at Northrepps.[81]

28th May 1866
'Lisa', 'Pris' and 'Isa', working at Northrepps

Relations on the lawn at Northrepps Hall (1866). Hannah herself in the middle (she was tiny), her only two surviving children, Thomas Fowell, Ellen's father, and Uncle Charles with the beard – and their wives and children Pris, Isa, Effie and Sarah Maria. Effie's husband, Miles, was also there with their two small children, Grace and Harry.

Ellen's grand-daughter, 'Kisty', tells us in her book, *A family sketchbook 100 years ago* that later that year (May 1866) Ellen's father sold Leytonstone House and bought an estate in Hertfordshire, on which was being built their 'Victorian dream of a house', designed by Waterhouse, in diapered red brick, called Easneye. Until it was finished the family lived for the time being at Ham House, Upton, the former home of Samuel Gurney and his family, quite near to Leytonstone.

While their belongings were being moved into Ham House, the family once again went to Northrepps. This time the woods were full of bluebells and other flowers, including wild tulips, narcissi and summer snowflake, which they mercilessly dug up to put in their gardens.

We shall leave Ellen's family preparing for Christmas 1866, with a brief summary of what happened to them.

Ellen did not draw so much as she grew older and became involved 'in the grown up world'. Just after her twentieth birthday Ellen married a distant cousin, Robert Barclay, in February 1868. They had eight children, and made their home at High Leigh, Hoddesdon.

The rest of the family moved into Easneye [Saxon for 'Water Island'], not far from High Leigh in 1869.

The last Buxton to live at Easneye was Henry Fowell Buxton (1876–1947). At this time London was being bombed during the Second World War. As the bombing continued, children from demolished homes were taken in. As the war dragged on, the house became more established as a children's home for the London County Council. The elderly owner Thomas Fowell, lived in a few rooms on the ground floor. With the coming of peace and his death, the house was turned into a reception centre for deprived youngsters from London.

Today Easneye is home of the All Nations Christian College, the foremost college for training missionaries in the world. Here students come from all nations, with over thirty nations being represented in any one year.

The College purpose statement states: 'The purpose of All Nations Christian College is to train and equip men and women whom God has called for effective cross-cultural mission throughout the World'.[82]

Easneye

25

Northrepps Through the Eyes of Priscilla Hannah: From her own Collection of Photographs and Paintings (c.1860s)

The following pages include a selection of photographs taken around Northrepps Hall together with some fine water colours, painted by Priscilla Hannah, which have been reproduced by the kind permission of Verily Anderson Paget.

Autumn 1864: A Buxton/Johnston/MacInnes family photograph. Granny is the seated white bonneted lady with Buxtons either side of her. Back row standing: Emily Buxton on stilts; Louisa Buxton; Aunt Rachel; the almost twin-like Pris and Isa; Charles Buxton; Rev. D.F. Wilson; Effie MacInnes; Uncle Fowell and Miles MacInnes with a young Harry in the basket. Seated from front to back: the Buxton children – Barclay; Chenda; Ethel. Behind them: Grace MacInnes; Sarah Maria Wilson; Ellen Buxton.

26

An End and a Beginning (1867–1872)

The family circle about Hannah Lady Buxton had grown smaller as Priscilla Hannah's siblings married and left Northrepps, to make their own homes elsewhere. By 1870 Priscilla Hannah alone would be with her grandmother, her constant companion. 'My dear Priscilla, my one fixed inmate, watches closely over me,' her grandmother wrote in affectionate appreciation.

[In 1858 Andrew had married Charlotte Anne, daughter of the Rev. George Trevelyen, rector of Malden-cum-Chessington, Surrey; Effie had been married to Miles MacInnes since 1859 and was living in Carlisle, with a young family of her own. In 1863 Sarah Maria married the Rev. Daniel F. Wilson (one time Bishop of Calcutta); young Fowell, having removed to South America in 1866, there married Alice Douglas, the daughter of a Scottish rancher in 1869. A picture of 'Isa' and Dr Arthur de Noé Walker's marriage in 1869 is included in the colour plate section.]

[Dr Arthur de Noé Walker was a nephew of General Sir George Walker, who was distinguished for the part he took in the Peninsular War (1808–13). Arthur was also a grandson of Mrs Walter Riddell, the friend and correspondent of the poet Robert Burns.

Born in 1820, the son of a naval captain, who served under Nelson, Arthur entered the Indian army, and served in the China expedition of 1842, when he was wounded. Retiring from the service with the rank of captain, he studied medicine and, having volunteered his services as a surgeon during the Crimean War (1853–56), was present at the capture of the Redan and other engagements. His gallantry in attending the wounded under fire was celebrated in verse by his old friend, Walter Savage Landor, who, shortly before he died, committed his writing desk with its contents to Dr Walker's care, thus ensuring the preservation of many interesting mementos and manuscripts.[83]

After their marriage the Walkers moved to London, eventually settling at 10 Ovington Gardens.]

Priscilla Hannah once again had cause for concern over her grandmother's health when, in the spring of 1867, Hannah had a severe illness. She was taken ill at Northrepps, but was removed when she became better for a visit to Colne House. Here, however, she became very unwell with cough and fever.

Colne House, May, 1867

Mr and Mrs Fowell Buxton with Hannah's two granddaughters and grandson had arrived on Saturday evening, and in the evening of Sunday Grandmamma Hannah had been as usual brought down in her chair into the drawing-room. Words fail to give the picture when the party assembled to say verses and hymns. Only those who know the beautiful room, the fine conservatory, the view from the windows of the declining sun throwing the shadows across the bright green lawn, can the least fancy the scene, nor can I adequately describe the individuals composing the groups at the bow window. On the Ottoman seat, Grandmamma, so diminished in size, delicate, refined, in a rich black silk dress, with a shawl of a thin material bordered with white, very feeble, but animated, summoning all to come close by her, her hand clasped in that of her dearly beloved son Fowell, he so gentle, loving and cordial with her. Then on the chairs and stool of various heights, the grandchildren grouped round her, and beginning at the youngest, each in turn repeated a portion of scripture or hymn.[84]

From this time Hannah's memorials are filled with letters to the family, describing her and Priscilla Hannah's life. These would probably have been dictated to, and written by, Priscilla Hannah. Hannah and her brother Dan, as the only survivors of eleven brothers and sisters, grew increasingly close in their old age and wrote frequently to each other.[85]

June 1867 – To Daniel Gurney:

I am become deaf, so that I am deprived of the pleasure of hearing my grandchildren, though I like a cheerful looking party about me. This I have now. May we both be kept in peace, receiving Christ into our hearts, or rather, let us hide ourselves in Him.

December – To Daniel Gurney:

What weather we have had! Sorrowful wrecks; one under the lighthouse. The miserable men had taken to their boat, and were all four washed up together and buried in one grave. Miss Wilkinson saw a wreck on Monday, and the life-boat turn from it while six men were on board, and then saw them fall into the sea and be tossed about for a time, before they were drowned, all but one. Two more wrecks since; one went down, the other on to the shore, but the men saved. In one was a woman who had been lashed to the mast! What suffering must they all have undergone! We feel for these as near to us. But how fearful the many besides, and the cyclone in the West Indies.

December – To Effie MacInnes:

Darling Effie,

You would be surprised to see how comfortable we are. Three young ladies just come to stay, if I like, which I at once refuse! It is so very agreeable to me to be left alone. I could often wish to have more time over past things. Priscilla and I agreed yesterday that we must not dine till a quarter past seven. I get too little time going up at six, but do not incline to shorten our reading hours. I do not often go out, and we are not at all dull. I enjoy this warm drawing-room, and am really low sometimes in my great comforts, when I know the sorrowful need of others who do not lie down as I do at night with every possible indulgence; and peace in Christ graciously added to all.

What a decided course was your grandfather's. We have been reading some of his early life today, how few like it now.

February 6 1869 – To Lady Buxton:

My most beloved Catherine the weather is so delicious, and your five and Priscilla as if the cork was just out of the effervescent bottle, all so exuberant in life and talk and play, with apples, oranges and luncheon devoured with great spirit. We had a beautiful drive on Friday.

February 24 – To Daniel Gurney:

Dearest brother, your enclosed of the certificate of my birth has been amusing to me, as it shows I have never known my true birthday, but have always thought it was September 15th and not October 15th; no doubt on our dear mother's death, no one knew accurately, and September 15th was adopted, so that I am a month younger than I thought.

I left Ham House probably forever on Monday. It is a sorrowful wind up there, and yet there is nothing forced in it. The separation from it and the family is like the ripe fruit falling. Fowell's new house [Easneye] is ready. It is a beautiful house. I wish to see Charles' [her son's] house, 'Fox Warren' once more.

In June 1870, after visiting the graves at Overstrand, Hannah writes, 'How I love them, and those others within the ruins. How have I felt the body to be the Lord's, though not redeemed here from its suffering and death, yet preserved in Him, to be restored and made like Him and be found with Him, perfected and united, soul and body!'[86]

At the close of 1870 and the beginning of 1871 Hannah writes to Daniel, 'I have been visiting with you in mind, in the desire and confidence for us both at our age, to be in Christ. I am well and have had a merry Christmas with Priscilla, my only one and the Bosworths. We may thank God for our peace, and warmth, and food and clothing. Dreadful what others suffer.'

Hannah herself describes her life in her last year, 1872, in which her youngest son Charles died in Scotland leaving her with one survivor, Fowell, of her original eleven children. She writes to her brother, Dan: 'Catherine often joins me in the drive or comes up with the girls to dinner and at home I am quite rich now with Effie and Sarah Maria, besides my constant companion Priscilla. So without much excitement we have pleasant little variations and most truly I desire to give thanks for the great mercies I enjoy – such merciful indulgences.'[87]

Some of Hannah's last letters show that she herself was feeling she might be nearing the border-land, and as the spring of 1872 advanced it became more and more, the unspoken anxiety of those about her. Ever since the death of her son Charles, she had been more feeble and infirm, and though mind and spirit were as vigorous as ever it was plain to Priscilla Hannah that the flesh was failing.

On Saturday, 16th March, her son Fowell came to her with his wife, and she enjoyed their company exceedingly. She drove to Colne House on Tuesday, 19th March, but did not leave the carriage, and on returning home enjoyed the group of grand-daughters in the bow window of her drawing room, with their primroses and violets. Wednesday opened with further weakness. In the afternoon she enjoyed her usual books, and then asked for some verses, as was her daily custom. [Although her eyesight had began to fail from the age of forty, so that Priscilla Hannah had read to her, in her last years it had improved to the extent that she had been able to read for herself.] Lady Buxton read the passage, 'When thou passest through the waters I will be with thee, and through the rivers; they shall not overflow thee...' All was peace and cheerfulness around her. Priscilla Hannah's preparations for dinner were undertaken as usual with customary exactness. It was then the summons came. She said, 'My flesh and my heart faileth, but God is the strength of my heart, and my portion forever.'

She had no final illness; she simply lay on the bed, the exhaustion increasing, till at about 9.00 p.m. she gently expired.

A few days later her children, grandchildren, and great-grandchildren, with many others were gathered to attend her funeral. She was laid to rest in the vault, in the ruins of Overstrand Church, beside her husband and others of her family.[88]

St Martin's Church, Overstrand

In the eighteenth century the roof of Overstrand Church fell in and, instead of re-roofing the whole church, a partition wall was built across the nave. The western portion was used as a church to accommodate around 140, while the eastern was left in ruins; here several of the Buxtons of Northrepps hall are buried.

[Hannah Lady Buxton died aged eighty-eight. This was an exceptional age to have reached, given that by 1878 the average age of death for Quakers was fifty five and a half years and for the general population only thirty three years.][89]

Priscilla Hannah now found herself, at the age of twenty-nine, free to take an active rôle in her own life. Her appearance was now rather like that of her elder sister Effie – immensely aristocratic, with a noble bearing, an aquiline nose and the high cheek bones of the Johnstons.[90] She was very much the new woman, archetypically English Victorian in her ambition and determination to channel her energies into any deserving causes.

Whether any romantic prospects ever arose for Priscilla Hannah is unknown. Perhaps with her restricted life in caring for her grandmother she did not have the opportunity to meet the right man. Or perhaps she had chosen to remain unmarried in order to retain her freedom to pursue her philanthropic works, for at this time married women lost all legal standing and claim to their inheritance and earnings and became solely dependent on their husbands. However, there were those whose husbands permitted them to work for causes dear to their heart. One such, close to Priscilla Hannah, was of course her great aunt Elizabeth Fry, though it had been considered that such women found their work in the public sphere slowed by 'domestic cares'.

There is no doubt that she would have discussed with her grandmother what part she might play and in what activity she might engage. Certainly she reflected on her great aunt Fry's beliefs that every woman had a vocation and was called upon to leave for a time her home and family, to devote herself to some good cause. Elizabeth Fry had succeeded in finding her own sphere of activity. Other women, she was aware, might not be as fortunate as herself in finding a field of endeavour, or in being able to pursue it; many, in spite of good intentions and high hopes, found themselves limited to the usual charities of gentlewomen. But Priscilla Hannah was convinced that there was a sphere of usefulness open to all women, and if they could make the opportunity, they might then achieve much.

The following year, 1873, saw her embark on a 'new beginning' – she now joined Miss Adeline Paulina Irby in the Balkans.

[1873 also saw John Henry Gurney and his two sons Jack, twenty-four, and Richard, nineteen, take up residence at Northrepps Hall. The tradition of Gurneys living at Northrepps continues to this day].[91]

PART THREE

'The Unspeakable Turk' and
'The Angels of Mercy'

Adeline Paulina Irby

26

Introducing Paulina Irby and her Work

Adeline Paulina Irby was born in 1831, the youngest daughter of Rear Admiral the Hon. Frederick Paul Irby, of Boyland Hall, Long Stratton, Norfolk. He was the second son of the second Lord Boston, and had entered the navy during the Napoleonic Wars, serving in the North American and home stations and taking part in the blockade of the French coast. For two years he was senior officer of a squadron off the west coast of Africa, engaged in suppressing the slave trade and in supporting the British settlements there. He had no further service after 1813, and retired to live the life of a country gentleman in Norfolk. His first wife died in 1806, and he married in 1817 Frances Wright, daughter of Ichabod Wright, the banker, of Nottingham; of his second family of three sons and three daughters Paulina was the youngest daughter. The Admiral was a man of great energy, courage and charm, a country gentleman only in the sense that he lived in the country; handsome, unconventional, even flamboyant in his mode of life; a personality robust and lively and fascinating enough to outweigh the indiscipline of his temper and habits. He was not particularly public spirited, but he was strong in his beliefs, and his years of service off the coast of Africa had inculcated in him a violent hatred of the slave trade in all its aspects; he became the active supporter of his friend and Norfolk neighbour, Thomas Fowell Buxton, in the anti slavery campaign. Paulina's mother was as beautiful as the Admiral was handsome, but with a style of looks cooler and less vibrant; equally her temperament was more reserved.

The Admiral died in 1844, and when her mother died six years later, Paulina felt herself to be very much alone. She made her home with her married sisters, spending the greater part of her time with her sister Frances, whose husband, Lewis Lloyd, a wealthy landowner and banker, had homes at Monk's Orchard at Addington in Surrey and at 29 Hyde Park Gardens, in London.

Paulina, living in luxury with her sister in London, was unhappy. She had felt a sense of neglect and non-adjustment through her childhood and early womanhood. The good looks of her parents had somehow passed her by; she inherited much of her father's vigour, ability and courage, but lacked his gaiety and charm. She became serious and intense, wanting to do something useful with her life. She was intent on learning, and carried on with a variety of studies — classics and languages as well as dabbling in science. In seeking to educate herself more fully, she became interested in the education of women and she joined with other young ladies, including Octavia Hill and her friend Louisa Twinning, in assisting in the newly opened classes for women at the Working Men's College in Great Ormond Street. (Men's classes were held in the evening, and afternoon classes were organised for women.) But the inspiration that her friends were finding in doing good works was lacking with Paulina. A lifetime spent as Louisa Twinning's was, in improving the conditions of workhouse inmates, had no appeal for her. She was too proud, too conscious of her own superiority to the poor and the ignorant. Paulina would have liked to have found a cause of her own, but had not found one that had an urgent appeal for her, an appeal that would sustain her for a lifetime of devotion.

Then, around 1859, she began to travel with her friend, Miss Georgina Mary Muir MacKenzie. There is no evidence of how and when they met. Now Paulina began to test her abilities and her interests in new fields of accomplishment. Tentatively at first, they followed along the usual routes of the English traveller abroad, accompanying Georgina's mother to Holland, Switzerland and Italy. Then, growing confident and more daring, they began to travel alone farther afield, two English ladies, with only a maid to attend their needs.[1]

Late 1859 saw Paulina and Georgina MacKenzie make a fact-finding journey across the Carpathians. This resulted in a publication which contained an account of their arrest as possible pro-Slav spies. Not many Victorian travellers could claim the distinction of having been arrested as spies and this incident certainly gave an individual flavour to the account of the journey *Across the Carpathians*.

Paulina first took up her residence in Bosnia-Herzegovina in 1866 and in 1870 with the assistance of Miss MacKenzie founded what would be the first of a number of institutions for the education of Serbian boys and girls. They also became most active in all kinds of charitable work to relieve the Balkan peasants from the outrages and horrific conditions they were suffering at the time.

However, by 1871, the partnership of Paulina and Miss MacKenzie as friends, as travellers, as writers and as benefactresses had been broken. Miss MacKenzie now retired from the Balkan scene due to her failing health.

On Paulina rested the responsibility of promulgating the objectives that together they had conceived and worked for. By the time Miss MacKenzie died in 1874 Paulina had committed herself to the management of the schools for an indefinite period.

At least she was not alone. After the summer of 1872 spent in England, where she had tried hard to woo approval and help from Florence Nightingale, whom she greatly admired, Paulina returned to Bosnia in the autumn of 1872 accompanied by a new friend and colleague, Miss Priscilla Hannah Johnston.

27

The Eastern Question

After the death of her grandmother in 1872 Priscilla saw her sphere of usefulness in helping to promote education among the South Slavonic Christians of Bosnia at Sarajevo. Ladies of the Victorian era travelled far and ventured forth on many perilous journeys in 'the spirit and in the flesh'. But few could have travelled further than Miss Adeline Paulina Irby.[2] Her first travelling companion on the 'Balkan Scene' was Miss Georgina Muir Mackenzie. Partnership lasted a decade (1859–1870) being terminated only on account of Georgina's failing health which had suffered terribly as a result of the hardships endured by the two ladies. Notable among their benevolent works for the South Slavs of Bosnia was the founding of a school for future teachers in Sarajevo.[3]

Paulina Irby and her work was already known to Priscilla, for Paulina's father Admiral Irby had been associated with her Grandfather and his fight to 'emancipate the slaves'. As the families were neighbours in Norfolk there were also connections in business and social activities. Admittedly Paulina's family were landed and ennobled, while Priscilla's had a professional background, but in the matter of philanthropic works Priscilla's references and connections were impeccable and far more authoritative than those which the Irby family could claim.[4]

Initially, Priscilla contented herself with assisting Paulina with the administration and organization of running her school in Sarajevo. However, the ladies became more and more concerned by the increasing disturbances in the Balkans and the inability of Austria to suppress violent uprisings (1875–1879) and more and more concerned about the plight of the refugees. Their benevolent work developed into an extended effort on behalf of refugees from Turkish reprisals on the Bosnian rising.

For several centuries the Turks had ruled much of the near east and south-eastern Europe. But in the nineteenth century the Ottoman Empire was threatened by the tide of nationalism which caused the Christian peoples of the Balkans to rise in revolt, the insurgents suffering terrible atrocities at the hands of the Turks; the situation being intensified by the interests and rivalries in the area of the great powers, notably Russia.

Fearing that the disintegration of the Ottoman Empire might leave the Mediterranean trading routes and the route to India open to Russian threat, the then Conservative Government supported Turkey. However, a feeling of outrage began to emerge from the British Public at this support given to an oppressive power. The public grew to despise the backward and barbaric Ottoman Empire, and to sympathise with the struggling nations. The opposition was led by Mr Gladstone, after the Bulgarian massacres of 1876.[5]

At this time Paulina addressed a number of letters to *The Times* describing the outrages and condition of the fugitives. The ladies appealed to friends at home for contributions to the Bosnian and Herzegovinian Fund. So great were the effects of this publicity that many thousands of pounds were placed at their absolute disposal. In July 1877 a large meeting was held at Willis's Rooms, at which Thomas Carlyle was present and supportively contributed his immortal phrase about the 'unspeakable Turk'. Mr Gladstone delivered an eloquent address on behalf of Miss Johnston and Miss Irby, resulting in much support for their work and many subscriptions to their fund.

Mr Gladstone and the great powers of Europe began to seek ways to bring pressure upon the Ottoman Empire which might result in the reform and pacification of its provinces. When in 1877 Russia declared war on Turkey it was feared that Turkish troops would inaugurate a final campaign of 'pillage and massacre' on the remnants of the Christian population. However, the dominant elements of the Austro-Hungarian Empire, the German and Magyar would never countenance a war against Turkey on the side of the Slav cause, Austria having earlier signed a secret convention with Russia promising to maintain a 'benevolent neutrality' in the event of war. Should the dismemberment of the Ottoman Empire occur it would become necessary as a safeguard to Austrian interests that they should annex the provinces of Bosnia and Herzegovina. The Austrian occupation eventually began in June 1879 as a result of the Treaty of San Stefano which effectively saw the dismemberment of the Ottoman Empire. However, the Austrians did little in the early years to try to win over the Bosnian people. A fresh rebellion broke out in 1881 in protest at the enforcement of conscription on Bosnians to serve for three years in the imperial army.[6]

As a result of her many years of first hand experience of the suffering caused by what, in her opinion, was 'Turkish misrule' Paulina developed strong political views, which she was not afraid to express. Priscilla, on the other hand, was content to work quietly in the background, entering neither upon controversy nor politics. Yet she contributed much to the smooth running of their schemes in terms of practical organisation and detail.[7]

Writing in 1893, Paulina detailed their achievements: £40,912 3s. 4d. had been collected and distributed by the 'Bosnian and Herzegovinian fugitives and Orphan Relief fund' in the period of four years, from 1st October 1875 to 13th June 1879. The number of refugees who had received help from the fund was a quarter of a million. In Strimca alone twenty-seven thousand people were clothed, fed, and housed; two hundred and fifty thousand along the borders of Dalmatia, Croatia and Slavonia, 'did not perish because of the fund'.[8]

They had set up the native machinery and by constant nagging of officials had kept it working. Their constructive achievements in those years amounted to schools being maintained; an orphanage coming into existence; children cared for; schoolmasters found and trained; local popes being engaged by the ladies to attend to the building of roads and houses; trees planted where there had been none. They had also organised the guides who went over the mountains and the muleteers who drove the caravans. All were friends and helpers. By 1879 Priscilla and Paulina had under their direction a considerable organisation.[9]

As for the Bosnian refugees, it had been surprising enough for them that someone had cared, that someone had come to their aid. At the beginning of 1876 Priscilla and Paulina had been viewed with suspicion by their refugees – there had been an uneasiness as to their motives, distrust in their intentions. Like those from their government, were they really pro-Turkish? By 1879 instead of mistrust there was something akin to reverence: Miss Johnston and Miss Irby had worked for them and worked with them and fought on their behalf.[10]

The two ladies had become their champions, their 'Angels of Mercy'. For Priscilla's part, in true family tradition, she had joined Paulina because there was work to do. That it was in Bosnia was of no great importance; that she could help to alleviate the suffering of others was.[11]

Paulina first met Miss Nightingale in 1869 through her parents, William and Fanny Nightingale. They invited her to their home, Embley Park, Hampshire to meet Florence and a friendship between the two women slowly began to develop.

Miss Florence Nightingale (1820–1910). 'Pioneer of modern nursing'

That the friendship developed at all was much due to the domestic difficulties in which Florence found herself. Paulina was only too pleased to devote her summer time visits to England to caring for Florence's ageing parents, thus allowing Florence to devote her time to work. However, this was somewhat detrimental to Paulina's own work. So after the death of her father in 1875, Florence determined that 'Paulina's feet must be turned back to the path of duty'.

There was much that Florence admired in Paulina and her work with Priscilla, and she was always prepared to show her support for her friends in practical ways. Her contributions to Paulina and Priscilla's fund were frequent, and she also allowed her name to be used by Paulina in her reports, knowing full well that her approval of the fund was of great value in its promotion.

The very characteristics that Florence admired in Paulina, she also found drove her so often to plain exasperation; and her wholehearted devotion to 'Her Dearest Florence' could be very trying. Nevertheless, Florence Nightingale's irritation did not interrupt their friendship. They corresponded and met regularly for another twenty years.[12]

28

Priscilla Hannah, 'Angel of Mercy' (1872–1884)

Priscilla in 1872 was without experience of travel, the Balkans or the Slavs.[13] For Paulina it was pleasant to have a companion during the months at Sarajevo, and it certainly made travelling less wearisome than when she had made the journey Eastward by herself. It was also satisfying to be able to impress Priscilla along every stage of the route with her knowledge and experience. Priscilla, eleven years younger than Paulina and only just emerged from the insulation of her sheltered home and happy family background, was more than somewhat dazzled by her friend's wide range of experience, and more than a little in awe of Paulina herself.[14]

For Priscilla and Paulina a pattern for their lives was established: a pilgrimage each autumn to Sarajevo, the months there from October to May devoted to the school and pupils; then return in early summer to England. Their travelling at least could be accomplished more easily than when Paulina and Georgina had first set out on their explorations. The journey from Vienna to Paris, by rail, could be made in two days, in the comfort of wagon-lits.

The journey Eastwards was less easy, the speed of the journey being a burden rather than an advantage. From Tuesday evening in Paris until Thursday in Vienna was too short in time for their minds to adjust from thoughts of home and family to preparations for 'what lies ahead.' It was preferable for them to travel slowly. They would stay overnight in Hanover to see Priscilla's niece at school there, stop a while in Prague to talk with Paulina's numerous Czech friends, pause for a day or so in Vienna. From Vienna they travelled by rail out of the Austrian division into the Hungarian, to Agram (Zagreb) in Croatia, where they would spend one or two nights, then by a smaller train to Sisak, a small town on the Sava River in the region of the military frontier.[15]

The night spent at Sisak they regarded as their half way stage, where the West receded and the Orient loomed very near. In the public rooms of the inn alongside the River Quay, the mixture of race, costume and languages signified that they were approaching a vast frontier. From here they would take the steamer that went down the Sava. Other passengers included a mixture of Hungarian Officers, Serbian Merchants, Turkish Officials and Bosnians. The little steamer was neutral, neither east nor west. Yet looking on either bank the demarcation was complete. On the one there were bulbous church spires, bare-legged and bare-armed Croatian women kneeling with their washing at the edge of the water, the dull western colourings of black, white and grey. On the opposite bank, there were minarets, fezes, red turbans and the muffled dark shapes of cloaked women. They would leave the steamer at Brod, with Sarajevo still some one hundred and forty miles away.

At Brod came the formalities of the Turkish administration, and after that the hiring of a vehicle for the last stages of their journey. Sometimes they would travel in the Austrian post-cart, which once a week made the trip to Sarajevo, but this was little more than another spring-less cart, piled high with hay and with room for three passengers. It was preferable for them to hire a whole cart for themselves and their baggage, and, with an escort, make the journey at their own pace.[16]

This last stage of their journey, as well as being uncomfortable was depressing. It was pleasant to look ahead to the school and the girls, but

Brod in Bosnia

Sarajevo in the 1860s

it was shattering to be 'plunged back into a world of medieval spectacle and barbarism'. They found it heartbreaking to see the signs of stagnation and decay. It was never easy to make the adjustment back to this tempo of life. For Paulina it had engendered a passionate hatred for all that Turkish misrule stood for; for Priscilla, imbued with all her family tradition of progress and idealisms, it came as a shock and a disbelief that such things should be allowed to happen, that it was 'easier to do nothing than to do anything'. On arrival at Sarajevo their spirits lifted as they looked out across the plain at the city, Damascus to the north, with its gilded domes of one hundred and fifty mosques, the white minarets reaching up to the sky, surrounded by hills, the old ruined castle on the heights. For Priscilla and Paulina it was the end of their pilgrimage eastwards.[17]

Bosnia, Summer 1875[18]

In returning to Sarajevo in 1875 Paulina proposed that they leave England earlier than usual, towards the end of July, in order to spend some time travelling through Bosnia on a 'recruiting expedition' to obtain new pupils for the school; she was determined that it should not 'fade away'.

Before they left London confused reports of another uprising of the Christian population of Herzegovina had filtered through to English newspapers. But Paulina saw no reason for she and Priscilla to change their plans. After leaving the steamer at Gradiska, they were taken by canoe across the river Sava to where the 'Oriental barbarism, dirt, squalor, and misery marked the frontier line of Asiatic encroachment'.

The next day Priscilla and Paulina began their recruiting tour of Bosnia. They travelled by cart to Banja Luka, where they were received uneasily by their friends there. The family having come under suspicion from the Turkish authorities, this visit made their position even more difficult. Our two ladies realised that on this occasion they were not very welcome guests and that they themselves were also under suspicion. Outside waited the Zapteih who had followed them to the house. As they left they were accosted by him and ordered to appear before the Turkish Police Official. But our ladies, as always, stood firm by what they considered their rights as Englishwomen. They turned upon the Zapteih and demanded instead that he should take them to the Governor as they wished to travel on to Travnik and required an escort. The superiority of their demands was not on this occasion put to the test. However, after being advised that their projected tour was very unwise at that moment in time, they finally agreed to change their plans and return to Gradiska, much as they 'regretted the loss of a visit to the lake scenery of Bosnia and the old historic fortress and Castle of Jajce'. Their return on Sunday, 15 August proved a wise decision, for that night the insurrection in Bosnia broke out.

Priscilla and Paulina refused to be daunted. But when Paulina pointed out that, should two English ladies be killed by the Turks, the public outcry would surely help the cause of the Bosnian Christians, the reply they received was short: 'Perhaps, but not you two ladies.'

They left Brod by the Austrian post-cart on 17th August to make the quickest possible journey to Sarajevo, travelling through the night and the next day. All the warnings that they had ignored seemed to be coming true. To the two ladies it appeared they were too late – that Sarajevo must already be a devastated city. It was a relief to see as they crossed the plain the minarets still standing and the city lying shimmering in the heat.

Their arrival was unexpected, but all within the schoolhouse was peaceful, even flourishing, and three new pupils had arrived. However, the rest of the city was in a panic. Everyone waited, fearful that the uprising in the north had spread throughout Bosnia. They were given no rest at the schoolhouse, as it was besieged by Christian merchants, begging that they might seek shelter under their supposedly invulnerable (because of its English occupants) roof.

Priscilla and Paulina, having reached Sarajevo, determined to leave at once. They now believed the revolt might well be as widespread and as bitter as they had been warned it would be. Under those circumstances the school and themselves might be in danger. They decided 'to turn these adverse circumstances to the furtherance of our educational plans and carry off the most promising of the pupils to continue their training in Prague. They would take five of the best pupils to the Bohemian Higher Girls School in that city'. At the school in Prague there would be a continuation of the Slav background and tradition. Hastily they put their plans into operation.

It was one thing to decide to leave Sarajevo with five pupils, but permission and passports had to be obtained from the Turkish Governor who, when approached by the two ladies, begged them to remain in the city for fear it would give a bad impression and evoke even stronger feelings of panic amongst the Christians. But they believed the situation was too dangerous for them to stay on just 'for the sake of keeping up the appearance of the Turks'.

It was a small party – five pupils, two teachers, their maid and Priscilla and Paulina – that left Sarajevo early on the morning of 23rd August in a convoy of four carts. Paulina described the road as 'being as quiet as a grave'. In a short while they saw evidence of the brutality which had occurred earlier: 'Bodies drifting along with the current; the corpse of a man who had died slowly and agonisingly from heaps of burning coals that had been heaped upon his chest.' It was not a pleasant journey for they were in fear that at any time trouble might be around the next corner. In spite of their permit Priscilla and Paulina feared that some official might forbid their passage, though Priscilla had anticipated such a difficulty and had collected western costumes which the girls might wear. Just before reaching Brod the girls changed into European clothes and, thus attired, the party approached the town. But there had been no need to worry – the efficiency of the few days before having lapsed, barely a question was asked, their documents scarcely looked at. Five minutes later they stood on Austrian soil.

By mid-September the number of refugees in the military frontier was estimated at 20,000. An attempt was made to spread the influx of population by sending the refugees further in to the interior villages. But many of the huddled groups could not bear to be sent away from the sight of their native lands. Priscilla and Paulina had seen enough of the refugees' misery and suffering in those few days travelling for them to appreciate the need and conceive the part they could play during the uprising.

'They would return to this frontier to bring relief to the refugee children. They would establish orphanages and schools. Thus they would be working towards two ends, the immediate one of relief, and in the long term, by furthering education of the native Bosnian they would be preparing him for the day when he could return to his country, free from the Turk and oppression, ready and more able to establish his own Slav state.'

After leaving the five girls and two teachers at Prague, by the middle of September 1875 Priscilla and Paulina were on their way back to England. On arrival, Priscilla went to stay with her sister, Catharine de Noé Walker, in London.

England, Autumn 1875[19]

Little interest had been aroused in England by the news of the July uprising in Herzegovina. Since 1874, when the Conservatives under Disraeli had come to power, the long established 'Turcophile' policy of England had been more actively pursued and official reports of insurrection were carefully regulated. But all reports told of Bosnian Christians fleeing across the borders.

On 28th August, former Foreign Secretary and Prime Minister Lord John Russell, impatient with the policy of the Conservative Government, wrote to *The Times*, offering £50 as a contribution towards the support of the Bosnian refugees. The immediate result of his actions brought together a 'conference of the Friends of the suffering Rayahs'. The meeting pledged itself 'to assist in every legitimate way to obtain the removal of the evils under which they suffered'.

But the British public remained largely unconcerned with the fate of the Christian Rayahs. Brief accounts of hostilities continued to appear in the papers, reports which were conflicting, confused, exaggerated, inaccurate, as well as unpleasant and horrific: Christians assembled in church to attend a holy day service had been attacked and massacred; the insurgents had had the better of an encounter with the Turkish army and had made off with eight hundred noses; Turks were defiling churches, destroying altars and pillaging; the number of Turks killed yesterday was not 10,000 as reported but 1,000 etc. Not even these accounts could arouse the public conscience, nor the appeal by the metropolitan of Serbia to the 'Christian peoples of Europe, in the name of Christianity and humanity, to assist the unfortunate starving men and women and children of Bosnia and Herzegovina'. By now the numbers of refugees exiled from their country were astronomical: 50,000 in Montenegro, 30,000 in Dalmatia, 25,000 in Serbia, 40,000 in Croatia. The Bora wind from the east had begun to blow, and the refugees were dying in their hideouts among the caves and the rocks. In Ragusa an international committee for the relief of families and wounded in Herzegovina and Bosnia had been set up, but their efforts were concentrated on the refugees around Ragusa. As Priscilla and Paulina saw it, help was needed along the rest of the frontier. On the 16th November a letter from Paulina appeared in *The Times*, simply headed 'Bosnia and Herzegovina':

> ...I cannot refrain from making an appeal to the English public on behalf of the Bosnian and Herzegovinian refugees... It is impossible that these unhappy people should return to their homes, for they no longer exist... Much is being done by the Austrian Government and by the local committees to relieve the immediate wants of the sufferers; yet I cannot believe that the English public will be unwilling to help towards the special work of rescuing and providing for the orphans and destitute children who are in sore need of being looked after. I propose that together with Miss Johnston, to reach the Bosnian frontier in the beginning of December, and, putting myself in communication with the local committees, personally on the spot to apply the funds entrusted to me.

'The Bosnian and Herzegovina Fugitives Orphan Relief Fund' had now come into being. Amongst many influential religious men, patrons also included Paulina's friends Dr Humphrey Sandwith and Miss Louisa Twinning, and Priscilla's sister, Mrs Walker, her brother in law, Miles MacInnes, and her brother, Andrew Johnston as Vice-President. This fund did not receive particular prominence as the 'Conference of the Friends of Suffering Rayahs' had evolved into the more positive shape of 'The League in Aid of the Christians in Turkey' and the public, largely in ignorance, subscribed more to this better known fund.

Priscilla and Paulina had been extremely active since their return to England. A small pamphlet about the aims of their fund had been distributed and, in order further to arouse the interest of the public, letters had been published in magazines and newspapers, in which Paulina impressed the public with her knowledge and expressed her own opinion of the possible future for Bosnia as part of a Christian state; Serbia already gave 'promise of strength and tact sufficient for the task'.

A somewhat confusing circular also appeared, appealing on behalf of both the 'Bosnian and Herzegovina Fugitives Orphan Relief Fund' and for the continuation of the work of the 'Association for promoting Education among the Slavonic Christians of Bosnia and Herzegovina', with contributions being received for both causes.

The text continued this confusion of the Fund and the Association. The directresses, Miss Johnston and Miss Irby, intended to reside at Gradiska and there 'to meet the needs of the starving, demoralised, half-clothed, homeless children by housing, feeding and training as many as possible of the refugee children, whether boarding them out in native families; by establishing small Orphan homes; by finding work for the mothers, or by such other means as the Directresses' personal acquaintance with the country and language, applied on the spot, may enable them to discover and employ.' The list of first donations impressively included many relatives and friends of the ladies. It also included a £50 donation from Florence Nightingale, with whom Paulina often stayed and who was quick to point out the confusion and contradictions. 'She (Paulina) talks about housing Orphans, then in the next breath talks of their mothers!'

In *The Times* on 14th December there appeared an advertisement for the fund – £555 had been collected and three hundred pairs of blankets had been despatched to the north Bosnian border. By Christmas Day the fund had reached £900.

Priscilla and Paulina left England towards the end of December, actually a month later than intended. Paulina was now displaying the half-hearted attitude which was anathema to Florence Nightingale. 'If only she be allowed to stay on at the Nightingales.' Florence was adamant. 'Paulina had appealed to the public for their help in carrying out their work; she had set out their aims and intentions and from the public she had collected money for that purpose. Now she must accept the responsibility; she had her duty to perform, which could not be done in the comfort and ease of England.'

Florence, however, agreed that, with the assistance of her own cousin, William Shore Smith, she would help with the affairs of the Fund in London. Paulina was given full instructions by them as to what was required from her: she was to keep careful accounts of all that she spent, she was to write often and tell them exactly what they were doing, she was to keep to their objectives as set out in the brochure, and she was not on any account to meddle in politics, comment on politics or show any political leanings. Their mission was one of relief; in all else she must be strictly neutral.

Croatia and Slavonia (January to July 1876)[20]

On reaching Agram they had planned to make their headquarters at Gradiska. It had seemed straightforward and simple enough set out in a brochure, but in the reality of the military frontier these aims seemed far removed from the overwhelming scenes of suffering which greeted them. The plans and objectives set out in London so categorically, and subscribed to by friends, relations and the public generously, proved to have so little relation to the actual situation as to show that they had been perhaps too superficial in the estimation of the needs of the refugees – an underestimation which could not have been comprehended by Florence and Shore back home in the safety of England. All Priscilla and Paulina could do in those first few weeks was to travel about the region, observe the conditions of the refugees and try to establish some contacts.

They travelled by sledges, stopping at each village to enquire as to the numbers and conditions of refugees. These were not very pleasant journeys for the two ladies to undertake. In some places they dared not stop as smallpox and typhus were raging. From all they saw they concluded that the refugees were in far greater need of shelter, food and clothing; a project for setting up a school for the refugee children now seemed unnecessary and impractical.

By the end of January, they had found no orphans, had started no schools; they had handed out around 300 blankets, had distributed some £20 for clothing for children, had talked with mothers and had given sugar lumps to their children. Priscilla had also been distributing little shirts which she had made. What is more they had now also begun to show sympathy with the refugees, having been told of dreadful Turkish maltreatments. Paulina, in fulfilling her instructions, duly wrote back to England of these proceedings. A letter appeared in *The Times*, of which Florence was very critical, summing it up thus, 'From its contents; its style; its tone; she talks of pretty scenery, of a ball at the Inn, and of having coffee and wine; she has allowed her report to descend to the level of a tourist letter … it appeared it was calculated not to bring in money.'

February came, and no schools had been established, no orphans found and their relief work remained unorganised. Shore frequently wrote from England enquiring as to what exactly were the aims of the fund; facts and more facts were required as to how they were spending the public's money. Paulina pleaded their difficulties: no available buildings were suitable for schools, and no teachers could be found. In truth, she wrote, while the children and their mothers were so in need of clothes and food, education did not seem so important. Once again Paulina came in for criticism from Florence and Shore as to exactly how they were spending the money entrusted to them. This time an account written by Priscilla was sent to England:

> As the special aim of our fund is educational, I hope we have not been too niggardly in not spending more on relief. As the necessities of the People are very great, I hope we have not spent too much on relief, neglecting the special aim of our fund ... We are trying to arrange homes for children. When one decoy duck comes, many other ducklings will follow.

As far as Florence was concerned Paulina had now failed in carrying out their planned works and following the instructions set out by herself and Shore.

Their first two months of inactivity had been a useful period for establishing contacts and acquainting themselves with the situation along the frontiers, however, and at the end of February the two ladies had some positive facts to report back to England: arrangements had been made to open two schools for the Bosnian children. They had found a young crippled schoolmaster who could take charge of a school with 161 children under twelve years old in one village; in another village nearby a young man was prepared to take charge of the other school. For schoolrooms they had acquired two empty houses and the schools themselves would be supervised by a committee consisting of professors. They had also found two little orphan girls (one with a mother) who would be boarded with the local schoolmaster.

On receiving this latest letter Florence wrote to Shore, 'At last their work is taking shape, thanks to you. I wish we could have induced her (Paulina) to give up the word "orphans" and substitute the words "gutter children" or "waifs" or something to that effect ... There are no orphans, or at least we don't hear of any, or only of ones with mothers.' Of the letter Paulina had sent to be printed in *The Times*, Florence, carefully editing it, did succeed in removing any contradictions, as well as being generally vague about orphanages and schools: 'Let the people think the schools are orphanages if they wish.' The political phrasing was also moderated. The final letter which appeared in *The Times* on 13th March however did give a graphic picture of the destitution, misery, discomfort (for the ladies), and their achievements – as well as details of the moneys spent.

Miss Nightingale and William Shore Smith, however critical of Paulina's character and actions, worked hard on behalf of the two ladies. They drafted the next round of circulars to be distributed to stem the public's continuing indifference to the plight of the refugees. Such interest as there was being centred around Ragusa, every visitor and English tourist still stepping off the Austrian Lloyd steamers were immediately made aware of what the insurrections meant. There were smoke-filled skies where villages had been burnt by the Turks, vultures circling over places where a week earlier there had been a battle and, visible to these visitors, the refugees begging in the streets.

With the focus on Ragusa it was only Priscilla and Paulina with their small fund who were working for the Bosnian refugees along the more inaccessible frontiers of Croatia and Slavonia. They had less than £1,500 from public donations, plus their own money and their own toil to carry out relief work, and they were spending freely of their own money — none of their expenses were charged to the fund, nor the cost of the advertisements and the printing and despatching of circulars; they were paying half the cost of carriage and despatch from England of blankets and material. Nevertheless, by the end of March four schools with four school masters had been organised, and there were prospects for more schools. The two ladies' reputations had been enhanced.

As Priscilla and Paulina's standing among the refugees grew so also was their position, politically, made more delicate. Paulina's pent up anger and bitterness now exploded in a series of letters to Florence. They expressed anger against 'England's pro Turkish policy', and bitterness against the 'smug comfortable English, ignorant of the conditions of existence among the refugees or the blight of life under the rule of the Turk'. In writing this Paulina now failed in her final instruction, 'to remain neutral'.

Priscilla and Paulina would be able to return to England for the summer, satisfied with their achievements in the last six months. Eight schools had been established, for four hundred children; more than three thousand women and children had been clothed and fed; they had also, just as importantly, vaccinated the school children after, having ordered their own supply of vaccines. However, they were constantly aware that it was such a small proportion of misery they had been able to relieve. They hoped to collect more funds during the summer months in England, but they could not be sure that the amount necessary to sustain their work would be forthcoming.

As the two ladies were planning their return to England, alarming reports of a new revolt in Bulgaria began to filter through, the first news of atrocities inflicted by Turkish troops and Bashi-Bazouks upon the Bulgarians appearing in the *Daily News*. In England the conservative government stood firm by its Pro-Turkish policy. When questioned about the new atrocities in the House of Commons, Disraeli replied that 'the trouble seemed to have begun by strangers burning the villages without reference to religion or race ... The disturbances seem to have ceased and information received does not justify the statements in the *Daily News*.'

England, Summer 1876[21]

Priscilla and Paulina arrived back in England at the beginning of July, just as Serbia and Montenegro, rejecting the warnings of the great powers, declared war on Turkey.

On their arrival in London they were pleased to discover that there had been a change in public opinion and growing disquiet with the Pro-Turkish policy of the Government. The public's disgust and horror had been fuelled by the increasing number of accounts of atrocities recounted by Edwin Pears, the correspondent in the *Daily News*. *The Times*' reports were equally appalling: '100 towns destroyed, 25,000 massacred, 1000 children sold as slaves, 10,000 imprisoned: all these crimes perpetrated with the utmost damnable outrages and tortures.' Disraeli's reply when questioned about these further atrocities was that 'he doubted whether 10,000 were imprisoned, and as to tortures, he believed that among the people in question it had been customary to terminate the connection in a more expeditious manner'. To the English public this was offensive and it was not right, nor proper that Britain should continue to support this heathen and barbarous race. Priscilla and Paulina, however much they might privately agree with these sentiments, had no desire to be involved in a public agitation against government policy.

Priscilla, as soon as she had settled in London, was busily employed in trying to organise relief. She was at once in touch with Dr Michael Laseron and arranged that he should set off for Belgrade to investigate conditions of hospitals and the wounded. She quickly collected £500 from the family circle for his expenses, and was able to write to the *Daily News* on 26th July that he was ready to leave and that on his return an appeal would be made for funds for nurses and medical supplies. Priscilla's scheme met with great success and resulted in the appearance of 'The Eastern War Sick and Wounded Relief Fund' in August, which was immediately absorbed into the 'National Aid Society' with a sum of £20,000 being allocated for the war under the name of the 'Turco-Serbian Relief Fund'. For the two women the special purpose of their own fund was now occupying a secondary place in their interests. In spite of this, Florence Nightingale, now falling short of her own high standards of strict non-involvement wrote:

> Good cheer to your efforts to help the sick and wounded of both sides, and bring them hospital and medical necessaries and comforts too. I hope, in this heartrending war ... a war which will, please God, at last bring freedom, the safety and blessings of home, of industry, of progress – all that Englishmen, Women and children most prize.

The gaze of the British Public was now firmly fixed upon the territories of the Ottoman Empire in Europe, on the battle fronts along the borders of Serbia and Montenegro, but more especially on Bulgaria. The Bulgarian revolt of 1876 was savagely suppressed by the Turkish Troops, especially the ill-disciplined irregulars known as Bashi-Bazouks. The terrible accounts which had appeared in the *Daily News* and had been dismissed by the Disraeli Government as being exaggerated were now proved correct.

The horror aroused by the reports of J.A. MacGahan, the special correspondent who had been sent by the *Daily News* to verify and report on the spot facts helped to bring about the autonomous state of Bulgaria in 1878 at the Congress of Berlin. The facts themselves were terrible enough but the horrific details described by MacGahan inflamed the public's imagination, emotions and conscience:

> *The Turkish Atrocities in Bulgaria, 2nd August 1876*
> *The Daily News Correspondent Reaches Batak. J.A. MacGahan*
>
> Down in the bottom of one of these hollows we could make out a village, which our guide informed us it would still take an hour and a half to reach. This village was Batak. The hillsides were covered with little golden fields of wheat and rye. But although the harvest was over ripe, there was no sign of reapers. The fields were deserted and the harvest was rotting in the soil.
>
> As we approached our attention was directed to some dogs on a slope overlooking the town. We turned aside from the road and passing over the debris of two or three walls, and through several

gardens, urging our horses up the ascent towards the dogs. They barked at us in an angry manner. I observed nothing peculiar, until my horse stumbled. When looking down I perceived that he had stepped on a human skull partly hid among the grass. It was quite dry and hard, and might, to all appearances, have been there for two or three years, so well had the dogs done their scavenging. A few steps further there was another, and beside it a part of a skeleton, likewise white and dry. As we ascended, bones, skeletons and skulls became more frequent, but here they had not been picked so clean by the dogs, for there were fragments of half-dry putrid flesh still clinging to them ... All of a sudden we drew rein with an exclamation of horror, for right below our horses feet was a sight that made us shudder. It was a heap of skulls intermingled with bones from all parts of human bodies, skeletons, nearly entire, rotting clothing, human hair and putrid flesh lying there in one foul heap. It emitted a sickening odour and it was here that the dogs had been seeking a hasty repast when our untimely approach interrupted them. Bones were strewn in every direction where the dogs had carried them off to gnaw at them. The town reminded one somewhat of the ruins of Herculaneum or Pompeii. Next we saw the bodies of two children with frightful sabre cuts in their tiny skulls. The number of children killed in these massacres is something enormous. They were often spitted on bayonets and we have eye witness accounts of babies being carried about the streets on the points of bayonets. The reason is simple. When a Mahometan had killed a certain number of infidels then they were assured of paradise. Here in Batak the Bashi-Bazouks in order to swell the amount were known to have ripped open the bellies of pregnant women and killed the unborn infants. There was not a house beneath the ruins that we did not see human remains...

The church was not a very large one but as we approached we saw that the whole of the little church yard was an immense heap to a depth of three or four feet of festering humanity partially covered with rocks in a vain attempt at a burial by those who had been ordered to bury the dead some weeks after the massacre. They had only partially succeeded for the dogs had done their work here too. There were bodies of little babies with their hands stretched out as if for help, children who had died shrinking in fear, young girls who had died weeping and begging for mercy and mothers who had died trying to shield their little ones, all lying there festering in one horrid mass. It was a fearful sight.

Bashi-bazouks ravaging a village, taking women and animals

A Turkish guard with the heads of captured insurgents

They were silent enough now. There are no tears, nor cries, no weeping, no shrieks of terror, nor prayers for mercy. The harvests are rotting in the fields and the reapers are rotting here in the churchyard.[22]

MacGahan further reported on 18th August: 'A bagful of human heads from Baz was emptied in the streets at Jambuli before the house of the Italian Consul and eaten by dogs.' On the 22nd August he wrote: 'The bones of two hundred young girls first captured and then kept for a fate worse than death – kept for several days – suffered all that weak suffering girls could suffer at the hands of brutal savages.'[23]

Through September the agitation swept across the country in an indiscriminate wave of anti-Turk feeling, cutting across traditional lines of political and religious alignments. Public meetings and the drawing up of proclamations critical of Government policy expressed the public's feelings. Side by side with these meetings went a wave of generous giving. By the end of September there were numerous relief funds, all advertising and all receiving generous contributions. Now the poor fugitive Bosnians and their orphans came at the bottom of an ever growing list of funds.

For Priscilla and Paulina it was a period of great activity and much exasperation. Paulina for her part tried to bring before the public the difference, geographically and racially, between the Bosnians and Bulgarians in a letter to the *Daily News*. But the public's eyes and ears were still enraptured by the word 'Bulgarian'. In comparison with other funds Priscilla, and Paulina's grew slowly. Priscilla's brother, the MP Andrew Johnston, wrote on their behalf: 'The principal maintained by the two ladies was that of giving only such reproductive help as would enable them (refugees) to help themselves.' He spoke of Miss Irby's association with Bosnia and the work undertaken the previous winter by her and Priscilla. As a result the sum of £1,000 was allocated to their fund.

The women in England had been no less moved by the plight of the poor Bulgarians and their men folk. A presentation to Queen Victoria was made of a petition of 44,000 signatures. Women up and down the country were eager to help more positively.

'Clothes for Cold' was an objective that women could appreciate and do something about. Almost immediately 10, Ovington Gardens, the London home of Mrs Catharine Isabel de Noé Walker, Priscilla's sister, became a warehouse of used clothing, and a hive of activity of volunteer ladies packing and sorting. By October sufficient had been collected to make up 100 bales.

The scene in the Drawing Room of 10 Ovington Gardens. A few of the active ladies and their assistants opening parcels of clothing kindly given. They are sorting or laying it out ready to be packed by the hydraulic press

In that short summer of 1876 Miss Irby and Miss Johnston had been brought into the forefront of the agitation. It was paradoxical that because of the misfortunes which had befallen the Bulgarians the two English ladies who had been working in obscurity for the cause of Slav freedom should now become heroines and experts.

Paulina had not only been openly and vehemently critical of the Turkish maladministration, but had been prepared to back her criticisms with her personal knowledge of incidents. She had also been friendly with too many of the wrong people: Serbian politicians; Slav agitators; Bosnian Patriots. But in the summer of 1876 it was no longer indiscreet to have friends among the 'semi-barbarians'. Paulina now returned to her work more proud and less obsessed by her wish for Florence Nightingale's approbation.

Priscilla and Paulina, returning to Croatia in the Autumn of 1876, were richer in money and very much richer in the regard they had won from the English public.

Slavonia, Autumn 1876[24]

When Priscilla and Paulina left England in October the agitation was already diminishing in intensity. The truce with the ending of the war in Serbia meant the return of surgeons and nurses who had performed so valiantly on the battlefields.

On the borders of Bosnia in the north the ladies, returning to their work, discovered that in their absence strong pressure had been brought to close the schools for political and religious reasons. They had come under suspicion; it had been suspected that the setting up of the schools was all part of an Orthodox plot; that the schools were meeting places where Bosnian refugees were to gather arms before descending upon the Catholic population to massacre and rape. Common sense, however, soon prevailed and they were allowed to remain open, proving their importance to the refugee population and the authorities.

In the six weeks between mid-October and the beginning of December it proved possible to double the number of schools. Teachers now came forward, suitable buildings were placed at their disposal. Priscilla and Paulina had established their position.

The responsibility for the organisation in managing sixteen schools lay with the two ladies. Those living in remote villages slept the night at the school house, and for these additional food, blankets and heating were provided. Those living closer had to leave the security of the school house early so as to make the journey home in daylight before the wolves came out along the roadsides.

Each Sunday the schoolmasters came to report to the two ladies at their hotel in Pakrac to receive pay and supplies from their benefactresses. Thursday was market day in Pakrac and Priscilla and Paulina were often besieged for hours on end by refugees and pretext Bosnians begging for blankets, food and clothes. Their organised relief was distributed from the villages, where the schools formed centres for obtaining information and distribution.

The Hungarian authorities remained suspicious of the schools and the two directresses who maintained them. It was possible for the administration to show its disapproval of their activities in wearisome ways. Those bales of clothing and blankets so laboriously sorted and packed at 10 Ovington Gardens reached the Austrian-Hungarian frontier, there to remain held up by customs regulations. After the ladies complained to the foreign office, early in January 1877 the Austrian Government conceded that clothing and blankets, but not food, might pass free of duty.

The picture of Priscilla and Paulina at the end of 1876 was more organised and cheerful. However there were others whose plight was now even more grim. The pope of a village near Knin in the mountains of Dalmatia had written, begging that they should come to the aid of refugees in that area. The two ladies decided that they must leave the schools in Slavonia and Croatia to attend to this more urgent work. But first their affairs must be put in order. The schools were left in the care of Professor José and funds were deposited at Pakrac, to be drawn upon for aid as required.

There had been other requests for their services. Concern had been expressed about the plight of the refugee Herzegovians and they had also been urged to take over the aid in Ragusa. If they could not be everywhere themselves at least they had money to distribute. In England donations were steadily flowing into the fund.

A supply of clothes and blankets was sent in advance to the pope at the village near Knin and, as 1876 came to a close, Priscilla and Paulina set off on their journey south to that village.

Knin and London – January to July 1877[25]

The journey from Zara was eight hours of discomfort in an open cart, accompanied by a bitter and penetrating wind. They were in Dalmatia where the mountainous landscape made every aspect connected with the refugees more tortuous. It was as they had suspected: the state of the refugees around Knin was far worse than in the north. In these surroundings the last traces of amateurism were stripped from Priscilla and Paulina. Gone were the references to 'bright angel faces' and the talk of prospects for a Slavonic future. Here among the desolation of the mountains their work was reduced to its bare essentials. People were dying for 'the want of a farthing of bread'. Paulina's first act of relief was immediately to order much needed supplies: £1,000's worth of Indian corn.

Knin itself was a small town, important in medieval times but now consisting of one street, a river and a bridge with an old fortress towering above.

From their house in Knin the two ladies planned to make regular distributions, under their own supervision, of food and clothing. They would also endeavour to establish centres of relief at other villages. Soon after their arrival they went to the village of Strimica, taking what supplies they had; there the population of six hundred had swollen to nearer six thousand. But for many help had come too late – the new grave yard was already over full. Priscilla wrote to her brother, Andrew, telling him of the scene at Strimca. Thus one day's work for Priscilla and Paulina in January 1877:

It is impossible to describe, and impossible to forget. We stood all morning at the window of a shed in a courtyard surrounded by high walls; we had with us only sufficient cloth for one shirt for every child and a biscuit of black bread. Over three thousand Bosnians pressed about us, crowding over the walls, pressing close at the gate while the children filed in – or were carried in – or came crawling in – to raise their thin arms to the window, to lift faces suppurating with small pox sores, to show pot bellies of starvation, with the bitter wind whistling through the crowd, catching at the ragged clothes, making feeble frames falter. To six hundred children we gave food and material, taking down the name of each child. Then when it seemed we had reached the last of the children, and the end of our strength, there came a great shout, and the courtyard was suddenly filled with more children, more mothers, more babies, two hundred more holding out their hands, crying out for food and clothing. We had just enough for all. Eight hundred children in one day were given some means of protection and some sustenance to keep them alive for another day. It was little enough but if a distribution of this kind could be made each week, then lives would be saved.

In the year 1877 the two ladies were joined by Mr Arthur Evans, writing for the *Manchester Guardian*. In his first report from Knin early in February he gave a general picture of deplorable conditions, of fresh outrages by Bashi-Bazouks on Christian villages, of small pox and famine and typhus. But the misery of the refugees about Knin was nothing compared with his description of the refugees living in the caves just over the border in Bosnia:

> ...a great black opening in the rock, from which, as we climbed up to it, crawled forth a squalid and half naked swarm of women, children and old men, with faces literally eaten away with hunger and disease ... In another small hole, I saw a shapeless bundle of rags and part of the half-hidden pale face of another woman stricken down by the disease of hunger ... Then slowly tottering and crawling from an underground lurking place at the bottom of the pit, there stumbled into the light an old man, so lean, so wasted, with such hollow sunken eyes, that he seemed nothing but a moving skeleton – it was the realisation of some ghastly medieval picture of the resurrection of the dead!

Even to these caves did the helping hand of the two ladies reach. By midsummer those who had survived the winter had been rescued and rehoused in comparatively comfortable sheds.

Meanwhile, back in England, questions about Bosnia were raised in the House of Commons, about the state of the province and the outrages that had occurred. Since his emergence from retirement the previous summer, all Mr Gladstone's interests had been centred on the Eastern Question. He had been an admirer of the previous travels of Miss Irby and Miss Muir Mackenzie. Mr Gladstone had now become an admirer of the relief work of Miss Irby and Miss Johnston. He gave talks, written up at length in the newspapers, with his praise of the ladies there for all to see.

After a six-week visit to England, the main purpose of which was Paulina's preparation for the new edition of her *Travels* much encouraged and supported by Mr Gladstone, the two ladies returned to Knin in April just as the uneasy peace that had existed all year was disrupted. It was not certain what would be the immediate outcome of the fresh hostilities, but the ladies were sure the number of refugees would increase daily.

Whilst the two ladies were in England, Mr Evans, who had remained in Knin to help with their relief work, had uncovered fresh tales of atrocities which he now recounted to them.

Refugees among the mountains of Dalmatia

Because of the hardships they had endured as refugees twenty-three families had returned to their village of Ocievo. Promises of security had been given by authorities in the district. However, their village had been attacked and pillaged by a force of a hundred Mussulmen; the head of the village elder had been cut off and paraded in the Turkish town of Kulen Vakuf. The next Sunday, Turkish forces returned – four to five hundred Bashi-Bazouks – and 'a general scene of plunder and rapine followed'. Some escaped and fled over the border. It was these whom Evans had sought out and questioned. He set down in a report some of the horrific details he had been told: 'A woman with her baby in her arms; the baby had been removed by the simple expedient of cutting off the woman's arms: of an impalement at Gabella in Herzegovina: of the Christian Rayah who had been captured by the Turks, split like a lamb and roasted alive...'

This report, when it appeared in the *Manchester Guardian* was powerful; readers, including some who were MPs, were profoundly moved. However, there were still those who dismissed the atrocities as highly 'exaggerated' or 'pure invention'. At the beginning of May Paulina wrote to Mr Gladstone, enclosing a letter she had drafted for *The Times* and asking that he should endorse it. The said letter appeared on 17th May – an account of another incident of atrocities. The ladies were trying to ensure that he and the public received the facts and believed these horrific incidents were truly taking place.

The strain was beginning to tell and in early June Paulina wrote: 'We must go away soon; the heat is knocking me up, at least in Knin where the marsh makes the air so bad. It is no use staying under these circumstances, and we must go in any case to Slavonia.' However, they could not leave until they were certain their relief work was reasonably well organised and that distributions of corn would continue to operate smoothly in their absence. It was July before they would return to Pakrac.

In her heart Paulina now knew that the only solution to the five hundred years of 'Turkish Misrule' and two years of insurrection was in fact for the Austrians to occupy Bosnia. Back in England many influential people agreed with Paulina's judgement.

On the 16th July, MPs, politicians, peers and philanthropists of both parties were present in force to acclaim Miss Johnston and Miss Irby and their work at a large and influential meeting held on behalf of the 'Bosnian and Herzegovinian fugitives' in Willis's Rooms, at which Thomas Carlyle was present to show his feelings about the 'unspeakable Turk'. *The Times* gave full coverage to the meeting in two and a half long columns on 17th July. Two resolutions were put before the meeting:

1. That this meeting desires to express its sympathy with the refugees from Bosnia and Herzegovina in their distress and sufferings, as described in the recent despatch of Consul Freeman to Lord Derby.
2. That the efforts of Miss Irby and Miss Johnston in relief of the sufferers are worthy of the admiration and gratitude of Englishmen; and this meeting earnestly desires that they be supported.

Speaking in support of these resolutions gave the gentlemen present ample opportunity to express their admiration of Miss Irby and Miss Johnston, and to state their own views on the 'Eastern Question'. Then the meeting settled down to its main business, a speech by Mr Gladstone in which he delivered another accolade of the ladies' work and a condemnation of the evils of 'Turkish Misrule'.

Mr Gladstone, who on rising was received with loud cheers:

The resolution I have risen to support draws us aside for a moment from the direct and principal purpose of this meeting. It calls upon you in the earlier part of it to record your admiration of the conduct of Miss Irby and Miss Johnston, and your gratitude for the services they have rendered (Applause) I will not stop for a moment to express a doubt whether your feelings will answer in all respects to the warm terms of that resolution. If we have lived into the day when an assembly of English men and English Women is incapable of, or indifferent to, or lukewarm in the expression of admiration for such conduct and of gratitude for such services, then we indeed have lived into the day when humanity has altogether lost its bloom (Applause). It is impossible in my opinion to overrate the honour that is due to these ladies (Hear! Hear!) I have had the satisfaction – the distinction, I will say – of personal communication with Miss Irby when she was in London a few months ago, and I must say that I never witnessed a nobler or simpler example of entire self-devotion to the cause of good – of good unmixed with evil, of good unmixed with suspicion, of good so pure that the pursuit of it was an honour and a privilege to all those who could indeed appreciate such a pursuit. I speak here in a hall which has long been the traditional scene of the festivities of this wealthy and luxurious capital; and the recollection of those festivities suggests and enforces the contrast between our life and the life of these two ladies. They have voluntarily sacrificed whatever attractions are to be found in the gilded saloons of London or whatever higher attractions are to be found in its rural retreats, to devote themselves to unceasing and wearying labour, with no small share in their own persons of many whose physical privations which they are working so indefatigably to relieve. And they have done this not for the sake of obtaining your plaudits. (Hear! Hear!) The machinery of public meetings has been far from their idea. What they have thought of has been to dedicate themselves, their own energies, their own time, their own fortune, and – indeed in tranquillity, and yet it might have been so in obscurity to a great and beneficial work. (Hear! Hear!) It is only the enormous extension of that work, it is only the occurrence of these tremendous calamities unanticipated that Miss Irby first undertook her mission of Philanthropy – that makes it necessary not for these two ladies but for their friends at home to call upon the public to resort to the machinery of gathering together a large assembly to listen to the account of their labours and to share in their labours and thereby to do something towards conferring that fame which they cannot lose, but which they have never sought (Applause). Now my Hon. friends who have immediately preceded me have observed that we are here without any distinction of political colour. The fact that one has moved and the other seconded, and that I rise to support the resolution and the prominence of many who are on the platform and in the body of the room afford the clearest testimony in proof of the assertion (Hear hear) and it is most important that it should be understood how absolutely, how completely, the purpose of this meeting is disassociated not only from politics in the ordinary sense, but disassociated also from Eastern politics (Hear! Hear!) There are two great controversies going on, the controversy of a tremendous and bloody and, perhaps a cruel war; and a controversy in political life upon the Eastern Question. Scarcely less sharp than conflict of the sword which is now pursuing its desolating course in Eastern Europe. From both of these equally this cause of today is separate. I wish this was to be more clearly understood because there are many undertakings, in themselves perhaps well judged. I still not undertake to pronounce upon them certainly in their intention benevolent, in respect to which doubt and scruple may honestly be raised. I will not say a word against those who have thought it their duty to institute a distinct and separate fund for the purpose of providing necessary clothing and comforts for one of the armies engaged in this great war; but our case is not like their case (Hear! Hear!) I will not speak except for the purpose of drawing a distinction, either in favour of or against another plan which commands itself to many most excellent persons, the plan of raising funds for the relief of the sick and wounded on both sides in this campaign; because with respect to that also I feel myself that much may be said which is of an argumentative and of an ambiguous character (Hear! Hear!). In this case there is no such association of all. It would be easy to discuss the manner in which the misery now existing has been brought about, but with that we have nothing to do on this occasion. It is not necessary, nor is it desirable to enter largely into the details which have been abundantly supplied in the reports from the spot, and which are perfectly indisputable in all their painful particularity. The want of food, of clothing, of shelter, of fixed abode; the pangs of hunger and the ravages of disease the mother with her children fading and falling around her; fever and pestilence, which always follow on the heels of want – all these form a dreadful assemblage; and the picture that they fill is a picture of vast extent. And you may judge for yourselves what would be the condition of those refugees were they to return home, when you find them preferring all these terrible calamities to returning to their own country, because these calamities, whatever they may be, do not destroy liberty and honour – and especially the honour of women – and do not extinguish hope (Applause). It is now for us in some degree to say whether that lamp of hope shall be fed by the bounty London can administer. You have been reminded of the vast expenditure of this luxurious capital, of the entertainments we bestow on one another for social enjoyment, and that we spend as much in a few hours as would be sufficient to support many hundred families in Bosnia. Let me add one suggestion. I will ask you to think not only of the expenditure of London, but the waste of London. Think of that which in every house in London is recklessly cast away by which human life could be sustained. I believe that a very small proportion – not of the expenditure properly so called, but of the sheer idle waste of London – would be sufficient to place all Bosnians in a condition of real comfort. You are told that £15,000 have been found by English bounty, down to the last accounts, for the purpose of mitigating the distress of Bosnia and Herzegovina. That you must admit is a trifling sum. What do you think of the £15,000 which at present represent the sum total of English bounty when we are told that the Government of Austria, which has not been renowned in former times for any romantic generosity has spent half a million of money. I believe that to be a great understatement, for I believe undoubtedly that what Austria has given in sheer hard cash for the relief of these people is over one million (Cheers). And while I admit that they have the responsibility of neighbours, yet I cannot see that their responsibility is greater than ours. I should be the last man to recommend that the government of this country should substitute the easy machinery of a public grant for the free flow of private and general benevolence still is the case that we as a nation, have had as much to do with the causes of this deplorable state of things as Austria has had (Cheers). I do not speak of anything that has been done within tens and scores of years; and I speak of it, not for the purpose of praise or blame, but to strengthen my appeal. When I conjure you to believe that this is no far-fetched call of a romantic philanthropy, but it is an earnest exhortation to you to listen to the claims of an urgent and proximate obligation incumbent upon you. The only scruple that I am able to conceive as occurring to any mind is to be found in the natural argument, why don't the refugees return to their homes? This is a natural scruple, especially when we find the Ottoman authorities continually inviting them to return to their homes, and the landlords, who have had too much to do with driving them away, now find their consequences in their own lands desolate, their own incomes cut off, their own interests paralysed, anxious for them to come back. It is one thing to destroy confidence; it is another thing to re-establish confidence. We may be sure, from the severity of the sufferings of these people, that causes which prevent their return are but too real and too substantial, and you cannot have a stronger proof of the sufficiency of those causes than that of the Austrian Government have expended so largely money drawn from the taxation of their subjects to support the refugees. Holy upon it, that if it had been possible to do so in any sort of way consistent with humanity or decency, the Austrian Government would – perhaps ought to have driven these refugees across the frontier and bid them bear their own burden of life, whatever it might be, within their own borders. On the contrary they have not taken such a course, but they have chosen rather to administer what was quite insufficient for relief considering that it came from the taxation of Austrian subjects. They have papers laid before Parliament in the spirit of last year, and not one of the particulars is subject to the smallest doubt. A party of twelve refugees were encouraged by the consular authorities, they accordingly to go to their homes. Arriving there they find themselves encountered by a body of their landlords with other followers. These landlords massacre the twelve refugees and the troops appointed to be their escort stand by and look on. This was reported home, and Lord Derby on reading the report conceived that indignation with which it should fill every breast. He wrote in a becoming tone to the British Ambassador of Constantinople and wished that the parties should be detected and punished. Immediate inquiry was promised further remonstrance proved to no avail and the promise passed away as with the passing wind. No fruit whatsoever came of it, no redress was afforded, no punishment was inflicted. Under these circumstances, you will well understand how reasonable it is on the part of these refugees to stay where they are and trust themselves to the mercies of God rather than fall into the hands of man. (Cheers) I am sorry to quote a case of that kind because it involves reproach. I wish now to illustrate the only argument to prove that the refugees are unable to return. I wish to illustrate it in a manner more agreeable to my own feelings and to yours, and to answer the same purpose. It is a very remarkable case, which is to be found stated in one of the reports of Mr Consul Freeman; and which happily is disassociated from questions of controversy. The report is dated the 5th June, and it explains to us a particular case in which where there happened to be a good Mussulman landlord, the rayahs, the peasantry, instead of encountering the evils attendant upon removal to another country, very naturally, very sensibly, and very much to the honour of all parties remained at home. Consul Freeman said, 'I cannot refrain from mentioning one pleasing incident in connection with the flight of the Christian peasants from the neighbourhood of Banialuka. On my late journey from the town of Gradishka, in the midst of the general desolation, I was surprised to see in one locality some houses standing and certain fields cultivated, such is the condition of that country.' And we may believe there is no exaggeration in the statement when we are told that from one third to one half of the agricultural population have been driven from their homes – that he tells us it was a matter of surprise to him when he arrived at a certain district and found some houses standing and fields cultivated: He proceeds, 'On inquiry I found they belonged to a rich Turkish proprietor named Yusuf Bey Sibich. When insurrection broke out and all the peasants were flying, and the Mussulman landowners were seeking refuge in the towns, Yusuf Bey engaged twenty Albanians to guard his country house, and then calling around him his rayahs, he told them that if they wished they were at liberty to fly with the rest, and he would not prevent them, but that he intended to defend his property to the last. If, on the contrary they would stand by him, he would not desert them and he trusted that this mutual protection and confidence would bring them all scatheless through the difficulty'. Glad I am to have the opportunity of mentioning a Mussulman's name in this country, at this time which we can receive with honour. (Cheers) Yousuf Bey had always been a good and liberal master, and his peasants without exception determined to remain faithful to him, and up to the present moment not one, it is said, has either joined the insurgents or fled to Austria. There can hardly be a more striking proof than this of the extent to which the Turkish landowners are responsible for the present insurrection.' (Cheers) These peasants are but a sample of the general population of the country – a population backward in civilisation, much more so in all respects than the Servian, more backward in industry than the Bulgarians; but it is a population well disposed, inclined to perform their duty, and to do well for themselves and others had they but the chance. This case affords a moral demonstration that it is attributable to political intrigue or foreign agitation, but a real pressure of calamity which is not only painful but debasing and intolerable, that has driven these unhappy persons into their present condition of exile in which position you are called upon to administer them such mitigation of their case as circumstances permit. To a certain extent, perhaps the cause has been injured by the chief labours in it. The time has come, whatever be their scruple, however unwilling they may be to enjoy the celebrity they deserve but of which no one can deprive them when the urgency of their work and the sacred nature of the call it makes, the hope that great assistance we can give, renders it imperative that these things should be made widely known throughout the land to which we belong. You have had the advantage of hearing the personal testimony of Dr Zeimann, who is entitled to be a sharer in the honour, as he has been a fellow labourer with these ladies in their good and benevolent work. As to the facts, there is no doubt; as to the motives that can govern you, there is nothing to divert the stream of your benevolence or to introduce into the case it may be permitted to us as Christians and Human beings may not be without an adequate response and that something worthy of the name of England will pass forth in the bounty of England for the relief of the distressed Christians of Bosnia and Herzegovina (loud Cheers).

The Earl of Shaftsbury in his acknowledgement of Gladstone's eloquent address now spoke. In conclusion, he desired '… to especially appeal to the ladies of England to help their sisters, Miss Irby and Miss Johnston, whose exertions prompted him to think that he would rather command a detachment of ladies than a whole army of gentlemen.'

The proceedings then terminated. Many subscriptions were announced and others received at the close of the meeting brought up the day's total to about £900.[26]

When the meeting broke up the influential gentlemen went off to their clubs and dinners and their comforts; in Pakrac, Priscilla and Paulina sat in the indifferent comfort of their hotel and tackled the complex problems of trying to house, to feed and to clothe the two thousand children in their schools. When they did hear of the success of the meeting they were proud, and grateful on behalf of Priscilla's brother for organising and arranging such a meeting. It was no mean achievement to have persuaded such a large number of busy men to spend an afternoon at any meeting that touched upon the Eastern Question. Priscilla's concern was '… for the cause alone, the cause of the weak, the starving, the ill.' She was content that increased appreciation and understanding of what they were doing would bring forth an increase in their resources, and hence an improvement in their achievements.[27]

London, Pakrac and Knin – August 1877 to May 1878[28]

The atmosphere in London in August 1877 was infinitely more bitter than the previous summer. 'British Interests' in the near east were at stake, with the Russian advance in Turkey threatening the route to India. The anti-Russian, pro-Turkish factions bellowed for war and the pro-Russian, anti-Turkish factions criticised the Government and argued for peace.

Just as the previous summer, this year saw the introduction of many new funds, the difference being that most were now concerned not with relieving the refugees, but with addressing the suffering on the battlefields. Appalled by reports of the fighting, it was to these funds that the public now generously subscribed.

The summer of 1877 found Priscilla visiting her sister, Catharine, and her husband Arthur de Noé Walker at Ovington Gardens. Paulina firstly stayed with cousins in London. From being an honoured guest in London she went to Somerset to stay with E.A. Freeman and his family. His daughters knew from their own experiences in Ragusa just what Priscilla and Paulina had been achieving. They could speak with her on knowledgeable terms about the country and conditions there.

From Somerset she then went to Derbyshire, where she spent five weeks caring for Mrs Nightingale, whose eyesight was now failing badly. This was also Paulina's time of real rest and recuperation; time too for work and to prepare a new report on their activities.

Florence was rigid in her day's routine. She now spent most of her time in her rooms and in the five weeks Paulina was there she was to be granted just one hour each day to be with Florence. This harsh régime made Paulina knuckle down and work on her report and letter writing, for at each granted visit Florence would enquire of her day's work. Without this regime it is very likely Paulina would have fallen back into her habits of emotional talk and political arguments, which would have resulted in her report being rushed and haphazardly written.

[The following are a selection of letters of appeal for funds from Miss Priscilla Hannah Johnston to the British Public through Sophia May. These are letters which appeared in the Quaker publications of the time, *The Friend* and *The British Friend*. They are reproduced by the kind permission of Jennifer Milligan of the Religious Society of Friends in Britain, London.]

BOSNIA.

AGAIN I have gratefully to record the steady sympathy of Friends in this very practical part of the terrible Eastern question. At the end of last month I sent £100 to Miss Johnston, and already the alms so kindly entrusted to my care amount to another £100.

It is a great delight to me to receive this help, especially just now, as Miss Johnston is in England recruiting her overtaxed strength, and it is my desire to lay in her hands on her leaving us in October (in company with Miss Irby) a proof of our admiration of their Christian heroism, in the form of a substantial sum with which to carry on their work. It is a work which many of us desire, with aching hearts, should be carried out, but which we are ourselves unable to effect.

These ladies deliberately resign all that is comprised in a luxurious life in England, and choose to pass the winter abroad, side by side with the tortured and dying Sclavonian fugitives, in scenes of incredible suffering, amid diseased and starving people, only longing to imitate *in degree* the great Master, to heal and comfort some. Surely it is a great privilege for us to aid them in their loving mission.

As regards the clothing I would just remark, that as I hope to send garments for 300 of the poor little ones, I shall be extremely obliged if those friends who desire to aid me in this, will, *as soon as convenient*, send me their names and addresses, stating for how many children (and if girls or boys) they will kindly send me clothing. One *warm strong* garment is all that these poor creatures expect. If the material is much worn it might be lined with coarse flannel or strong serge.

If possible, I should be glad to receive such gifts by the end of October, but I imagine that during the whole of next winter they will be required.

SOPHIA MAY.

Bruce Grove, Tottenham, London.
Eighth Month 19th, 1877.

Miss Johnston writes:—

"The work of the 'Bosnian and Herzegovinian Christian Fugitives' Fund' is going on satisfactorily during the short visit of Miss Irby and Miss Johnston to England. They hope to return to the refugees in the beginning of October, to help them as far as possible through the terrible winter which is coming. There must be far greater want and suffering than ever, because the Austrian allowance has lately been much reduced, being now only about a halfpenny a day per head, many of the poor people not receiving anything, and numbers of fresh fugitives arriving.

"The twenty-one day-schools are going on well : 2,000 children are fed, clothed and taught. To enable the children to attend during the winter, it is necessary to supply them with warm clothing. It is earnestly desired to collect worn but strong and warm things for children (principally boys) between six and sixteen. New goods have to pay a very heavy duty and can be procured good and cheap in the country.

"Miss Irby and Miss Johnston only ask for children's clothes ;—out-grown school suits, flannel shirts and great-coats, will be thankfully received by Mrs. Malleson, 29, Queen's Square, London, W.C.

"The schools and the maintenance of about sixty orphans will be continued. All money besides will be spent on corn and hut-building for the starving houseless refugees. Miss Irby and Miss Johnston will gladly answer letters addressed to them at 158, Leadenhall Street, London, E.C."

BOSNIA.

It is always a rest and refreshment to see a streak of golden light under heavy storm-clouds, and we often there trace an outline, as of a grand city, far away in some region of brightness, rendered only more striking by the death-like darkness and silence around.

And surely those who regard the cause of Christianity as the cause of Heaven, and work with glad, if tried, hearts and hands for the thousands of *Christians* now turning out to die on a foreign soil, can discern one streak of light amid the clouds that hang over them, and the outline of a better country than that in which no corner is granted them for a bare existence.

Two ladies, with skilful hands and loving hearts, are travelling, this bitter night, from the luxury of English drawing-rooms, to the Austrian frontier of Bosnia, for the express purpose of passing the winter amid this mass of starvation, disease, and death, that they may, as far as possible, clothe the naked, and feed the hungry, and comfort the dying; may we, through the terrible season before them, as we sit by the cosy fireside, remember them with loving prayers, and by *practical* aid also.

Two days ago I conversed with Miss Johnston on her grand mission, the latest report of which she gave me, extracts from which I subjoin. All my kind helpers will be thankful to learn that their contributions amounted to a *farewell gift* of £250, which I laid in her hand, and for which, and the magnificent presents of clothes, sent me for her, she desires her deep gratitude. "I am humbled," she says, "by so much goodness and kindness!" From Tottenham, Stoke Newington, London, Brighton, Stratford-on-Avon, Bristol, Leicester, Sheffield, Kendal, &c., such presents of carefully made, or of good, though worn, clothing have been given to me, that our store will dress the 300 children promised, *without* allowing Miss Johnston to touch the sum placed at her disposal, which will now be devoted to hut-building, or to buying food. During November I shall gratefully accept sums for clothing (5s. is the average price of a child's dress). After that I propose setting on foot a Christmas present for Miss Johnston, in the shape of as large a sum as I can raise for her work, to give the ladies a little pleasure at the time of the Christian's *great rejoicing*. As *half-a-crown* will keep one little orphan for a month, may I ask that those who take an interest in this work will save a little donation towards it from amid the luxuries of our happy Christmas time; on no account would Miss J. desire to take it from English or other sufferers. Next month I hope to have news direct from the East for the very kind workers, who may then fancy the little Bosnian children smiling with delight over the warm, snug dresses, and their daily hunch of bread.
SOPHIA MAY.

Bruce Grove, Tottenham,
Tenth Month 18th, 1877.

"All Knin, the whole neighbourhood up to the Triplex Confinum, bless you, the English people; for, but for you, instead of 27,000 over 50,000 would have been now under the earth.

"Sixteen huts, holding each from ten to twenty, have been built at an expense of £4 to £5 each. They are made of planks, and walled round with stones. More are in progress, and we hope to build enough before the winter to house the wretched dwellers in caves.

"By far the most satisfactory and hopeful part of our work are the schools. The first of these was opened in March, 1876. There are now twenty-one day-schools, containing about 2,000 children. Every child receives a New Testament as soon as it can read; later a Bible. Up to this time the only reading books, so-called, have been the Serbian Testament, and a selection of the National Songs of Serbia. The children, if they are to be taught, must be clothed and kept from starvation; they are such poor little pale things, with a mere thread of a pulse, but might be rosy merry children had they but a little more food. We give each a piece of bread daily. In the school at Plavno in Dalmatia, besides the day scholars, thirty-nine orphans are boarded and lodged, under the care of the excellent parish priest and his wife, and his brother, who was a schoolmaster in Bosnia. We employ twenty-one Bosnian schoolmasters, for the most part young men, some of them trained in Belgrade, Neusatz, or Banialuka. We are careful to supply them with books and newspapers; in a more civilised land than their own, and under better influences, they are in a position to fit themselves for future usefulness in their native country. The twenty who are in the neighbourhood of Pakrac in Slavonia are under the superintendence of Professor Josics, the director of the Serbian training-school for teachers. The professors have employed their summer vacation in giving practical courses of instruction to those twenty schoolmasters, who have spent six weeks at Pakrac at the expense of the Fund to improve themselves by this opportunity, and prepare the course for their own pupils during the next half-year.

"For these schools, and for a number of orphans boarded out to attend school, we incur an average monthly expense of £300.

"To meet this expense for the next half-year we have placed £2,000 at deposit account.

"Our recent purchase of £3,000 worth of Indian corn, together with some payments shortly due, leaves us with nothing beyond a few pounds. We implore further contributions. We have no funds left; none to buy food to save the bare lives of these starving Christian fugitives, stripped of all they possessed. £1 worth of Indian corn will keep one of them alive for four months. We beseech your help.

"A. PAULINA IRBY.
"PRISCILLA JOHNSTON.

"*September 21st, 1877.*"

Donations received at Messrs. Twinings' Bank, 215, Strand, London; and by Sophia May, Bruce Grove, Tottenham, London.

BOSNIA.

In this time of sore pressure, when doubtless many aching hearts are raised in prayer for the victims in the awful struggle so lightly treated by some as the "Eastern Question," let us look diligently for the seeds of future blossoms, amid the utter and sickening desolation of one of the fairest gardens of Europe. A few such at least are collected for us by the ever-diligent hand of Priscilla Johnston, in whom the self-sacrificing spirit of her noble grandfather (Sir T. F. Buxton) works on with marvellous energy.

With some funds in hand, and hoping for the continued support of her friends during the winter of terrible endurance before her, she set off last month for her field of action. On arriving at Novska, Slavonia, after travelling from 4.30 a.m. till 2 p.m., and visiting at once one of the schools, she wrote me the following description. I beg that any who desire more exact information about the schools, or about *any branch* of the work, will write to me for reports (of which I have a large quantity) or for other details:—

"*Novska, Slavonia, Oct. 29th.*

"To-day we have arrived among the fugitives, and have had a delightful visit to our first school. We went in quite unexpectedly, and woke a smile on 120 poor little faces, and saw how capitally everything was going on. All the 120 were able to read and afterwards relate in their own words what they had read; singing, arithmetic and geography. They eat up about eight shillings worth of bread every day, and look quite flourishing, but I should have been sorry for you to see their rags and the remains of the clothing we gave them last November, which they have worn since and have almost worn out. After our little peep at more prosperous lands, poor Slavonia looks more deplorably miserable than ever. Dr. Ziemann was told most distinctly by all the Consuls in Bosnia that the return of the fugitives was at present out of the question. There is not even the usual pretence of order in the country. Stray bands of Bashi-bazouks scour the land, murdering and robbing as they choose."

Priscilla Johnston writes again from Palcratz, Nov. 12th, 1877:—"We have now visited nine schools which are joyfully attended by these poor refugee children. I wish you could hear the shout of welcome when we appear, and see the eager eyes fixed on the teacher to know who will be allowed to read or repeat, and show us how they have got on since we left them. These hungry little creatures each receive a piece of brown bread, which they eat happily in the sun, outside the school, about eleven, keeping a piece for supper. The number of the children orphaned during the last few months is appalling. Hunger and disease have ended the sorrows and anxieties of hundreds of poor fathers and mothers, and from all sides destitute children are brought, and we are implored to take them. As many as we possibly can we shall rescue; but the support of a child costs about ten pounds a year, and our funds are heavily drawn on."

Since the collection of £250 was presented, and the 300 sets of garments (given almost entirely by various Friends) were sent off, duty and carriage free, I have had sums sent me amounting to £30, and trust all the kind donors have duly received our warm thanks. This sum I intend to send (with what additions may come during November) to P. Johnston for the children's clothes, in accordance with the wish of the subscribers; and up to the 20th of Twelfth Month I shall gladly receive warm strong clothes for them (though I am sorry to have to state that the duty on new goods is one shilling per suit). After this month I propose making a special collection for Christmas, and would venture to ask that those mothers who, in their luxurious homes, are making large provision for their carefully attended little ones, will remember the orphan children of Bosnia, whose murdered parents have fallen victims to this horrible "Eastern Question," and who live and learn contentedly on a piece of bread a day and one scanty set of clothes per year! Without our help even these necessaries of bare life cannot be obtained.

It will give me the greatest pleasure to receive little sums from children and others unable to spare much from the multitude of "home charities"; and if anyone desires to send a message of love and cheer to our Christian heroine in her hard contest with varied difficulties, I will gladly forward any such note.

SOPHIA MAY.
Bruce Grove, Eleventh Month 17th, 1877.

BOSNIAN REFUGEES.

The readers of the *British Friend* are kindly interested in the sufferings of these poor people, the victims of Turkish cruelty, the *unoffending* victims; for they are mostly old men, women, and children, against whom is no allegation of wrong, except that they profess the Christian faith, so we venture to request insertion for recent information respecting them, which, alas! gives a sad picture. While yet the summer lasted, there was something to be had in the fields; by closely following and carefully searching after the diggers of potatoes, a few handfuls of rejected or overlooked potatoes were gathered up. But even this has now failed, and the first frosts are setting in with starvation and misery. It is only too probable that the sum of 27,000 deaths, which have already occurred from starvation, will be greatly augmented before the winter is over. Dr. Ziemann, who is almost overwhelmed with work and distress, writes: "And now I have returned to our unhappy sufferers, and ask you what shall be done with them? Verily it is no use to them that Englishmen take a great interest in the war, and watch the result with deep concern. Methinks history will tell it as one of the 'curiosities' of modern diplomacy, that Russia was fighting for the political existence of the Bosnian Christians, with England, Austria, Germany, and France on the watch to see how far Russia can or dare do it—whole Europe in excitement about the result, and in the meantime the poor Christians *die* — DIE, forgotten and uncared for, die for want of bread and in despair! I know there are people outside of the diplomatic circle, with sound hearts and heads, who are calm enough to think of the poor sufferers! In fact, my balance sheet proves it. But we must do more. I cannot put the case more interesting than in the plain figures relating to the work. Here are 100,000 people, or more, unprovided with good clothing and proper shelter; winter is coming; their hardships and privations, now great, will later on be simply awful. Shall we help them, or shall they perish? In the name of justice, in the name of humanity, I ask, Shall they perish?"

A very interesting report of their work has been issued by Pauline Irby and Priscilla Johnston, dated September 17th, 1877—just before returning to their labours among the fugitives. It presents a picture of the state of the poor people, an epitome of the efforts for their relief, and the formal narrative of the ladies. They say:—"More than 250,000 fugitives have crossed the Bosnian and Herzegovinian frontiers into Austria, Servia, and Montenegro. Of these, thousands have perished, but the number is kept up by fresh arrivals."

The *Times* correspondent, writing from Vienna, Sept. 23rd, 1877, gives the number in Austria alone as exceeding 115,000. In the beginning of the year the official report gave 119,000.

The allowance made by the Austrian Government is 5 kreutzers a-day (1d.) to women and children; men receive nothing. It has been calculated this makes about 2 kreutzers a-day per head. It is barely sufficient to keep them above ground as living skeletons, whose spark of life may be put out by the least accident or illness. We spent over £7000 between January and August, in Indian corn, in order to supplement this allowance. Our aim was to give to 10,000 persons in the most needy neighbourhood of Kuin, 12½ lbs. of Indian corn once a fortnight; but we have been quite unable to carry this out. We entreat for money to enable us to do so.

A letter, dated 11th Sept., tells us of the death of a mother and two children, of starvation, at Stermica —fresh fugitives. The writer, a well-known merchant of Agram, says—" The real misery will now begin. I am firmly convinced the winter will kill half of these poor creatures, who are living for the third year on crusts. . . . . Sixteen tents holding from 10 to 20, have been built at the expense of £4 to £5 each. More are in progress, and we hope to build enough before winter to house the wretched dwellers in the caves."

There is a little brightness in one side, however. "By far the most hopeful part of our works are the schools. The first of these was opened in March, '76. There are now 21 day schools, containing about 2000 children. Every child receives a New Testament as soon as it can read—later, a Bible. The children, if they are to be taught, must be clothed and kept from starvation. They are such poor little pale things, with a mere thread of a pulse, but might be rosy, merry children if they had a little food. We give each of them a piece of bread daily. For these schools, and for a number of orphans boarded out, we incur an average monthly expense of £300. To meet this expense for the next half-year, we have placed £2000 at deposit account. Our recent purchase of £3000 worth of Indian corn, together with some payments shortly due, leaves us with nothing beyond a few pounds. We have no funds left to save the bare lives of those starving Christian fugitives. £1 worth of Indian corn will keep one of them alive four months."

The latest news is contained in a letter from Priscilla Johnston to a lady in Edinburgh, dated Oct. 29th, 1877. "I think I must send you a line to tell you we are again among our poor fugitives, and have to-day had a really delightful visit to the first of our schools; 120 bright, intelligent pairs of eyes brightened up as we unexpectedly opened the door and went in. We found them in capital order, all able to read and pass satisfactorily a little examination in Scripture, &c. These children look quite flourishing on the 8s. worth of black bread which is given among them every day. We had the great pleasure of meeting Dr. Ziemann at Agram, and arranging our plans for the winter, so as to work harmoniously in different districts. He takes the parts in the neighbourhood of Agram, and we Sclavonia and Dalmatia. I need not tell you, however, that the utmost we can do will be grievously little in face of the want and misery of the coming winter.

Dr. Ziemann's funds are very low, and we cannot help him much from ours as every penny is bitterly needed. Good, excellent man! he takes the condition of these poor people most sadly to heart. We hope he will come to Packratz very soon, and have a look at some of our schools, which he says are the 'solution of the Eastern question.' I am to have a little treat to-morrow—2d. each—to celebrate our arrival. It is not out of the fund, only a private affair of mine.—Affect. yours, P. Johnston."

We are collecting and sending all the money we can to help to save the precious lives that have survived the three years of distress. We are also sending out blankets, which are imperatively needed, whatever the duty and cost of transmission; and half-worn clothing, especially boys' clothing, is asked for. The girls are more easily provided for, as some spinning and weaving were accomplished in the summer. The heavy duties charged on new clothing prompts the request for the half-worn, and we have despatched two small bales, and shall continue to forward goods up to the third week in 12th Month. We are very grateful to the dear friends who have helped us so kindly, and it is scarcely necessary to add, we shall gratefully receive and transmit any further aid entrusted to us.

For the Edinburgh Women's Committee,

E. Wigham, 5 Gray Street, Edinburgh.

Sums received since last acknowledgment in the *British Friend*:—A Friend, per J. C. Newsom, Cork, £1; Isabella Morrison, Carlow, £1; Joseph Masquillan, Wexford, £1; Mary Pim, 1s. 1d.; A Friend, 10s., per Jane Saddler; Sarah Fenwick, Perth, £1; J. G. Stirling, Landown Lane, Wavertree, £3 10s.; E. R. Constable and Joseph Bell, £2 1s; James Glenny, Waverley Lodge, Melrose, £2.

SLAVONIA.

"If thou seest the oppression of the poor, and violent perverting of judgment and justice in a province, marvel not at the matter, ; for *He that is higher than the highest regardeth.*"—Eccl. v. 8.

These words come with strength and comfort amid the complicated distress and suffering revealed in every letter from the friends of the still perishing nation of the Slavonians. And indeed it is a high privilege to labour in a cause on which our Heavenly Father promises to look and to aid those sufferers whom He is "regarding"; may we not even feel that one way in which He does *regard* them, is by opening the hearts of others, among His children, to hasten to their rescue?

The January gift of £100 has been made up and sent off, and I have at present about £26 in hand; how much all is needed will be seen by the subjoined papers.

SOPHIA MAY.

Bruce Grove, Second Month 17th.

(*From Priscilla H. Johnston.*)

"*Knin, January 14th,* 1878.

"We are indeed thankful for the Christmas gift (£200). Now that there is such grievous want in England, we cannot expect and do not receive nearly so much help as we have hitherto done, so that your labour of love is doubly acceptable. Ours has been a peculiarly sad Christmas and New Year. Our best girl, one of those we took from Bosnia to Prague in 1875, who had been a faultless inmate of our school for five years, died, the Friday after Christmas day. She was about eighteen, as good as gold, a sincere Christian, an industrious and zealous scholar.

"Bright hopes were fixed on her soon taking her place as the first native Bosnian schoolmistress; but the Master has called her for a better and happier service in His presence. . . ."

"*Knin, 21st January.*

"You can fancy the cold (at Plavno, where Miss J. had been) was pretty severe, as we find it necessary to go to bed in full walking costume—muff, jacket, gloves—to ensure our ever waking again. . . ."

The following have been kindly placed at my disposal by Andrew Johnston, Esq., brother to the writer, Miss Johnston :—

"*Knin, Dalmatia, January 21st,* 1878.

"After seeing the caves and their wretched occupants last spring, we felt that the first thing we ought to do was to provide some better shelter before the winter. Twenty huts, the building of which provided for months of honest labour for the men, and one good large stone house, where the feeding school is, and where the thirty orphans live, were seen from the top of the last hill when we reached Plavno on this last visit. Under the walls of the house we saw in the distance a large group of the inhabitants—in fact, all who could stand the bitter cold and high wind which was blowing—to welcome their 'mothers,' as they chose to call us. There were the thirty well-clad, well-fed orphans, not to be recognised as the little scarecrows of last year—the thirty feeding-school children looking anxious to see if we had brought any of the much needed clothing for them, then the mass of poor ragged fathers and mothers hemming us all in. . . . . We asked particularly to see one child, a little boy we had found and sent to Plavno almost the last day before we left Knin in the summer. Never had we seen such a skeleton as he was. He was actually dying of hunger, and his face was like a skull. We were too late to save his little sister, who died a day or two after she had tottered out to receive a loaf of the bread we were distributing at Sternica. The boy is now strong and well, but it will be long before he loses his wasted, hungry look. . . . . Though the 242 inhabitants of the huts are well sheltered, they are wretchedly ill off for food, and, above all, for fuel. A few sticks were burning on the ground in the middle of each hut, and round these little fires were sitting and lying dozens of forlorn and ragged children, none with more than a shirt on (a mass of rags strung together and patched in every direction), and the poor wistful mothers. Everywhere we heard praises of the huts—how dry they were, and oh, how much better than the holes and caves in the damp, cold ground! . . . In nineteen of the huts there was not an article of furniture. . . . . We had only six blankets with us, and these were given to the sick, of whom there were two or three in every hut. We had sent four sacks of clothing on the day before, and we were able to give one article at least to all the most naked. . . . . Twelve loads of corn are going to-morrow, and blankets will be sent shortly. . . . . Our hearts were cheered by seeing another generous gift from Edinburgh of £150, and we cannot thank our kind, good friends enough."

In a postscript to Miss Johnston's letter, Miss Irby mentions a poor sick woman whom they saw lying on the floor in one of the huts, with her head on her daughter's lap. "Next day she lay in the same position—no bed, no blankets—but they were thankful for shelter. The roads were almost impassable with ice at the time, and the cold is intense."

BOSNIAN RELIEF.

The readers of the *British Friend* cannot fail to be deeply touched by the following extracts of letters just received from Priscilla Johnston, and Paulina Irby, and those kind friends who have so generously contributed will be glad to know that their gifts have been so timely, and so well administered.

Extracts of letters from Priscilla Johnston and Paulina Irby:—

KNIN, March 15th, 1878.

"I have just returned from a very sad, but in some ways successful, expedition to visit some caves in which fresh fugitives found refuge just before Christmas. Those sad scenes are so much the same, day by day, that we fear a description of them must be wearisome, but it seems they are not, at least to our kind Edinburgh friends, our faithful supporters. We had hoped that all the inmates of our wretched caves were comfortably housed in our Plavno huts, but it appears that long after they were built and occupied, a fresh band of fugitives crossed the frontier in December, and could find no better shelter than some caves about two hours' distance from Knin, in a rocky, barren valley. Last Saturday, on our way from some much more distant caves, to the inmates of which we had before sent blankets and clothing, we passed those to which we have been to-day. We had nothing with us then, and darkness was quickly overtaking us, but we saw enough of the miserable inmates to take the first opportunity of carrying them some help. Human beings so brought down or nearly naked I had never seen. One pretty little girl, about 10, eager to have a peep at the strangers, I saw vainly trying to make the tattered rag of an old sacking shirt cover her sufficiently to come forward, but she had to hide behind the others. One old, old man, his poor limbs shivering through many holes, seemed more anxious to make us notice his only child, a tall, pretty girl about 15, telling us she could not ask herself—she was deaf and dumb—and imploring us to give him something warm to cover her with. Some little packets of coffee and sugar I think cheered the hearts of the old and sick, and with the promise of speedy help we were obliged to leave them. To-day, well armed with blankets, ready-made clothing out of empty sacks, new strong linen, children's clothing, and bread, all carried in sacks by two horses, we set off up the valley, and soon came to the first dwelling, half cave, half a ruined mill or bridge. Out of the entrance streamed 35 poor creatures, men, women, and children, some hardly able to crawl, and stood or sat on the ground round us. We asked them to group themselves into families, and all keep in their places, and first produced the beautiful warm blankets, lately sent us by M. Frankovich, of Fiume, wrapping the shivering invalids and mothers with naked, crying babies in their thick folds. Then one or two blankets were given to each family, according to the number of its members. One blanket we consider enough for three or four, for the poor dears must lie so very close in the crowded dwellings. The next sack contained a capital suit of sacking, strong and lasting, for each of the men. Thin linen was measured off for the women and big girls, evidently a great treasure, and the children were clothed in nice little red flannel dresses, with a long strip of warm material wound round and round their waists, and each given a good piece of bread to make their happiness complete. Then we should have liked you to see the scene! A cold wind was blowing, but the sun was bright, and the little munching red figures being admired by ragged fathers and mothers made a picturesque foreground to the dark hut and the stern hills all round, Miss Irby superintending from the top of a white horse, and receiving petitions for absent husbands and sons gone to get wood from the hill. There were six or seven of these, so that hut must shelter more than 40 inmates.

"Soon the little horses were reloaded, and we on our way about two miles further up the valley, to a veritable cave in the side of a little rising. Smoke was coming out of a hole in the top, and below there was an opening which looked wide enough for a sheep to pass through, but out of which crept, one after the other, 16 human beings, looking, if possible, more miserable than those we had just left; but this was because there was such a large proportion of sick and very old. These 16 were soon joined by some families from a cave across the river, which was crossed on a narrow plank by mothers and fathers carrying and dragging *bunches* of white, thin-limbed children, and again we separated them into families and gave to each and all. One touching little party, standing alone, consisted of a man and little boy about 3, both with as little on as it was possible for them to have. The mother had died two years ago, the man explained, while he proudly and tenderly dressed his little boy in his red flannel garment, and wrapped the blanket round his own almost bare shoulders. Next to them was a family consisting of a young man and wife, with three sickly children, the youngest crouching in the arms of the old tottering grandfather, and sharing his blanket, while he carefully fed it with tiny morsels of the loaf we gave him. Those poor people expressed more pleasure and gratitude than is usual; and many trembling voices asked God to bless us for coming to help them.

"A long way beyond, too far for us to reach to-day, are other caves and miserable dwellings, but stores have already been sent there. To-morrow we are going to find out more caves in another direction, and take supplies, as we did to-day.

"It is vain for us to try to express on our own behalf, or on behalf of those poor refugees, the gratitude we feel for those whose labour and generosity enable us to help them, or to tell how deeply the help is needed. We hope you will have seen a letter written here last Friday, by Mr. Stillman, a correspondent of the *Times*, about the refugees. He was here five days, during which he saw one of the Stromeritza distributions to 1,000 people, and visited Plavno.—Gratefully and affectionately yours,

"P. H. JOHNSTON.

"*P.S.*—I must reopen my letter, and put in one or two violets from a bunch brought here to us to-day by a poor little orphan boy, who, with two little sisters, was left utterly destitute and alone lately in one of the caves, and is now provided for with a kind Dalmatian woman. The violets are an offering of pure gratitude from the child."

poor hunted "dwellers in the earth," the life which is fast ebbing away.

At present I have about £84 to send for their relief. This sum, with any additions, will be sent off at the end of the month; already I have apprised Priscilla Johnston of its coming.

Next month I shall set on foot a fund to assist the survivors in rebuilding their ruined and bloodstained houses, and it will give me the greatest pleasure if a few others could make a little collection for the same object. In case of any one desiring to do so, I will just remark that the best plan seems to be that of simply sending round copies of Miss Johnston's letters, &c., to those in the neighbourhood likely to assist, and calling in a few days to receive what they are willing to give, since persons are quite glad to hear of a quick and safe way of helping the suffering Eastern Christians. I will supply papers with pleasure for this purpose. When I receive sums *without* any directions for their use, I will continue to send them to Miss J., for her to apply as most needful, as hitherto.

SOPHIA MAY.

Bruce Grove, Tottenham,
Third Month 20th, 1878.

"*Kimri, Dalmatia, March 11th,* 1878.

"MY DEAR MISS MAY,—It is too long since I wrote to you, but our time is so filled up. Last week we had a visit from Mr. Stillman, a correspondent of *The Times,* and he wrote a letter from here about our fugitives, which I hope will be printed. . . . . On Saturday we made a very interesting expedition to find out about some caves which we had heard of as being inhabited. From our windows we can see a mountain, about ten miles off, its bare sides here and there streaked with sun, and altogether a most bleak and dreary object. We were told that just under it were some caves filled with a most miserable set of fugitives, but, no very exact information being obtainable, we thought we had better see for ourselves. Indeed, after our expedition, we no longer wondered that the caves had been rarely visited by officials or any one. A two hours' drive, and three hours' walk and scramble, over the rocky paths, brought us to the first. It was more the ruin of a house than a cave; part of the walls were standing, and a miserable family had taken up its abode there. . . . .

"I have seen sad sights enough, but this exceeded all. It was after sunset when we reached the last cave, of which nothing was at first seen except a little hole in the ground, from which smoke was ascending, and lower down an opening, large enough for a sheep to pass through, which served as a door.

"Our guide, a Bosnian, called down the upper opening, and suddenly came forth from below, as from the sepulchre, one after another, about thirty half-naked, starving forms, men, women, and children; some carrying little ones in their arms, whose naked, thin limbs hung out like sticks. We were surrounded with the poor creatures in two or three minutes. One miserable woman, who had given birth to a child two days before, had run after us—her ragged skirt and only garment fluttering in the cold wind, which was blowing on us straight from the south, and her poor limbs shivering—to beg for something to cover her and her babe. She was a widow with four children, her husband lately killed by the Turks. . . .

"We had some packets of coffee and sugar, and a few little garments with us to cheer those sad hearts, and we are arranging to take a good supply of blankets (six bales of which have just arrived) and strong calico for shirts in a few days. It was piteous to see a little girl, about ten, in vain endeavouring to cover herself with her few tatters of an old sacking shirt, and hiding behind the others. Out of another cave swarmed about fifty more of these gaunt, ragged, hunger-stricken people. One old woman, like a skeleton, laid her hand like a bird's claw on my knee, and said, 'Help us; we are dying of hunger and sorrow.'

"To-day and to-morrow these poor dwellers in the earth are sharing in a distribution of corn, salt, and bread, and on Wednesday we hope to visit them again; but it is a miserable and hopeless existence they are now leading, few and small the alleviations.

"If, and whenever, a safe return to their own country is permitted, we shall help to our utmost, in seed, implements, cattle and building materials, but money is going fast now to keep them alive. Of this we are certain, the Bosnian fugitives cannot return as they are even if order is restored; for they have neither seed, implements, nor horses, and the land is a waste, sown only with blood for the last two years."

SLAVONIA.

THE following letter, just received from Priscilla Johnston, tells its own tale of awful suffering. There is no need of words of mine, except, as my heart is bowed down, and my eyes fill with tears, to thank with a double earnestness those kind friends who allow me the privilege of sending their gifts, and so, of giving back to these

In September Paulina reported that that year they had spent £7,000 between January and August on Indian corn alone; sixteen huts had been built; twenty-one schools were supported and attended by two thousand children; the monthly expenses for the upkeep of orphans and schools was £300. More funds were urgently needed … 'We have no funds left, none to buy food to save the lives of these starving Christian fugitives, stripped of all they possess. £1 worth of Indian corn will keep one of them alive for four months. We beseech your help.'

Up to the 21st September 1877 they had received £22,422, spent £20,226 and set aside £2,000 into a deposit account to be drawn on for the maintenance of the schools. They had received £7,000 in the two months since the meeting at Willis's Rooms, which was actually half the amount received the previous year over a two month period. The two ladies were concerned there would be no prospect of more relief until spring 1878: 'There must be another winter of starvation and misery for refugees already weakened and emaciated, now living for their third year on crusts.' However, one grateful Bosnian merchant heartened the ladies by writing, 'All Knin bless you the English people, but for you instead of 27,000, over 50,000 would have been now under earth.'

By the end of August the Turkish Government was claiming that the insurrection in the provinces had been stamped out. Priscilla and Paulina knew otherwise.

The ladies were back in Slavonia by the end of October. A letter from Paulina appeared in the times on 14th November reporting their progress:

'Since our return we have visited five of our schools and find them in very satisfactory condition … In the first we entered unexpectedly and found two Bosnian teachers and one hundred and twenty children at work…' She went on to give another account of the devastation in the country, the letter ending thus: 'To maintain these poor people alive … is surely a Christian duty, incumbent not on Austrian hospitality alone, but on the hospitality of all Christendom. The greatest distress has always been among these 250,000 fugitives from Turkey, but their cause has been sufficiently pleaded.'

Arthur Evans' report from Pakrac appeared in the *Manchester Guardian*:

The hope of Bosnia, Miss Irby and Miss Johnston's children

The scene of the English ladies' labours is indeed an oasis in the lengthening waste of human misery. The schools are well equipped with Blackboards and globes, the rooms are decorated with stories from the bible sent out by missionary societies in London and in each was a picture of St Sava. The children are bright eyed and eager to learn. The teachers are equally eager and effective in their role. The children are being taught, what few would have had the opportunity to learn in their own country, simple arithmetic, spelling, reading and writing in their own alphabet and tongue. They are also being taught that they are Serbs and Bosnians. The schools are on Austro-Hungarian territory, the children dwell on Austrian soil, but they are being taught to look forward to a time when they would be able to return to their own land, when their own land would no longer be Turkish but 'true Serb'.

Such widely circulated publicity proved to do more harm than good for the schools. It served to make the Hungarian authorities subject them and those responsible for them to closer scrutiny. The schools had always been viewed with distrust and suspicion by the more extreme Roman Catholic population in Croatia and Slavonia, and by the Hungarian officials, though the ladies had successfully thwarted an earlier attempt in the autumn of 1876 to close them down.

At the beginning of 1878, in a background where outside pressures were changing the situation in the frontier regions, if the provinces were to be occupied by Austria-Hungary factions then no encouragement could be given to an education that emphasised the glories of the Serbian past. The schools on the military frontier now became the victims in the struggle between the Magyar, Roman Catholic and Orthodox elements in the Austro-Hungarian Empire. The new Governor acted not against Priscilla and Paulina, for they were English subjects with powerful friends behind them, but against the schools.

Professor José and his assistant teachers were now forbidden to supervise the schools and accused of behaviour 'dangerous to public order and tranquillity'. They became the victims of 'politico-religious' persecution. However, the Governor did not wish to lose the benefit that the schools and the English money brought to the refugees; he was prepared to let them continue under the supervision of a Roman Catholic Croat. This person proved totally unfit for the task of supervisor.

Priscilla and Paulina, struggling with this problem from the distant location of Knin, felt they had no alternative but to cease to maintain the schools. The authorities had neither money nor inclination to support schools for Bosnian refugee children, so in February 1878, the schools closed.

Had the ladies been present perhaps such drastic action might have been averted. As it was they could not leave Knin, for there they were indispensable. It was thought '... better that the memory of the schools and what the English ladies had done should remain untarnished, and that the closure should be fixed squarely and firmly on Hungarian Officialdom and ancient religious rivalry.' Once again Paulina had declared her political beliefs. It was noted in official circles that Miss Irby and her actions must be closely watched.

There was one consolation, however. With less money to be expended on the schools, there was more to spend on corn at Knin. But by spring 1878 Priscilla and Paulina were coming to believe that however much they had to spend, however large their stocks of corn and clothing, still the queues of outstretched arms would be waiting when all supplies had been exhausted.

When they had come to Knin a year before they had thought that they had reached the depths of human misery; now after the third winter they knew otherwise. Priscilla and Paulina, working on through the winter to spring of 1878, were bowed down with the sordid drudgery of their ordeal, which became even harder to endure. Every delay in the diplomatic field meant less chance for survival for so many refugees. Arthur Evans spoke of the problems facing the ladies: 'Miss Irby is much exercised as to why the diplomats are delaying ...the seed time is passing away and in three weeks time it will be too late for the refugees to return, even if supplied with corn.' On Easter Day he had accompanied the ladies to a village four hours drive away from Knin. He continued: '... They had distributed corn to four hundred and seven families, over three thousand people in eight hours. There was to be another distribution the next day for those who had received nothing.'

Meanwhile, back in Britain the political atmosphere which had been turbulent at the end of 1877 now, at the beginning of 1878, reached a new frenzy as Russian troops advanced and Turkish defeat became inevitable. Powerful voices spoke out against war and two large rallies were held for the opposing parties, one in Trafalgar Square, the other in Hyde Park. Attempts to keep them separate were in vain and there were violent clashes. While Britain waited to hear the terms of Russia's settlement with Turkey at San Stefano, the Government made preparations for war with the enormous sum of £6,000,000 being voted to army and navy estimates. In Dalmatia Priscilla and Paulina continued their fight against starvation and destitution. But was there going to be any further interest in England in the fate of the starving Bosnians? Miss Nightingale summed up the situation in a letter to her cousin, William Shore Smith: 'I have at last had a full account from Miss Irby of all their works (they are wonderful) almost too late ... I am afraid it is too late for people to give money to the sick and starving. They will say "We shall want it all for ourselves!" (War seems very near.)'

June 1878 to June 1879 – The Austrian Occupation[29]

Instead of war, at the end of June 1878 a European Congress was held at Berlin. The conviction that there must be no dismemberment of the Ottoman Empire, which had shaped the policy of the British Government for so long, was now abandoned. The treaty of San Stefano recognised the independence of Serbia, Roumania and Montenegro. Russia took Bessarabia, Cyprus became British and Austria was entrusted with a mandate for the occupation of Bosnia and Herzegovina. Paulina had long since accepted that the provinces would become part of the Austro-Hungarian Empire. Her only consolation was 'that it was to be occupation not outright annexation'. Her dream of Serbia enlarged to become a Slav state must remain a dream.

Priscilla and Paulina had hoped for some settlement in the provinces by spring 1878, that the refugees might return to their devastated lands in time to sow their crops for next summer. But politicians had no thought for the seasons of cultivation – seed time passed, summer and autumn and once again there were no crops to be harvested, and still the refugees huddled over the border, and still the two ladies fed and clothed them.

By the summer of 1878 they had increased the scope of their activities. Another item was now added to their supplies: they must purchase pick axes, for the ladies had now become employers of labour with a force of six hundred Bosnians engaged on road making in the village of Plavno. They could see no end to their labours until spring 1879 when the refugees would be able to return to their lands with some chance of being self-supporting.

Priscilla and Paulina travelled back through Bohemia in July 1878 to make their customary three months summer stay in England, to rest and to renew their requests for funds. Their many friends, as usual, were only too eager to help.

On their return to Pakrac at the end of October they found that the refugees were to be transported back at once. Spokesmen pleaded in vain with the authorities '... that they might remain in familiar and friendly surroundings rather than set off into a wintry waste to search for villages that had been destroyed and homes that no longer existed.' But it had been ordered that the refugees must be repatriated, and so they were, in the depths of winter. The authorities had, however, anxiously awaited the English ladies' return in the hope that provisions from their fund might help the refugees on their journey. Priscilla and Paulina hastily bought up all the stocks of blankets and shoes that they could find in Pakrac and distributed them. Next morning they watched as the sad

The distribution of corn by Miss Irby and Miss Johnston – a list of places in Dalmatia with numbers and amounts given, January and February 1879

Refugees on the Austrian border

caravan set out on a three to four day journey. Some three hundred people – those who had not fallen by the way to be frozen where they lay, and those who had not been tipped from rafts as they were ferried across river – weak and worn from suffering, starvation and disease, their possessions limited to the rags upon their backs, were driven south to Knin, there to cross the mountains to where an Austrian official of the new Bosnian administration awaited them. It was no wonder that there was a growing belief that the brutality was deliberate, part of a policy devised by the Hungarian authorities to reduce that proportion of the Bosnian population that was Orthodox and Serb.

In January 1879 the process of repatriation was continuing in Dalmatia. The condition of the returning refugees grew worse. Arthur Evans set out to investigate for himself the conditions of these 'victims of official atrocity'. This resulted in the damning of Austrian policy in his article, 'A relief expedition in the Bosnian mountains', in which he gave detailed descriptions of the suffering and the dying refugees dwelling in caves and huts. He related that '...the population in the first twelve were all dead or soon to die. To those who received Miss Irby's and Miss Johnston's bread and corn a further expectation of life was given; but this would be to no avail, merely a postponement of the inevitable.'

The following further letters of appeal for help from the British Public, which appeared in *The Friend* and *The British Friend* are reproduced by kind permission of Jennifer Milligan of the Religious Society of Friends in Britain, London.

June, July and September 1878

DISTRESS OF BOSNIAN REFUGEES.
LATEST NEWS FROM PRISCILLA H. JOHNSTON.

Very lately the following letter reached me from this worthy great-niece of Elizabeth Fry, with an earnest entreaty for more aid from England, as all readers will see not without good reason:—

"*Knin, April 16th, 1878.*

"To-day we have paid out for corn the last kreutzer we had in hand here, and though some money is on its way to us from London, most of it is already portioned out, and in a few weeks we shall have no more. The 12,000 fugitives who have been actually kept alive by our fund in this district must sink into a condition which it is misery even to think of.

"Besides our help they have only the Government allowance of five kreutzers a day (and only about four in every five receive that), and they have to pay one kreutzer per head per day as rent to the poor Dalmatians in whose huts and sheds they are crowded. I send you a little bag which exactly holds the quantity of raw Indian corn which can be bought for five kreuizers, and you will see that we are not wrong in saying that without the English help which has been given these people must have perished."

"Will you get the little bag filled with Indian corn and look at it as a day's food for each hungry man and wasted baby! Our hearts fail when we think of these people, now so well known to us, left with nothing but that little bagful. If, indeed, it comes to this, we must go away and not wring our hearts with the sight of misery we cannot prevent. Last Saturday we went again to those wretched caves, and the poor inmates poured out with their pinched, patient faces, and crowded round us with their sorrowful tale, 'When would the next distribution be? 'Ah! we have nothing! we cannot wait till then.' The want was so real and terrible that they were called to receive corn again yesterday; and to the joy of the poor mothers a nice bundle of flax was given to each—employment for long and listless hours, and at last the long-forgotten comfort of a whole clean shirt.

"There is a place called Verlika, about twenty miles from Knin, at and near which there are about 4,000 fugitives whom we visited last week. These have been living and dying on the five kreutzers, for we have only been able to give them corn for two distributions. The misery of those people it is impossible to describe—almost frantic with want, the half-naked emaciated creatures pressed round us, everywhere stretching out their wasted hands and imploring us to help them; mothers thrust forward their little skeleton children, their cage-like forms only too visible through the tatters which hung about them, and kissed our clothes and feet in gratitude for the little we had done for them. And these weeping, thronging beggars, all had once their little home, a plot of land—held in fear indeed of their cruel masters, but with no thought of starvation and beggary. It was sorrowful indeed to see their despairing looks when we drove away, though we knew they would soon be cheered with the news of the 2,000 florins we had left to be honestly earned with work. It is now our great desire to give relief in this manner to those who can work, while continuing our help to the widows, orphans, and sick, and to-morrow 191 Bosnians will be at work road-mending close to Knin. In two places near this it has been already for some time going on. The poor men are far too weak and hunger-stricken to do a full day's work, but they hold on as long as they can gladly and thankfully.

"Our great want now is more money for corn to keep these poor people alive till they can return to their own country. Our means of helping were never so wanted or so near their end as they are now...."

PRISCILLA H. JOHNSTON.

It will be a comfort to the readers of this distressing letter to know that, through the constant help of many Friends, I have been able to send again this month £100 to P. H. Johnston; also that the War Victims' Committee, on reading the account, decided to add another £100 to the fund. Should any one feel inclined to respond to her entreaty for more aid, by collecting a little amongst friends or neighbours, I shall be glad to send copies of the above letter, printed ready for circulation. Very few persons who read these terrible descriptions refuse a contribution if politely solicited.

The family of Priscilla Johnston are very grateful for the support rendered by Friends and others to their sister,—and send warm thanks, which I gladly hand on to all the workers, some of whom amidst severe affliction, or even on beds of sickness and pain, are working for her in her noble, sad mission.

SOPHIA MAY.

Bruce Grove, Fifth Month 20th, 1878.

BOSNIAN REFUGEES.

During the time of the Yearly Meeting one hour was given to hearing details of the distress in Bosnia, and of the efforts for relief administered by Paulina Irby and Priscilla Johnston. The following extracts are from a letter of most recent date:—

"KNIN, DALMATIA, *11th May, 1878.*

"We must now give a worse account than ever. We feel almost in despair; for the money goes fast, and we have only about £40 in hand to-day.... The Austrian Government is now anxious for the return of the fugitives; and last week Baron Rodich, Governor-General of Dalmatia, came here to visit the fugitives in different places, with the object of persuading them to return, telling them that the allowance (for some time given only to women and children) will very soon be entirely stopped. The answer of the poor people everywhere was the same—'We will starve, but we will not return till Bosnia is under a Christian Government.' Baron Rodich told us this himself. In proof that their fears are not groundless, news have just come from Strimnitza (two hours from Knin, and on the frontier) that three men from among the fugitives had gone over for wood, had been found by one of the bands of armed Turks, or Bashi-Bazouks, and had been murdered. The bodies were found shockingly mutilated—ears, noses, and tongues cut out—eyes destroyed.... We have not been able to afford a distribution at Strimnitza for a month. The three hundred sacks of corn cost £193.... We can only feel what must be the state of the women, little children, and the old and sick, lying about in the huts and caves. We have resolved to give at least one more distribution at Strimnitza.

"The people at Kinnesi Polje, numbering over three thousand, are in terrible distress, for we have been obliged to draw in.

"Our walks and rides close by bring us everywhere into most touching scenes—the human misery is in such contrast to the lovely scenery, the burst of flowers and foliage, nightingales pouring out their songs from every tree and bush; and then, creeping by tens and twenties from every hut and shed, come the piteous groups, and over and over we hear the same tale, so evidently true—'We are dying of hunger; O give us something, for God's sake!' The poor mothers drag and carry the wasted, pallid children to show us; and in every hut we look into there lies one, often more, too ill even to crawl to the door—lying on the hard uneven earth floor, happy if able to rest their heads on an empty sack rolled up, but often with no pillow but a thin wasted hand. A neighbour uncovers the face, and we think, 'Surely merciful death has come at last;' but the sunken eyes unclose, and are turned on us beseechingly. Even the promise of a supply of corn next day seems a mockery; but what can we do more with thousands in the same condition round us?.... Returning in the sunset yesterday evening from a visit to a group of huts, the Bosnian who was with us (to hold the horses, &c.) remarked, 'Ah, but if it were not for you there would not be one of us living now!' I could not help saying to Miss Irby, 'Then, would it not have been far better for them if we had never come? Is this living death a boon?'

"We are establishing three more feeding schools here, when every day great bowls of polenta will be joyfully devoured by one thousand hungry children. They sit in tens and twelves round each bowl.... A mother standing by said to me, 'If it were not for this, my children would have nothing.' So we struggle on, if with sad hearts."

The response to the appeal was prompt and generous. The following are the sums handed to J. and E. Wigham, 5 Gray Street, Edinburgh; and an equal amount, we are informed, has been sent through Sophia May. A note from P. Johnston to Edinburgh workers, dated "June" 8th, 1878, returns grateful thanks for this help. She adds:—

"Things here are as bad as ever, but we hear on all sides with thankfulness that the pressure of distress will be rather relaxed in July, owing to the fall of prices before the closely-approaching harvest. The heat is becoming very trying, but we hope to be able to bear it some time longer.... Strimnitza has had a distribution this week, thanks to you."

Robert Doeg, Stanwix, £2; H. H., M. J. H., and S. H., Bulford Mill, £2 11s.; James Cochrane, 6s.; Alex. Allen, Dublin, £2; Ellen Allen, do., £1; W., £1; Eleazar Lewis, Ontario, Canada West, £1; Senhouse Martindale (4th subscription), £10; H. Webster, £2; Jane, Frank, and Alfred Webster, 10s. each—£1 10s.; Margaret Capper, Hammersmith, £5; Louisa Peet, £1; Hannah and Marianne Burgess, £5; M. Dawes, £1; Ellen Claro Grace, 10s.; E. W., 2s.; Per Marianna Crowley, Alton, £1; A. F. Fox, £2; Collection at Meeting-house, £12 7s. 10½d.; Jane Little, £5; Schools at Kingston-on-Thames, 17s.; Friend, 5s.; Isaac Hull, 10s.; G. Satterthwaite, 10s.; Mary H. Pease, £10; H. and J. Hewitson, Leeds, £30; C. Richardson, £2.

NEWS FROM BOSNIA.

It is with a melancholy pleasure that I lay before the friends of the Slavonian Christians the interesting letters just received from Miss Johnston, who is now in England for two months of rest before another of her terrible winter campaigns, assisting Miss Irby in their grand work on the frontier. In reply to the kind inquiries of those who are willing to help me again this autumn in sending out bales of clothes, I would suggest two modes of procedure. First, to procure from Miss Johnston a pattern of the simplest boy's suit needed, and set the sewing circles to work early, making a little collection afterwards, when the clothes are made, to pay for duty and carriage; or, second, where this is not practicable, to collect worn boys' clothes from friends around, and employ the poor, to whom it is desired to give help, in strongly mending and patching them, thus helping our own poor people as well as the foreigners. As the "orphan girls" also require clothes, I shall gratefully receive warm garments for them. May I ask those friends who intend to assist me in this little enterprise to let me know, early in October, about how many children they will be able to clothe? last winter we sent garments, or money to purchase them, for many hundred children. I promised to clothe 300, and think my kind friends doubled the number,—could we promise Miss Johnston the same help this year?

Although, partly from the impression that Bosnia was now free, the funds have fallen off very much, yet I am thankful to have a donation of £33 to give this month, and shall most gratefully hand to Miss Johnston any sums, in one large gift, before she leaves England in the middle of October. As I am likely to be abroad during September, I would ask all desiring to add to the fund, or to gain information, during that month, to write to Miss P. H. Johnston herself. Address, A. Johnston, Esq., 158, Leadenhall Street, London.

I trust that for one more winter her kind friends will make it possible for her to feed and clothe these desolate little children.

SOPHIA MAY.

Bruce Grove, Tottenham, Eighth Month 18th, 1878.

"*Eighth Month 14th, 1878.*

"We had to grieve you often enough with descriptions of the sufferings of the fugitives from Turkey: what will you say if we tell you that things with them are unchanged at this moment—that all the hunger, homelessness, weakness, and despair, are now going on as badly as ever? For not one of the refugees has yet been allowed by the Austrian Government to return to Bosnia, and, indeed, the histories in the newspapers of the fighting and disturbance in that province more than account for this state of affairs.

"Yesterday we sent off a fresh table of dates for the distribution of corn, as arrangements had only been made for continuing them till the end of August; but we see there is no hope of their not being wanted for many weeks to come yet. Then come the cold autumn nights, and soon the dreadful winter will be upon them. We are again in great need of help. It is thought by many that since peace was proclaimed the needs and sufferings of the fugitives must have ceased, but we are eye-witnesses to the fact that at no time has the want been greater than it is now.

"Happily, when we were obliged for health to leave Dalmatia, we were able to place the continuance of the relief in the hands of trustworthy agents, *as long as we can supply them with funds*. Hundreds of children are still living on the daily meal of bread they receive at our schools, and there are more than one hundred orphans for whom we are entirely responsible now and for the future. Miss Irby is in constant correspondence with our helpers and with the schoolmasters.

"We shall be in urgent need of blankets, and warm clothing for the children, but money to buy bare food is even more necessary and important; and we must run the risk of being called importunate, when we plead most earnestly for more help for these long and deeply-tried fellow-creatures. If, and when, they return to Bosnia, they will want everything, for they will find their homes ruins, their fields waste, and it is not yet known whether Austria will supply cattle and seeds and building materials. The funds we have now in hand will only support our twelve thousand of the fugitives for the next month or six weeks of exile.

"As to clothes, whatever happens they will be wanted. I cannot truly say that I think it worth while sending any but very strong boys' things, the prejudice against European clothes for girls and women is so strong. But we shall exceedingly want endless quantities of strong boys' clothes for the schools. They joyfully and thankfully wear them. Then our orphan girls will want things, and of course must take what we choose to give them. The native clothing is very expensive to buy, as each family only grows and spins enough for itself, and the homespun linen and cloth last many years till clothes become real heir-looms. I will not again attempt thanking you, for you are so entirely with us in the work that it would be like thanking ourselves. But I think you know what we feel.

"Most affectionately yours,
"P. H. JOHNSTON."

More articles followed, savagely critical of the Austrian regime in Bosnia. Mr Evans and the *Manchester Guardian* were deemed to be too outspoken, and the British Consul in Ragusa was called upon to warn the journalist against making further attacks on the Austrian administration. The authorities next turned their attention to Miss Irby. Paulina was closely associated with all Evans had said and had herself been outspoken and intense in her opposition to Austrian policy. The matter of her schools and their pro-Serb character was still a matter of concern to the authorities. In early 1879 the ladies had set up four more schools about Bihac for the children of the returning refugees, but the authorities were quick to suppress them. When Paulina approached officials about returning to Sarajevo and re-opening the school there, she was rebuffed; they were not certain they wanted Miss Irby and her companion to return to Bosnia.

Paulina was defiant. To her friends in England her high-handed attitude and behaviour to the Austrian Government was the cause of much anxiety. Through Evan's articles and by her own statements she appeared to be trying to arouse public opinion in England and to turn Bosnians against Austria. Priscilla, however much she was deeply concerned about this highly volatile episode in their companionship, was powerless to control the dominant and determined character of Paulina. Even her adored friend, Florence Nightingale, no longer believed that anything she might say or do would influence her in any way. She expressed her concern: 'I tremble every time lest she should any day shut the door upon herself and her great work (I think Austria is rather patient with her). She has been told (and rather gloried in it) that she is stirring up Bosnians against Austria and there is enough truth in the accusation for it to make us all tremble.'

However, after much pressure from 'influential friends' of the ladies the Austrian authorities relented. Miss Irby's reputation stood so high among the Bosnians, it would be less than sensible to make a martyr of her in their eyes. She was told the school in Sarajevo could re-open.

The two ladies went on with their relief work about Knin and, against the advice of friends back in England, they returned to Sarajevo. It was a busy time for the two English women: Paulina updated Florence of their activities: there was not only the distribution of relief to see to and the road works, but they had now to plan the future of the children in the schools, the orphans and the apprentices. There were also nine older and more able boys who were being trained to be schoolmasters, and who were to be sent to various villages in Bosnia to set up schools. 'This must be very much a secret project which I am planning with the schoolmaster of Plavno, with all to be done as if nothing were doing lest the Government should stop it ... The Serbian Government has just bestowed on us the Cross of Takova, in common with a crew of rogues, villains and adventurers, and a few honest men. It is not a desirable distinction in Austria, but probably won't do any harm.

In June they were finally to leave Knin to return to Sarajevo. There, back in the old school premises, they planned a new beginning.

> Priscilla Johnston writes:—"We cannot but look forward to the winter with heavy hearts, knowing so well as we do what suffering must be borne, what numbers must perish, and how little we can do. Miss Irby and I left the fugitives in the end of July, in the full expectation that two months more of exile, at the outside, were before them, and that they would be allowed to return 'home' to their beloved Bosnia in time to build some kind of shelter from the cold of winter. But now there is no hope of this return till next spring. As we are very anxious that the day-feeding schools should remain open and full all the winter, we make an especial appeal for strong, warm second-hand clothing for the children,—ages from six to sixteen—chiefly boys. The reason why we ask for clothing which has already been worn is that the Customs duty on new things is very high. If friends who are so kind as to make things will get them worn for a week or two by some cottage children, the clothes can then honestly pass as second-hand. Blankets, old or new, are greatly needed for the sick and infants.
> "Parcels directed to Miss Irby or Miss Johnston, care of Messrs. Bayley & Co., 1, Cousin Lane, Upper Thames Street, E.C., will be received and gratefully acknowledged."

Letter from Priscilla Hannah Johnston to *The Friend* September 1878

Priscilla's final years in Bosnia – 1879–1884[30]

When Priscilla and Paulina returned to Sarajevo in 1879 everything was changing. Austrian armies had taken over the town. The flags hung black and yellow where before they had been green. Austrian officials clustered about the town, establishing a new efficient Germanic administration. At least now that Bosnia was Austrian it could no longer be a barrier between east and west. Means of communication reached down more easily into the provinces, and the medieval Orient no longer began at the river Sava. By 1882 the railways had arrived at Sarajevo; it was possible then to reach England in four days.

For the two ladies there were many adjustments to be made. Their horizons were suddenly restricted, everything now being much more limited in numbers and scope. Whereas before they had been used to thinking in thousands, now in 1879 sixty-six children were gathered in

Sarajevo in the care of Miss Johnston and Miss Irby. These included the five pupils who had returned from Prague, together with a few pupils who had remained to shelter in the school, watched over by the caretaker and his wife. There were the refugee children from Slavonia and Dalmatia, the orphans and the lost who had survived the mountain snow. It could no longer be called a 'school for the training of schoolmistresses'. It was a home, an orphanage and a school for forty-one boys and twenty-five girls. Their future for the moment was bound up with the lives of these children, although they did anticipate a time when the boys would be old enough to be apprenticed or might return to their villages. This, however, would not be for a considerable number of years, as the youngest boy was five years old and the youngest girl a one-year-old baby.

Further letters to *The Friend* and *The British Friend*, published during 1879

FIRST MONTH 1, 1879.] THE FRIEND. 17

FRESH NEWS FROM BOSNIA.

IN laying before the friends of the Slavonian Christians the terrible intelligence contained in the following letters, I beg those whose tender hearts suffer most deeply from sympathy with them to allow me to add a word of comfort. Many of those so cruelly dragged out to die on the way to their former homes have been for one or two years under the self-sacrificing and loving care of Priscilla Johnston. From her, especially, the little ones* who with such joy attended the daily schools, have heard and seen what Christian love really is, and have with great pleasure learned the sweet stories of our Saviour's life of healing and blessing on earth. May we not then trust that the dear Lord who so loves children, and so comforts the broken-hearted, has thus first prepared these down-trodden, ignorant people to understand a little of His love and then taken them to Himself? This thought consoles me greatly, and I trust it may soothe the grief of many who cannot think without

* Salutations from London Yearly Meeting, 1857.

tears of the terrible sufferings of these innocent people. When they have once fully accepted the faith "as it is in Jesus," they appear able to *rest* in Him, amid all these horrors, in the spirit of Job when he sang, "Though He slay me, yet will I trust in Him."

A few days ago I conversed with a Bulgarian pastor, most of whose family were horribly murdered, and whose aged mother was driven to insanity and death by the fearful scenes around her. With a marvellous calmness, and without one touch of bitterness, he told me of the fate of his family, adding, "I found only skulls in the courtyard of our house;" and if harsh words were used against the savage perpetrators of these crimes, they came from my lips, not from his. Such an instance of faith and of rest in Jesus should surely stir us up to greater reality in our high profession. He spoke warmly, as an eye-witness, of the constant and practical kindness of the Russians to their Turkish prisoners, confirming what others have already said on this subject.

It will cheer all the kind workers to know that again a large amount has been raised this month for P. H. Johnston; and I am sending her £150, as our Christmas gift, for the purchase of food, clothes, and blankets.

In conclusion, I must thank, very, very warmly, the multitude of friends who allow me the great privilege of handing their substantial aid to the otherwise perishing sufferers.

SOPHIA MAY.

Bruce Grove, Tottenham, Twelfth Month 16th, 1878.

"*Paleralz, Slavonia, Austria, Nov. 16th, 1878.*

"My dear Miss May,—I got your card, and was mindful of your wish that I should send you something for *The Friend* by the 16th; but we did not get among the fugitives till the 9th, and then we had to make inquiries and hear and see a great deal before we could write off about their present condition. The order that they were to go only came here on the 10th, and since then the confusion and misery have been bewildering. It is the most cruel, as well as foolish, plan that ever was made, and if carried out fully must end in more than half dying during the winter. Bosnia is merely a desert —no houses, no food even to be had for money; the roads and land flooded, bridges broken, and, more than all, bitterly cold and unhealthy. This last week we have had heartrending scenes before us, and we have heard pitiful stories. Groups of half-starved, almost naked, sick, hopeless people, imploring with tears to be only allowed to stay till the spring. Mothers with babies only a few days old obliged to set off, tottering from weakness, and without a thing in the world. On Wednesday, 300 were to go from here, and we had been hard at work fitting out the most miserable with opankés and blankets. Carts were got together, and the women and children packed in. The sad procession was just starting when a telegram arrived to say the river was overflowed, and they must stay where they were. But many had already been sent off, and there they are on the road, often entirely without shelter. A mother and four little children died on the very road from cold and exhaustion, and were found by some one we know. Two poor women had babies on the journey; one died and the baby. On Monday, fourteen children from one of our schools were drowned in the Save while they were being taken across. It is almost impossible to believe any so-called Christian Government could in the nineteenth century be so inhuman and barbarous. The poor people themselves seem to be reduced to such bitter despair and hopelessness that it is all one to them what becomes of them. They are like a herd of starving, over-driven cattle, not knowing where to turn or what to do. We shall have a terrible winter; for if they go we must send and take food and clothing to them in their misery, and if they stay it will be the same as the last three winters. General Philipovich has so mismanaged the occupation, that the fugitives could not be back at the right time, and now, it appears, merely that he may show his work complete, he has ordered that they should go back towards the end of November. The authorities everywhere have expostulated, but hitherto without success. We do not know what will happen this next week. Numbers of destitute children are left high and dry when the people move, and we must take them and provide for them. They are constantly being brought to us. We shall have about 200 on our hands. We have extorted permission to keep two of the schools going for these orphans.

Very affectionately yours,
P. H. JOHNSTON.

The following letter has been received by a lady in Edinburgh from Miss Johnston:—

"*Palcrats, Slavonia, Nov. 30th,* 1878.

"We arrived in the midst of the preparation for the departure of the fugitives in this district. They were to go off in two days, so we at once set about supplying the poor travellers with blankets and opankés, and giving what help we could. After all, the journey had to be given up because of the floods, and the fugitives are still here. About 20,000 from various parts were got over into Bosnia, and these are dying in hundreds, totally unsheltered and starving. No preparation or provision was made, and the repatriation has been carried on recklessly and cruelly by the Government order. Nearly everywhere the local officials have protested against it, but little heed has been paid to what they say. The miserable Bosnians—old, sick, infants of two or three days old, dying mothers—were forced to leave the poor shelter they had been in for three years, and start on a journey through miles of mud and marsh, often of several days' length. No wonder that so many died on the road. Many old people and children died each night. The rapid overflowing of the Save put a merciful stop to this for a time, and many of the worn-out, weary creatures have returned to their temporary homes. We hear that to-day and to-morrow those who are already on the way, lodged in the villages close to the frontier, are to be driven across and set down each to find his way to the ashes of his former home. Winter has already set in, and nothing can exceed the misery and suffering of these doubly-persecuted creatures. They are full of bitterness about the Austrians, whose coming was to have brought peace and happiness, but who begin by almost greater cruelty than the Turks. So many orphans are left to be helped and provided for. We have obtained special leave for our two schools here to continue till the spring—a girls' and a boys'—with two of our best Bosnian teachers. . . . We are going to see after the orphans in Dalmatia, whence the greater part of the fugitives have already gone over into Bosnia to villages near the frontier, where we hope to be able to visit and help them. We were surprised and very grateful to see in our list £42 from Edinburgh. It does, indeed, show the real pity and interest felt for those poor refugees that their wants are thought of in a time of calamity such as it is in Scotland. Miss Irby sends her love to you and all kind helpers."

A correspondent of *The Daily News* writes as follows:

"On Thursday morning some 300 were just starting for Berbir, when a telegram arrived to say the inundations were so high that the departure was to be delayed till further notice. From other villages the fugitives were already on the way, and that night several caravans, amounting in all to about 300 persons, arrived together in the village of Okucane. One of these caravans had returned from Gradiska, the waters having been too high for it to proceed. That was a miserable night in Okucane, numbers having to remain out shelterless in the cold mist and rain; but the scene last week near the river can hardly be imagined. Weary, sullen men, trudging behind the carts piled with women and children and their poor possessions. Women and children, too, on foot, up to their bare knees in mire. One must have seen the mud in the lands of the Danube and Save to picture it, and it is worth seeing once as the veritable Slough of Despond. One poor, weary woman, with her child on her back, fell in the mud and was choked to death. Little children—I know not exactly how many—met the same fate; fell down, and were choked in this hideous mud. After two or three days' tramping on foot through wet and mire, many sickly ones have perished by the wayside. A little cross here and there along the road now marks the spot where, last week, one and another sank down, died, and was buried."

It is difficult to ask for money at a time when there is so much ruin and distress at home; but from the above it will be seen how impossible it is to refuse effort to obtain the aid which the devoted ladies, who are risking health and life on behalf of the sufferers, so earnestly entreat.

FRESH LETTERS FROM BOSNIA.

Perhaps at no time in the memory of most of us, was the whole world (as it often seems) so groaning with unutterable distress as now, and the only way to meet our daily work properly is to ask for calmness, and trust, and courage, to continue doing the little we can do to any, in whichever cause we seem able to be of most use. Some may think it out of place while such distress prevails at home to ask for help still for the poor Slavonian Christians; and yet as long as such brave and devoted almoners can be found as the Misses Irby and Johnston, we may surely spare yet a trifle to keep them at their terrible post; for, without our help, every bitter night, while we are enjoying the ample comforts of home, these Slavonian fellow-Christians of ours are slowly but surely freezing to death beside their few smouldering sticks, almost naked and without food! The following extracts from recent letters need no comment—except that Friends will see that it is their donations which enable the ladies to keep many of these sufferers alive, who otherwise must have been starved or frozen to death. Since last month's account I have made up a collection of £70, and have £40 in hand, which will soon follow.

SOPHIA MAY.

Bruce Grove, Tottenham,
Second Month 13th, 1879.

From P. H. Johnston:—
"*Knin, Dalmatia, Jan. 20th, 1879.*
". . . I have waited, before giving myself the pleasure of answering your delightful letter, to be able to tell you the result of an expedition we have been sending into Bosnia, for the relief of the returned fugitives, who are living and dying there in the utmost misery. Mr. Evans, who took charge of the caravan, returned yesterday, bringing a most grievous history of the suffering he has seen." [Extracts from this account are subjoined.] "We sent twenty horses loaded with bread, flour, and clothing; and shall do this as often as our means allow. It is quite clear that the returned fugitives cannot exist without help till the next harvest, and that without gifts of implements and seed-corn there can be *no harvest.* . . . I wish you could see the number of hungry ragged little boys, who make their way over from Bosnia to see us, and to beg to be taken back to school; their poor little school-books, bag, and treasures carefully preserved, and their piteous entreaties to us to take them back. We can only clothe and feed them, and send them away happy with a Testament; keeping, of course, those who have no one in the world to take care of them; the answer to our question is so often, 'No one but God and you.' . . ."

THE BOSNIANS—LETTER FROM P. H. JOHNSTON.

Knin, 7th June, 1879.

My Dear Miss May,—I can only send one line for we have a distribution on hand to-day, and there is no time—but one word of thanks we must say! Last night arrived a telegram from my brother telling us of another £500. It is delightful to be able to call hundreds more of these wretched, hopeless creatures, to be fed and cheered and put in the way of helping themselves. Miss Irby is now arranging who to send for, *i.e.*, which districts want most.

Such heat has set in that every movement is labour. Happily the sufferings of the Bosnians are greatly diminished by it, and we have no more urgent petitions for blankets.   *   *   *

Knin, 11th June, 1879.

Your letter of 2nd came after I had written to you. We are stopped in the middle of a large distribution, for want of small change, and so I have the opportunity of sending you a line.

We are thankfully and hopefully giving out the money which has come in, in answer to the appeal suggested and circulated by you.

If only the poor down-trodden, spiritless, pauperized creatures are thrifty and industrious, those reached by our help *have* the means of a fresh (very small certainly) start in life.

On the way to Strinitza last Saturday, we passed numbers of Bosnians driving sheep, lambs, kids, and pigs back into Bosnia. They had received money from us and had gone to Knin on market-day to make their purchases. As there is plenty of grass for the animals, this is an unmixed benefit. We thought how much pleased you would have been if you could have seen the treasures being carefully driven, and stopped to rest and refresh wherever there were water and grass. A well-fed sheep will give a good deal of milk, then there is the wool and the profit of the lamb, whether kept or sold.   *   *   *

I don't think I told you of our last "rescue." A girl of 13 crawled and tottered here apparently dying: the doctor says she has no complaint, but was in the last stage of starvation. The old woman we sent for to wash her said afterwards she had never seen such a fearful sight as this girl. Our German servant tells us she is like a skeleton. Her hands and arms are like sticks, but her state is impossible to describe. We are doing our utmost to save her, but the doctor thinks it very doubtful if she can live. She says she had been living on grass and leaves. Such a beaming smile of gratitude comes over her poor, sad face whenever she sees us. Of course the charge of her devolves on our good Anna, who feeds her up and watches over her. If she lives we shall take her with us.

The heat is becoming almost unbearable. * * *

Very affectionately yours,
P. H. Johnston.

JOY IN BOSNIA.

It is indeed true that the darkest hour comes just before dawn, and how lovely and refreshing is that dawn to those who have watched through the long, dreary night! Such a dawn our friend Priscilla Johnston is delighting in, and very warm and loving thanks does she send to those whose efforts, through our Father's blessing, have rolled away at last the darkness hanging over the sad land of Bosnia. Some weeks ago she wrote me word that their funds were all but exhausted, and that they must, unless helped again in their work of rescue, soon come away, as they could not stay there to *see the people die* of hunger and exposure.

Again she wrote, begging me to *telegraph*, if her appeal to the Yearly Meeting met with a response, as, she said, "we are nearly *penniless*." Judge, then, of her delight, at receiving first £500 "from some good liberal," calling the hopeless people round her, and sending them away, with food, seed, and tools, "hugging the latter with joy;" and, soon afterwards, £500 again, chiefly from Friends. The number of donors is so great that we cannot here publish names, but I may just say that I received at the time of the Yearly Meeting £120; since then I have been enabled by my kind friends to add £50, and already about £12 more has reached me.

As P. H. Johnston is wishing to supply all the villages near her, before leaving Knin, I have asked her to advance for us up to £50. Therefore any friend wishing to help still, will feel that it is not too late to send a trifle for seed, tools, or animals. When the ladies leave Knin, they will occupy themselves in making provision, for the next *six years*, for the numerous orphans of the murdered Christians, left *desolate*, but for their kindness and love; and as I am very desirous to help them in this beautiful work, I shall with great pleasure receive the name of anyone wishing to become a yearly subscriber, or to make a donation towards a fixed income, and shall gladly receive from 5s. upwards for this purpose. I subjoin extracts from the most cheering letters referred to above, and add many, many thanks to all workers.

SOPHIA MAY.
Bruce Grove, Tottenham, 21st of Sixth Month, 1879.

Knin, June 7th, 1879.

MY DEAR MISS MAY,—I can only send one line, for we have a distribution on hand to-day, and there is no time; but one word of thanks we must say. Last night a telegram arrived from my brother telling us of another £500, and this we feel sure is owing to your labours. It is delightful to be able to call hundreds more of these wretched, hopeless creatures, to be fed and cheered and put in the way of helping themselves. Miss Irby is now arranging whom to send for, *i.e.,* which districts want most.

Such heat has set in that every movement is labour; happily the sufferings of the Bosnians are greatly diminished by it, and we have no more urgent petitions for blankets. . . .

Knin, June 11th, 1879.

Your letter of 2nd came after I had written to you. We are stopped in the middle of a large distribution for want of small change, and so I have the opportunity of sending you a line.

We are thankfully and hopefully giving out the money which has come in, in answer to the appeal suggested and circulated by you.

If only the poor, down-trodden, spiritless, pauperised creatures, are thrifty and industrious, those reached by our help *have* the means of a fresh, though very small, start in life.

On the way to Strinitza, last Saturday, we passed numbers of Bosnians driving sheep, lambs, kids, and pigs, back into Bosnia. They had received money from us and had gone to Knin on market day to make their purchases. As there is plenty of grass for the animals, this is an unmixed benefit. We thought how much pleased *you* would have been if you could have seen the treasures being carefully driven and stopped to rest and refresh wherever there were water and grass. A well-fed sheep will give a good deal of milk; then there is the wool and the profit of the lamb, whether kept or sold. . . . I do not think I told you of our last "rescue." A girl of thirteen crawled and tottered here apparently dying; the doctor says she has no complaint, but was in the last stage of starvation. The old woman we sent for to wash her said afterwards she had never seen such a fearful sight as this girl. Our German servant tells us she is like a skeleton. Her hands and arms are like sticks, but her state is impossible to describe. We are doing our utmost to save her, but the doctor thinks it very doubtful if she can live. She says she had been living on grass and leaves. Such a beaming smile of gratitude comes over her poor, sad face, whenever she sees us! Of course the charge of her devolves on our good Anna, who feeds her up and watches over her. If she lives we shall take her with us.

The heat is becoming almost unbearable. . . .

Very affectionately yours,
P. H. JOHNSTON.

BOSNIANS REPATRIATED.

So many friends aided the poor Bosnians in their exile and sore distress, that the following extract of a recent letter from Priscilla Johnston to a lady in Edinburgh will be interesting to them. No wonder it felt strange to return to the capital of Bosnia after all that had passed. The little company of girls, to whom allusion is made, was sent to Prague in the beginning of the insurrection that they might be gaining instruction to aid their country when the troubles should be over—little did they think how long and sharp those troubles would be! Now a little insight is given into the new plans for their benefit projected by their devoted friends. The extract is dated

"SERAJEVO, *July 30, 1879.*

" . . . . We are in the midst of much business, but I must find time to send you a note to tell you how we are getting on. We left Adilsberg on the 9th. The next day was spent on the Save. And we reached Brood in the evening, to start in the middle of the night by the new railway, which is opened half the distance to Serajevo. It was a very interesting and curious journey to us, as you can fancy, and we lost nothing of the country or people as the train went slowly along, for the carriages are only small cattle trucks with benches on two sides and we could see all around. The journey lasted from 3.30 a.m. to 8.30 p.m. We reached Serajevo on Saturday night, and were welcomed by the nine children we had sent from Knin, all looking the better already for the change from the heat of Dalmatia to this delicious, almost mountain air, and rejoicing in the large airy house and garden. Since then has been a busy time getting things in order and beginning lessons.

We heard of the death of our dear little Anitza who was left near Prague with Miss Walker. She was the cleverest and best of all our girls, a most true and devoted little Christian, and the one who had most longed to return to help her own country.

I hope to send you soon a translation of a letter she wrote to Miss Irby four days before she died, and of a little prayer which Miss Brook found written by her. She is the third we have lost since we took the party to Prague. The rest now return to finish their own education and to teach the younger children. Next week 15 more orphans from Rickrutz and then eight or nine from Plassis, we shall have in all 28. Fifteen boys will live in a separate house with the Bosnian schoolmaster and his wife, and we shall keep two very little ones with the girls. The poor starved girl I told you about is gaining health and strength and is very industrious in housework. School work seems almost beyond her power at present. We hope to train all the clever and willing ones as future schoolmistresses, and the rest as useful servants. The girls do all the house work of the home and help in cooking and washing. We have only one servant within doors.

We are very glad to find a young woman, who, as a child, was in the school, now earning a good living, and supporting her mother by washing, learnt here. And two more established as nurse and cook with the wife of the French Consul.

The dearness of living here alarms us a good deal, prices have risen enormously. We have a sum reserved for schools and orphans, but out of it we have to support several day schools which have been set agoing in Bosnia, and any how it will not last long under such heavy demands. We shall be most thankful for help in the autumn and winter, when we intend to issue a little account of, and appeal for, the orphans left on our hands. We shall also be glad of good, strong, already worn clothes, as there is great difficulty in getting anything here.

> *Serajevo, August 24th, 1879.*
>
> My dear Miss May,—... We are so very busy that I fear you will have but a short letter; the principal reason of this is that all our three governesses are ailing, one girl dangerously ill, and others poorly, and all the work these various incidents necessitate must be performed in heat rarely below 80°; but it is our hope and desire to lead a quiet regular life, and not be *always* overpressed. I am head nurse, and am often to be seen scampering about with little trays of food, and dressing wounded feet, &c.; I suppose we must not expect ever to be free of ailments in a large party of children, most of whom have been permanently weakened and injured by starvation. ... I was to have left Serajevo about September 1st, but now I hardly know how to leave Miss Irby with sickly helpers and children, and no one to stand by her; I believe I shall be in England during October and November. We have hardly had time yet to turn to the great question of how we are to keep all these children, but we are sure at least of your help. It is grievous to hear of the destitute orphans in and near Dalmatia; people write imploring us to keep them on where they are—boarded, cared for, and taught under a man we can trust; but it cannot be done under nine guldens a month each child (about 15s. 6d.), and there are thirty boys utterly destitute. If we can we shall keep them through next winter, getting rid of them as fast as little situations or apprenticeships open up for them to earn their own living. As you will have seen in the papers a great calamity has happened here from which we were preserved, but, like everyone else, we suffer much indirectly, for prices have risen enormously, and the daily expenses of our household grow alarming. But I do wish you could see the fat, happy children, shouting and laughing in the garden, and when they are all tucked into little clean, comfortable beds.
>
> A foundling kitten, a poor little starved thing I found mewing in the yard of an empty house, now grown fat and strong and named "Sunbeam," is competed for, and sleeps in one or other little bed with the children. There is high joy when I come in and go round. ... It is all such a wonderful contrast to their former life, as you can suppose. ...
>
> Very affectionately yours,
> P. H. JOHNSTON.

In August 1880 Priscilla gave an account of daily life that was simple, hardworking and devoutly Christian:

> We have only one indoor servant so that the girls do everything by turns, so that each gets a share of house and kitchen work, washing, cow keeping and a little gardening. Besides they have five hours schooling daily, and make and mend all their own things and the boys' 'underclothing'. The boys are kept equally busy with indoor and outdoor activities. As well as carrying wood and water, some of them can also scrub floors and sweep cleverly, and they consider it an honour to be employed in this way ... Twice a week the whole house is washed, on other days swept. Sunday is a happy day of rest and scripture reading.[31]

In 1881 it became necessary to extend the school house. The house which had seemed so large and superior when it had been built in 1868, with its two storeys, its large high rooms and the long gardens that stretched down to the river Miljacka, could now barely accommodate all the girls. The boys had been installed in another house, which had been purchased nearby, under the care of a 'kind, stirring Serbian widow'. Now a new roof was put on and additional rooms built. Much disturbance was caused in the street outside by the laying of new drains. This year their travelling sequence had been different: Paulina stayed in Sarajevo throughout the summer to supervise the alterations, which she found to be 'a very trying time due to the considerable noise and disruption'. Priscilla and the English teacher had made the journey back to England.

Further letters which appeared in *The Friend*, concerning Priscilla's final years in Bosnia.

Seventh Month 3, 1880.]   THE FRIEND.   199

PRISCILLA JOHNSTON AND THE ORPHANAGE IN BOSNIA.

Those who have worked and prayed for the orphans under the care of P. H. Johnston and her friends, during four years of terrible trial, will be deeply thankful to hear of a company of hearty, lively, merry little children, forgetful of the horrors of their babyhood, as the result of the self-sacrificing work of these two ladies.

The following letter—lately received, and written very much for those kind readers of *The Friend* who are supporting in great measure these little ones in their happy "home"—tells all what they will chiefly wish to know, and will be felt by many a rich reward for the trouble they have taken in this satisfactory work.

SOPHIA MAY.
Bruce Grove, Tottenham, Sixth Month 17th, 1880.

Extract from the latest letter from P. H. Johnston:—

"MY DEAR MISS MAY,—. . . . Our large family of orphans so fills up my time that there is hardly any left for sitting down to read or write. My work begins at 6 a.m., so I am up at 5·30. Our matron is gone (whether for a holiday or permanently is not yet decided), so that a good deal more is thrown on us in the actual management of the school. We have now twenty-six girls and thirty-eight boys on our hands, besides many boys already placed out to learn trades and earn their own living.

"We are breaking up the orphanage in Dalmatia now, as we could hardly supervise it from such a distance. Sixteen of the children arrived here under good care last week, and there will be about ten more to come here, or be provided for till the end of July. The boys sleep in a neighbouring house, which we have bought, and are under the care of a clean careful widow woman. They all have their meals and learn here, and at other times are busy working in the garden under the charge of the gardener and his wife. . . . .

"I wish you could just peep in upon us, I am sure you would be pleased and interested in our busy hive. From 9 till 12 a.m. lessons are going on in the schoolroom and two class-rooms; thus there are two hours for dinner and recreation, three hours more school and needlework in the afternoon; housework is got through from six till nine in the morning, and the girls take turns to be in the kitchen helping the cook, our only servant indoors.

"To-morrow one of our girls is going to a nice situation, which we have found for her with the wife of an engineer (quiet and respectable people), for we are bringing them all up to earn their own living, either as teachers or servants. Our eldest is already of great use in the house; she makes all the bread, and milks the cows, but has no gift for learning.

"The two next, who have been with us ten and seven years, teach the two younger classes, and take charge of the children generally at meals, &c.; they are both good and steady girls, and devoted to the school. These two know German and English, besides being very forward with their other studies; one of them comes from a village about six hours' distant from Serajevo, and her great hope is to go home and establish a school there as soon as she is qualified. The other will, I hope, always remain with us. . . . .

"Very affectionately yours,
"P. H. JOHNSTON."

OUR LITTLE BOSNIANS.

Autumn has come, so winter will soon be here, and Priscilla Johnston is already considering how the large family of little Bosnians, under the care of herself and Miss Irby, are to be clothed when the severe weather comes, of which we know but little in England.

She has written to me for assistance in this work, and as she concludes her letter by saying, "Will you ask the Friends?" I give it almost entire, and will very gladly take charge of any clothes which the English mothers can spare, or old stock from shops. Next month I hope for a little statement of the past year from P. H. J., to lay before the yearly subscribers on the collection of their kindly promised subscriptions.

As regards girls' clothing Miss J. says, "We shall also be glad of a moderate supply of good warm girls' things."

SOPHIA MAY.

Bruce Grove, Tottenham, N.,
Eighth Month 18th, 1880.

"*Serajevo, July 15th,* 1880.

"MY DEAR MISS MAY,—I have been wishing to write to you ever since the bale arrived containing the boys' clothes you sent us, to tell you of the delight they gave to the children, and how very acceptable and helpful they are to us. Our boys were almost in rags, and had only one suit each for Sundays and week-days; for we find everything bought here is so very dear and bad that it is no use trying to get their things here. We had an amusing scene fitting the boys out, and when it was finished they looked like a party of nicely dressed little English gentlemen. The caps were especially admired and coveted; the eight youngest had them. We have so thanked you. . . .

"In spite of the long summer before us, we are beginning to consider anxiously about winter clothing, especially for the boys, for we are clear that in spite of the heavy carriage and duty, it is much cheaper to get it from England than to attempt to buy it here. *Will you help us still?* We shall want twenty very strong warm suits for working days, and the same for Sundays and holidays. Clothes already worn answer much better than new, as they fit better, and trousers are better than knickerbockers, for the great cold of Bosnian winters. I think in the summer holidays in England a great many mothers will find their sons have outgrown their last winter suits; and though I know how many there are who want clothes in England, I feel sure some of those who have been so wonderfully generous to, and sympathising with, these poor Bosnians, will remember our boys. We have now twenty-four, but we hope to get four at least into situations before the winter. Those we keep are all under twelve, except two invalids of fourteen. We have already placed out twelve to learn trades, and they are all doing well. Their masters clothe them and feed them, and they mostly spend their Sundays with us. We had looked forward to difficulties in our mixed party of boys and girls, but we have never had one from that cause. The boys sleep in another house, but are all here for the day, and mix freely with the girls, doing a good deal of the heavier house-work and carrying water. There are several little sets of brothers and sisters among them, and it is pretty to see the motherly interest of the girls in the boys' conduct and clothing. Miss Irby has engaged a German lady to come out, as it is necessary for our children all to learn German, as the country is to belong to Austria. Miss Walker will not return.

"Affectionately yours,
"P. H. JOHNSTON."

OUR LITTLE ORPHANS IN BOSNIA.

The following letter, lately received from Priscilla Johnston, will be of interest to the many kind friends who continue by their subscriptions to keep up this delightful home for the otherwise utterly homeless little ones, and at the same time an explanation of the anxiety felt lest the interest in it should flag. For four more years the two ladies expect to depend very much on English help in educating and placing out their great family; after that time they hope that with but little assistance they can maintain the few who may still be too young, weak, or backward, to work for themselves. It will gladden many loving hearts to read of the Christmas rejoicing of these once-suffering and starving children.

Warmly thanking those who have enabled me to send so much aid already, I commend this bright letter to their attention.

SOPHIA MAY.

Bruce Grove, Tottenham,
Second Month 20th, 1881.

Serajevo, Bosnia, Austria.
January 15th, 1881.

MY DEAR MISS MAY,—I am very glad to be able at last to sit down and answer your delightful New Year's letter. You and I have been equally busy, I think, lately; I am so glad to hear of the success you have had in your labours for the Boys' Home. My great press of work came to an end with Miss Irby's return on January 1st, but since then we have had the great business of preparing, with scanty material, the immense treat for our forty-one children, of a Christmas tree. And now directly that is happily over, I am rightsiding and making preparation for setting off homewards for a holiday. I did long for you on Thursday evening (the New Year's day, Old Style) when our good Governor-General, the Duke of Wurtemburg, came to help us to distribute the presents from the tree. He is such a dear fatherly old man, and takes so real and detailed an interest, that the children's joy was quite unchecked by his presence, and the clatter and fun were deafening—reaching a climax when the topmost doll was cut down by a tall young A.D.C. with his sword, being too high to reach otherwise. Our family is just now in high health and spirits; there is a very bright, busy spirit in the house, and all is going well; but at times, when I was single-handed during the autumn, when some of the children were very ill, it was all I could do to struggle through the work, day and night. With only one servant and two rather delicate governesses, I was thankful indeed to be in thoroughly good strong health myself, for there were some days when I was the only grown-up person about the house. We have a charming young German governess, but she is very delicate, and has had already three really sharp attacks of illness, with, of course, no one to attend to her but me, in addition to the rest of my occupation. I have I know been remiss about writing, but I don't think you want our gratitude *expressed*. You know how true and hearty it is. We are much cheered by hearing of the £230. Bosnia has now become such a very dear place that we are sometimes doubtful if we can go on keeping so many children. We are going to place a girl out now with the Bible Society's colporteur's wife, as kindermädchen; but it is most difficult to find respectable places here for girls, and ours are necessarily a little spoilt for "echt," Bosnian houses. They are particular about cleanliness and order—not reigning attributes in this country.

Very affectionately yours,
P. H. JOHNSTON.

[Tenth Month 2, 1882.] THE FRIEND. 261

ANNUAL ACCOUNT OF THE BOSNIAN ORPHAN HOME.

Extract from a letter from Priscilla Johnston to Miss May, dated Rickerby, Carlisle, September 5th, 1882:—

"I am hoping to return to Bosnia soon. In the meantime I have excellent accounts from Miss Irby of the welfare of her large household. She says that this is a critical time for the school, and that she hopes to be able now to get it authorised by the Government to send out schoolmistresses into the country. Without this Government recognition we cannot do anything for the education of any girls besides our own in poor, downtrodden, miserable Bosnia. It is Miss Irby's earnest desire to spread the benefits of civilisation and education which the children we have been able to rescue are receiving; and to combine this with the care of starving, destitute little ones.

"Since last autumn we have received seven new children. Our house was already pretty full, but each of these seven was in such urgent need of shelter, food, clothing, everything, that we could not bear to turn one away. Miss Brooks, our excellent helper in the work, writes:—'Two more children were taken in about three weeks ago, sisters. The youngest such a poor, puny little thing that I thought it could scarcely be two years old, though it is really three. When I saw it for the first time, and it was put down to run about, it looked, with its small head, legs like sticks, and hollow eyes, just like a little monkey in clothes. But it is wonderful what kindness and care have already done for it. I noticed even two days after it was brought to us a change in its little face. There is no longer that monkey-like expression, it looks happy and contented, and I sometimes hear it laughing and running about quite gaily. This is the youngest member of our large family, and is the special charge of one of the elder girls, who took to her from the first. Indeed all the girls are very kind to the little mite. I fitted these two children out with clothes from the store of things sent us by Miss May.

"Milë, the little fellow who was brought here in a box, is growing a big boy; one of the big girls is his 'aunt,' and she looks after him. Iovanka, a girl of about seventeen, went to a nice situation in the spring. She often comes to see us on Sunday afternoons, and stays for the Bible-lesson. We have now altogether twenty-seven girls and one boy in this house, and eleven boys in another—thirty-nine in all. We have had our summer examination very sucessfully. It was said that of all the examinations at the various schools in the town, ours and the one at the Jewish school were the best.

"We hope for the continued help and sympathy of the Friends. I think if any one could see our rows of happy, healthy children, and could contrast the scene, as we can do, with the poverty and terrible suffering in which we found them, they would feel thankful to have been the means of giving these blessings to children so direly in need of them. . . .

"We shall be extremely glad of good, warm clothing, either new or worn, for boys and girls of all ages."

Although before long the annual report, &c., will be sent round to subscribers, yet I will just add, for my friend P. H. Johnston, that I shall again this year gratefully take charge of clothes or money for our little friends in the orphan home.

SOPHIA MAY.

Bruce Grove, Tottenham, September, 1882.

By 1884 the school numbered thirty-three girls and five boys. Their lessons included German as well as the essentials of a Serb education. The entire expenses of the school, clothing, feeding and supplying of teachers fell on Miss Johnston and Miss Irby; and contributions towards the sum of £400, which was required each year, were most welcome.[32]

In 1885 came another break in the pattern: Priscilla returned to England and her sister Euphemia's family, the MacInneses, for good. In 1884 she was with Paulina in Sarajevo, but by 1885 Paulina was the sole directress of the school. Carlisle directories for 1885 list Priscilla as residing at The Beeches, Rickerby Village. There is no record of why she returned to England. It is only possible to surmise.

During the years of insurrection there had been essential work to be done, each day and every day, and in the actual striving and coping. In their new life in the 'Austrian' Sarajevo there was no great drama, just a humdrum round of lessons and children growing and petty domestic difficulties. Perhaps she felt her work here was complete and she could be of help to others elsewhere. 'She had played her part on the open stage of humanitarianism, and had done her duty as a Buxton and a Johnston and a great-niece of Elizabeth Fry.'[33]

OUR BOSNIAN ORPHANS.

By way of Annual Report this year I will give recent accounts from Miss Irby's and Miss Johnston's pen, adding that I shall most gladly receive all subscriptions, gifts of clothes, &c., as usual.

This is the last of the six years during which I asked for help, for the little fugitives, most of whose parents had been barbarously murdered or hunted to death by the Turks. It is with deep gratitude to all who have assisted in the work, that I look back on the five years already past, and note that during that time we have sent for the support of these helpless ones £1,606 15s.

As several of the children are quite too young and tender to be sent out, even into the best situations, I shall be very thankful if some of our friends will continue their subscriptions a little longer.

Miss Irby also begs me to add that the school (which part of the undertaking was commenced years before the last massacre of the Christians) will be continued as usual, if the funds make it possible ; but that it will require the assistance of those interested in these down-trodden Sclavonian Christians to make it at all efficient.

SOPHIA MAY.

Bruce Grove, Tottenham, September, 1884.

Miss Johnston writes this summer (1884) as follows :—

"There is now a most happy flock of little children, all girls except one, a boy of about five ; their little voices and steps are rarely quiet about the house and garden, except when they are at lessons, and meals, or asleep in their little beds. I wish you could see them at their first lesson in the morning, clustered round Miss Brooks, repeating their texts and hymns, and learning new ones. She says, 'Now, Milka, say me a verse about God.' Baby Milka quickly answers, 'God is love.' 'Sofitza, how does the Bible teach us that we should behave to each other?' 'Do unto others as ye would they should do unto you,' says Sofitza : others chime in with, 'Love one another,' 'Let love be without dissimulation,' &c.—showing that the repetition of the verses is not merely parrot-like, but that they understand the meaning and application. Some of the elder girls are very fond of the little ones, and proud to show off their attainments. One of them is constituted knitting mistress to the babies, who daily collect for an hour of severe labour with wool and needles, resulting in the production of some very creditable work from the little fingers. The first stocking is always a great triumph and cause of rejoicing. Of course these infants are not supposed to do any of the housework, but it often surprises me how quickly and nicely they can clear and neaten the playground and yard, and how delighted they are to be entrusted with a broom and have a little task of sweeping appointed them. Two of the elder girls are now regular teachers of fourteen little ones in two classes, for two hours every morning, and have brought them on very nicely in reading, writing, and spelling. Those of the elder ones who are being trained for teachers are taught German, arithmetic, and dressmaking by a German lady ; grammar, history, &c., by a teacher of their own nationality, and various subjects by Miss Brooks—who also gives Scripture lessons daily. There are several of the girls who can cook, wash, milk the cows, and do house and needlework very well, and they are in demand as wives and servants, but it is not easy to find safe situations for them where they would be carefully looked after. Our Sunday evening hymn singings with the harmonium are a great pleasure, and the girls know quite enough German to enjoy the number of beautiful hymns and translations in that language ; we are never allowed to stop till nine o'clock, their bed-time, has fully arrived. They pick up new tunes very easily and sing them about the house, and at their work."

One of Priscilla's final letters concerning her work in Bosnia, dated August 1884

PART FOUR

Aunt 'Pris' of The Beeches, Rickerby Village, Carlisle (1885–1912)

Aunt 'Pris' of Rickerby

29

Introduction

In 1885 Priscilla, having returned to England now came to Carlisle to be nearer to her sister, Effie, the wife of the banker and MP, Miles MacInnes of Rickerby. In September 1884 the MacInneses had been deeply saddened by the death of their eldest son, 21-year-old Harry. By moving to Carlisle, Priscilla would be 'on hand' to support her beloved sister through this distressing period. She took up residence at The Beeches, Rickerby Village, near Carlisle. Here she resided with her good friend Miss Amy Beevor, the retired headmistress of Carlisle High School for Girls.

The Beeches, Rickerby Village, the country home of Aunt 'Pris' and Miss Beevor. Also in residence at the time were Emily Jane Casey, parlour maid; Jane Elizabeth, servant; and Mary the cook. Today The Beeches is home to the Cawley family.

For the rest of her life she was known as Aunt 'Pris' to all the Johnston and MacInnes young relatives: Aunt 'Pris' who was interested in good works, who was particularly attached to animals to the extent of being mildly eccentric in her attentions towards them. It was Aunt 'Pris' who had a horse trough built on the bridge at Stanwix and who arranged for an annual supper for the local drovers.'

Bosnia, as the years went by, was forgotten, pushed away into the recesses of her mind and never talked about. No legends grew up in the MacInnes family of Aunt 'Pris' and the Bosnian children, of the starving refugees she had helped to keep alive, of the journeys by cart through snowdrifts and blizzards, of the treks by horse over the bare mountains in blistering heat, of the Cross of Takovo which had been awarded to her for her great services. When she died in January 1912 there were no reminders that for some thirteen years of her life Priscilla Hannah Johnston had worked and lived abroad, 'in the Balkans'. Only one relic remained: a 'Bosnian boy's costume' preserved in an attic, its source and its history unknown.

Once settled in Carlisle Priscilla found plenty to employ her. In her life, both in private and in public she devoted her energies to good works for the poor and the suffering in the area. 'Her purse and ear were always open to the tale of sorrow and need, and yet she was not readily deceived.' Priscilla would sometimes say that her affinity with the hungry and the needy was due to a practical experience of insufficient food. There were many poor and destitute whose needs she discovered for herself by personal contact with them in their homes. At this time around 10,000 people were living in the cramped and squalid housing in the area of Carlisle known as 'The Lanes'. Here malnutrition and disease, especially tuberculosis, were rife, causing a quarter of all deaths. Up to a quarter of children did not live to see their first birthday day.[1]

However, Priscilla did take some time out from her philanthropic work in Carlisle, returning periodically to visit her extended family at Cromer, one such occasion being recorded thus in the 1904 Overstrand Church Parish Chronicle:

> The church bell at Overstrand was used for the first time after being recast, on Sunday, October 16th. The old bell which summoned the villagers to church for nearly 300 years has for a long while been seriously cracked. Miss Johnston, grand-daughter of the late Sir T. Fowell Buxton, Bart, most kindly took the matter up this summer, while staying at Cromer, and collected sufficient money

from the late Fowell Buxton's direct descendants to have it restored. The bell bore the date Anno Domini 1605, and the mark of William Brand, Bell Founder, of Norwich and Alice his wife. Additional metal has been added so as to make the bell larger and to give it a deeper and richer tone; it can now be heard all over the village. A brass tablet will be put up in the church with the following inscription:

<blockquote>
'TO THE GLORY OF GOD
The bell of this church, bearing date 1605
was recast in 1904.
The work was undertaken by descendants of
Thomas Fowell and Hannah Buxton
In grateful memory of their bright example.'[2]
</blockquote>

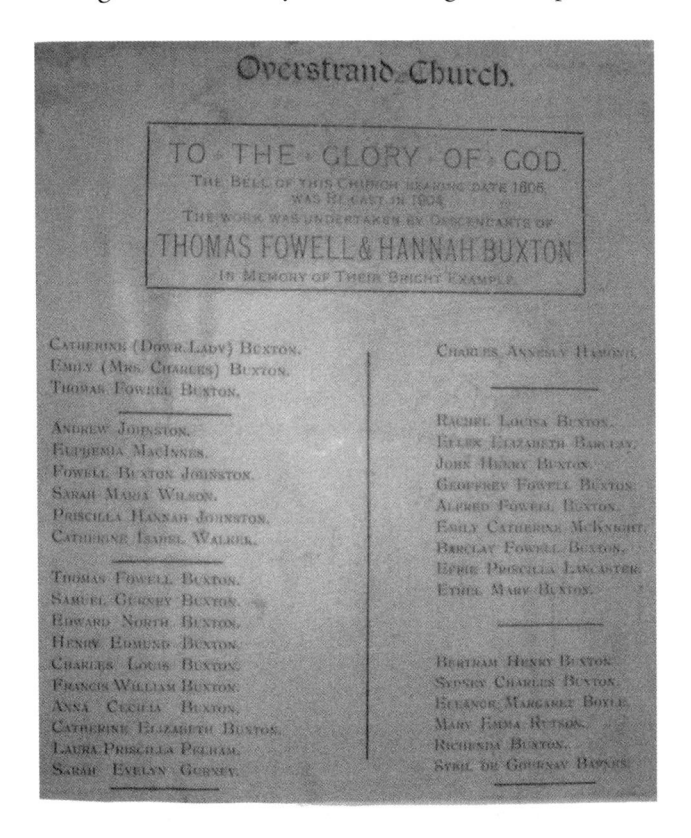

The Memorial Tablet in Overstrand Church, commemorating the occasion of the restoration of the Bell

281

At Carlisle Aunt 'Pris' became fastidious to a fault in her personal tastes and little inclined for society with a large 'S'. She made many gatherings happy on summer evenings at her country dwelling, and bettered the fare in many a cottage home. That the guest was poor was the greatest reason for providing the daintiest dish.

From her mother's family, having inherited a passion for freedom and a hatred of oppression which in her gentle personality found practical embodiment in her work for animals, she became a generous supporter of the philanthropic institutions in Carlisle, taking a particular interest in the Society for the Prevention of Cruelty to Animals, with which she was associated since its inauguration. For a time becoming joint secretary with Mr G.F. Saul, who later occupied the post on his own. In connection with the latter organisation she started the 'drovers' supper' in around 1892, for some years being responsible for this at her own expense. Eventually, the Society recognising the beneficial results of this annual opportunity of getting in touch with 'the man with the willow wand', eventually assumed financial responsibility through the generous donations of money and kind given to them with an almost lavish hand by butchers, livestock breeders and trades people of the area. At the time Cumberland was proud to boast imitators of the plan up and down the country.

Her interest in the welfare and kind treatment of animals was not confined to this country. She was also secretary in England, almost from its inception, of the Naples Society for the Protection of Animals. She was also behind the movement for the establishment in the district of the kindred organisation, the National Society for the Prevention of Cruelty to Children, which also found in her a generous friend.

Her other charitable works included a warm support of the Carlisle Charitable Organisation Society. Liberal by birth and education, she viewed with no misgiving the social legislation which terrified many of her sex and standing. Her gentle exterior hardly prepared her fellow workers for her shrewd hits at their 'too ready acquiescence of the existing social conditions.' Long before the gospel of physical culture was preached and practised by the social worker, she started a drilling class, held at the ragged school[3] for girls; it was the forerunner of the girls' clubs which later began in Carlisle.

She also joined in the experiment of carrying the slum children of the Caldewgate area of Carlisle to the fresh air of the nearby Solway seaside resort of Silloth. What began as an experiment in 1894 soon became a regular four-outings-a-year event. Over the next eighteen years Aunt 'Pris' saw over 23,000 poor children from various parts of the city enabled to spend an afternoon at the seaside. A complete immunity from accidents characterised these outings from the beginning, and when regard is given to the difficult nature of the work this was certainly a splendid achievement. The work was un-denominational and all members of the committee paid their own expenses. Activities were also funded by several subscriptions donated by the readers of the *Carlisle Journal*.

For a number of years she was a member of the Carlisle Board of Guardians, which had been set up to oversee the running of the Fusehill Workhouse. More than one reform at Fusehill was due to her suggestion and influence. However, she never claimed or desired the credit for such improvements, being simply content that they should be effected. Priscilla also became one of the vice-presidents, and a devoted adherent of the British Women's Temperance Association, which held its annual meetings in The Friends Meeting House, Fisher Street. She was also a much valued worker on the general committee of the Carlisle District Nursing Association.

As the years passed and her eyesight and health failed she withdrew from many activities and rejoiced to see her place filled by others, but in the hearts of those who mourned her passing, her place could never be filled.[4]

Introducing The MacInnes family of Rickerby

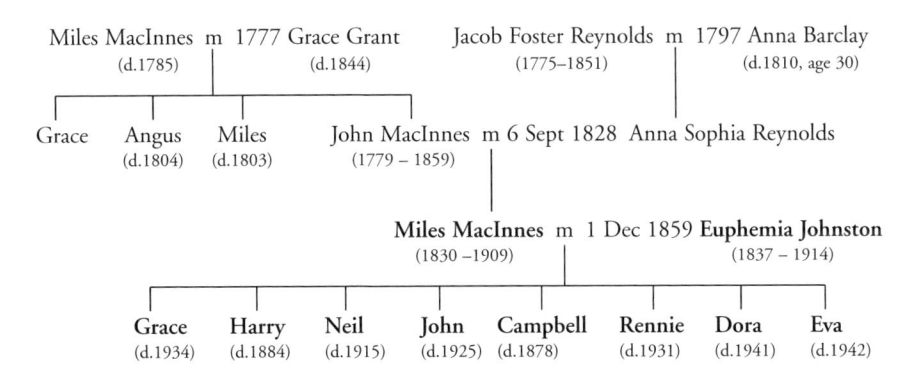

Miles MacInnes m 1777 Grace Grant   Jacob Foster Reynolds m 1797 Anna Barclay
     (d.1785)   (d.1844)   (1775–1851)   (d.1810, age 30)

Grace   Angus   Miles   John MacInnes m 6 Sept 1828 Anna Sophia Reynolds
         (d.1804) (d.1803) (1779 – 1859)

                    Miles MacInnes m 1 Dec 1859 **Euphemia Johnston**
                         (1830 –1909)   (1837 – 1914)

Grace   Harry   Neil   John   Campbell   Rennie   Dora   Eva
(d.1934) (d.1884) (d.1915)(d.1925)(d.1878)   (d.1931) (d.1941)(d.1942)

The first MacInnes family memorials are to be found on a tombstone in the churchyard in the Parish of Sleat in the Isle of Skye. The Miles MacInnes there named who died in 1730, was the great-great-grandfather of the Miles MacInnes of this book.

In an old manuscript the following account is given of the origins of the family name of MacInnes:

The Clan of McInnes are of Argyle, and are descendants of Lochaive, for a long time the chief supporter of William Wallace; and whose castle of Dunstaffnage served partisans of Robert Bruce, as a place of refuge, and of a meeting for the first parliament he summoned; and which advantage, and other eminent services, he derived from the zeal and ability of a younger, said to be the second son of the above named Lochaive, who was made governor of the above mentioned castle; and his name being Eneas, his genuine descendants took the name of M'Eneas, spelt by them M'Innes. Some branches of them took the name of Campbell.

However another and more probable derivation is that of MacAngus. The writer of the Brave Sons of Skye says: 'The Clan MacInnes, cinah Angus or Clann Anglaise is of common origin with Clan Macdonald and derives its name from MacAngus, meaning "Son of the bow".' [Miles MacInnes was told whilst travelling in Skye in 1894 by a Miss MacKinnon, that the first MacInnes who came to Skye was called 'Neil of the Bow' because he came to teach the MacKinnons how to shoot.]

The name Miles is not, as might be supposed, derived from the Latin name for soldiers (miles) but is distinctly of Gaelic derivation. Mal, son of.[5]

The oldest family record is a marriage settlement made by Miles MacInnes in 1777 to Grace Grant. She was the eldest daughter of the Revd. William Grant, for many years minister of the Highland parish of Kilmonivaig in Lochaber.

As a girl Grace went to visit friends in Skye. She was married young and never left the island till she left it as a widow with four little children, John, Grace, Angus and Miles, who was born after his father's death. Travelling in the Highlands was simple in those days, and she rode on horseback, with all her children in panniers. She settled in Inverness for the rest of her long life, and died there in 1844 aged 86.[6]

John MacInnes would often later recall leaving Skye as a fatherless boy at five years old. As a young man, in November 1799, he was admitted to the service of the Honourable East India Company. On the 6th of September 1828 Anna Sophia Reynolds was married from Bury Hill (the home of her Grandfather Robert Barclay) to John MacInnes, then a colonel in the Bengal Army. Sophia was of the Society of Friends, and her marriage with a soldier separated her from the Society, as it was not then allowed and she was in fact disowned.[7]

After the wedding journey John took Sophia to the Highlands to introduce her to his mother and his Scottish relations and friends.[8] Their son, the Miles MacInnes of this book, was born in 1830 in the beginning of the reign of William IV.

In 1902 at the age of 72 Miles recalled his early life thus:

> In the early part of their married life my father and mother took furnished houses in London, Edinburgh and elsewhere, but always spent many months in Scotland every year to be near my grandmother and Aunt Grace.
>
> I was born in Edinburgh, 11th April 1830. The yearly journeys between London and Inverness stand out as golden days in my recollection. We were not very fond of the long sea voyage on the east coast by 'North Star' which took two days and three nights or longer, but we often went via Liverpool to Greenock. There were fine steamers on that route when there was no railway communication between England and Scotland. From Greenock we took the 'Rob Roy' steamer, which was small enough to pass through the Crinan Canal; we landed to sleep the first night at Oban, and the second at Banavie.
>
> My father was always a keen traveller, and after my grandmother's death (1844) he frequently took us abroad. In 1845 we went to Hamburg; in 1846 we went to Switzerland; in 1847 we were at Sea View, Isle of Wight and in 1848 my father took me to Paris for the first time.
>
> My schooldays began in 1838 when I went as a border to Miss Joyce in Church Row, Hampstead. Miss Joyce was a first rate teacher. She made us absolutely accurate, and grounded us in grammar splendidly.
>
> From Miss Joyce I went for one term to Mr Harper, at Mortimer near Reading, but was soon moved to Mr Greig, a curate at Wanstead Church. I remained there till the summer of 1843 and went to Rugby in August. Miss Joyce and Mr Greig had taught such habits of accuracy that I went up the school quickly, and I passed through two forms in my first 'half'. I left Rugby on 11th October 1849 with tears in my eyes, and went up to Balliol College, Oxford next day.
>
> At Rugby I was very keen on football. At Oxford I used to play hand fives and row, and, being always more or less 'fit' when a fresh oar was suddenly wanted in the Balliol 'Torpid', I was taken into the crew, and remained there. We were then high on the river 2nd

or 3rd. I was light, and pulled 'bow' or 'two'. At the end of my last summer term in 1852 I was one of a scratch eight, with R E Bartlett as cox, who rowed from Oxford to London.

My degree in December 1852 was disappointing. I had never dreamed of a 'first', but many friends commiserated me on taking a 'second'. I had begun to read for a Mathematical Honours when I first went up to Oxford, but gave up – a great mistake, which I have always regretted.

My parents had always hoped that I should be ordained, but I was not prepared to offer myself for ordination, and when I left Oxford, my future occupation was not fixed. My father consulted Bevan Braithwaite about studying Law, but it was finally settled that I should go to my uncle J G Fry, to learn business in London.

Just one week after this decision to enter on a commercial life, Mr Head invited me to Rickerby; my father and mother had stayed at Rickerby once or twice. Mrs Head was a cousin of my mother, her father, Thomas Woodrouffe Smith, made or inherited, a large fortune as a Russian merchant and my grandfather, J F Reynolds, was one of his executors. At the time of my invite Mrs Head was then on her deathbed, and I was told that they both wished me to come to Rickerby on a long visit to work in the bank and eventually it was intimated that I might succeed to their property, if I proved suitable for the position. I was too much surprised to say much, but next day I called on my old schoolmaster, Dr Tait, then Dean of Carlisle, and talked over the invitation with him.

I returned to Rugby till 3rd December 1853, when I came back to Rickerby, and began that residence, which with various breaks, has now lasted more than forty eight years, just two thirds of my life.

The Heads had no children, they had for some time been considering which of her near relations should be chosen to succeed them. Probably her imminent death induced them to take definite action, and invite me to Rickerby.

I began, at once, to go to The Old Bank and my coming to Rickerby was evidently a great interest to Mrs Head, who was then slowly dying from a incurable disease. Mrs Head died 8th February 1854.'

It was during this period that Miles would meet his future wife. Having spent some time at Rugby with his future brother in law, Mr Andrew

Johnston, Miles was now introduced to Andrew's sister Euphemia. She had been invited to stay and attend a garden party which was being held in the grounds of Rickerby mansion.

In 1910 Miles' brother Angus recalled their first visit to the Heads at Rickerby taking place in 1844 thus:

> As we were journeying south after my grandmother's death in the autumn of 1844 we came by coach from Glasgow to Carlisle. At the familiar corner, where the Brampton and Scotch roads join, the coach was stopped, a note was handed in, inviting us to alight there, and get into the handsome barouche lined with blue and crimson (this is a very vivid memory of mine) and we were told that a cart would meet the maid, and the luggage, at the coach office in Carlisle.
>
> Thus we first entered the house that was to mean so much to us in after years! A bell hung in a tree as we passed the lodge, warned the house of our arrival. The Heads were kindness itself in their hospitable welcome. The house was conducted with old fashioned propriety. I think the dinner hour was four o'clock, for which solemn occasion the ladies, Mrs Head and Mrs Graves, came down in the regulation evening costume, with pelerines and mittens prepared to spend the rest of the day in needlework and talk.
>
> We little thought during that visit what a part Rickerby was to play in our family story."[9]

[Mrs Graves, her faithful companion before marriage had lived at Rickerby all through Mrs Head's married life, and remained in charge of house and all household matters, till her death in 1866.]

The village of Rickerby is pleasantly located about one and a half miles north-east of Carlisle. Rickerby or Richardby, was a mesne manor under Linstock, and formerly belonged to the Tilliols; afterwards passing to the Pickerings, Westons, Musgraves, Studholmes and Gilpins. In the last named family it continued for three generations and from them a Mr Richardson purchased what remained unsold off to the tenants.

The place appears in the 'Calendar of Inquisitions' 1237, as Ricardeby and in 1297 as Ricardby: and it was in the possession of Richard Tilliol in the early 12th century. The significance of the name is said to have been 'The Farm of Richard'.

The estate, comprising the mansion, the land that later was formed into the park we know today, and a farm contiguous to the village, came

Rickerby Mansion

into the possession of the late Mr George Head Head in 1832. As time passed he extended his purchases in that direction and to the northwards, until he owned all the land from Eden Bridge to 'the keepers plantation' at the nearby village of Linstock, and from the River Eden to the Brampton Road, nearly as far as Whiteclosegate. Later, Linstock Castle and the farm belonging to it was also added to the Rickerby Estate.

On first taking possession, Head swept away all the hedges on the Carlisle side of the mansion house, and had the park tastefully laid out, and planted with the vista-like clumps of trees now growing there. For at that time the expanse of land lying between Eden Bridges and Rickerby Beck consisted of a number of small fields sub-divided by hedges. [However 'legend' has it that a previous owner, James Graham (d.1820), whose second son was James Reginald Topin Graham is in fact responsible for the layout of the trees in Rickerby Park. James junior was a major in the 2nd dragoons (Scots Greys). He was in charge of the Heavy Brigade at Waterloo, where he was wounded by a Frenchman and left to die. Eventually he was saved by a young English soldier. In remembrance of this, according to hearsay, the trees in the park were planted to represent the battle.][10]

Head also laid out the place on the lines of a 'model village' with trim and neat houses standing well back from the road, and having a wide expanse of grass in front of them. Behind however, a narrow lane, less than three feet wide separated them from a high garden wall.

The road from Stanwix formerly ran between hedges, and passed close to the mansion, crossing Rickerby Park by a balustraded bridge a few yards lower down than the existing bridge. The old bridge, blocked up at the ends, remained in position for many years.

The surroundings of the new bridge – which was built to carry the road circuitously away from the mansion – used to be more picturesque than they are now, for a fine beech tree overhung the far corner. The rivulet was fringed with bulrushes, and among them, and around the beech, in summertime, gorgeous dragonflies disported themselves.[11]

During the Heads' time the MacInnes family were frequent visitors to Rickerby, one or two of the family were born there. On one of their visits they went up in the first balloon in Carlisle. But it did not become their home until after Mr Head's death in 1876.

George Head Head wished to find someone to take over Rickerby. The Heads had no children, Mrs Head had no nieces or nephews but she did have six cousins. It was decided to have each of the cousins to stay in turn and to leave Rickerby to the one they liked best. According to Miles and Effie's grand-daughter, Jean MacInnes, 'Mr Head did not mean just to choose an heir for a stately home; he was deliberately choosing someone who would run a real Christian home, and continue all his good works. That meant supporting the Ragged schools in Caldewgate and the Reformatory for young criminals at Stanwix.'

It was in December 1853 when he was aged twenty three that Miles first came to Rickerby as one of the 'cousins on trial'. Head decided in favour of Miles MacInnes when he saved the bank. Miles worked in Head's bank in the 1850s. One day George Head arrived at Court Square to find that he had forgotten the key. It was 9.40 am, but Miles fetched the key from Rickerby in twenty minutes. If the shutters at the bank had not been taken down at 10.00am there would have been a 'run on the bank'. (Later when Rickerby House became Eden School there was an annual 'Key Race' held at the school.)

By George Head's will the banking interest and beautiful Rickerby estate overlooking the River Eden was left unfettered to Miles MacInnes, regarded as a worthy successor. But he would not have been able to take up the position and live there had he not inherited ample means from his father, General John MacInnes of Fern Lodge, Hampshire, as well as having the proceeds of the lucrative Corn Trade business in Mark Lane, London.[12]

[After his 1859 marriage to Euphemia Johnston, Miles who had previously lived with Mr Head at Rickerby, took a house at Stanwix. They lived there until the death of his younger brother in 1865, when Miles went to London and became a partner in the firm of Horne, Son and MacInnes, Corn Factors, Mark Lane, taking his late brother's place in the business.[13]]

Miles MacInnes   Euphemia 'Effie' MacInnes

Both Miles' father and his mother's family were Conservative, thus Miles' early life was wholly conservative. Also from the age of twenty-three to twenty-nine he had lived under the roof and was partner of George Head, a Tory and treasurer of the Carlisle local constituency party. Between these two periods came ten years of Rugby and Oxford where all that was vigorous and hopeful among the younger masters, and nearly all that was so among the leading boys in the school, was ranged on the liberal side. Under the influences of those ten years, Miles became and remained through life a consistent, while moderate, liberal. Moreover he married into a family who were on the side of reform.[14]

After taking up his residence at Rickerby, Miles was soon drawn into the public life of the City and District, and was early thought of in connection with Parliament. However it was not only as a public servant, but as a family man that Miles was remembered. His influence with the family was sustained by prayer. Breakfast followed Prayers. But by giving so much time to his family he did not neglect his other duties. Business often called him away. He was a railway director and a banker.

It was through his support of the Temperance cause that he was asked to represent the Hexham division of Northumberland. He had travelled one day to speak of the cause at Hexham. A few months later the committee for Hexham Liberals approached him and said they had heard him that day and had decided they would like to invite him to stand as their candidate. Though he had for some time abandoned the idea of entering Parliament he felt he could not refuse their appeal and was duly elected as MP for Hexham three times. He was in Parliament from 1885 to 1895 during which time the most important business was Gladstone's Irish Home Rule Bill. These ten years of his Parliamentary life were a time of much interest, and he loved to share the interest.

Miles MacInnes was Vice-Chairman of the Cumberland County Council for many years. He was Chairman of the Eden Fishery Board and from the winter of 1876 he was a director of the London and North Western Railway Company. Miles and his family also sat along side Aunt 'Pris' on the committee of the RSPCA. Having identified himself with the work of the church, he took a special interest in missionary work, being Vice-President of the Church Missionary Society.

Education became compulsory in 1872 and the School Board built more schools. Still Miles continued to run the school at Rickerby until the teacher, who had been there for forty years, died. Then the children were transferred to the Board School at Stanwix. Caldewgate Schools were taken over by the Board and rebuilt. But Miles MacInnes continued until the day of his death walking into Carlisle before church every Sunday morning to hear the Caldewgate Sunday School boys say their verses.

In 1903 the School Board was abolished and the work given to the Education Committee of the County Council. At which time Miles became the first Chairman of the Committee.[15]

Like her husband Mrs Effie MacInnes was greatly interested in good works, especially missionary and temperance work. Drawing room meetings in support of these and similar objects were frequently held at Rickerby,[16] to which, more often than not, Aunt 'Pris' and philanthropic friends would be found in attendance lending their support. Later her nieces, the Misses MacInnes would be seen to take their places on various committees and supporting causes alongside their dear mother and aunt.

At this time Rickerby was indeed the happy hunting ground for all who desired to plead the cause of the poor and needy, the sorrowful and sinning.[17]

When the MacInnes family moved into the Rickerby Mansion it became a most delightful and happy home, of which Miles was the pivot. But while there was liberty, there was no licence – in some ways they were very strict. The object of both parents was to promote all that was lovely and of good report. Miles' influence with his sons was sustained by prayer – each child in early life went alone to either parent for their morning prayers.[18]

The day at Rickerby began with family prayers at 8.30. No sooner did the gong sound, than the step of the master was heard in the passage, and on the stair, unless indeed, he was already in his library, dealing with letters that the post had brought before seven. He made family prayers a great reality. They began with a hymn, to the harmonium, then a short Bible passage, on which he would occasionally give a short, simple comment to bring it home to the hearts of the hearers.

Breakfast followed prayers and at breakfast there was much cheerful talk on matters private and public. Very often the newspaper was read aloud. After breakfast Miles would go to his library, generally for a very busy morning, but however busy, he was always ready cheerfully to give his interest and attention to any intruder who came to him for advice.

Fishing was his favourite recreation, as well as his great refreshment. He would spend whole days by the river, casting a very straight line. The party from the house would often join him for luncheon in the hut – sausages cooked on its little stove, and hot coffee. As many as ten or twelve might squeeze into the hut by the riverside.[19]

There were many dinner and garden parties at Rickerby, but the family were not allowed to dance, go to the theatre or even play games with cards. After dinner some cheerful games such as forfeits were played and pictures were drawn.

Miles and Euphemia had eight children, whom their Aunt 'Pris' loved dearly. The oldest, Grace, was fourteen when they went to Rickerby. There are sketches of her with her governess. According to her brothers who drew the sketches 'she threw chairs at her governess and blew her up with a rocket'. However Miles' grand-daughter, Jean MacInnes recalls that, 'It was very likely the boys who were the naughty ones not Grace.'

Harry, Neil and John went away to school. In the holidays when they returned they had the top room in the tower for their games and hobbies. Its walls were hung with pictures of themselves in any teams they had managed to get into at school and with stuffed birds and fish they got in the holidays. Campbell, Rennie, Dora and Eva were still in the nursery.

There are no ghosts at Rickerby, but there is however one ghost story. One summer evening the girls were sent to bed at about 9 o'clock. It was such a lovely night that they persuaded their governess to come for a walk among the rhododendrons growing thickly behind Gurney Terrace. The governess was a nervous lady and was also worried in case she ought not to have been out so late. When a white figure loomed out of the dark bushes in front of her she turned screaming and fled – much to the amusement of John, who was the ghost dressed in a sheet.

Rennie was later a bishop, but even bishops were at one time naughty little boys. On Grace's 21st birthday her father gave her a brooch with a diamond in it. 'Oh I say,' said Rennie, 'diamonds write on glass' and he went to the window and wrote R. M. I. on it. It could still be seen for many years after.

The best toys at Rickerby were actually invented by Effie MacInnes and made for her by the estate joiner. The first was a box of bricks big enough and light enough to build wonderful castles and, as the children grew older, well balanced enough to make scale models.

And, mimicking Effie and Pris' own childhood toys at Northrepps, there was a rocking boat, large enough for four quite large children. It could be turned upside down to make a bridge, a coach or a lion's cage big enough to hold any boy who wanted to be a lion. The original boat was rocked by many and various children for over 60 years, until it was removed to an aunt's house in London where in 1941 it was 'blitzed'.

Of course there was no television or radio but the Rickerby family had more fun of their own making. They played paper and pencil games in which they drew cartoons and wrote verses about each other and all the events of the day. There are fishing and shooting and picnicking sketches, often in deluges of rain. One lovely picture is a picnic covered in umbrellas and underneath is written 'Good for turnips and fishing'. Another entitled 'Going to bed at Rickerby' shows nothing but a lot of pairs of feet going upstairs. At one time the family brought out a handwritten newspaper called *The Rickerby Journal* in which they made fun of agricultural papers by giving ridiculous farming advice.

As the children grew up they added more and more animals to the family. First, of course were the horses, who were not only pets but an essential means of transport. One was called 'Mr Speaker' because its master was an MP. At a later stage, when grandchildren fought for the privilege to ride on the box with Mr Tanner, the coachman, the horses were called Eden and Nile. Mr Tanner was also an amateur artist, making oil paintings of the horses in his spare time.

Eva was so fond of horses that the family said she knew what visitors had called if she could see the ears of their horses over the stable yard door. This must have been from the nursery window. The children had a parrot in a cage, and it was said that their father once went to stop the boys shouting and found only the parrot! They kept rabbits and tried experiments with carrier pigeons, sending messages to friends at Dalston. There were numerous dogs and cats. One cat in particular was called Sir Bartle Frere after a politician of the day. Eva kept a scrap book 'Odds and Ends of many friends' and in it is a Valentine sent to her by one of the boys but pretending to be from Bartle, in which he had cut out a cat's head and pasted on to it the body of a man with a gun surrounded by rabbits.

Rickerby was always full of flowers. There were herbaceous borders both inside and outside of the walled gardens. One year a very rare aloe that flowered once in only one hundred years, flowered in the green house and gardeners came from far and wide. Once they had a pot plant so tall that visitors saw the pot as they came in at the front door but did not see the flowers until they were upstairs on the landing.

Rickerby was a very open house to many friends and relations. Elizabeth Fry, always known as Aunty Fry, visited Carlisle in September 1818 to inspect the conditions of the women's prison, which she deemed satisfactory, but it is not known if in later years she ever visited Rickerby. However the terrace part of the garden was always known as the Gurney Terrace and her picture hung in Rickerby.

Besides numerous relations and friends a number of famous people stayed at Rickerby. Charles Kingsley, the well known English clergyman, poet and historical novelist, and his sister visited. One year when the Royal Show was held at Carlisle the Kitikuri (Prime minister) of Uganda stayed there and caused great excitement driving around the show in the Rickerby wagonette. General Booth, founder of the Salvation Army, came to stay for some meetings. Much to the amusement of the young MacInneses the local paper records that 'A large crow [*sic*] watched and cheered while Mr MacInnes received the General at the station.' One visitor arrived as a very old lady dressed in black, come to take a meeting. Mr MacInnes received her with great courtesy and talked earnestly about the meeting but joined in the fun when he found out it was in fact Dora dressed up.

In 1900 a typical arrival at Rickerby is recorded thus,

> Hansom dashes up with a hollow sound on the stones under the portico. Miles hurries up fingering his waistcoat pockets and extends a cordial hand to the arrival. Neil marches up and says 'Bravo'. The hall fills with pleasant folk, Dora sails forward, exclaiming in Dora's most singular nice voice, 'Oh there is –' and shakes hands. Then Effie with uplifted hand glides majestically, swathed in filmy shawls and pats the arrival on the shoulder and says 'Dear –'.[20]

The year of 1901 marked the visit to Rickerby of Effie and Pris' nephew Edward Johnston on the occasion of his engagement to Greta, who had been vouched for by Rickerby. Edward later recorded, 'Rickerby has been quite excited, I never knew I had such friends. It is beautiful that everyone thinks we were for each other.' However there was only one real objection from the family point of view, Edward broke it to his Aunt Pris as gently as he could saying that after all she might get over it, but the fact was Greta did not really care for cats. Aunt Pris took it very well saying only, 'None of the husbands and wives have, we must not expect it of outsiders.'[21]

Miles felt intense love for his children, and every detail that concerned their welfare and happiness meant so much to him. The boys would always say, 'It's no fun without father', if it seemed doubtful whether he would be able to go with them on some expedition and everyone felt it was flat if he was not there. Although the MacInneses could be very strict in many ways with their children, out of doors the girls were given more freedom than most girls of the day. Sometimes they went to the Solway or to the lakes. In the winter they flooded the Willows [a field near Rickerby] for skating – sometimes by the light of bonfires. They went on camping and shooting trips upon Cumrew fells with their brothers. Mr MacInnes was always so particular, both in skating time and shooting, to impress the utmost care upon his children, to take all reasonable care to avoid accidents, himself having had a foot seriously injured in a shooting accident some years earlier.

Deep sorrow threw dark shadows over that happy home life – shadows that could never pass away as, sadly for the MacInnes family, the eight children did not all grow up. In March 1878 Campbell, the fourth boy, died of scarlet fever at school at Wimbledon. He was within a month of ten years old, and all who remembered him knew what a beautiful and brilliant child he was and how great was the promise of his future, both for mind and body. On 22nd September 1884, three weeks after his twenty first birthday, their eldest son Harry met with instant death while climbing on the Alps, near Villar in Switzerland. Neil and Eva stayed at home and ran the home farm and the breeding of hacks and carriage horses. John was a clergyman. Rennie and Dora were missionaries, first in Egypt and then in Palestine. Rennie became bishop in Jerusalem.

The three surviving sons went on to marry. Rennie in August 1896 to Janet, daughter of the Revd Canon Carr, of Holbrooke Hall, Derby. John, in September 1899 to Ethel, daughter of Mr Dashwood, of Wilton House, Shenley and Neil, in January 1904, to Armine, daughter of the Revd Canon Hoare, vicar of Aylsham. The three new homes gave Miles unfeigned pleasure. Each grandchild was welcomed in its turn. 'I enjoy my grandchildren far more than my children,' Miles said to one of his sons. 'I have all the fun and none of the responsibility.' In the 1870s sketches were painted of him giving Bible lessons to his own family and in the 1900s there are photographs of him teaching his grandchildren.[22]

Jean MacInnes recalls,

> The first time my parents met was at a garden party at Rickerby for the crippled ladies from Strathclyde House. My mother [Miss Hoare] had met my aunts and been invited by them to stay at Rickerby. When she arrived the party was in full swing and my father [Neil MacInnes] was down on the terrace, above the river throwing sticks in the water to make the dogs race to amuse the old people in their chairs. He said afterwards that he made his mind up there and then on the terrace. The next day the family all drove out to the fells. Neil said his sisters could go in the carriage but Miss Hoare must come with him in the gig.
>
> They were married in Norfolk. After the honeymoon they came back to Rickerby where the people were so pleased to see him that they took the horses out of the carriage and pulled it themselves through the park. Mr Little, the game-keeper, speaking on behalf of the men said, 'They say that in Cumberland when strangers come, we Summer them and Winter them and Summer them again, but we won't wait that long for Mrs Neil.'

She continues,

My grandmother [Effie] as usual thought out wonderful parties. The 'birthday child' always wore a wreath. There was an Easter egg hunt, when my brother found a golden egg. It was in the gutter of the roof and he had to get a ladder to fetch it. There was always a golden egg at Rickerby Easter egg hunts. All the smaller eggs were shared out at the end so that no child was left with none.

Then there was the rat party. Uncle John dressed up as the Pied Piper and all the children came to the party dressed as rats. We followed the piper round the garden but when we got to the door in the wall of the old drying green we turned back to the house. I have never forgotten the disappointment as I had really thought we were going through that door into the fairy hill.[23]

Family recollections of Miles' last two months of an unclouded holiday time were full of many vivid and bright pictures. In July he went to Scotland with Neil and Armine, who were delighted to be his companions and caretakers. Miles greatly enjoyed the journey and returned refreshed.

Back home at Rickerby the eleven grandchildren were backwards and forwards. There were afternoons at Silloth, to see John and Ethel's children, who after leaving Rickerby, were there for sea air, and to whom

Miles and Effie MacInnes and eleven grandchildren August 1909. Jean MacInnes 'is the fat baby with red hair'. The kilted boy standing far right is Gurney, the future husband of Mrs E.J. MacInnes of Cumbria

it was a great pleasure to share with 'grandfather' the pleasures of the shore.

There were two garden parties at Rickerby in 1909, on August 24th and September 7th, for old and young. All eleven grandchildren were present. They were photographed with their grandparents, just before guests began to arrive. The pony and donkey took many children on much coveted rides, up and down the front of the house. One child asked if there was anything to pay.

There were delightful days on the fells, when he would walk with the dear sons as they were shooting and he would often walk in and out of Carlisle.[24] However, on Tuesday 28th September 1909 Mr MacInnes, now in his 79th year, motored into the town and, having a variety of business to transact, sent his motor car back to Rickerby. On his return he took the tram as far as Stanwix and proceeded to walk the mile home through the park, but feeling unwell he rested for a short time in a house on the way. The tenant accompanied him through Rickerby Park, but it was characteristic of Mr MacInnes that before reaching the house he asked this man to accompany him no further, lest the family should be alarmed, but to watch till he reached the door. At the door Mr MacInnes turned and waved his umbrella, and entered the house without telling anyone that he had been unwell. He arrived at his residence about quarter past one and joined the family at luncheon, taking part in the conversation round the table and appearing nothing more than perhaps a little tired by his morning's work. Suddenly as the family sat round the table, his eyes closed, his head fell back and there were some deep breaths. Restoratives were quickly applied; he was laid on the sofa mattress on the floor. The doctor was at Rickerby in an incredibly short time, but no doctor was needed to tell them that the tender, loving spirit was gone. Indeed it was the family's belief that death must have actually occurred almost at the moment that the sudden change in his appearance was noticed, 'For him all parting pain and sorrow were over – that he was seeing we believe – knowing as he was known, in the presence of the Master whom all his life he had loved and served.' Had he lived two months longer, Mr and Mrs MacInnes would have celebrated their Golden Wedding for which arrangements were in preparation.

On Saturday 2nd October, the beloved remains were laid to rest, in the same grave, with his two sons in Stanwix churchyard. A London and North Western Railway lorry, covered by a deep, scabious-coloured velvet pall drawn by horses from the farm, bore the oak coffin through the park.[25] Ten minutes before his death, Mr MacInnes was asking about the oak tree that had been felled near the house a few years earlier, and spoke of the need to use its well seasoned timber. None who heard him speak about this favourite tree thought that it would give the best of its heart for this last solemn service to him.[26] It is not too much to say that of the great company who gathered in the church, and around the open grave, there was not one who was not drawn there by love and respect.[27]

30

Introducing her Friends and Fellow Philanthropists Miss Amy Beevor and Miss Mary Ellen 'Polly' Creighton

Miss Amy Beevor

[Miss Amy Beevor and Aunt 'Pris' were in fact distantly related through the elopement and subsequent marriage of Miss Juliana Mary Beevor and Sir Robert John Buxton of Tibenham, on 22nd May 1777.]

Miss Amy Beevor was born at Hampstead on 31st December 1852. From 1868 to 1886 she then lived at Hargham Hall, Norfolk.

On the 18th August 1885 her father died at the age of sixty-two. Her mother, Sophia Lady Beevor, now openly assumed the family management. However, Beevor finances were already stretched and Amy felt she should now play her part. She had been educated entirely at home, yet in 1886 at the age of thirty-four, she obtained the post of assistant mistress at Notting Hill Girls' High School, where she proved her worth as an excellent teacher. She remained there until September 1892 at which time she was appointed, by the Girls' Public School Company, headmistress of Carlisle Girls' High School, then situated on Castle Street. (In 1909 it moved to Victoria Place, becoming Carlisle and County High School for Girls, where it remains today, although in much extended form, as St Aidan's County High School.) She continued to hold this position until December 1902 when she retired.[28]

Miss Beevor, who was a very gifted lady, took the greatest personal interest in all her pupils. After the severance of her official connection with the Girls' High School and the school guild, she was a frequent attender at prize-giving ceremonies.

An estimable lady, she was deeply interested in educational, social and philanthropic work. For many years she was honorary secretary of the Cumberland Branch of the National Union of Women Workers. The work of the Charity Organisation Society also claimed her sympathy, and she served on the local committee. She was warmly interested in the welfare of the Blencathra Sanatorium, a hospital for patients recovering from tuberculosis, and the local branch of the RSPCA, serving on the committees of both these organisations. She was also a member of the Carlisle Insurance Company.[29]

In 1909, having already retired from her teaching post in Carlisle – though her home and friends were there, of course – she left everything in order to help her brother Hugh, who had been widowed on 17th April. His sons were already away at school, but they would need his attention during the holidays, and how could he best look after his young daughter alone? The redoubtable Amy came to the rescue, in her usual practical fashion, returning to Norfolk for a time to care for his children. Whilst, Hugh, who upon his retirement took a trip round the world to get over his bereavement. On his return it seems he decided to live at the family home, Hargham Hall, whence Amy accompanied and certainly stayed for a while, until the eldest child, Bridget was old enough to cope with running her father's house.[30]

She then returned to her friends 'up North' in Carlisle and once again took up residence with Aunt 'Pris' at The Beeches until that lady's death in January 1912, after which Amy resided at No 9 Eden Mount, Stanwix.

After the outbreak of war in 1914 she was appointed by the Canadian Red Cross to look after Canadian Soldiers in Carlisle hospitals.[31]

The Creighton family c.1870. Left to right: James, their father Robert, Polly and Mandell

Miss Mary Ellen Creighton (1849–1944), otherwise known as 'Polly', whose grandfather came to Carlisle from the Scottish Lowlands, was the daughter of Robert Creighton, a cabinet maker who also entered civic life, and Sarah Mandell Creighton, daughter of a yeoman farmer of Carlisle Gate, Bolton.[32] Polly was thus a distinguished member of an honoured Carlisle family, the members of which made themselves famous in their day and generation by their outstanding ability and the manner in which they at all times gave their services freely and voluntarily to their fellow citizens.

Polly was born in 1849. The following year her mother, Sarah, died unexpectedly from an unknown illness, leaving her father to bring up three young children with only slight memories of their mother. He never re-married, nor ever spoke of his wife to his children again. Soon after, his unmarried sister, always referred to as Aunt Jane, came to live with the family and remained for many years. Polly's father, Robert, was Mayor of Carlisle in 1866. Her brother, James Robert (1844–1896), became Mayor twice and in 1889 the first honorary freeman of the city, making him one of the greatest municipal representatives Carlisle has ever had,[33] so much so that after his death the citizens of Carlisle erected a stone memorial to him. This memorial stands at the south end of the Eden Bridges, opposite the Civic Centre, on the city's main traffic roundabout, Hardwicke Circus. It is an impressive stone pillar, thirty-one feet tall, displaying a figure of St George slaying the dragon, the whole edifice placed on a substantial stone eight-step pedestal; it features the following inscription:

> On his death bed he sent a message to his fellow citizens expressing his profound conviction that the greatness of England depended upon its capacity for local self-government. He trusted that Carlisle would never be without a due supply of men who regarded it as both their duty and their pleasure to devote their seal and energy to the promotion of the welfare of the City.[34]

Her brother Mandell Creighton (1843–1901), Bishop of London, was a famous historian, who became the first editor of the English Historical Review and author of many books.

As a child Polly had first resided with her family in quarters above their shop on Castle Street, Carlisle. Here Robert ran a successful cabinet-making and decorating establishment which became renowned for manufacturing quality furnishings for gentry houses and mansions of the county. The family later moved to the nearby village of Kirkandrews.

While her brothers enjoyed an extensive education, sadly for Polly, her education, a brief few years at a girls' boarding school, was cut short after her father had a paralytic stroke in 1870; she had no choice but to share in his caring. She never married and spent her entire adult life in Carlisle, engaged in civic and private philanthropy, taking an active and prominent part in the many charitable and other good causes for the welfare of the community.[35] All her work was done in such a quiet, unostentatious way that only those working with her knew of its extent and importance. Her gentle and sincere manner made her approachable at all times. It was this which placed her on such good terms with youth, and which enabled her to reach out to and help, quite humble people. She was especially interested in the advancement of education and social welfare, and the furtherance of women's influence in public life. She was devoted to the cause which used to be called 'emancipation of women', but her great love of children permeated all her work.[36]

Her home at number 14 Warwick Square, and latterly at number 1 Eden Mount, became a centre for those interested in education, public work and social welfare. Many were the stories she told, with keen wit and a twinkle in her eye, of her adventures with the girls of the GFS [Girls' Friendly Society] Club, which she ran for so long in days when manners were rougher and people more candid. She never lost touch with old members: her post bag frequently brought letters from those married and settled overseas, some of whom it was her proud boast to have visited in their new homes. Then there were the boys and girls boarded out by the city whom she visited regularly, calling them 'her children'. It was amazing how she could enter into their thoughts and those of their foster mothers in all the numerous difficulties and troubles that arose.'[37]

For a number of years Polly, in conjunction with other prominent local ladies, organised a club for girls working in factories. This was in connection with the Association for the Care of Friendless Girls, and she subsequently served on the Executive Committees of both organisations. For a period of eight years she acted as secretary to the local branch of the National Council of Women, becoming president on two occasions. This Council took a prominent part in the appointment of health visitors for the city of Carlisle.

She was an associate of the Girls' Friendly Society from its establishment in the 1840s, the aim of which was to encourage more 'responsible parenting', both in moral and educational matters (by ensuring, for instance, that girls remained in regular school attendance until aged fourteen, in the days prior to the Compulsory Attendance Act of 1876). From 1906 she was closely connected with the Babies' Welcome and School for mothers, of which she also became president, at all times displaying a keen interest in the most important branch of work as a member of the Health (Maternity and Child Welfare) Sub-Committee. She also took a prominent part in the erection of the Blencathra Sanatorium for the treatment of tuberculosis patients and of the open-air school in the Newtown Road district for child sufferers from this pernicious disease. She acted as a governor and member of the Cumberland Infirmary Committee and a member of the Carlisle and District Nursing Association, as well as serving on the Executive Committee of the Charity Organisation Society from the beginning of its work in Carlisle until it developed into the Council of Social Services.

However, she was especially interested in the education of children, feeling that this had been one of the major omissions in her own life. She became a member of the Education Committee from the time of its formation in 1903.[38]

When Miss Amy Beevor came to Carlisle as headmistress of the Girls' High School, the two women became close friends, and thus was the friendship forged with Priscilla Hannah Johnston. These three great women tirelessly worked together for many years to raise the standard of public work.

31

The Origins of Some of Priscilla Johnston's Philanthropic Work in Carlisle

The establishment of the RSPCA and other humane societies[39]

The early pioneers of the RSPCA faced derision and contempt for their belief that laws should be passed to bring to an end the suffering of the 'Brute Creation' at the hands of humans. This is the story of how a handful of men with a vision overcame prejudice, ignorance and selfishness, and how their courage and persistence educated public opinion to recognize the claims of animals for justice.

Priscilla Hannah's grandfather, Sir Thomas Fowell Buxton, sat as chairman at the first meeting of the SPCA (for it had not yet been granted the Royal seal of approval). He was of the school of thought which believed that '... English People could not learn to be kind to animals until they learned to be kind to one another.' So it could be said that his fight against human injustices went 'hand in hand' with his fight against animal injustices.

The first suggestion that animals should have legal protection seems to have been made by an anonymous writer of an article in the *Gentleman's Magazine*, in 1749, in which he denounced the brutal sport of 'cock-throwing'. This sport consisted of throwing sticks at a fowl tied to a post until the bird was fatally injured, and to make the game last longer the bird's feathers were sometimes greased so that the sticks would glance off its back. In his article the hen speaks. She pleads with the company for kinder treatment, and concludes, 'Perhaps legislature may not think it beneath them to take our sad case into consideration.' Legislature, however, did nothing for animals until 1822; birds were not protected by law until 1835.

It must be remembered that at that time there was no law in this country for the protection of animals. A man could do what he pleased

Bull baiting

Bear baiting

with his own animal. A servant who injured one of his master's animals was liable to be prosecuted, not for cruelty to the animal, but for malicious injury to his master's property. The master had only to prove that his servant was actuated by malice. Thus on 4th October 1790, a man was prosecuted at Bow Street for tearing out the tongue of a horse. This offence was a little too brutal even for the people of those days. The newspaper report of the case describes the offence as one 'at which humanity must shudder. How completely depraved the mind of the man capable of committing an act of such cruelty as is alleged against the prisoner.' The man had pulled the tongue out of the horse with his left hand, and 'with more than brutal violence' had beaten the horse over the head with the butt end of a whip for upwards of ten minutes. The report concludes: 'The offence is capital, and if he should be found guilty we believe few will be found to repine at the punishment of such a wretch'. But as malice was not proved the wretch was acquitted.

The eighteenth century closed as it had begun so far as the treatment of animals was concerned, with suggestions and entreaties for reforms. But words were soon to be translated into deeds.

Further articles and books were written, and sermons preached, but, apart from some isolated prosecutions for egregious cruelty, the first serious attempt at legislation for the protection of animals was made in April 1800, when Sir W. Pulteney introduced a bill to stop bull-baiting. When this first humane measure was introduced the sport had fallen into disrepute and was generally regarded as one of the amusements of the lowest of people. Still, those who wished to abolish bull-baiting laid themselves open to the charge of interfering with the amusements of the people. It was considered that the '... amusement was a most excellent one. It inspired courage and produced nobleness of sentiment and elevation of mind.' The bill was lost and two years passed before a second attempt was made to suppress bull-baiting.

William Wilberforce, whose love for animals was as ardent as his sympathy for human slaves, made a long speech in support of the second bill, but this second attempt also failed. However, at the next elections Mr Windham, representative of Norwich in Parliament, who had been the 'stumbling block' for the bill was unseated. There were other members of famous Norfolk families, notably the Gurneys and the Buxtons, whose views on the subject of cruelty to animals were in harmony with those who wished to put down bull-baiting, and the electors of Norwich declined to be represented in Parliament by an advocate of that barbarous amusement.

At this time, those who were working for the alleviation of the suffering of their fellow creatures were more successful than those who were trying to secure laws for the protection of animals. The same spirit of humanity which animated William Wilberforce in his efforts to abolish slavery, and Sir Samuel Romilly in his work for reforming our criminal law, now also inspired Lord Erskine to bring a bill in the House of Lords to prevent cruelty to animals in 1809.

Lord Erskine was Lord High Chancellor of England and his bill was for 'Preventing Wanton and Malicious Cruelty to Animals'. It passed through the Lords but met with much opposition in the Commons, and was eventually lost. Within a few months of the rejection of Lord Erskine's bill, the first society for preventing cruelty to animals was established in Liverpool. This was called the 'Society for the Suppression of Wanton Cruelty to Animals', but it was short lived. Supporters soon discovered that without the aid of a law one can do very little, and the country was still without that law.

In 1816, the Attorney-General, Sir William Garrow, moved for leave to bring in the 'Stage Coaches Bill', the object of which was not so much to prevent cruelty to animals as to protect the lives and limbs of His Majesty's subjects. The Lords rejected this bill, saying that 'no persons would agree as to what was and what was not over driving'.

In 1821, Richard Martin, member for Galway, brought in a bill to prevent the ill-treatment of horses and other animals. The Commons laughed at him. The suggestion that asses should also be protected from cruelty was greeted with laughter so loud that *The Times* reporter could not hear him speak. One member suggested that if a bill for the protection of horses and asses were passed, he should not be surprised to find some other member proposing a bill for the protection of dogs. 'And cats,' added another member. Although Martin's bill eventually passed through the Commons, despite many petitions in its favour, it failed in the Lords.

Undaunted by his failure, Martin tried again the following year. This time 'Martin's Act', as it came to be known, the first law for the protection of animals, was put on the statute book. 1822 was thus a memorable year for animal lovers (and, indeed, animals) – England had begun to be humane.

A number of successful prosecutions followed, Martin himself being prominent in seeking out and apprehending offenders.

Martin knew where an offender would be likely to be found, and he went out himself and found two offenders. He took a turn into Smithfield during horse market day and in consequence, two men were taken into

Richard Martin, MP

custody by officers for offences under the Martin Act. The first, who gave his name as Samuel Clarke, had been observed beating a horse with a large whip in so cruel a manner, that the poor animal was completely wealed from its shoulder to tail. The beast could have done nothing to merit such punishment as it was standing quietly tied up. Clarke said that he had brought the animal to market for sale, but it was standing very sleepy and dull. He acknowledged that he had hit it a few times to make him show the appearance of a little spirit and life. The other prisoner, David Hyde, was charged with beating a horse, which he was riding to the market for sale, over the head with the butt end of his whip in a most cruel and wanton manner. This brutality seemed to be the result of the same motive as that of the first prisoner. The two fellows were each convicted by the mitigated penalty of 20s each. [The minimum penalty under Martin's Act for cruelty to an animal was a fine of ten shillings.]

The Revd Mr Arthur Broome had long cherished the idea of starting a society to protect animals from the cruelties which had generally been accepted as part of everyday life. On the passing of Martin's Act, Mr Broome saw the chance of his ideal becoming a practical reality, and so he set about the formation of a society in earnest. In *John Bull,* 3rd November 1822, there appeared the following advertisement:

> At a meeting of Gentlemen, lately held at Old Slaughters Coffee House, St Martins Lane, the Revd. Mr Broome in the Chair, it was resolved,
> 1. That a society be formed for the purpose of preventing, as far as possible, the cruel treatment of brute animals.
> 2. That a committee, consisting of Twelve Members, be appointed to prepare the outline of a plan for the establishment of such a society.
> 3. That the Revd. Mr Broome be requested to accept the office of honorary Treasurer and Secretary to the proposed Institution.
> 4. That the cordial thanks of this meeting are given to Richard Martin, Esq. MP, to whose praise worthy and indefatigable exertions, in the cause of humanity, the Public are indebted for a Bill introduced by him into Parliament and passed into a law entitled 'A Bill for preventing the cruel and improper Treatment of Cattle.' Communications from persons who are willing to co-operate with the Society in its benevolent design are requested to be addressed to the Secretary, free of postage, at Messrs. Whitmore and Fenn's Booksellers, Charing Cross.

No record exists of what transpired, so that one can only suppose the effort failed. However, Mr Broome evidently felt optimistic as to the ultimate formation of his pet society, and strove to finance it to the best of his power. He himself employed a man as inspector to watch for cruelty – probably the first man ever to have been so employed.

Early in 1824 Arthur Broome found that the activity of propaganda took up so much of his time it seriously interfered with his clerical work. Consequently, he resigned his living and devoted his whole time to the realisation of the one objective which demanded his individual attention.

On 16th June 1824, a meeting for the formation of the society was again called at the Old Slaughterhouse. Richard Martin was among those present at the first meeting, along with Wilberforce. Thomas Fowell Buxton, MP, was in the chair, 'a member of the well known Norfolk family, several of whose descendants are ardent workers for the cause.' In his opening speech Buxton explained that their object was not only '... to prevent the exercise of cruelty towards animals, but to spread amongst the lower orders of the people, especially amongst those to whom the care of animals was entrusted, a degree of moral feeling which would compel them to think and act like those of a superior class.' Buxton mentioned that Mr Broome had employed a man named Wheeler 'to keep an eye upon the men who brought cattle to Smithfield Market', adding that during the past six months Wheeler had secured the conviction of sixty-three men for cruelty to animals.

Two committees were formed, one to superintend the publication of tracts, sermons, 'and similar modes of influencing public opinion' and one 'to adopt measures for inspecting the markets and streets of the Metropolis, the slaughter houses, the conduct of coachmen, etc.'

During the first year, the Society successfully prosecuted in 149 cases of cruelty to animals. Its anniversary meeting was a very happy one. The members had good reason for being in an optimistic mood. There had been a change for the better in the conduct of the Smithfield drovers; the Society had lived down some of the ridicule with which it had been assailed at its formation; many sermons on its behalf had been preached; many tracts distributed in schools; inspectors had been successfully employed; and branches of the Society had been formed at Wakefield and Liverpool. In spite of many vicissitudes, the Society gathered support. In 1835 it was honoured by receiving the patronage of the Duchess of Kent and Princess Victoria, and from that moment its continued existence was assured. On her accession to the throne in 1837, Queen Victoria renewed her patronage and in 1840 extended it by graciously permitting the Society to use the prefix 'Royal'. The members celebrated by increasing their efforts on behalf of animals and in the year 1837 the number of successful prosecutions was 270, double those of the previous year.

Her Majesty also assisted the Society by her frequent expressions of disapproval at the wearing of birds on hats, osprey and other feathers, the use of bearing reins on horses, and of the mutilation of animals.

Though every day brought fresh examples of the need for the work of the new Society, public support was, unfortunately, very meagre, and in the following year (1826) the committee was faced with serious financial difficulties. As secretary, Arthur Broome was held legally responsible for the Society's debt, and as he had sacrificed his profession for his new work, and had therefore lost his stipend, he was not in the position to meet his debts. He was cast into prison, another sacrifice for his ideal, but Richard Martin and Lewis Gompertz (subsequently the second honorary secretary of the Society) went to his rescue and he was liberated.

The year of 1827 was the blackest of all the years in the history of the Society. At one time the committee were on the point of deciding to pay the outstanding debts themselves and to dissolve the Society. But they persevered and contrived to hold three meetings in 1827.

One can readily imagine that Arthur Broome, deprived by his own enthusiasm for this work of his clerical stipend, had to find other means of subsistence, and evidently this work, whatever it was, began to occupy much of his time. In consequence of this we find in the minutes of the meeting held on 29th February 1828, that the committee passed the following resolution: 'Resolved that this Society feel highly indebted to the Revd A. Broome for his services as honorary secretary, and regret that he should find it inconvenient to attend to the duties of the office, and that Lewis Gompertz be requested to accept the office of honorary secretary.'

Arthur Broome did remain a member of the committee, and continued to take an active interest in its work, and was present at several meetings of the Society. In the report of the Society for the year ending 5th May 1832 (the first printed report in existence) Arthur Broome's name appears as founder and as a member of the committee. This is the last mention of him in connection with this work, for in the following year's report his name does not appear and no mention of his death at Birmingham on 16th July 1837, is made in the Society's records. All efforts to discover his grave have failed. Many of the graves in the churchyard in which he was probably buried have been removed and so it has not been possible to do honour to the resting place of the founder of the Society. He seems to 'have slipped out of this world unwept, un-honoured and unsung'.

Having rescued the Society from its debt, Gompertz set out to increase its activities and to attract the support of the public. In 1829 he wrote a tract on the objects of the Society, which gives us a 'pen picture' of the many forms of cruelty prevalent at the time, including the following: Sheep were driven 'for above a hundred miles' to market, and were goaded through the crowded streets, where after vainly attempting to allay their thirst in filthy gutters, they dropped from exhaustion. Sometimes their ears were torn off by dogs, sometimes their eyes were 'knocked out and their legs broken by drovers'. The slaughter houses were from ten to twelve feet underground, and into these the sheep were flung. The method of slaughter was 'according to the un-controlled fancy of the slaughterer'. Oxen were compelled to travel for many days with little or no food, they were killed by 'repeated blows of hammers on their heads'. Calves were packed into carts with their legs tied together, and afterwards kept for days in the underground slaughter house where they were slowly bled, to make the veal flesh white. During the process their mouths were 'kept closely muzzled with straps lest the public should be attracted by their moans'. Horses and donkeys were driven to death. Various animals were caused 'to mangle each other in public theatres and pits'. Bulls were baited for several days, eels were skinned alive, pigs were whipped to death. In the streets 'one heard the unceasing sound of the lash.'

In 1831 Gompertz resigned due to disagreements, however he was thanked for his work in redeeming the Society 'from a state of exhaustion and debts'. In spite of the lack of public support, the Society's committee declined to be pessimistic; they had undertaken the work of preventing cruelty to animals, and they intended to go through with it, with or without public support. Undaunted by the fact that the Society could not pay its way, and feeling that they could not make much headway with the public, one or two members of the committee resolved to see what they could do in Parliament. They decided, therefore, to try to improve then enforce Martin's Act by increasing its scope. The Society advanced a little way towards its goal; in 1835, its progress was more marked and was in fact, apparent even to the callous public.

That same year (1835) the Joseph Pease's Bill went before Parliament, a Bill which aimed at protecting all domestic animals, dogs of course included. This Bill passed through the Lords without discussion and received the Royal Assent on 9th September. This new measure provided a maximum penalty of forty shillings and a minimum of five shillings for cruelty to any animal. By this Act, keeping or using a place for baiting bulls, bears, dogs or other animals or for cock fighting, became punishable.

At the annual meeting of 1835 it was decided to have a Humane Drivers Fund, so that ladies might reward some of the men and boys who treated their animals well. The fund did not long remain in existence, not through lack of support, but there were no humane drivers to receive the awards. A little note in the report of 1835 is of great interest: 'It may well be worthy of consideration whether metal labels might not be very beneficially granted by the Society to those drivers who receive certificates of good and kind behaviour.' This custom of giving 'metal labels' in the form of brass badges of merit was subsequently inaugurated and began instantly growing in popularity at many shows held throughout the country.

The public were now learning to be kind to animals and all domestic animals were now protected by the laws passed in 1835. But many acts of gross cruelty were of common occurrence, and I propose to glance at a few of them.

Around that time, certain people in London gained their living by stealing cats, skinning them while they were alive, and selling their skins for 'imitation fur'. The skin of the female cat was preferred to that of a male, and it was supposed that a live animal could be skinned more easily than a dead one.

The young Victoria, who was extremely fond of cats, knew of this form of cruelty and wished to aid the Society in its war against that 'detestable race, the cat skinners' who 'tore the skins from the quivering frames and the victims of this brutality have been allowed to survive for many hours of intolerable anguish'. The Society prosecuted several persons for skinning cats alive. A constable who gave evidence at the trial of a young woman charged with having stolen thirteen cats stated that 'with a piece of baited liver she enticed the poor things into her reach, and then whipped off their jackets. In a few minutes they were struggling and sprawling skinless on the ground, and he had trouble of disposing them.' The case was dismissed due to there being no law for the protection of cats, however there was a certain Paving Act which provided penalties for people who created a nuisance in the street. At the conclusion of another cat skinning case, the magistrate fined the offender forty shillings for creating a nuisance by throwing the carcasses of the cats into the street. [At a similar case many years later in 1859 the maximum penalty of three months hard labour was inflicted; when the offender was taken out to the prison van his fellow prisoners booed him.]

Horses were then regarded by many people as mere machines, but there was some hope that a better time was in store for them; it was thought that horses would be superseded by steam. The public were demanding that coaches should be faster, but with increased speed accidents were more frequent and more severe.

The report of 1838 states that the Society had employed 'three powerful horses in assisting to draw carriages of all descriptions up Holborn and Ludgate Hills. The Society does not now provide such trace horses at hills. It found that carters, knowing that such horses were provided for them, gave their own horses the maximum load which they could pull on a level road. The provision of trace horses at hills thus encouraged rather than diminished cruelty to horses. One man finding his horse was unable to pull a laden cart out of mud, lit a fire under the horse and burned it.'

The worst horses must have been those in the night cabs of London. Slaughter men would sell on condemned horses to night cab drivers, the dark hiding the fact that the horse was 'badly broken down'. These horses were worked until they dropped dead. Many once fine horses who were deemed to be unfit to carry on hunting were sold on to 'draw coals from mines'.

It was during this period that the Society first sent inspectors to watch over ponies and donkeys employed on the sands at seaside towns. Many holiday makers were prosecuted. The Society prosecuted two men who rode a donkey round a field until it fell from exhaustion; they then beat it with sticks, tore out its tongue, and otherwise mutilated it. These men were sentenced to six weeks hard labour.

The provision of additional gas lamps was sought for Smithfield market in order to cut down on the use of lighted torches, a continual source of terror for cattle and sheep.

Mention is made in the 1837 report of cruelties to birds. 'Birds' eyes were put out to make them better songsters. It had for some time been the practice to employ pigeons to carry intelligence of the result of races and such matters; but lately they have been employed to carry news of the state of French funds for the purpose of stockjobbing. To prevent the news from reaching this country, persons have been stationed on the cliffs to shoot them as they come over.'

This brief glance at the records of the Society gives one a rough idea of the cruelties of this country when Princess Victoria, a girl of sixteen, came to their aid.

Queen Victoria's interest in the Society and its work never flagged. At the close of 1876, Her Majesty gave the Society a photograph of herself and Princess Beatrice for reproduction in *Animal World*, the official magazine of the Society. In December 1881 she commanded the Society prepare a medal, to be known as the 'Queens Medal', for presentation to some of its conspicuous workers. The design of which was submitted by the Queen who, when noticing that there was no cat among the animals depicted upon it directed that a cat should be placed in the foreground.

In 1835 the Society had embarked on the beginning of 20 years working towards the prevention of cruelty to dogs. There had been several scares of Hydrophobia in the early part of the nineteenth century, and more than one attempt was made to pass a Bill 'To prevent the spreading of canine madness'. While these scares prevailed stray dogs were cleared off the streets by the police. Local by-laws contained provisions for dealing with stray dogs.

An act of 1835 nominally protected dogs from cruelty but it did very little for them and left untouched the chief form of cruelty, the employment

QUEEN VICTORIA AND PRINCESS BEATRICE WITH THEIR
FAVOURITE DOGS.

From a photograph presented by Her Majesty to the Society.

THE QUEEN'S MEDAL.

To face p. 94.

of dogs as beasts of burden. Dogs were worked in this way because they were much cheaper than horses, ponies and donkeys, because they cost so little to keep, and because a dog-cart paid no tolls on the roads. Any attempt to suppress this cruelty was met with the objection that to do so would deprive many persons of their means of living. However in January 1836 Robert Batson, a member of the Society's committee, prosecuted a man for 'half starving three dogs, covered in sores, being used in a dog-cart'.

On 1st January 1840 the new regulation prohibiting the use of dogs as beasts of burden in London (only) came into force. Gradually town councils in other areas of the country introduced their own by-laws preventing the use of dog-carts in their respective boundaries It was not until 1855 that a bill was passed which included this clause.

Soon after the passing of this 1855 bill the first dog show was held in 1859, and was soon followed by others. With greater public interest in well bred dogs came an increase in the custom of 'cropping' the ears of dogs of certain breeds. This practice was illegal, having been outlawed by the bill of 1835, and carried a fine of six pence, but detection was difficult, as a man could not be prosecuted for 'owning' a dog with cropped ears. The act of preventing the 'cropping' of a dog's ears solely for fashion was next on the agenda for the Society. At this time the painter, Sir Edwin Landseer, who was a vice-president of the Society, invariably refused to paint a 'cropped' dog or a 'docked' horse. However it was not until early 1889 that the Kennel Club's committee began to concern itself in bringing about the abolition of 'cropping', but little was done until 1895 when the Kennel Club then passed a rule that no dog born after 31 March 1895, nor any Irish Terrier born after 31 December 1889, could, if cropped, win a prize at any show held under Kennel Club rules. Irish Terrier fanciers had been to the front in helping to bring about this reform.

[In 1860 the home for lost and starving dogs at Battersea had been founded by a Mrs Tealby, of Islington, her brother, the Revd Edward Bates, and a Mrs Major, after coming across a half starved homeless dog whilst they were out walking one evening. The two ladies afterwards tried to found a private refuge for dogs, but it was soon evident that the refuge would be too large an affair for private enterprise. An appeal was then made to the public by means of letters to the papers for support, which was soon forthcoming.]

While the Society had been engaged in securing the emancipation of dogs, the need of other reforms for the benefit of animals became plainly apparent.

In 1843 the attention of the public was again drawn to the shocking cruelties to horses in the knackers yards, horses which of course, should have been put to death quickly and painlessly. In many cases worn out horses were left to stand in the knackers stables until, so famished with hunger, they could be found to be gnawing at each other's manes and tails for want of food; and consumed with thirst, they dropped from sheer exhaustion and they became a prey to rats and other vermin. The living and the dead were heaped together until the living succumbed to their tortures. It was considered a little cheaper to leave the poor wretches to die in this fashion than to kill them. Thus early in 1844 a petition from the Society complaining of the inadequacy of the laws relating to knackers yards was presented to the House of Commons by the Hon. F.S. Wortley, and later in the year a bill for the regulation of knackers yards was introduced.

Humanitarians of the time now began to notice other signs of increased interest of the public in the welfare of animals. Veterinary surgeons now began to use anaesthetics when operating on animals, and the general public uttered the first protests against inadequate sentences passed on offenders found guilty of cruelty.

Another important measure now prohibited the sale and use of poisoned grain. The practice of destroying small birds by poisoned grain had become very common, and some measure for the protection of birds was certainly overdue. Having protected birds from being massacred in the fields, people naturally thought of the risks which other animals now incurred of being killed by poisoned food, and so the Poisoned Flesh Prohibition Bill was passed.

The rapid passing of these measures shows plainly enough that by this time the public were on the side of the animals. People who saw cases of cruelty to animals wrote to papers. Thus, letters appeared in *The Times* protesting against the brutal cruelty of drivers to the horses used in carting gravel for the building of the Thames Embankment in 1865. Soon afterwards the same paper drew the attention of the public to the practice of torturing calves by bleeding them to death in order to obtain 'white veal'. In the same year protests were made in the papers against the cruelties inflicted on cattle and sheep on board ship and in railway trucks at home. The public's attention also turned to the plight of the 100,000 or more animals working below ground. [However the Coal Mines Act was not passed until 1911.]

In May 1869 the Baroness Burdett-Coutts laid the foundation stone of the Society's headquarters in Jermyn Street. The Baroness also now formed the 'Ladies Humane Society'. Among the duties of this committee was the work of introducing humane education into the schools of the country. To teach young people the duty of kindness to animals was considered the most important department of its work. While the Society was thus pressing forward its work among children, one of its members suggested the establishment of another branch. The Society protected animals from cruelty, but many children were in equal need of protection from ill treatment. This humane person [name undiscovered] was clearly thinking ahead of his or her time. A branch of the Society was not then formed, but in 1884 a separate society for this object, the 'National Society for the Prevention of Cruelty to Children' was founded. A branch being founded at Carlisle in 1892, the NSPCC became another charity in whose works Priscilla Hannah Johnston took a great interest.

The *Carlisle Journal* of Friday 1st July 1892 reported thus on the meeting held on the 24th June in the hall of the County Hotel concerning the formation of this branch:

> The Chairman in opening the meeting said the only objection he had heard against the establishment of a Society of this kind in Carlisle was that they were so very kind and good to their children that there was no necessity for anything of the kind; but he was told by those who knew better that it was a mistaken idea to suppose there was no cruelty to children in their old City.
>
> The Revd Benjamin Waugh, of London [Director of the Society] who was then called upon, explained the work and objects of the Society, which was formed eight years ago. Prior to that time he pointed out that nothing was done to prevent cruelty to children, but since then the Society had dealt with cases involving the welfare of 44,405 children, and had landed 2,800 men and women in gaol, whilst 16,000 had listened to the warnings of the Society and had mended their ways without being prosecuted. The great majority of the prosecutions were for neglect and starvation, with respect to which he gave many painful illustrations, showing that except for the methods of the Society they would have escaped detection. Three years ago, he stated, there was no law in England to prevent a man starving his children, whilst it was the law of the land that if a man starved a puppy he might have three months

imprisonment. The Society had however raised the baby to the level of the dog.

Having referred to other alterations which had been effected in the law for the benefit of children, he claimed that the Society had proved itself worthy of support, and concluded by showing that a change was required in the law with reference to baby-farming and child insurance, in connection with which subjects he mentioned the case of a woman in whose charge fourteen children died in two years, eleven of them being insured.

The Bishop of Barrow then moved the following resolution: That in view of the beneficial effects of the operation of the NSPCC in many parts of the United Kingdom, it is hereby resolved that an aid committee be established for the district.

The Revd J. Christie seconded the motion, remarking that some of them who had sat on the by-laws committee of the School Board knew that there were many cases of flagrant neglect of children.

The resolution being carried, a committee was afterwards elected to appoint an executive and communicate with the central Committee for incorporation; and at the conclusion of the meeting several ladies and gentleman, at the invitation of Miss Johnston of the Beeches, partook of tea at the hotel. At a meeting held subsequently, it was agreed to guarantee £150 per annum to ensure a permanent officer for the district.

It was not until the year 1900 that protection was afforded to wild animals, whether free or in captivity by the 'Wild Animals in Captivity Protection Act'. It was later repealed by the 'Protection of Animals Act' of 1911, which incorporated it in substance. By means of this short and practical measure the scope of the Society's work was greatly increased, and a wide loophole which had allowed the escape of numerous offenders for acts of cruelty, sometimes of the grossest nature, was effectually sealed.

From 1835 we may pass to the Prevention of Cruelty to Animals Act of 1849. This act was for the next sixty two years the most important statute existing for the protection of animals. It repealed the previous act of 1835, widened the class of existing offences, and, in general now gave much greater scope for humane activities.

Since its inception the Society had found cause for concern at the methods of slaughtering animals. They now turned their efforts into trying to discover an instrument for the humane killing of animals. In pursuit of this goal the Society carefully examined the various methods employed in the slaughterhouses. The most common instrument was of course the pole-axe, but there was more than one kind of pole-axe. A method named after its originator, a Mr Wackett, needed the employment of two men. One man held a short bolt on the head of the beast, and the slaughter man, using a mallet, drove the bolt home into the skull. In some places a guillotine was used for killing the animals; sometimes an animal was shot with an ordinary gun and the Spanish method of killing was by the use of a large dagger.

There followed an important trial of various slaughtering instruments held at Liepzig, however no improved instrument was forthcoming until 1895, when Mr Greener, of 68 Haymarket, London, acting as agent for a Swiss inventor, Mr Stahl, of Zurich, introduced a pistol for slaughtering cattle. The barrel of the pistol was fixed to a disc. After modifications this became the instrument which was used at the Carlisle abattoir, under the management of Mr Dodds.

It was not until 1907 that the RSPCA humane cattle killer was invented. This invention owed its existence to the Boer war. Captain Derriman (general secretary 1905-1908) its inventor, had been a transport officer in South Africa. In the course of his duties he frequently had to have disabled trek oxen destroyed, an operation which was usually effected with the help of a service revolver. But occasionally it was difficult to use the weapon at close quarters. This difficulty suggested the idea of attaching a pistol barrel to a shaft, which enabled the operator to stand clear of the animal when firing. By 1911 800 humane killers were in use in private and public slaughter houses and other instruments for humanely killing animals had been invented.

While the Society was occupied with this task of finding a humane method of killing animals it was also engaged in trying to bring about the abolition of 'obscure dens where slaughtering was entrusted to the scum of the people', the private slaughter houses. In 1882 the London Model Abattoir Society was formed for providing sanitary and humane methods of killing animals for food.

It must be remembered that the Society could not take one and only one view on this subject for there were those members who were vegetarians who objected to animal destruction for food. There were also those who as meat eaters had no such objections, however they did object to the destruction of animals subjected to painful experiments. This resulted in the passing of the Cruelty to Animals Act of 1876, which regulated the practice of vivisection and stated that only persons holding a licence from a Secretary of State should perform painful experiments on animals. The Society confined its attention to ensuring, so far as it was able to under the Government system of inspection, that the provisions and safeguards of the Act were properly enforced. However, owing to the fact that many experiments were taking place in secret, prosecutions were extremely difficult.

This was not so in the all too public display of the cruelty inflicted on animals by the drovers in and around the markets. To prevent cruelty to animals when they were being driven or brought to slaughter was not a simple matter either, for 'the custom of the trade' was accepted by some magistrates as an excuse for brutality. It was suggested that heads of families should instruct servants not to accept any joint from a butcher which had the appearance of a wound or a bruise on it. The butcher would then entreat the drovers to abstain from ill-treating the animals.

The work of the Society had now grown to such an extent that branches were being founded all over the country. On the 7th November 1879 the local *Carlisle Journal* reported, 'In connection with the Cumberland and Westmorland branch of the Royal Society for the Prevention of Cruelty to Animals, an inspector [Inspector Craigie] has now been stationed permanently at Carlisle. The recent appeal for local contributions to the funds of the Society has not yet met with much response in the shape of actual gifts of money, but it is hoped that now that the officer is at work, subscriptions will flow more freely into the treasurer's hands.'[40]

The earliest reference in RSPCA publications to a branch in Carlisle, Cumberland or Westmorland appears on page 21 of the February 1880 issue of the *Animal World* (the RSPCA Magazine) where there is a list of 'Branches of RSPCA and Kindred Societies' which includes a branch at Carlisle with T.H. Godding as Secretary.[41] Owing to the large area covered by the Cumberland and Westmorland branch, however, it experienced mixed financial fortunes over the next decade, resulting in its 'near folding'.

On the 8th November 1889, the *Carlisle Journal* reported, 'The Secretary in reading the annual report pointed out that there was ample work in Carlisle alone for one officer, and appealed for support to enable the Society to maintain a sufficient number of officers for the district. The annual statement of accounts showed that there was raised for the year £293 0s. 4d. of which £265. 17s. 10d. was remitted to the Parent Society.

The expenses for printing, advertising and other things amounted to £27 2s. 6d. The total amount of the subscriptions for previous years was only £50.'[42]

On the 4th November 1892, the *Carlisle Journal* reported:

> The treasurer's statement showed that the total receipts for the year, amounted to £229 10s. 6d. as against £214 4s. 8d. for the preceding year. Taking into account that the cost of maintenance of each officer amounted to £250 per annum, it must be seen that the funds of the branch were still quite inadequate to maintain two officers at present employed, and that therefore it continued to be largely dependent upon augmentation from the Parent Society. This was far from being as it should be, and it was felt that a strong effort should be made to place the branch upon a more independent and satisfactory basis, and upon one more worthy of two counties of the size and importance of Cumberland and Westmorland.
>
> In reply The Bishop of Carlisle pointed out that they [the Parent Society] ought to remember that the diocese of Carlisle though territorially large was, in regard to population, small, not being more than two thirds of the population of the City of Liverpool. That was a fact which ought to be borne in mind by the Secretaries of many of the Societies in London who, from his experience, were in the habit of coming north and saying 'Oh, this is a great County, a large diocese,' thinking it was a kind of 'happy hunting ground' for them, but not sufficiently remembering that the population was comparatively small, and that it was a population moreover, composed largely of agriculturists who had been hard hit lately. Therefore while they pleaded for an increase of revenue he thought on the whole he should congratulate the Society upon the increases there had been in the income during the year. There had also been a large increase of convictions for cruelty, 28 more than the previous year, and the number of warnings had been 570, as against 320 last year.'[43]

However the following year's annual meeting showed their fortunes had taken a turn for the better: 'The annual report stated amongst other things that during the past year the work of the Society had been carried on in Cumberland and Westmorland with unabated activity ... In spite of the depression of trade in West Cumberland, the subscriptions of the Whitehaven auxiliary were in excess of those of last year – £34 9s. as against £32 13s. 6d. and that auxiliary was congratulated upon having maintained as energetically as ever their share of the work.'

The Chairman congratulated the friends of the Society upon the large attendance and upon the report. But as friends of the Society it seemed to him that prevention was better than cure, and he was sure much might be done amongst children by introducing into all elementary schools Humane Reading Books. He also thought that much might be done in the Sunday Schools, '... as the Bible abounded with teaching on the subject. (Cheers)'[44]

It was also around this time in Carlisle, as Co-Secretary [with Mr G.F. Saul] of the Cumberland and Westmorland branch of the RSPCA, Priscilla Johnston, with an eye for improving standards, believed that only good could come from befriending 'the man with the willow' [the drover and his stick]. True to form, for a number of years, at her own expense she organised the annual Carlisle Drovers' Suppers (as mentioned earlier), bringing together all manner of people from the trade. Here they would be entertained by an excellent musical programme, where a number of local butchers - Mr John Bell, Mr George Rigg, Mr Corrie, Mr Bell of Tait Street and Mr Bell of Bowman Street, all keen to display their highest standards – provided quality meat, and also assisting in carving and serving throughout the supper.

Although these suppers were initiated by Miss Johnston, who supported them up until the final year of her life, the function eventually became organised by the RSPCA. It was run to a very great extent on subscriptions in money and kind given to them, in respect of Miss Johnston, with an almost lavish hand by the local butchers, breeders, trades people and the public in general.[45]

A glance at the annual reports of the RSPCA shows how far reaching the influence of its work for animals, which starting in a small way in 1824, now extended to all parts of the globe.

It is not possible in the space at my disposal to refer to the founding and the works of the Society in other countries, but one such off-shoot is deserving of attention: the Naples Society for the Protection of Animals, of which Miss Johnston, almost from its inception, was Hon. Secretary.

The Naples Society for the Protection of Animals was founded in 1891 by Princess Mele Barese (nee Mackworth Praed) of Italy. It met at first with little pecuniary support, and would soon have collapsed but for the magnificent and repeated gifts of its treasurer Mr J.H. Buxton (cousin to Miss Johnston, by the 1845 marriage of her uncle, Thomas Fowell Buxton and Rachel Jane Gurney of Leytonstone).

For some years it had to struggle constantly against the violent opposition of the people and the indifference of the authorities; but it steadily won both over to its side and by 1903 employed 22 inspectors at work not only in Naples and the neighbourhood, but also at Rome, Genoa, Alassio, Bordighera, Brindisi and Sicily.

In the Society's office there was a room fifteen feet square and ten feet high, the walls of which were covered from floor to ceiling with thousands of spiked curb chains and other metal instruments of torture confiscated by the inspectors who, in the course of the first thirteen years of the Society's being had destroyed the enormous number of 222,000 sticks and 27,000 stakes used for beating animals.

The annual report of the 1st June 1903, which was carried in the form of a letter addressed to the readers of *The Times*, stated that at the annual horse and donkey parades a steady improvement had been seen year by year in the care bestowed on the animals. A large number of the cab horses in Naples, which were formerly lame, miserable, thin and covered with sores were now in splendid condition. It also included the following appeal by 'PORTLAND' of 2 Grosvenor Square, London: 'I regret to learn that the income of this admirable society has recently fallen off considerably: and I appeal to the generosity of your readers to assist it in carrying on its serious and much needed work.'

The yearly report released in June 1905 from Naples stated that during 1904 its inspectors had confiscated about 26,000 sticks and stakes used for beating; besides 1,105 spiked bits and many other instruments of torture. They had prosecuted 3,094 cases of which 1,070 were for beating, 835 for overloading and 945 for sores. Three persons had been convicted for plucking fowls alive and two for blinding decoy birds to make them sing at night. The Society had also suppressed the disgusting exhibition of the Dog Grotto near Naples, where for centuries a dog had been plunged into carbolic acid gas to show that the latter will not support life and then released after terrible struggles, only to be subjected again to the same process twenty or thirty times a day for the amusement of sightseers. The Society had prosecuted the owner of the Grotto several times without success. Finally, after agitating in the Italian newspapers, it induced the Italian government to forbid the spectacle. It had also caused the local authorities throughout Southern Italy to prohibit bull baiting.

In England, where Priscilla served as its Hon. Secretary *The Times* regularly carried appeals on behalf of the Society.

The following letter appeared in *The Times* on Monday 4th June 1906:

NAPLES SOCIETY FOR THE PROTECTION OF ANIMALS.

TO THE EDITOR OF THE TIMES.

Sir,—I venture to ask you again to publish in *The Times* an appeal on behalf of the Naples Society for the Protection of Animals. When founded by me in 1891, with the generous assistance of Mr. J. H. Buxton, who is still its treasurer, the society's district was limited to this city; but its work now covers the greater part of the provinces of Naples and Salerno, while there are branches at Carrara and Girgenti. It has 16 inspectors, who during 1905 had extra animals attached to 21,780 overloaded carts, destroyed 28,490 sticks, confiscated 1,865 iron instruments of torture, and secured 4,451 convictions. The society does not, however, confine itself to the prevention of cruelty, but distributes literature inculcating kindness to animals, gives prizes for the best-kept horses and donkeys, maintains drinking-troughs, and plants trees on cabstands to shelter the horses from the intense heat of the Italian summer sun.

Our work is not without personal danger. Ten days ago the honorary director was injured by a fall of rocks, owing to his having remained behind during the blasting of a quarry at Carrara in order to rescue a fallen bullock; last month he was assaulted by a carter; and 19 attempts have been made to assassinate him. We who carry on the work are willing to risk our lives for it if only we receive the means to continue it, and I appeal once more to my generous compatriots, begging them to help us in our arduous undertaking.

Contributions, both great and small, will be thankfully received and promptly acknowledged by Miss P. H. Johnston, The Beeches, Carlisle, or by Mr. Leonard T. Hawksley, 2, Via Vittoria, Naples, Italy.

Yours truly,

E. L. M. (PRINCESS) MELE BARESE (née Mackworth Praed), President of the Naples Society for the Protection of Animals.

Naples, May 30.

In the years after Miss Priscilla's involvement with the Society, it continued to work tirelessly for animal welfare. During the First World War nearly £200,000 was raised and used to alleviate the suffering of animals caught up in the hostilities. This included the building of 500 kennels in England to accommodate the dogs who had been faithful companions to soldiers in the trenches when they returned home after the Armistice.

In gathering up the threads of the Society's work during its first 100 years, the outstanding impression one gets is of the steady and natural growth of the Society's influence on mankind as a whole. It has been the story of gradual achievements, which have brought about many changes in the country's manners, customs, and thoughts barely dreamed of by those who first conceived the idea of founding such a work.

The Story of District Nursing[46]

The first organized district nursing in England began in 1840 with the English Protestant Sisters of Charity, subsequently called 'Nursing Sisters', though the foundation came into being through the labours of Elizabeth Fry. The nurses, who were supplied with uniforms and lived in a 'Home' in Devonshire Square, Bishopsgate, took no vows, but visited the sick poor under the direction of the clergy.

In 1845 the famous tractarian leader, Edward Bouverie Pusey, established the Park Village Community in Regents Park. The nurses of this community received no special training, and much religious ritual was bound up with their daily routine. The Sisters of Mercy, founded by Priscilla Sellon at Devonport three years later, likewise had no regular training at first. This movement spread to Bethnal Green and to Pimlico, later amalgamating with Pusey's community.

In 1847 the eminent London ophthalmologist William Bowman (afterwards Sir William Bowman, Bt.) emphasized the need for a training institute for nurses, and in the following year the community of St John's House came into existence at 36 Fitzroy Square, in the district of St John the Evangelist, St Pancras, from which it took it's name. Later the House moved to Norfolk Street, Strand, and in 1907 to Queen Square, Bloomsbury. In 1919 the Nursing Sisters of St John were taken over by St Thomas's Hospital as a private nursing organization.

The year 1859 is a memorable one in the history of district nursing, for in that year William Rathbone, a prosperous Liverpool merchant and philanthropist, engaged Mary Robinson, the nurse who had attended his first wife in her last illness, on a trial period of three months to visit poor patients in their own homes in the Liverpool slums. When, after much discouragement and many rebuffs, her work began to bear fruit, Rathbone tried to recruit other suitable nurses, but found that none was available. He then consulted the Royal Infirmary Committee and undertook to build at his own expense a training school and home for nurses. Its objects were to train nurses for work in the infirmary and for visiting the sick poor in their own homes; also to look after well-to-do private patients. The Liverpool Training School and Home for Nurses in Ashton Street was in operation by 1st May 1863.

In 1866 Liverpool was divided into eighteen districts and a nurse allotted to each district, hence the term 'District Nursing'. Ladies resident in the city superintended the work of the nurses, paid for their lodgings, and provided medical comforts and food for those of the sick too poor to supply their own needs. In 1876 a matron was placed in charge of each group of nurses and the groups were concentrated in district homes. In 1898 the district nursing activities of the Training School were transferred to the Liverpool Queen Victoria District Nursing Association (so named because of the Queen's Jubilee in 1887) which was used to develop district nursing.

The first association to give nurses trained in hospital an exclusive district nursing training was the Metropolitan and National Nursing Association, founded in 1874 by William Rathbone in accordance with Florence Nightingale's suggestions for improving the nursing service for the sick poor. Two years later Florence Lees was appointed its first superintendent, at 23 Bloomsbury Square.

Associations similar to the Liverpool body were established at Manchester and at Salford in 1864, and at Leicester in 1867. Soon the rest of the UK, and many other countries, would follow suit.

Queen Victoria devoted £70,000 of the 'Women's Jubilee Gift' to furthering the 'nursing of the sick and poor in their own homes by means of trained nurses', and, largely through the efforts of Miss Nightingale and the great surgeon Sir James Paget, who were convinced of the importance of training nurses for district work, the Queen Victoria Jubilee Institute for Nurses was founded. In 1899 it was granted a Royal Charter, adopted the Metropolitan and National Nursing Association as its nucleus in London, and subsequently became affiliated with the Liverpool and other associations. At the Diamond Jubilee in 1897, and on the occasion of the Queen's death in 1901, further sums were given to promote district nursing throughout the British Isles. The greater part of the sum raised as a national memorial to Queen Alexandra was also devoted to this cause.

The report of the Cumberland Nursing Association, of which Priscilla Johnston was a much valued worker, appeared in the *Carlisle Journal* on the 24th October 1905 stating that:

> Doctors throughout the country recognised the immense value of the services which they had derived and could derive from having

fully trained nurses at their disposal to carry out their injunctions in attending cases for which they were called in. Those who chiefly benefited were the poorer classes of the Country. Though at first they were perhaps somewhat indisposed to receive some of the nurses into their homes, had now themselves come to recognise the valuable aid which those women rendered to them in their homes in cases of sickness and distress. A Dr Lediard believed that the ladies of this county by their work had established a sympathetic bond between the rich and the poor, and he congratulated the Association on that circumstance.

When Queen Mary became Patron in 1925, the Institute was renamed the Queen's Institute of District Nursing, and in 1932 it was provided by the National Birthday Trust with new quarters at 57 Lower Belgrave Street. By 1948, 2,716 associations were affiliated with it.

The 1904 origins of the Carlisle Charity Organisation Society

The Carlisle Charity Organisation Society, to which Priscilla Johnston latterly became a subscriber, was not truly established until 1904, though its formation had been proposed some twenty years earlier, along with proposals for the foundation of what appears to have been an early form of 'Meals on Wheels'.

In the *Carlisle Journal* of 7th February 1880 there appeared an article concerning the annual meeting of the Carlisle Dispensary Subscribers. Of Carlisle's charitable institutions the Dispensary claimed the first place in seniority, having been founded on 1st July 1782.

Under the heading 'Provision For The Sick Poor In Carlisle. Annual Meeting Of The Carlisle Dispensary Subscribers' the *Carlisle Journal* states that it discussed establishing a Sick Provision Fund in the city. Canon Prescott spoke.

> It had been suggested, but had been thrown out at the last meeting, that it would be very valuable to have in this City a Charity Organisation Society or Institute equivalent to that which should include the Sick Provision Fund of which they had been talking. However the present view was that establishing a Charity Organisation Society was a little bit in the clouds, too large. This sick persons' fund might very well be affiliated to such a Society afterwards. He did not see his way to

such a Society being formed just yet. If the Mayor should think fit at any future time, whether long distant or only a short period hence, to try to institute such an institution as that he would co-operate in the carrying out to the best of his ability, but at present he thought it would be better to deal with that of establishing a Sick Provisions Fund, which they could go on with at once.

He observed that the proposal was to provide provisions of nourishing food and so forth for the sick who were attended to by the Dispensary medical men. It had also been suggested at this meeting that a room or two might be hired and to have a woman, who would be an honest, cleanly, able sort of cook and who would cook for the sick, who would attend regularly, say for instance three days a week.

He wished to bring the thoughts of those of well off connections that he should like the poor to receive gifts in kind and also information that any who were well to do would be glad to give a poor child, who was known to be sick a pint of milk for a fortnight or dinner for a week, and so give them gifts in kind.

By this means they might bring the thoughts of people of means absolutely into contact with those in the neighbourhood who were in want. He could not help thinking it would have a good effect on those who gave and those who received. He was quite certain that such a scheme could be carried out if they got the ladies generally to assist them in such a cause. (Cheers)

A Dr Elliot continues:

In many Towns in the Kingdom experiments more or less successful have been tried for supplying the poor. They had some years ago tried an experiment in where Soup of the very best quality was sold at a penny a pint, and yet leaving a profit. That institution was imitated in many parts of the Country and its good work was published far and wide.

A Mr Scott agreed that the scheme was feasible but thought he saw some difficulties: 'What if the "Sick Poor" were unable to come and get the food? ... every dinner or breakfast would need to be carried to them and they would require a messenger or somebody to do this.' He concluded that they had better commence the scheme small scale and enlarge the scope of it afterwards.

Canon Prescott declared he believed £100 to be the necessary expenditure at the very outset. The Mayor said that he would take steps for informing the public that donations would be gladly received; also annual subscriptions for carrying out the objects of the fund.

Subscriptions and donations given before the meeting amounted to between £30 and £40.[47]

The Carlisle Charity Organisation (CCOS) was eventually formed in 1904, operating from 38 Scotch Street with the Revd H. P. M. Lafone as Chairman. Miss Mary Ellen Creighton sat upon the Executive Committee and Miss Amy Beevor upon the general Committee. Aunt 'Pris' can be found listed among the subscribers.

	General Fund.	Relief Fund.	Pension Fund.	Emigration Fund.	Blencathra Sanatorium Fund.
	£ s. d.	£ s. d.	£ s. d.	£ s. d.	£ s. d.
Holy Trinity Poor Fund	...	0 8 9	...	...	...
Hodgson, C. B.	...	...	...	1 0 0	...
Hill, Miss N.	0 2 6	...	...	...	...
Hudson, Rev. Canon	1 1 0	...	...	...	...
Henderson, Miss A. F.	0 5 0	...	...	...	...
Hayton, F.	0 10 0	...	...	...	...
Henderson, Mrs M. W.	0 10 0	...	...	...	...
Howard, Mrs., Corby Castle	0 10 6	...	...	...	...
Irwin, Mrs., Lynehow	2 0 0	...	...	3 0 0	...
Johnston, Miss, The Beeches	1 0 0	3 0 0	0 13 0	...	...
Lafone, Rev. H. P. M.	1 1 0	...	...	1 1 0	...
Ling, C.	...	3 3 0	...	...	...
Lowry, Miss	...	0 4 3	...	...	...
Liddell, Mrs., Warwick Hall	1 0 0	...	...	...	...
Lawson, Lady	1 0 0	...	...	...	...
Lindow, Rev. S.	...	...	...	...	0 5 0
MacLaren, Dr.	1 1 0	...	...	...	...
Martindale, John	0 10 0	...	...	...	...
MacInnes, Miles	2 2 0	...	...	...	...
MacInnes, Miss	0 5 0	...	...	...	...
Mark, W. D.	...	0 2 0	...	...	...
Matravers, J. H.	0 5 0	...	...	...	...
Matravers, Miss M. H.	0 5 0	...	...	...	...
Matravers, Miss E. C.	0 10 0	...	...	...	...
Moses, Mrs.	1 0 0	...	...	...	...
Mayo, Miss	0 10 0	...	...	...	...
Nelson, James	0 10 6	...	...	...	...
Orman, Miss	...	0 13 0	...	...	...
Phillips, Rev. Canon	0 10 6	1 1 0	...	...	...

The 1904 CCOS report
Miss Johnston of The Beeches is listed in 'Subscriptions and Donations'

During the fifteen years prior to the foundation of the CCOS Aunt 'Pris', who at that time had still been in reasonably good health, became involved with the aims of the 'Provision for the sick poor in Carlisle', often visiting the sick and hungry in their own homes to discover their needs, and The Beeches was frequently the scene of a large gathering of these less fortunate locals sampling her fare.

One of the oldest such Charity Organisations in the Country the CCOS was indeed the fore runner to modern day Carlisle Council for Voluntary Service (CVS) which today operates from 27 Spencer Street, Carlisle.

With the creation of the Welfare State over 40 years ago times of illness and unemployment meant desperate hardship for many people. The aim of the CCOS was to organise efforts in providing charitable help in such cases.

The CCOS was made up of annual Subscribers, local people such as Aunt 'Pris' and her family and friends, who contributed a minimum of 5s. a year to be used for 'the improvement of the condition of the poor'. Each year the subscribers elected a committee who ran the Society. The committee reads like a 'Who's Who' of the great and good in Carlisle at the time. Many committee members were the daughters of wealthy families, who, unable to further their education or careers, were instead expected, in typical Victorian tradition, to carry out philanthropic works.

The Society worked in a very paternalistic fashion. Underlying their efforts was a belief that financial aid was not a right to be claimed by all, but should be awarded only to the most deserving cases. To establish which were the cases entitled to receive help, the Society set up a complex vetting procedure. Applicants were expected to call into the offices and fill in an application form explaining why they should be helped and providing references to their good character. This was then followed up with interviews of landlords and neighbours, as well as a home visit, which Aunt 'Pris' would often have carried out as part of her work for this Society and others. A report would then be compiled for the Executive Committee, upon which they would judge the case, and, if thought suitable, aid would be offered.

This aid varied depending on what was deemed to be most beneficial to the claimant: long term sick cases were sent to recuperate in the Sanatorium at Blencathra or by the sea side at Silloth; travel grants were given to help stranded travellers complete journeys home, or in some cases to emigrate; help was provided to find employment. As a rule assistance was made as a loan, the claimant being expected to pay the Society back when he or she was able.

Over time the Society found itself involved in a wider range of activities, such as the setting up of an emigration fund, a savings account, an employment register, pension scheme and a children's cottage home.

The CCOS was indeed the forerunner of the modern day Carlisle County Voluntary Service (CVS), one feature, of which Priscilla Johnston would wholeheartedly have approved, remaining at the heart of both organisations: the value of voluntary help.

By 1919 the organisation had become known as the (CCSS) Carlisle

Council of Social Services and moved to 10 Victoria Place. The yearly report of 1919 sets out this change, 'What is generally known as social work has appeared in the past as the efforts of the well to do to improve the conditions of those living in worse circumstances'. The report of 1920 defines the ideal of Social Service to be one worthy of support namely 'the removal of human sorrow, the clearing up of human confusion and the diminishing of human misery.'

At this time three district Committees were formed leading to the creation of the Carlisle Cripple Clinic (1926), the Clog Fund (1927), the Carlisle Housing Improvement Society (1929), the Mayor's Committee for the amelioration of the condition of the unemployed (1933), the setting up of Currock House Community Centre (1941), the Haigs homes at Harraby (1938), the Citizens' Advice Bureau (1939).

In 1944 the CCSS moved to 27 Spencer Street (which in 1953 was gifted to the Society by F.N. Hepworth), at which time they began a survey of all aspects of life in Carlisle.

The next few years saw the creation of the Welfare State and the expansion of the local Authority responsibilities. This took over some of the functions that the original CCOS had set up.

The Old People's Welfare Council was formed in March 1965 with nine old people's clubs functioning in the city. It was during this year that the CCSS moved to the Town Hall, leading to them setting up a Tourist Information Centre there.

In 1974 The CCSS changed its name to Voluntary Action, with this being replaced in line with the nationally accepted form as, Carlisle Council for Voluntary Service in 1979. The Old People's Welfare was eventually absorbed into Age Concern in 1983.

The CVS continued to evolve and in 1989 moved back into its home at 27 Spencer Street and has remained there ever since. Despite the name changes and the evolving emphasis over the last 100 years, one feature has remained the bedrock of the organisation, which, I am sure Aunt 'Pris' would have whole-heartedly agreed with: the value of voluntary help.[48]

The Story of the Board of Guardians[49]

The site which St Martin's College, Fusehill Street, Carlisle now occupies, was previously the city's General Hospital, originally the Fusehill Union Workhouse. The workhouse was administered by an official body known

The Fusehill Union Workhouse, erected in 1863, opened in April 1864 for the accommodation of 500 poor men, women and children

as the Board of Guardians, comprising of publicly spirited men and women who were elected by the rate payers in much the same way as the local councillors are today to serve on the City Council. Their period of office extended for three years but, on termination of this time, they could seek re-election.

The establishment of workhouses was a direct result of the Poor Law Act of 1834 which was intended to improve on the original Elizabethan Poor Law Act (1601) by extending the relief available to the poor while seeking to avoid any exploitation of the law by those merely looking for 'free hand-outs'. In order that the daily needs of the sick and destitute could be more adequately dealt with, it was decided to place those eligible for 'relief' in accommodation specially designated for those in need. Thus, from the best of motives, arose an institution which, largely through its portrayal by Charles Dickens in *Oliver Twist*, became notorious as one of the worst manifestations of nineteenth century hypocrisy and was memorably targeted by George R. Sims in his powerful, if somewhat histrionic, monologue *In the Workhouse, Christmas Day*. This is unfortunate for not all workhouses were like that ruled over by Mr and Mrs Bumble.

The Carlisle Board of Guardians, together with its counterparts in town and country areas throughout the land, owed its origin to the first

Poor Law Act passed in the reign of Queen Elizabeth I in 1601 – a necessary measure to alleviate the miserable plight of countless men, women and children.

Since the early days of Christianity, the plight of poor people had been a severe problem and before the year 1601, there had been no official approach or effort to help their condition. Their circumstances were deplorable, wages were small, food was expensive and many people, particularly in the larger towns and cities, were exposed to misery against which the law afforded no protection. Many of them lived, worked and died in the most appalling conditions.

Under the new Law of 1601, it was possible to help meet the needs of the unfortunate and destitute poor and this help was given by way of cash payments. Money for this, however, which was levied on what was known as the Poor Rate (subscribed by rate payers) was neither plentiful nor adequate. Yet many rate payers complained that it was a direct encouragement to thriftlessness. Many claimed that the cash relief was given to the poor at random (the more children a man had, the more money he received) and there is no doubt that some unscrupulous employers used to employ the poor because part of their wage would be paid from the rates.

This state of affairs continued until 1834 when the new Poor Law Act was passed, which was to extend the degree of relief to be afforded. To avoid any exploitation of the law, and in order that the daily needs of the sick and destitute poor could be more adequately dealt with, it was decided to build workhouses for the accommodation of those in need.

Another Act was to follow which had for its objectives the Medical Relief of the sick poor in separate accommodation, to be known as Poor Law Infirmaries.

This brief description then of circumstances and events formed the background of the policy which prompted the Carlisle Board of Guardians to acquire the site at Fusehill and later, to invite by open competition to qualified architects plans and drawings for the two main buildings, the larger to serve as the Workhouse and the other as the Poor Law Infirmary.

The successful competitors were a Bradford firm, Lockwood and Mason and this Italian styled design was converted into bricks and mortar at a cost, unbelievable today, of under £15,000. The imposing facades have not lessened over the years, and have been in use until the late 1990s: the larger building being the main block of the City General Hospital

The Board of Guardians of the Fusehill Workhouse. The lady in the centre with the white apron was Nurse Parker (also a friend of Priscilla Johnston), the first district nurse of Carlisle

and the other the birthplace of so many local children, the City Maternity Hospital.

Aunt 'Pris' would regularly attend the fortnightly meetings of the Guardians of the Poor of the Carlisle Union, held in the Board Room or dining room of the Fusehill Workhouse. Over the period of her involvement with the Board of Guardians she was elected to, and held positions on, several committees. With the resignation of Mrs Hetherington in November 1898 she was elected Guardian for the Botchergate Parish, which covered the Fusehill Workhouse. She also sat on the House, Hospital and Revision Committee, the Fusehill and Harraby Hill [Workhouse] Visiting Committee, the 'Clothing Committee' and – perhaps particularly dear to her heart – the Orphan Children's Committee.

As a member of the latter Aunt 'Pris' would frequently visit children boarded into foster care, checking they were happy and well, their chosen homes were clean and assessing by interview the suitability of the foster parents. All being well, 2s. per week for each child would be allocated to the foster parents to meet all the needs of the children in their care.

Aunt 'Pris' was also present at the April 1900 Orphan Children's

1897-8.

CARLISLE UNION.

LIST OF GUARDIANS.

CHALKER, Mrs. JULIA	8 George Street, Carlisle.
HETHERINGTON, Mrs. ANN	27 London Road, Carlisle.
JOHNSTON, Miss H. P.	The Beeches, Rickerby
ARMSTRONG, T. J.	Duncowfold
BELL, J. I.	22 Broad Street
BRISCO, RICHARD	Ghyll House, Wreay
BROWNRIGG, WILLIAM	Carleton
BULMORE, JOSEPH	18 River Street
BURNS, ROBERT	Caldew Terrace
COWEN, R. W.	Mill Ellers, Dalston
DALTON, PATTINSON	Cummersdale
FOSTER, WILLIAM	45 Chiswick Street
GIBSON, JOSEPH	27 English Street
GILL, T. L.	Scuggar House
HODGSON, RICHARD	Midtown, Burgh
HODGSON, ROBERT	Beaumont
HODGSON, T. H.	Newby Grange
IRVING, WILLIAM	Rockcliffe
LAING, DAVID	3 Paternoster Row
LITTLE, ROBERT	Norfolk Road
NICHOLSON, J. W.	10 Clementina Terrace, Gloucester Road, Carlisle
PATTINSON, M. H.	Chatsworth Square
POTTER, THOMAS	Gatesgill Hall
RITSON, JOHN	5 Cecil Street
ROBINSON, THOS.	Cargo
ROBINSON, WILLIAM	11 Broad Street
SCOTT, JOE	74 Etterby Street, Stanwix
SIBSON, THOMAS	Grinsdale
STEWART, RICHARD	14 Hart Street, Carlisle
TEASDALE, ANTHONY	Scotby
THOMLINSON, R. H.	34 Port Road, Carlisle
THOMPSON, GEORGE	Devonshire Terrace, Stanwix
TYSON, THOMAS	Moorhouse
WALSH, THOMAS	2 Warwick Square
WANNOP, JOHN	Tithe Barn Farm, Warwick
WATERTON, Rev. G. W.	Warwick Square
WATT, JAMES	Knowefield
WILSON, Rev. JAMES	Dalston Vicarage

The 1897–98 Carlisle Union List of Guardians, with Priscilla Johnston third from top

Committee meeting which voted to petition Parliament in support of the bill for the prevention of the sale of intoxicating liquor to children under the age of sixteen years, and in 1903 when the Committee petitioned Parliament in support of the Employment of Children Act.

Meeting attendance records published yearly by the Board of Guardians show that Aunt 'Pris' continued her work tirelessly for the benefit of the less fortunate, attending 23 out of 26 meetings. It is only in the results for the year ending 14th April 1905 that we begin to notice a fall in her attendance to 14 out of 26 meetings. Almost certainly this decline was due to her failing health, yet she continued her committee work throughout the summer until the 19th October 1905, when ill-health forced her reluctantly to resign from all her positions.

From the records of the minutes of the Guardians we find that Priscilla Johnston's letter of resignation, expressing her utmost regrets at her circumstances, was read out at a meeting held on the 30th October 1905. The following Friday, 3rd November, the *Carlisle Journal* report of the meeting read thus:

RESIGNATION OF MISS JOHNSTON

A letter was read from the Local Government Board notifying that Miss Johnston had resigned the office of Guardian for the Botchergate Ward of Carlisle.

The Chairman said they were losing a very useful and efficient member of the Board through Miss Johnston's resignation, for which they were doubly sorry owing to the cause, which he believed, was ill-health. He proposed that the Board write to Miss Johnston and express the regret of the Board.

Mr W. Foster said he had much pleasure in seconding the motion. Miss Johnston had been a member of his committee for a considerable period and he had always found her a useful, painstaking and sympathetic member of the Board.

A meeting was held on the 13th November, at which a letter dated the 10th inst. from Miss Johnston of the Beeches, thanking the Board for their kind expressions concerning her resignation, was read.

With the passing of time and the improvement in social conditions throughout the land, many inequalities were to become apparent in the Poor Law as governed by Orders and Statutes by the Board of Guardians and in the early part of the century, the more forward looking of public men and women were calling not only for their reform but their abolition.

It was not until 1929 however, that the Local Government Act of that year proposed the abolition of the Board of Guardians and the transfer of their complex functions to the County and Borough Councils, or, for short, to the Local Authorities. This Act came into operation on 1st April 1930 and whilst it did not greatly change the organisation of the Workhouses and the Poor Law Infirmaries, it certainly sparked off the impetus by which the stigma was to be erased from the public mind. The term Workhouse was replaced by Institution and the Poor Law Infirmary by the Municipal Hospital each being controlled by the former and the Health Authority by the latter.

In general, the more progressive of our institutions and hospitals under the former Board of Guardians were to benefit even more by the broader and more enlightened approach and interpretation of the new Act.

At Fusehill, the Hospital was governed by the Public Assistance Committee until October 1938 when it was completely remodelled and upgraded with the Health Committee as the governing body. Application at this time was successfully made to the General Nursing Council for recognition of the hospital as a General Training School for Nurses.

At the outbreak of the Second World War in September 1939, the existing premises at Fusehill were scheduled by the Ministry of Health to come within the Emergency Medical Services for the treatment of war casualties and others. The civilian occupants were largely evacuated and during the next eight or nine years many members of HM Forces received hospital treatment there. Some patients arrived in convoy direct from the scene of battle but by far the greater proportion were admitted from the surrounding camps over a wide area.

After the war in 1945, it was destined that the premises should not singly revert to their pre-war function for, in July 1948, we saw the birth of the Welfare State with the National Health Service as an integral part. In short, the Welfare State could be described as an acknowledgement of the right of the individual to live without the imposition of charity and a proclamation that medical facilities should be available to all persons, regardless of their station in life.

32

The Death of Miss Priscilla Hannah Johnston in 1912

It is easy to understand how by 1905 Aunt 'Pris', now in her sixties, should suffer from deteriorating health after a lifetime spent in the care of others. We have seen how as a young woman she took on the responsibility of caring for her aging grandmother. While abroad she had regularly worked eighteen hours or more a day in difficult and distressing situations, whilst under great, unceasing stress not to mention the exposure to hunger and disease which had stricken so many. Then, following her arrival in Carlisle and during the 27 years of her life there, she had worked tirelessly on one committee or another solely for the good of others without a thought for herself. Now, constantly urged by her family and friends to take life easy, Aunt 'Pris' finally conceded. Her eyesight, as well as her general health, had been failing for a number of years and she had been under the care of Dr James Brown Bird, a physician of 84 Warwick Road.

By 1905 she had begun to withdraw from the forefront of her many activities. However, she continued to lend her support to one of the causes dear to her heart, and that for which she is most remembered in Carlisle, by remaining a treasurer for the Naples Society for the Protection of Animals.

In her final years, Aunt 'Pris' can be found listed as having made countless donations and subscriptions to many individual charities she had supported but with which she was now no longer able to be actively involved.

Her death is recorded thus in the *Carlisle Journal*:

DEATHS

JOHNSTON – At The Beeches, Rickerby, Carlisle on the 15th January. Priscilla Hannah, third daughter of the late Andrew and Priscilla Johnston. In her 70th year. Funeral Stanwix Church 2.15, Stanwix Cemetery 2.30 Wednesday. No flowers.

The grave of Priscilla Hannah Johnston in Stanwix Cemetery, Kingstown Road

Immediately after the death of Aunt 'Pris' tributes to the memory of her life and good works poured into the local newspaper. The *Carlisle Journal* printed numerous appreciations from her friends and colleagues in the many associations and committees on which she had served tirelessly.

On Tuesday the 16th of January 1912 a Mrs Bardsley, addressing the annual meeting of the Carlisle branch of the Women's Temperance Association, referred to the death of Miss Johnston. She told her audience they were all aware that Miss Johnston was interested in Temperance work, the Nursing Association and the Society for the Prevention of Cruelty to Animals but she did not think anyone had the faintest idea of Miss Johnston's liberality to those in need. They knew she was a saint, but she did not know whether they were all also aware of what a heroine she was, her disposition having been so quiet and retiring. She continued:

> ... but in her younger days before the question of Bulgaria and Armenia came so much to the front, Miss Johnston was so filled with horror at the atrocities and miseries in those countries that she

herself with a friend collected about £2,000, and she went herself to those countries and went through all sorts of dangers and adventures among the mountains, and at the risk of her own life took corn and food to these perishing women and children who were hiding in the dens and caves of earth. In doing that she contracted a terrible illness, and they could hardly get her to speak of it.

She hoped that some day a sketch of Miss Johnston's life would be forthcoming '...for she was a heroine as well as a saint.'[50]

What was this mysterious illness? On her death certificate Dr Bird states that Priscilla's demise was caused by 'Pernicious Anaemia Exhaustion', a disease so called because it was invariably fatal – that is until 1924 when Dr Minton of Boston, Massachusetts began to give raw liver to some seriously ill patients and found they recovered. The raw liver supplied the 'intrinsic factor'. To keep a person well, however, required they eat half a pound of liver a day for the rest of their lives. Such, doses were more than most people could stomach so extracts of liver were made, but these were expensive. Then it was found that extract of dried hog's stomach was as cheap and effective as whole liver and only about 1 oz. a day of this was necessary.

Pernicious Anaemia is a condition categorised with diseases of the blood. It is always associated with an absence of the normal acid that should be secreted by the stomach, characterized by deficiency of the said 'intrinsic factor' resulting in severe mal-absorption and deficiency of vitamin B_{12}.

When we consider that Aunt 'Pris' herself would sometimes say that her affinity with the hungry and needy of Carlisle was due to her own practical experience of insufficient food during her years in Bosnia, it is interesting to note that one of the greatest causes of the disease is defective nutrition, perhaps as a result of a very poor diet or one lacking in animal products. There is no doubt that both the Bosnian refugees and their relief workers, who rather than deprive a starving child of food would gladly go without themselves, were exposed to such conditions.

Pernicious Anaemia is more commonly seen in the older woman and Priscilla would have developed the disease gradually, perhaps over several years; symptoms may not have become apparent until it was advanced. She became pale and began, uncharacteristically, to suffer from mental weakness and tiredness. She started to experience shortness of breath, palpitations and fainting attacks. She noticed that her tongue had become smooth and sore, that her feet were swollen and that she had attacks of nose-bleeding. As the disease progressed it began to affect the liver, resulting in jaundice and the development of a brown pigmentation affecting her nail-beds and skin creases in particular. The condition upset her digestive functions, causing failing appetite and consequent weight loss, dyspepsia, diarrhoea and often vomiting. Sometimes she would experience a sensation as though there were a lump in her throat that seemed to prevent swallowing.

This was a truly disabling disease to have struck one who had been so independent and keen always to be on the move, working for the assistance of others less fortunate, made all the more poignant if it was indeed contracted as Mrs Bardsley suggested in her address.

On Wednesday 17th January 1912 the mortal remains of the late Miss Johnston were interred at Kingstown Cemetery, the first part of the service taking place at the Stanwix church of St Michael the Archangel. The officiating clergy included the Revd P. Byard and the Revd G. Wheelhouse. Among the chief mourners were her sister Mrs MacInnes, Miss MacInnes, Mr Neil MacInnes, Mr Andrew Johnston (her brother), Miss Beevor and Miss Creighton. The large congregation included many who had found in her a warm friend and inspiring companion. Inspector Hampshire represented the RSPCA; the Mayoress, Mrs Scott-Steele also attended.[51]

The following evening, Thursday 18th January, the Drovers of Carlisle to the number of about 130 held their annual supper in the Queen's Hall function room. The function was dedicated to the memory of Miss Johnston; tributes to her work were paid and an address was given by her brother.

After the supper Mr G.F. Saul took the chair. In opening the proceedings he reminded his audience that they were here under the shadow of great sorrow and a great loss. Almost on the eve of the supper their dearest friend Miss Johnston had been taken from them. He would not take up their time in telling of Miss Johnston's character, for they knew it better than he did. But he might say that she was above all things practical and retiring. He did not think that there was a Drover here, however long he lived, who would not keep green in his memory the kind, good lady who had instituted this supper and carried on so successfully till she was claimed by a higher power. He then introduced Mr Andrew Johnston, who spoke thus:

> I feel this occasion very much. I have been in the habit of coming down to Rickerby House for Christmas for some years past now

and my dear sister at The Beeches invariably expressed regret that the supper came just after I was obliged to return home, preventing me from coming to see what this supper was and express sympathy with the objects which they had in view. She would have liked me to attend and say a few words.

Miss Johnston was younger than I, although she has been taken first. We were brought up under family traditions of love of our fellow creatures, whether they went on two legs or four, and I have always been thankful that as a child I was trained in those traditions from my dear grandfather downwards, who has been gone more than sixty years. We were taught that lesson from the beginning. Men and women are very much what circumstances make them. You know the old story of train up a child in the way it should go and it has a chance. A great many of our fellow creatures have never been trained in the kindness to others, and it is not their fault that they grow up coarse and unfeeling; but I am thankful to be able to speak with most hearty sympathy with everything that conduced to that feeling of mercy and sympathy that I have referred to. My sister gave up almost her whole life since she became a woman to work for her fellow creatures, for men and women or the dumb animals and I am sure that it was a happy life, unselfishness being the secret of happiness.

Mr Johnston concluded by emphasising how suffering could be alleviated by setting a good example in the treatment of animals. He referred in sympathetic and appreciative terms to his sister's love for animals and her efforts on their behalf, not only in this country but also in Italy. His words were greeted with applause.

At the request of Mr Saul the company stood in silence for a moment out of respect for the late Miss Johnston.

There then followed a programme of music and recitations given by Mr G.A. Lightfoot, Police Constable Saunders, Mr Andrew Sharp, Inspector Hampshire (song and Clarinet solo) and Mr Whitaker's orchestra.'[52]

The following week on the 22nd January the *Carlisle Journal* reported thus on the annual meeting of the local branch of the Society for the Prevention of Cruelty to Animals:

Since the report was prepared the death has resulted after a long illness of Miss Johnston, of The Beeches, ladies' Secretary of this branch since its formation. Your Committee cannot sufficiently express their regret at the loss of a colleague whose love for animals and incessant and self denying work on their behalf must be almost unique. They desire to place on record their deep sense of loss this branch has sustained through her death and their heartfelt appreciation of her inestimable services in the cause which she had at heart.

The Chairman added that he would like to refer to the death of the lady who had done so much for the Society and to whom more appropriate reference could not have been made. Miss Johnston was a very quiet and unassuming person, and during the whole of her lifetime she took a deep interest in everything which had to do with the cause of humanity, or that would alleviate the suffering of animals. In fact her chief aim and happiness in life was to help others, and this desire found expression in many directions. This branch of the RSPCA had no better friend and not only was she one of the first to help to start this branch but she was also instrumental in forming a much needed branch at Naples. Any of them who had travelled in the Southern part of Italy knew how much work of that sort was needed there, and he had been told how the efforts of this Society had done an immense amount of good. Thirty or forty years ago cruelty in Naples was almost a by-word. He need hardly say that Miss Johnston would be greatly missed, but her useful and well spent life would be a fragrant memory and inspiration for her family and many friends. (Cheers)

Finally he would like to express the obligations of this branch to Mr George Saul. They all knew what a lover of animals he was. Miss Johnston would be a great loss to him in his work for this Society, but he hoped he would not be discouraged and that he would continue to carry it on, and that it would be increasingly supported and grow and prosper in the County. (Cheers)

Mr Saul asked to be allowed to refer to the late Miss Johnston with whom he had been associated in his work for seventeen years. He was afraid his share of the work had been small; but he had done his best, though he had not been equal to Miss Johnston, whose motto was 'Deeds not words'. Whatever she set herself to do she did it, but with as little fuss and talk as possible. Another leading characteristic of Miss Johnston was her absolute self-effacement and dislike of publicity. What Miss Johnston had to do in public was always in some degree a strain on her. At the annual Drovers Supper she always went round amongst the men, helped to serve them and talked to them; but as soon as ever the work was over she sat down quietly in a chair and nothing more was seen of her, because her services were not required. Miss Johnston's was a life of self-denial and though they were left much the poorer by her death none of them would grudge her the rest she so richly deserved. (Cheers)

Mr John Bell [Butcher] associated himself with all that been said concerning Miss Johnston, saying that twenty years ago Miss Johnston had sent a circular to all the Butchers in Carlisle, and she afterwards told him that he was the only one who replied to it; but things were so different now that he believed that everyone of them would have replied to it had it been sent out today...[53]

On the 1st of March 1912 a transcript of Priscilla's will appeared in the *Carlisle Journal*:

WILLS AND BEQUESTS

Miss Priscilla Hannah Johnston, of The Beeches, Rickerby, who died on the 15th January last aged 69 years, left estate of the gross value of £16,052 3s. 7d. [£884,000] and probate of her will, dated 25th June 1910, has been granted to her brother, Mr Andrew Johnston, of Forest Lodge, Woodford Green, Essex, company director. The testatrix bequeathed to each of her sisters, Sarah Maria Wilson and Catharine Isabel Walker, 15 shares in the Alliance Assurance Company, Limited, and her household and personal effects in equal shares; 200 shares in the said Company upon trust for her nephew and niece, Andrew and Priscilla Johnston; 215 shares in the said Company to her nephew, Edward Johnston; 170 shares in the said company to her niece Hilda Walker; 55 shares in the said Company upon trust for Hubert Blount; 15 shares in the said Company to each of her nephews and nieces, Grace MacInnes, Neil MacInnes, Rennie MacInnes, John MacInnes, Dora MacInnes, and Eva MacInnes, Mary Louisa Wilson, Bernard Gino Walker, Claire Carr, Olive Carr, and Cecil Wilson; 100 shares in the said Company to her niece Olaf Johnston. The residue of her estate she left to her brother, Andrew Johnston. She stated that she had inherited the shares to the Alliance Assurance Company, Limited, from her father, who was auditor thereof at the time of his death, and being of the opinion that the Company is excellently managed and that the shares will therefore grow in value, she desired, but without creating a trust, that the several legatees will not, unless compelled to dispose of the shares bequeathed to them without giving one or other of her father's descendants the opportunity of purchase and she desired that a copy of her wish shall be given to each of the aforesaid legatees and be placed with the certificate of shares.[54]

33

The Opening of the Miss Johnston Memorial Watering Trough (1913)[55]

The gathering at the opening of the watering trough on Scotland Road, Kingstown, Carlisle

Such was the importance of the occasion of the opening of the Miss Johnston memorial watering trough on 27th June 1913, that the mayor and members of the corporation for Carlisle joined her dear friends Amy Beevor and Polly Creighton, along with many other friends, colleagues, and her family. The following account of the afternoon's proceedings appeared in the *Carlisle Journal* on the 1st of July 1913:

> On the afternoon of Friday [27th June 1913] in the presence of a large gathering of friends of the late Miss Johnston, The Beeches,

and of sympathisers with her work on behalf of dumb animals, a cattle trough and drinking fountain, which have been placed on the west side of the Scotland Road, near Stanwix cemetery, as a memorial of her work in the Carlisle district and abroad, were formally opened. The weather was fine.

Amongst those present were Mr and Mrs F.W. Chance Morton; Mrs and Miss Bardsley, Eden Hey; Mrs and Misses MacInnes, Rickerby; Miss Creighton, Miss Beevor, the Revd A.E. Palin, the Revd G.A. Barclay, the Rev. J. Howie Boyd, and Mrs Boyd, Miss Isabel Boyd, Mrs Scott-Steele, Mr and Mrs G.F. Saul, Mr W.A. Main, the Rev. G. Simpson, Mr Crowder, Mr Robert Crowder, Captain and Mrs Ruth, Mrs Edward Cooper, the Misses Cartmel, Mrs A.N. Bowman, Miss Mary Hodgson, Miss Cape, Mr and Mrs Bell, Mrs Bertram Carr, the Misses Benson, the Misses Sutton, Mr and Mrs Sparkes, Mrs James Morton, Miss Breton, Mrs MacKenzie, Mr and Mrs D. Laing, Miss Routledge, Miss Marshall and others.

The watering trough being made of possibly Dalbeattie or Aberdeen Granite was supplied by the Metropolitan Drinking Fountain and Cattle Trough Association. It arrived in the City by train and was

The watering trough, shown here in its original location

taken to the site by horse and wagon where it was unloaded by hand, with the aid of planks and then manhandled into position by a Mr Blakely who in 1985 recalled that it was one of the first jobs he worked on when he joined his father's business as a boy. He also recalled that in the 1930s it was moved to a site behind the Miles MacInnes hall, to make way for a housing development. The inscription was cut by Messer's. Laing and Beaty, and the City Council's workmen did the plumbing.

After a prayer had been offered up by the Revd A.E. Palin, Mr F.W. Chance, addressing the gathering, said they were met in a somewhat circumscribed area and under somewhat unusual circumstances to pay their tribute to the memory of a good woman. Miss Johnston, he thought, was one of the last persons in the world who would have wished to have any fuss made about herself. She was modest and unassuming, and never courted publicity, but he believed the form that the memorial had taken would have met with her unqualified approval. Very few people had lived in this neighbourhood who had done more good in their time in a very quiet manner than she. She had the good fortune to be brought up in a family whose traditions were all to the good and the help of others. He believed she was a grand niece of Mrs Elizabeth Fry, who at any rate was one of her ancestors; and she was related to the Buxtons and the Gurneys, whose traditions in life were all for the helping of others. Early in life she found that 'It is more blessed to give than to receive.' Though quiet and unassuming, Miss Johnston had a very marked individuality. Whatever she undertook she did in a most thorough manner. Perhaps some present did not remember her work in Bosnia, where, more than thirty years ago, she and Miss Irby went to give a helping hand to the children of refugees who had been driven out of the Turkish provinces. In those days that Country was very unsettled, and it entailed hardship, and even danger, to travel in it. She had often, when in that Country, to go on horseback. He had travelled in Bosnia, in Sarajevo, the capital in which he believed that the names of Miss Irby and Miss Johnston were still cherished. (Cheers)

After the Austrian occupation Miss Johnston returned to this Country, and for thirty years lived at The Beeches at Rickerby. During all that time she was always ready to help any good cause, more especially the cause of temperance and the prevention of cruelty to animals. She was a great lover of animals, and even in her childhood he believed that there came to her squirrels and other wild animals which never seemed to fear her. She acted as secretary of their local society for the Prevention of Cruelty to animals for many years, and, not only so, for she took an interest also in a similar society in the South of Italy, in Naples, where the need for one was very great. Among other things she established the Drovers Supper in Carlisle, and he ventured to say that the seed sown on those annual occasions had borne good fruit. (Cheers)

There was one lesson in particular, he thought, that they had to learn from such a life, and that was that much good could be done by people carrying on their work in a very quiet, unostentatious way. Miss Johnston never courted publicity, and she achieved her end by patient continuing in well doing. They all felt a great gap had been left by her death, and yet they hoped that others would come forward and fill her place to some extent. He hoped that this drinking trough would refresh man and beast for many years to

Master Michael Saul [the young son of Mr G.F. Saul, friend and colleague of Priscilla's, also a well known Carlisle solicitor of the time] then amid cheers, turned on the water, which began to fill the trough above for horses and cattle and beneath for the dogs and smaller animals. A round of applause was accorded and a little Terrier availed itself of the opportunity for a drink.

come and sometimes remind passers-by that there had lived in this neighbourhood a good woman who loved her fellow men and dumb animals, and of who it could be said, 'Sweet mercy is nobility's true badge.' (Cheers)

Mr G.F. Saul next spoke of the value of the late Miss Johnston's work in connection with the local branch of the Prevention of Cruelty to Animals, and said that it was through her efforts that the drinking trough was placed on Stanwix Brow. In those days memorials and testimonials were very much overdone, but this one was the golden exception which proved the rule. It was a fitting memorial of an unostentatious life spent for the good of Miss Johnston's fellow creatures.

Miss Beevor said she wished to tell the subscribers that the money required for the memorial came in freely, and she could have had nearly as much again. She had received many charming letters from old and young, rich and poor, and all expressed their gratification at the form the memorial had taken. She was glad to say that the Royal Society for the Prevention of Cruelty to Animals had undertaken the responsibility for the trough. They could not have had a more fitting memorial of Miss Johnston. It was not what she did, she said very little, but it was what she was, it was the force of her example and the strength of her character.

Mr W.A. Main, giving an account of the finances, said that the total amount collected was £111 ... a balance of £14 13s. 2d. had been left over. This Miss Beever was handing over to the Royal Society for the Prevention of Cruelty to Animals, who would have to pay the council £1 a year for the water, and who would also defray the expenses of keeping the trough clear.

Miss Sylvia Saul having turned on the water at the drinking fountain, cups were filled and handed round after which the children from Houghton and Kingstown led the singing of the National Anthem.

Later in the afternoon, by the invitation of Miss Beevor, the company had tea in the MacInnes Memorial Hall.

Miss Priscilla Hannah Johnston is also remembered in the Overstrand churchyard thus:

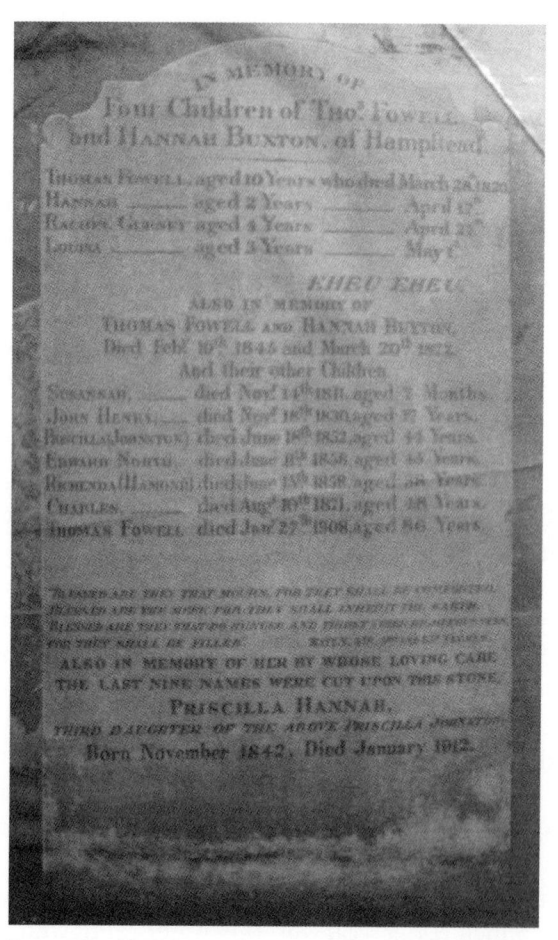

The Buxton Family Memorial Gravestone in Overstrand churchyard

EPILOGUE

The Legend of Miss Adeline Paulina Irby

After Priscilla's return to England in 1884, Paulina remained in Sarajevo. She made her last major journey in 1893 to America for the International Congress on Education.

Now the owner of a country estate and town house Paulina had settled down in Sarajevo as a permanent resident. The circle of friends in England had grown smaller with the passing years, and for many of them she no longer cared. She cut herself off from England. It was too far afield and was becoming distasteful in atmosphere and habits. She much preferred to now visit and travel in Italy.[1]

Never becoming reconciled to the Austrian rule of the provinces, her dream of the 'greater Serbia' did not diminish, with much political activity going on behind the school front. Her school was nationalist Orthodox, in and around the school and Miss Irby was a world of intrigue of violent patriotism. The school was the centre of the pro-Serb party in Sarajevo, 'all orthodox, wildly anti-Turk, and furiously anti-Catholic'. The Young Bosnia group was in secret communication with Serbia; there were smuggled papers coming into the house and other papers to be sent away by devious means, avoiding police checks; there was wild talk and grand schemes and, as a great defiant gesture, there was singing of nationalist songs with windows shut: with Miss Irby at the heart of it all.'[2]

The school remained open until her death which came quietly, almost secretly on the 15th September 1911. She had left instructions that there was to be no mourning, no grand funeral speeches at the grave side and that all her letters and papers should be destroyed. Not all these wishes were carried out, it was too important an occasion to be allowed to pass by unnoticed. Black flags were hung from the houses and the funeral became an occasion of public mourning with wreaths being sent from all over.[3] In London *The Times* of 18th September 1911 carried her obituary, short and factual:

> She had taken up residence in Bosnia and Herzegovina in the 1860s, had established schools and was most active in all kinds of charitable work, in 1876/77 she had written letters to *The Times* on outrages in the provinces. It is stated that she has left a sum of

500,000f. to Servian philanthropic institutions: A telegram from Belgrade states that news of her death was received with deep regret throughout Serbia, where her name was a household word.[4]

As the years passed much was written about her works. Pupils began to reminisce about the happy years they had spent in the care of the kind, grave faced lady who had watched over them and had attended to their education. Thus the legend of Miss Irby (her work and her friends) came into existence. By the 1930s the legend had grown strong enough to consider commemorating the centenary of her birth (wrongly believed to be 1833). After some delay the celebration took place in June 1934. It was an occasion of some national importance, with all of Yugoslavia (the new country, comprising Croatia, Dalmatia, Montenegro, Serbia, and Macedonia, had been created in 1918) taking part, and all religions participating. The commemoration was centred upon Sarajevo, where there was a parade with speeches at her grave, followed by a service at the Orthodox Cathedral, but all over Yugoslavia there were similar services. It was a gesture of appreciation and gratitude for one who had devoted so much of her life to Bosnia and the Bosnian Serb.[5]

The grave of Adeline Paulina Irby in the Serbian Orthodox Cemetery, Sarajevo

The grave of Adeline Paulina Irby in the Serbian Orthodox Cemetery, Sarajevo

> When I came to Bosnia I met one great and good hearted people, and the misery of these people aroused in me feelings of compassion, and I decided to make their misery less.
>
> Miss Adeline Paulina Irby 1908[6]

Andrew and Fowell 'Buxton' Johnston

Priscilla Hannah's brothers, Andrew and Buxton, grew up as different as two brothers could be. Andrew was tall, athletic and strikingly handsome with the straight nose and high cheekbones of the Johnstons, to which he added a wealth of beard in the Victorian manner. He was wise and upright in business, affectionate and kind at home, public spirited, philanthropic and, like his sisters, much given to good work.

In appearance Buxton was a modified version of his brother, though lacking his noble beard. In character he was opposite in almost every way. He was decidedly not wise in business, nor was he affectionate at home. He held no public office and took no interest in good causes. He

Andrew Johnston   Fowell Buxton Johnston

read Darwin's *Origin of Species* and became an agnostic. His granddaughter described him as 'the black sheep of what may well have seemed to him an almost oppressively snowy flock'.[7]

Andrew Johnston was born in the London house of his grandfather Sir Thomas Fowell Buxton on 23rd May 1835. He went on to be educated at Lowestoft, Rugby and University College, Oxford. Few forms of outdoor exercise did not at some time appeal to Andrew. In his younger days he was an enthusiastic mountaineer, later becoming a considerable traveller, always accompanied by his wife, who in spite of indifferent health, was ever his closest and most devoted companion. His pedestrian expeditions in the forest near to his Woodford home, and his affection for dachsunds, a breed of dog he kept for thirty years, were traits which the artist F. Carruthers Gould seized upon in his humorous sketch.

In 1858 he married Charlotte Anne Trevelyen, a friend of his sister Effie. On their honeymoon, Andrew's wife in writing to the MacInneses pinned in a scrap of the material of her dress and wrote against it 'Effie may like to fancy what I am wearing'. Thereupon Andrew snipped a fragment from a seam of his suit, pinned that in also and added 'Miles may like to fancy what I am wearing'. Andrew had hoped to carry on

THE CHAIRMAN
DRAWN BY F. CARRUTHERS GOULD.

The Chairman Sketch

the line of Andrew Johnston's that had come down to him unbroken from father to son for six generations. However this was not to be as their only child, Beatrice, died in 1860 aged two years.

Andrew was one of the first to join the volunteer movement, and in 1864 accepted a commission in the 7th Tower Hamlets, becoming Major in 1866. On his election for South Essex in 1868 he relinquished his military duties and devoted himself wholeheartedly to his political duties for six busy years. The election of 1874 restored the 'Essex Ten' with the Conservative Government and he never again sought re-election. In 1879 he began a second term of chairmanship of the Hand-in-Hand Fire Office; in January 1880 became one of the four chairmen of Essex Quarter Sessions; in March a Verderer of Epping Forest under the act of

1878, and High Sheriff of the County. He now devoted himself to codifying the rules for Quarter Sessions business, which later formed the basis of the Standing Orders used by the County Council. He had also been Justice of the Peace since 1866 and devoted himself with great thoroughness to mastering criminal law, with the result that he brought out in 1876 'A Pocket Index to Coke and Stone'. His special knowledge enabled him to make improvements of much value in the Summary Jurisdiction Act, 1879. On the formation of the Essex County Council. Mr Johnston was unanimously elected the first chairman, an office he held for 27 years, until increasing years necessitated his retirement, but his interest in County affairs continued unabated and only a few days before his death he saw one of the councillors about the purchase of a house at Woodford as provision for a girls school. He was always ready to speak in the interests of free trade on any platform in Essex, Suffolk (where he owned a small estate inherited from his father) or Norfolk, where his mother's family were prominent liberals. He became a great advocate of Temperance, and was for many years President of North Essex Band of Hope Union, and with his wife founded the 'Wilfred Lawson Temperance Hotel' at Woodford Green.

Andrew Johnston died on 1st March 1922 at the ripe age of eighty-six, after a life spent largely for others, at Woodford where nearly all his long life had been spent. His wife Charlotte Ann, died on 29th July 1921, after 63 years of happy married life and three days before her 85th birthday. On the occasion of their Golden Wedding in 1880 a sum of £1,000, raised by friends, was devoted to the provision of a large swimming bath, covered, warmed and lighted at Dr Barnardo's Boys' Home in Woodford.

He was buried at Ilford Cemetery after a remarkable service, conducted by the Bishop of Chelmsford at All Saints Church, Woodford Wells.[8]

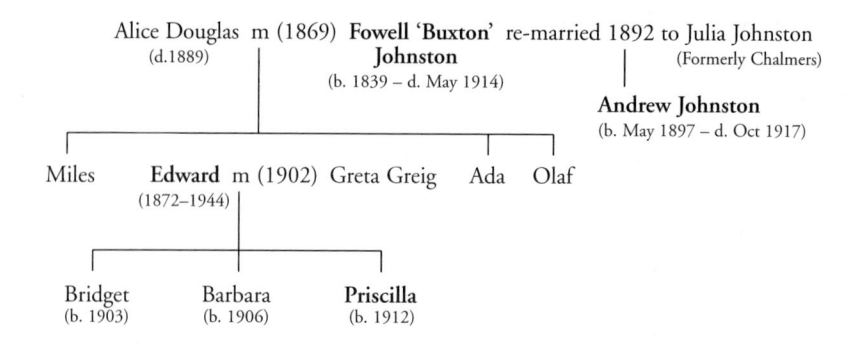

Alice Douglas m (1869) **Fowell 'Buxton'** re-married 1892 to Julia Johnston
(d.1889) **Johnston** (Formerly Chalmers)
(b. 1839 – d. May 1914)

Andrew Johnston
(b. May 1897 – d. Oct 1917)

Miles   **Edward** m (1902) Greta Greig   Ada   Olaf
(1872–1944)

Bridget   Barbara   **Priscilla**
(b. 1903) (b. 1906) (b. 1912)

Buxton, was described by his granddaughter, Priscilla, 'As being an enigma, an erratically brilliant ne'er-do-well, contrary, original and highly eccentric'. She continues, 'He bore a grudge against life from an early age. Firstly because his father took him away from Rugby prematurely, as he thought. In 1852 at the age of thirteen he and Andrew had been rushed home from Rugby to be present at their mother's deathbed. Secondly because he was thwarted in his plans for a career. He wanted to become a naturalist and to travel and explore. The best preparation for this, he thought, was to qualify as a doctor, but here his father intervened, telling him that medicine was 'not a profession for a gentleman' and putting him into a solicitor's office. There he kicked his heels, unhappy, bored and resentful, and when a friend enlisted in the army he impulsively did the same. Again a ripple of horror and distress spread throughout the family, but he could disregard it now he had got away.

He bought a commission in the III Dragoon Guards and went out to India but his military career was abruptly cut short by an illness so severe that he was not expected to survive. He made a complete recovery, however, and in 1866, at the age of twenty seven, he emigrated to South America where he bought a ranch, called The Arazaty in the province of San Jose in Uruguay. The place was remote – the nearest town was Monte Video but it took several days to get there. Buxton is said to have had a scheme for making soap from wild horses. Whatever he actually did it seems probable that he lost a great deal of money over it.

Three years after his arrival Buxton married Alice Douglas, the daughter of Adam Douglas, another Scottish rancher. Like the Johnston's, the Douglases who hailed from Coldstream in Berwickshire were bankers. Buxton and Alice were married at Buenos Aires. The bride's father had no money to buy them a present, so he gave her the most precious thing he had; her mother's tea-set. Alice came to The Arazaty and with her came her sister Maggie. Maggie was said to be always in a 'twitter' of anxiety, full of old wives' tales on subjects like health and hygiene. The two sisters proved to be every bit as pious as Buxton's sisters at home. He had escaped from one such family to find himself involved with another.

The couple went on to have four children, Miles born 1870; Edward born 1872; Ada born 1875 and Olaf born 1883.

[Edward became recognised as the artist of the family. For his sister, Olaf he produced a continuous stream of Victorian cats, all most carefully drawn and coloured. There were cat butchers with striped aprons, cat bakers with white hats, cat fishermen, cat nurses and cat postmen. For her birthday he made a sumptuous book containing a sequence called Aunt Balls' Dinner Party, after a cat of theirs called Airballs. Here cats are shown dressing for dinner and seated at a Beetonian feast in a Victorian dining room with rich wall-paper, appropriate pictures and heavy crimson curtains. Edward also went on to be described as 'possessing an unparalleled genius at the lost art of Calligraphy,' which he taught, firstly at the Central School of Art, Camberwell, before moving to the 'newly built' Royal College of Art in South Kensington in 1901, where he would remain until his death in 1944. Edward was also great friends with the MacInnes family of Rickerby; travelling with their son Neil. In 1939 Edward was made a Commander of the Order of the British Empire in the New Year's Honours List.]

His grand-daughter continues, 'Around mid 1875 Buxton and Alice sold the ranch and returned to England. Alice's health was already beginning to fail under the strain of the hard life and the local methods of midwifery. There then began a strange nomadic life spent in rented furnished houses and lodgings. Firstly settling at Torquay then South Norwood, Hastings, Ventnor, Turnham Green, Upper Norwood and Balham. Maggie continued to live with them and indeed grew more indispensable as her sister's health declined'.

She excuses her grandfather continuing thus, 'It is understandable that, for a man, a furnished house with an ailing wife, a fussy sister-in-law and children who spent half their time in bed with colds, might lack something of the charms of home life. Buxton was frequently away from home and is reputed to have found more congenial companionship elsewhere. As Alice's health failed to improve Buxton stayed away longer. What Buxton did at anytime after returning from South America is not known. He seems to have had a job sometimes and sometimes not. He had now got through most of his patrimony that was not tied up in trusts. However, his brothers and sisters were endlessly good and kind, whatever they may have thought of him personally they had a strong family feeling and sense of responsibility, with Andrew doing his best to see that his brother at least kept up appearances of respectability and did not disgrace him publicly. A man in his position could not have such a brother being seen about in the City.[9]

In October 1888 they moved into 25 Regents Park Road, London. The following August, Ada died suddenly; at this sad time Buxton forgot his agnosticism and knelt by her bed praying for her life. By this time Alice was completely bedridden. For the sake of her health in July 1890 they left London and moved to Plymouth. With Buxton out of a job again he had to borrow money from his sisters for the move. Alice died at Hampstead on 7th June 1891. For exactly a year after his wife's death Buxton lived with Maggie, Edward and Olaf in New Cross. At the end of that time he suddenly remarried and departed, leaving his children with Maggie. They would also visit with their Uncle Andrew at Woodford and with Aunt Isa (Catharine Isabel, Priscilla Hannah's youngest sister) in her London home.

Edward would meet his father at the National Liberal Club every Wednesday and woe betide him if he ever tried to put this engagement off. Edward's attitude towards his father was dutiful rather than affectionate but he continued to see him regularly in London and to spend occasional weekends with him at Kenly; where Buxton was now residing with his new wife and a baby son, born May 1897 which they named Andrew. As the young Andrew grew he began to show a brilliance, particularly in mechanical invention. A brilliant future was predicted for the child and it was hoped that he would make the name of 'Johnston famous'. But this was not to be as he was killed as a fighter pilot in the First World War, thus ending the unbroken line of Andrew Johnstons.'

Fowell Buxton Johnston was buried at Halesworth, where a tablet in his father's aisle says 'Captain Fowell Buxton Johnston, born 5th January 1839, died 22 May 1914'. Beside it is another tablet, 'Sacred to the memory of Andrew Johnston, Lieut. RFA, killed in Flanders 30 October 1917'. Below this is a wooden propeller inscribed 'Lieut. A. Johnston 30.10.17. RIP 21 Squad RFC'.[10]

Memorials to Fowell Buxton Johnston and his son, Andrew

In Memory of Mr Miles MacInnes

After the death of Miles MacInnes in 1909; at the suggestion of Dr Jex-Blake, then Dean of Wells, formerly Headmaster of Rugby, with the permission of Dr James, then headmaster, a tablet was placed in Rugby Chapel to the memory of Mr MacInnes, with a latin inscription by Dr Jex-Blake, which translates to:

'A twice elected Member of Parliament.
Through the North of England exceedingly well known,
In this man, while a wonderful sweetness
Was inbred in his very face and expression
So all his life through of the noblest character
There was a brilliancy and a loveliness,
Wise in affairs and highly expert,
By self control and most perfect courtesy
He had won the love of all the world,
Also as Christ's servant and Christ's herald
At home and far abroad of Christ's religion
He was a pillar, a champion, a model.'[11]

These recollections would be incomplete without a mention of the 'Miles MacInnes Memorial Hall' built on the glebe land on the east side of Scotland Road and at the head of Stanwix Bank, Carlisle. Very soon after he had passed away, an influential committee was formed under the leadership of Mr Chance, that there might be some public memorial to perpetuate the life, work and character of Mr MacInnes. It was felt that something that would be of use in the place where the chief part of his life had been spent, something that would appeal to all classes, would be most appropriate.

On 3rd August 1910, the foundation stone was laid by Mr Chance. Mr Howard of Greystoke presided over the gathering, and in his speech paid a valuable tribute to Miles' memory, saying, 'It was a privilege to be asked to take part in these interesting proceedings.' His connection with Mr MacInnes dated back for more than thirty years, during which time he had been closely connected with him. It had began with railway work, and continued with County Council work. He was also connected with Mr MacInnes for some time in politics.[12]

The Miles MacInnes Memorial Hall, at a cost of £1,830, was opened, free of debt, on 16th February 1911. In spite of its being a very wet day, the hall was filled with interested friends, both rich and poor, for the opening ceremony. Grace MacInnes was privileged to turn the key, and pronounce the hall open.[13] The *Cumberland News* reported, 'This would have pleased him as a practical man and a practical Christian.'

The hall then came under a committee, of which the incumbent of Stanwix Church was ex officio chairman, but its use was not limited to members of the Church of England.[14] The hall has since been demolished and today the site is occupied by flats, at the entrance of which there is a plaque bearing the inscription:

Miles MacInnes Court.
1987
Original Foundation Stone
1910.

Euphemia 'Effie' MacInnes (née Johnston)

In the four political contests which Mr Miles MacInnes had fought in the Hexam Division, Euphemia was ever at his side, and often spoke for him on Liberal platforms. After the death of her husband in 1909 Effie had continued to show her interest in Stanwix by having a barn converted into a hall which became known as 'The Welcome'. This was used as a gymnasium, reading room, for public meetings and for other purposes including the drilling of the Stanwix company of the Boy's Brigade until the opening of 'The Miles MacInnes Memorial Hall'.

After the death of Mr MacInnes, it was certain that the family could not afford to keep Rickerby, but decided they must keep it for the rest of Mrs MacInnes' lifetime. Five years later the MacInnes family left Rickerby, in the knowledge that 'Rickerby did not belong to us, but we belong to Rickerby'.

However Effie spent her last year residing with their son the Revd John MacInnes at the Whitehouse, Woodford Green, Essex. It was there that Effie, having been weak in health for some years, passed away on Thursday 5th March 1914. Only two weeks earlier their eldest surviving son, Mr Neil MacInnes, having passed away also.

At this sad time the *Carlisle Journal* recorded that, like her late husband, Mrs MacInnes was greatly interested in good works, especially missionary and temperance work; and drawing room meetings in support of these and similar objects were frequently held at Rickerby in by-gone years. Amongst the most valuable family possessions which she left were some books of pencil and water colour drawings, some of which appeared in the *Illustrated London News*.[15]

Early on the Saturday morning of the 7th March 1914 her body was taken, by her two clerical sons through the pretty woodland grounds at Woodford via Epping Forest to Euston Station for conveyance by train to Carlisle for interment in the family burial ground in Stanwix Churchyard. On arrival her coffin of plain oak was taken to Rickerby where it remained in the library until interment. On Wednesday 11th March a considerable number of family, friends, household servants, estate tenants and others assembled at Rickerby, and followed to the church, whilst others awaited the arrival of the procession at the entrance to the churchyard on Brampton Road. The clergy met the coffin at the churchyard gates, and the service in the church commenced with the singing of the hymn, 'How bright these glorious spirits shine'. The lesson was read by the Revd John MacInnes and the last of the prayers being read by her son, Canon MacInnes. [Canon Rennie MacInnes, who had spent a great deal of his life as a missionary in Egypt, and at the time was Bishop in Jerusalem.] The hymn after the lesson was 'Guide me, o thou great redeemer', which was sung by Effie as a girl of seventeen at the death bed of her mother.

At the conclusion the coffin was then borne out of the church by estate workmen to the grave where the remainder of the service was taken. She was buried with her husband, and their sons Harry and Campbell.[16]

It was not easy to sell a house in 1914, thus Rickerby House became a hostel for Belgium Refugees from the First World War, followed by Canadian Soldiers. After the Canadians it was used as an orphanage for children whose fathers had died fighting in the war. By 1930 these children had all grown up and the house became a boarding and day

Photograph of the MacInnes family grave

school for boys of eight to thirteen. When this school moved to Ecclefechan, Rickerby was bought by the Cumberland Education Committee and became Eden School. After the closure of this school the property became vacant and today the mansion house has been developed into exclusive apartments. The surrounding gardens and grounds are the executive housing development named 'Rickerby Gardens'.

The acquisition of Rickerby Park by Carlisle Corporation in 1922 came about largely through the efforts of the Carlisle Citizens League. The Corporation provided money for the employment of ex-servicemen to build and improve the roads and to lay the foundations of both a cantilever bridge and monument. The cenotaph was designed by Sir Robert Lorimer of Edinburgh and unveiled on 25th May 1922.[17]

Dr Arthur and Catharine Isabel de Noé Walker

Dr Arthur de Noé Walker became a devoted student of Italian art. Several of his pictures were presented by him to the Italian Government and hung in the Uffizi Gallery at Florence. On the walls of his Chelsea home hung many valuable works of art including a St Sebastian, which he believed to be by Andrea del Sarto.

After the death of his grandmother, Mrs Riddell, Arthur inherited a collection of Burns' autographs, amongst them being several of the poet's letters to Mrs Riddell.

Arthur himself died at the age of 79, at the family residence of 24 Carlyle Place, Chelsea, on the 2nd of October 1900.[18]

After the death of her beloved husband, Priscilla's youngest sister, Catharine Isabel, removed to Linden House, Manor Road, Woodford, Essex, where she died on the 18th March 1915.

Catharine Isabel's body was then conveyed to Carlisle where she was laid to rest in a plot of land owned by Miss Amy Beevor, 'next door but one' so to speak, to her sister Priscilla Hannah in Stanwix Cemetery.

Miss Amy Beevor

Miss Amy Beevor, who after the death of Priscilla had removed from The Beeches to Eden Mount, Stanwix, had been in failing health for some time and passed away there on 16th February 1918. The *Carlisle Journal* opined, 'By her death Carlisle loses a very estimable lady, who was deeply interested in educational, social and philanthropic work'.[19] Amy Beevor was then laid to rest between the two sisters, Priscilla Hannah and Catharine Isabel.

Amy had in fact purchased seven adjoining plots in the Stanwix Cemetery; four of them remaining empty to this day,[20] and it is not known for whom they were intended.

The graves of Priscilla Hannah, Amy Beevor and Catharine Isabel, Stanwix cemetery

Miss Mary Ellen 'Polly' Creighton

Miss Creighton's most distinguished work was in connection with the cause of education. During the 1880s she was a member of the Committee which induced the Public Day School Committee to establish in Carlisle the school which subsequently became the Carlisle and County High School for Girls. She was for many years Honorary Secretary of that Committee and in 1911 was appointed Chairman of the Governors for the school, a post in which her influence for good was invaluable.[21] Thus for over 32 years Miss Creighton presided over the affairs of the school and it was gratifying to her that her work was so appreciated by all connected with the school.[22]

Miss Creighton spent a great deal of time not only attending meetings of one Education Committee or another, but devoting additional time to studying at first hand the difficulties experienced in the schools and giving the teaching staffs the benefit of her help and advice, by making visits to every school at frequent intervals. Miss Creighton knew every teacher, not only in her work but in her home, remembered their faces and their names and took a personal interest in each one. Her visits were eagerly awaited in every school both by teachers and pupils and her speeches at prizegiving's and other school functions always held some telling phrase or some searching thought which could be carried away and made to bear fruit.[23] For example, 'The school is not there to supply a sufficient amount of education to carry a girl through life, but it is to be the beginning of a training which is to go on all her life.'[24] (Speech Day, 1894)

Miss Creighton was also recognised for her work as Chairman of the Belgian Relief Committee and also in organising and acting as Secretary of the Carlisle and District Women's League, a body of women banded together for the making of comforts and necessities for soldiers and sailors, in which work she bore her full share from August 1914 until the Armistice. The year 1921 saw her become a member of the Advisory Committee of the Carlisle and District State Management Scheme [for the control of liquor]. At this time she was appointed a magistrate for the city, serving the court with great distinction and ability.

On the 22nd September 1927 at a special meeting of the City Council, held in the Town Hall in the presence of a large and respected gathering, she became the first woman in Carlisle to receive the Honorary Freedom of the City, conferred 'in appreciation and acknowledgement of her services'.[25]

When Mary Ellen Creighton died on the 26th November 1943 having reached the age of 94, the *Carlisle Journal* reported the loss of 'An outstanding and greatly loved personality in the public life of Carlisle for many years...' The obituary continued:

> Miss Creighton, who was in her 95th year, had an accident a year or two ago from which she never recovered her physical strength, but to the last she retained her mental vigour and took the keenest interest in public affairs ... In view of her public services and the honour in which she was held, Miss Creighton might have been described as 'the grand old lady of Carlisle.' But she would personally have disclaimed any such title. She had a fastidious distaste of any form of personal flattery – a trait which she must have shared with her famous brother; for, although, as Bishop of London, Mandell

Creighton had to mingle in crowds, he never indulged in what has become known in more recent years as 'publicity hunting.' If Miss Creighton received some special commendation on her services, as sometimes happened at public meetings, she would ask for it not to be stressed in print.[26]

On the 4th December 1943 Speech Day for the Carlisle and County High School for Girls was held, falling just a few days after the death of Miss Creighton, thirty-two years Chairman of the Governors. During her last illness Miss Creighton had asked that her place at the prize distribution should be taken by Mrs Herbert Atkinson, Chairman of Carlisle Education Committee. Tributes to Miss Creighton's long service to the school were paid in the headmistress's annual report.[27]

On Saturday 3rd June 1944, what the Mayor referred to as 'a tribute in a tangible form' was paid by past and present scholars of the school to the memory of the late Miss Creighton when they held a fête and a sale at the school to augment the funds of the Miss Creighton Memorial Fund.[28] Finally, in 1948, an oak lectern was dedicated and placed in Carlisle Cathedral in her memory.[29]

Now we have reached the final page, and the people whom we have retrieved from a bygone era must make their way back to the place whence they came. But before we take leave of them let us pay them the tribute of a 'cheer'. They deserve it.

APPENDIX

The Buxton Family Tree

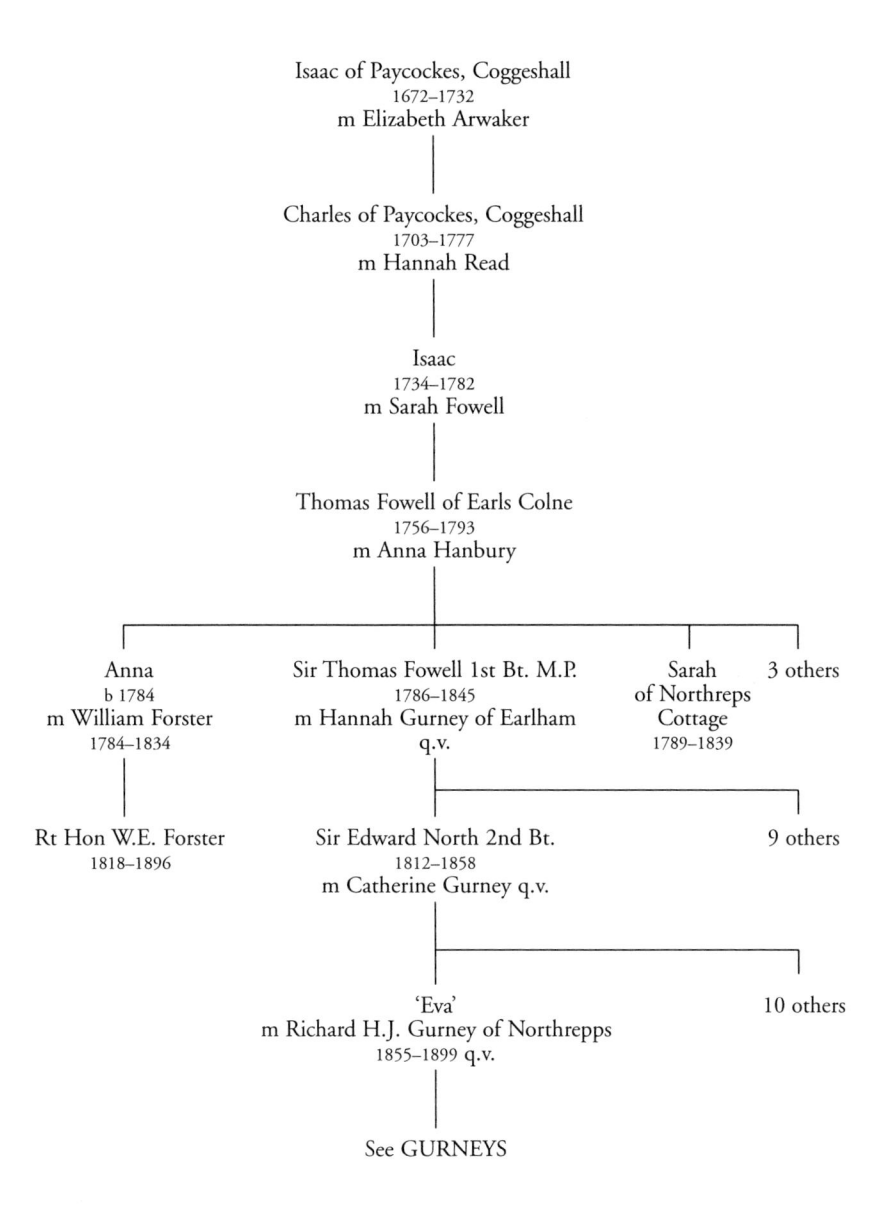

Isaac of Paycockes, Coggeshall
1672–1732
m Elizabeth Arwaker

Charles of Paycockes, Coggeshall
1703–1777
m Hannah Read

Isaac
1734–1782
m Sarah Fowell

Thomas Fowell of Earls Colne
1756–1793
m Anna Hanbury

Anna	Sir Thomas Fowell 1st Bt. M.P.	Sarah	3 others
b 1784	1786–1845	of Northreps	
m William Forster	m Hannah Gurney of Earlham	Cottage	
1784–1834	q.v.	1789–1839	

Rt Hon W.E. Forster
1818–1896

Sir Edward North 2nd Bt.
1812–1858
m Catherine Gurney q.v.

9 others

'Eva'
m Richard H.J. Gurney of Northrepps
1855–1899 q.v.

10 others

See GURNEYS

377

The Buxton / Gurney Family Tree

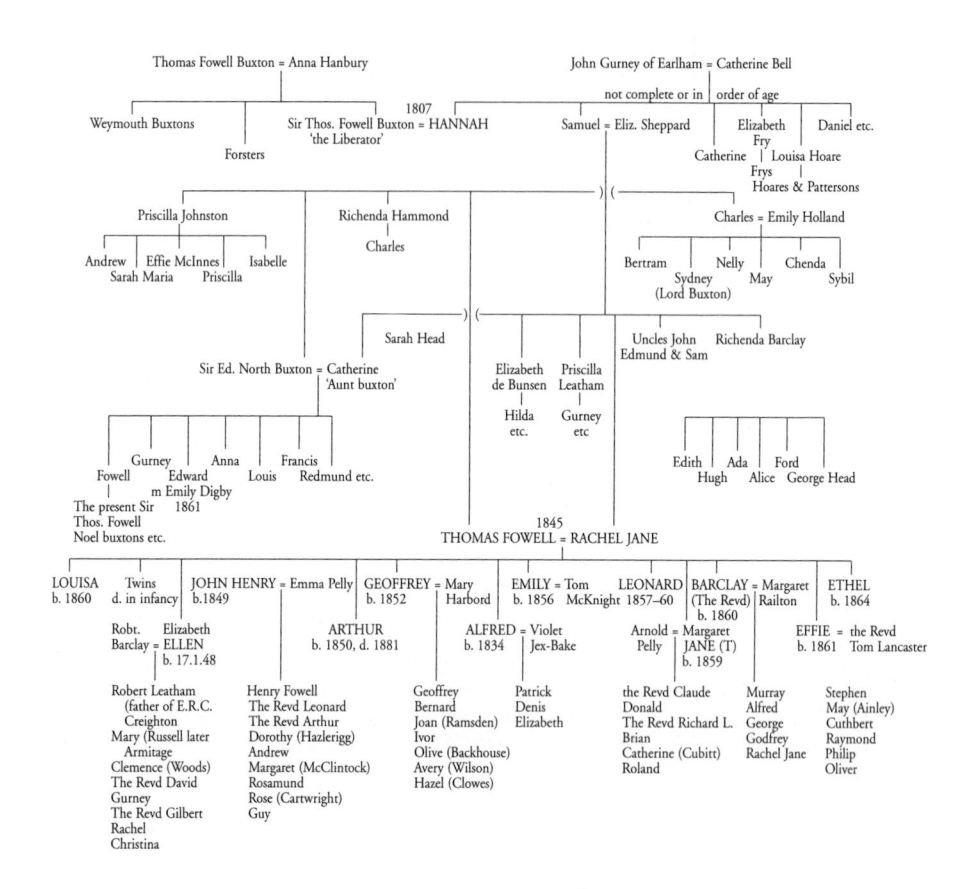

```
         Thomas Fowell Buxton = Anna Hanbury                          John Gurney of Earlham = Catherine Bell
                              |                                                 not complete or in  |  order of age
                        1807  |
   Weymouth Buxtons    Sir Thos. Fowell Buxton = HANNAH     Samuel = Eliz. Sheppard      Elizabeth        Daniel etc.
                         'the Liberator'                                                    Fry
          Forsters                                                          Catherine    |   Louisa Hoare
                                                                               Frys      |
                                                                                    Hoares & Pattersons

   Priscilla Johnston              Richenda Hammond                              Charles = Emily Holland
        |                               |                                                |
 Andrew | Effie McInnes | Isabelle    Charles                           Bertram |  Nelly      | Chenda
  Sarah Maria  Priscilla                                                      Sydney      May            Sybil
                                                                            (Lord Buxton)

                                )  (      Sarah Head              Uncles John   Richenda Barclay
                                                                  Edmund & Sam

         Sir Ed. North Buxton = Catherine      Elizabeth   Priscilla
                              'Aunt buxton'    de Bunsen    Leatham
                                                   |           |
                                                 Hilda       Gurney
                                                  etc.         etc.                Edith | Ada       | Ford
         Gurney  | Anna  | Francis                                                      Hugh     Alice    George Head
  Fowell  Edward   Louis   Redmund etc.
          m Emily Digby
The present Sir   1861
 Thos. Fowell                                         1845
Noel buxtons etc.                          THOMAS FOWELL = RACHEL JANE

 LOUISA   Twins       JOHN HENRY = Emma Pelly   GEOFFREY = Mary    EMILY = Tom      LEONARD   BARCLAY = Margaret   ETHEL
 b. 1860  d. in infancy  b.1849                   b. 1852          b. 1856  McKnight 1857–60  (The Revd)  Railton   b. 1864
                                                                                              b. 1860
          Robt.     Elizabeth          ARTHUR          ALFRED = Violet         Arnold = Margaret       EFFIE = the Revd
        Barclay = ELLEN             b. 1850, d. 1881   b. 1834   Jex-Bake       Pelly  | JANE (T)      b. 1861   Tom Lancaster
                b. 17.1.48                                                             | b. 1859

         Robert Leatham        Henry Fowell       Geoffrey     Patrick     the Revd Claude    Murray      Stephen
        (father of E.R.C.     The Revd Leonard    Bernard      Denis            Donald        Alfred      May (Ainley)
          Creighton           The Revd Arthur   Joan (Ramsden) Elizabeth    The Revd Richard L.  George   Cuthbert
        Mary (Russell later   Dorothy (Hazlerigg)   Ivor                        Brian          Godfrey    Raymond
          Armitage            Andrew             Olive (Backhouse)           Catherine (Cubitt)  Rachel Jane  Philip
        Clemence (Woods)      Margaret (McClintock) Avery (Wilson)              Roland                     Oliver
        The Revd David        Rosamund           Hazel (Clowes)
          Gurney              Rose (Cartwright)
        The Revd Gilbert      Guy
          Rachel
          Christina
```

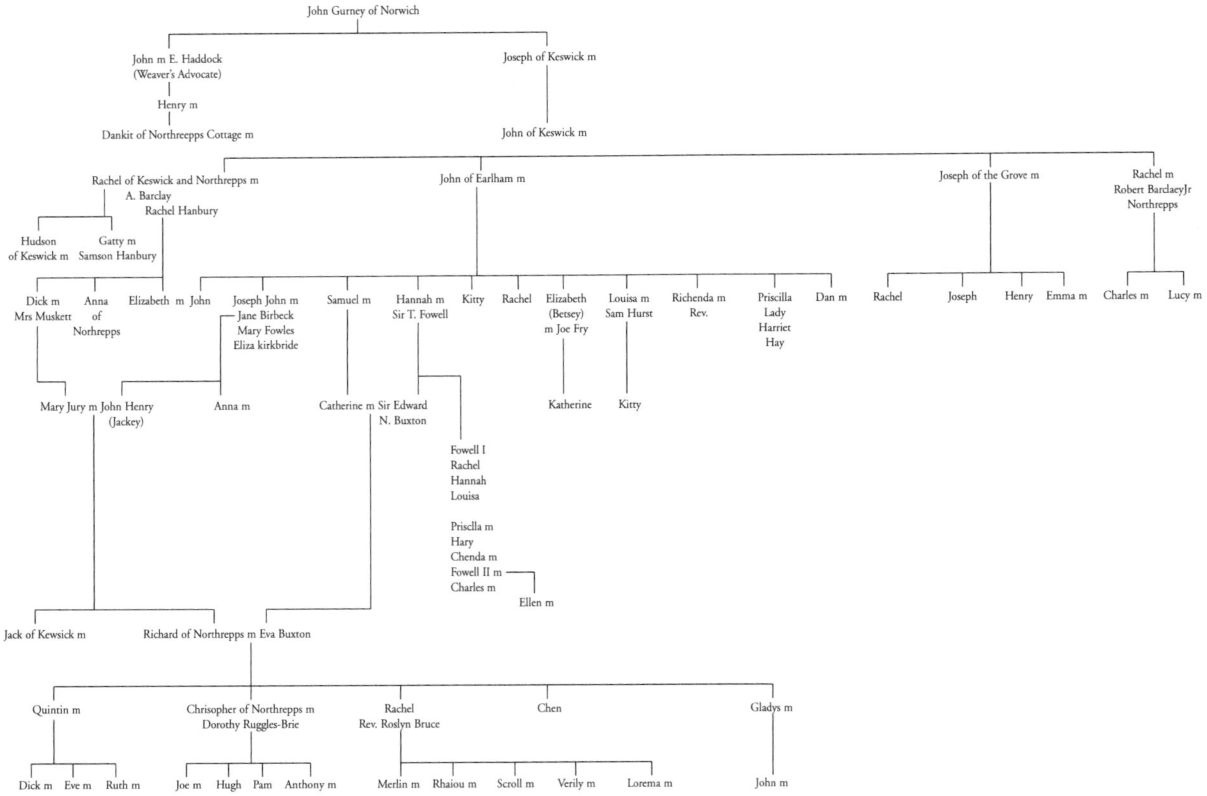

The Gurney Family Tree

The MacInnes Family Tree

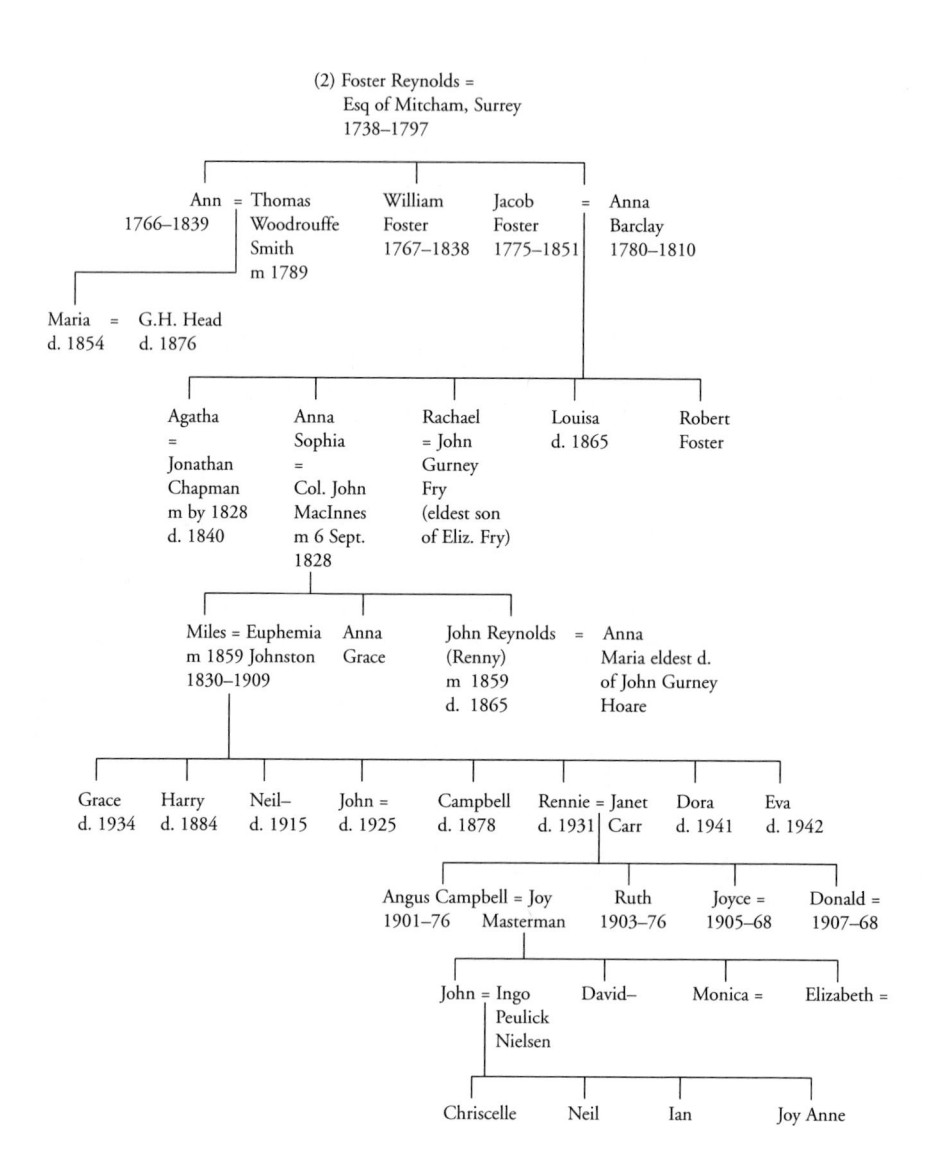

(2) Foster Reynolds = Esq of Mitcham, Surrey
1738–1797

- Ann = Thomas Woodrouffe Smith
  1766–1839   m 1789
- William Foster
  1767–1838
- Jacob Foster = Anna Barclay
  1775–1851   1780–1810

Maria = G.H. Head
d. 1854   d. 1876

- Agatha = Jonathan Chapman
  m by 1828
  d. 1840
- Anna Sophia = Col. John MacInnes
  m 6 Sept. 1828
- Rachael = John Gurney Fry
  (eldest son of Eliz. Fry)
- Louisa
  d. 1865
- Robert Foster

Miles = Euphemia Johnston
m 1859
1830–1909

Anna Grace

John Reynolds (Renny) = Anna Maria eldest d. of John Gurney Hoare
m 1859
d. 1865

- Grace d. 1934
- Harry d. 1884
- Neil– d. 1915
- John = d. 1925
- Campbell d. 1878
- Rennie = Janet Carr
  d. 1931
- Dora d. 1941
- Eva d. 1942

Angus Campbell = Joy Masterman
1901–76

Ruth 1903–76

Joyce = 1905–68

Donald = 1907–68

John = Ingo Peulick Nielsen

David–

Monica =

Elizabeth =

Chriscelle   Neil   Ian   Joy Anne

380

Certified copy of death certificate of Priscilla Hannah Johnston

CERTIFIED COPY OF AN ENTRY OF DEATH

Application Number PAS 6002642

REGISTRATION DISTRICT: Carlisle

1912 DEATH in the Sub-district of Stanwix in the County of Cumberland

No.	When and where died	Name and surname	Sex	Age	Occupation	Cause of death	Signature, description and residence of informant	When registered	Signature of registrar
180	Sixteenth January 1912, The Beeches Rickerby, Stanwix	Priscilla Hannah Johnston	Female	69 years	Spinster, Daughter of Andrew Johnston (deceased) of independent income	Pernicious Anaemia Exhaustion Certified by J D Bird M.D.	And. Johnston Brother Woodford House Wetheral	Sixteenth January 1912	George Liddle Registrar

CERTIFIED to be a true copy of an entry in the certified copy of a Register of Deaths in the District above mentioned.
Given at the GENERAL REGISTER OFFICE, under the Seal of the said Office, the 23rd day of April 2004

DYA 329008

Select Bibliography

Buxton, Sir Thomas Fowell, *Memoirs*, 2nd Edn, ed. Charles Buxton (London: John Murray, 1849)

Cresswell [Abridged from the larger memoir (by Katherine Fry and R.E. Cresswell), with alterations and additions.] (London: Piper, Stephenson & Spence, 1856)

Johnston, Priscilla Buxton, *Extracts from Priscilla Johnston's Journal and Letters, collected by her daughter E. MacInnes* (Carlisle: Charles Thurnam and Sons, 1862) [Includes an account of her childhood by her mother, Hannah Lady Buxton]

Jenkinson, Henry Irwin, *Jenkinson's Practical Guide to Carlisle, Gilsland, Roman Wall and neighbourhood* (London: E. Stanford, 1875)

Buxton, Hannah, *Memorials of Hannah Lady Buxton. From papers collected by her grand-daughters* (London: Bickers & Son, 1883)

Hare, Augustus J.C., *The Gurneys of Earlham* (2 vols) (London: George Allen, 1895)

McInnes, Anna Grace, *Recollections of the Life of Miles MacInnes* (London: Longmans & Co., 1911)

Fairholme, Edward G. and Pain, Wellesley, A., *Century of Work for Animals: the history of the RSPCA, 1824–1924* (London: John Murray, 1924)

Ensor, R.C.K., *England, 1870–1914* [*Oxford History of England, Vol. 14*] (Oxford: Clarendon Press, 1936)

Whitney, Janet Payne, *Elizabeth Fry, Quaker Heroine* (London: George G. Harrap, 1937)

Mottram, Ralph Hale, *Buxton the Liberator* (London: Hutchinson, 1946)

Woodham-Smith, Cecil, *Florence Nightingale, 1820–1910* (London: Constable, 1950)

Johnston, Priscilla, *Edward Johnston* (London: Faber & Faber, 1959)

Bett, Walter Reginald, *A Short History of Nursing* (London: Faber & Faber, 1960)

Kent, John Henry Somerset, *Elizabeth Fry* (London: B.T. Batsford, 1962)

Buxton, Elizabeth Ellen, *Family Sketchbook: a hundred years ago* [arranged by her grand-daughter, Ellen R.C. Creighton] (London: Geoffrey Bles, 1964)

Anderson, Dorothy, *Miss Irby and Her Friends* (London: Hutchinson, 1966)

Buxton, Elizabeth Ellen, *Ellen Buxton's Journal, 1860–1864* [arranged by her grand-daughter, Ellen R.C. Creighton] (London: Geoffrey Bles, 1967)

Anderson, Dorothy, *The Balkan Volunteers* (London: Hutchinson, 1968)

Anderson, Verily, *The Northrepps Grandchildren* (London: Hodder & Stoughton, 1968)

Oakley, Nigel W., *The Story of Easneye* (Ware: All Nations Christian College, 1972)

Vipont, Elfrida, *George Fox and the valiant sixty* (London: Hamish Hamilton, 1975)

Gooch, Michael and Sheila, 'The People of a Suffolk Town – Halesworth, 1199–1900' in *Pears Cyclopaedia*, 88th Edn., ed. L. Mary Barker (London: Pelham Books, 1979)

Matthew, H.C.G., *Gladstone, 1809–1874* (Oxford: Clarendon Press, 1986)

Carey, John (ed.), *Faber Book of Reportage* (London: Faber & Faber, 1987)

Carter, Anne, *The Beevor Story* (Fundenhall: A. Carter, 1993)

Kenyon, J.P., *The Wordsworth Dictionary of British History* (Ware: Wordsworth Editions, 1994)

Scott-Parker, Mary, *Forty Years On: Carlisle and County High School for Girls* (Carlisle: Bookcase, 1995)

Covert, James, *A Victorian Marriage: Mandell and Louise Creighton* (London: Hambledon, 2000)

Gavin, Adrienne E., *Dark Horse: a life of Anna Sewell* (Stroud: Sutton, 2004)

Gill, Gillian, *Nightingales: the story of Florence Nightingale and her remarkable family* (London: Hodder & Stoughton, 2004)

Trustees of CVS (compiled by), *100 Years of Service to the Community, 1904–2004* (n.d.)

Johnston, Mary, *History of Rickerby House and Owners* (unpublished papers, held at Cumbria Archive)

Newspapers and Periodicals consulted

The British Friend
Carlisle Journal
Carlisle News
Cumberland Paquet
Daily News
Essex Review
The Friend
Illustrated London News
Literary Gazette
Manchester Guardian
The Times

Notes

The following abbreviations are used to refer to works frequently cited:

CJ   Carlisle Journal
EF   Cresswell, Rachel E., A *Memoir of Elizabeth Fry by her daughter, Mrs Francis Cresswell* [Abridged from the larger memoir (by Katherine Fry and R.E. Cresswell), with alterations and additions] (London: Piper, Stephenson & Spence, 1856)
HLB   Buxton, Hannah, *Memorials of Hannah Lady Buxton. From papers collected by her grand-daughters* (London: Bickers & Son, 1883)
Irby   Anderson, Dorothy, *Miss Irby and Her Friends* (London: Hutchinson, 1966)
MM   McInnes, Anna Grace, *Recollections of the Life of Miles MacInnes* (London: Longmans & Co., 1911)
NG   Anderson, Verily, *The Northrepps Grandchildren* (London: Hodder & Stoughton, 1968)
TFB   Buxton, Sir Thomas Fowell, *Memoirs*, 3nd Edn, ed. Charles Buxton (London: John Murray, 1849)

Introduction

1. Priscilla Hannah Johnston's uncle, John Henry Gurney of Earlham, from 1864 frequently took his elder boy, Jack, to stay at Northrepps Hall. Richard, his younger son, was rarely fit enough to join the huge parties of grandchildren and stayed behind at Catton Hall where his lonely childhood was enlightened by Anna Sewell, the author of *Black Beauty*, who lived nearby and came to give him lessons.
   From Adrienne E. Gavin's, *Life of Anna Sewell 'Dark Horse'*, we also learn that in 1852 Anna Sewell's brother, Philip, and his wife, Sarah, had moved to Santander, Spain. Here Philip helped construct the Santander–Logrono and Bilbao–Tudela railway lines. He spent twelve years in Spain a well respected engineer.
   The Gurney family, which had previously acted successfully as yarn merchants had created Gurneys Bank in 1775. Now in 1864 on returning to England,

Philip and his family of seven settled at Clare House in New Catton, a suburb of Norwich. Philip took a positiion in the Gurney's bank in Norwich and when it became Barclays Bank in 1896 he became one of the directors.

In September 1864 Anna and her parents moved into the Whitehouse in Old Catton, which was situated across the road from the Gurney-Buxton's deer park. Here Anna and her mother, Mary, took up charity work. As the Gurney-Buxton squire of Catton Hall, saw to most of the charitable needs of Old Catton, Anna and Mary worked from the outset in Philip's neighbourhood of New Catton.

Anna Sewell

2. Hare, Augustus J.C., The Gurneys of Earlham (2 vols) (London: George Allen, 1895), Preface
3. The Gurneys of Earlham, p. 16
4. The Gurneys of Earlham, p. 18
5. The Gurneys of Earlham, p. 20
6. The Balkan Volunteers, p. 10
7. Thank you to Mrs June Cawley, of The Beeches, Rickerby, Carlisle for supplying this information on the care of the watering trough today.

Part One

1. Obituary of Miss Priscilla Hannah Johnston, *The Times*, 16th January 1912, p. 11.
2. Obituary of Sir Thomas Fowell Buxton, *The Times*, 22nd February 1845. p. 6.
3. *TFB*, inside front cover.
4. Obituary of Miss Anna Gurney, *Literary Gazette*, June 1857.
5. *NG*, p. 143.
6. *ibid.*, p. 144.
7. Obituary of Miss Anna Gurney, *Literary Gazette*, June 1859.
8. *EF*, p. 9.
9. *NG*, pp. 87–8.
10. *NG*, p. 90.
11. Carey, John (ed.), *Faber Book of Reportage* (London: Faber & Faber, 1987), p. 298 [See also *EF*, Chapter 7].
12. For further information see *EF*.
13. *EF*, pp. 1–2.
14. Kenyon, J.P., *The Wordsworth Dictionary of British History* (Ware: Wordsworth Editions, 1994), pp. 293–294. [See also Vipont, Elfrida, *George Fox and the valiant sixty* (London: Hamish Hamilton, 1975)].
15. *EF*, p. 2.
16. *ibid.*, p. 3.
17. *ibid.*, pp. 4–5.
18. Johnston, Priscilla, *Edward Johnston* (London: Faber & Faber, 1959), p. 23.
19. *TFB*, pp. 2–3.
20. *ibid.*, p. 5.
21. *ibid.*, p. 8.
22. *ibid.*, p. 8.
23. *ibid.*, p. 9.
34. *NG*, p. 92.
25. *TFB*, p. 9.
26. *ibid.*, p. 10.
27. *HLB*, pp. 8–9.
28. Johnston, Priscilla, *Edward Johnston*, p. 24.
29. *HLB*, pp. 1–4.
30. *NG*, p. 86.
31. *ibid.*, pp. 86–7.
32. *ibid.*, pp. 74–5.
33. *ibid.*, p. 80.
34. *ibid.*, p. 95.
35. *ibid.*, p. 126.
36. *TFB*, p. 28.
37. *NG*, p. 149.
38. Gooch, Michael and Sheila, 'The People of a Suffolk Town – Halesworth' 1199–1900', p. 128.
39. *ibid.*, p. 129.
40. *TFB*, pp. 394–6.

Part Two

1. Johnston, Priscilla Buxton, *Extracts from Priscilla Johnston's Journal and Letters, collected by her daughter E. MacInnes* (Carlisle: Charles Thurnam and Sons, 1862), pp. 74–6.
2. *NG*, p. 169, and *TFB*, p. 362.
3. *HLB*, p. 148.
4. *TFB*, p. 362.
5. 'The Royal Burgh of Kilrenny and Anstruther' (Tourist information leaflet).
6. Johnston, Priscilla, *Edward Johnston*, p. 28.
7. *Fifeshire Journal*, 27th July 1837. Courtesy of Mr Jim Addison.
8. Gooch, Michael and Sheila, 'The People of a Suffolk Town – Halesworth, 1199–1900', p. 129.
9. White, William, *History, Gazetter and Directory of Suffolk, and the towns near its borders* (Sheffield: 1844). Courtesy of the Norfolk and Norwich Millennium Library.
10. Gooch, Michael and Sheila, 'The People of a Suffolk Town – Halesworth, 1199–1900', p. 129.
11. *NG*, p. 182.
12. *ibid*, p. 196.
13. *ibid*, p. 197.
14. White, William, *History, Gazetter and Directory of Suffolk* (1844), 'Halesworth'.
15. *NG*, p. 16.
16. *Irby*, p. 72.
17. Johnston, Priscilla, *Edward Johnston*, p. 29.
18. 'Portrait of Andrew Johnston', *Essex Review*, Vol. 31, 1922.
19. Information provided by Brenda M. Gower, Suffolk Record Office, Lowestoft.
20. *NG*, p. 16.
21. *TFB*, p. 595.
22. *ibid.*, p. 596.
23. *NG*, pp. 202–203.
24. *TFB*, p. 599.
25. *ibid.*, p. 603.
26. *HLB*, p. 170.
27. White, William, *History, Gazetter and Directory of Suffolk* (1845), 'Overstrand', p. 761.
28. *ibid.*, p. 760.
29. *TFB*, pp. 605–606.
30. *NG*, p. 203.
31. *ibid.*, p. 203.
32. *EF*, pp. 580–2.
33. *NG*, p. 203.
34. *HLB*, p. 174.
35. Buxton, Elizabeth Ellen, *Family Sketchbook: a hundred years ago* [arranged by her grand-daughter, Ellen R.C. Creighton] (London: Geoffrey Bles, 1964), p. 11.
36. *HLB*, p. 175 and Johnston, Priscilla Buxton, *Extracts from Priscilla Johnston's Journal and Letters*, pp. 176–7.

37. White, William, *History, Gazetter and Directory of Suffolk* (1845), 'Northrepps', p. 760.
38. *NG*, p. 40.
39. *NG*, p. 73.
40. *NG*, p. 74.
41. *NG*, p. 74.
42. *NG*, p. 16.
43. *NG*, p. 17.
44. *NG*, p. 16.
45. *NG*, p. 19.
46. *NG*, pp. 23–4
47. *NG*, p. 40.
48. *NG*, p. 40.
49. *NG*, p. 26.
50. *NG*, p. 29.
51. *NG*, p. 30.
52. *NG*, p. 30.
53. *NG*, p. 31.
54. *NG*, Chapters 1 and 2.
55. *NG*, pp. 211–2.
56. *NG*, p. 213.
57. Gooch, Michael and Sheila, 'The People of a Suffolk Town – Halesworth, 1199–1900', p. 130.
58. *NG*, p. 49.
59. *NG*, pp. 50–1.
60. *NG*, p. 103.
61. *NG*, p. 44.
62. *NG*, p. 45.
63. *NG*, p. 150.
64. *NG*, pp. 152–3.
65. *NG*, p. 218.
66. The Nelson Room, Dickens World Exhibition, Downham Market, Norfolk.
67. *MM*, p. 123.
    *George Head Head. This unusual name came from a mistaken entry in a register.
68. MacInnes, Jean, 'Banks & Bankers: a History of Rickerby' in *CJ*, 3rd August 1934.
69. *Diaries of Miss Ellen Buxton* (unpublished). Courtesy of Mrs Ellen R.C. Creighton.
70. *Carlisle Journal*, 1st July 1915, p. 5.
71. Gooch, Michael and Sheila, 'The People of a Suffolk Town – Halesworth, 1199–1900', p. 130.
72. *Diaries of Miss Ellen Buxton* (unpublished).
73. White, William, *History, Gazetter and Directory of Suffolk* (1851).
74. *Diaries of Miss Ellen Buxton* (unpublished).
75. *CJ*, 1st May 1862.
*1. *Cumberland Paquet*, 3rd March 1863.

*2. *CJ*, 6th March 1863.
*3. *ibid.*, 13th March 1863.
*4. *Cumberland Paquet*, 17th March 1863.
76. Jenkinson, Henry Irwin, *Jenkinson's Practical Guide to Carlisle, Gilsland, Roman Wall and neighbourhood* (London: E. Stanford, 1875).
77. *ibid.*
78. Bulmer, T.F. (ed.), *History, Topography and Directory of East Cumberland* (Manchester, T. Bulmer & Co., 1884).
79. Information provided by David Bowcock and Susan Dench of Carlisle Heritage Offices; Jenkinson, Henry Irwin, *Jenkinson's Practical Guide to Carlisle, Gilsland, Roman Wall and neighbourhood*; Bulmer, T.F., *History and Directory of East Cumberland.*
80. Lanercost Priory (Guide Book).
81. *Irby*, p. 72.
82. Oakley, Nigel W., *The Story of Easneye.*
83. Family Obituary, *The Times*, 3rd October 1900.
84. HLB
85. *NG*, p. 237.
86. HLB
87. *NG*, pp. 239–40.
88. HLB
89. Isichei, Elizabeth Allo, *Victorian Quakers* (London: Oxford University Press, 1970), p. 168.
90. MM
91. *Irby*, p. 73.

Part Three

1. *ibid.*, pp.16–17.
2. *Irby*, p. 236.
3. *ibid.*, inside cover.
4. *ibid.*, p. 73.
5. *ibid.*
6. *Irby*, pp. 185–6.
7. *ibid.*, p. 203.
8. *ibid.*, p. 199.
9. *ibid.*, p. 210.
10. *ibid.*, p. 199.
11. *ibid.*, p. 203.
12. *ibid.*, p. 55.
13. *Irby*, p. 72
14. *ibid.*, p. 74.
15. *ibid.*, p. 81.
16. *ibid.*, pp. 82–3.
17. *ibid.*, pp. 83–4.

18. *ibid.*, pp. 81–92
19. *ibid.*, pp. 93–8.
20. *ibid.*, pp. 99–119.
21. *ibid.*, pp. 119–37.
22. Carey, John (ed.), *Faber Book of Reportage*, pp. 389 & 340.
23. *Irby*, p. 126.
24. *ibid.*, pp. 138–46.
25. *ibid.*, pp. 147–72.
26. *The Times*, 17th July 1877.
27. *Irby*, p. 171.
28. *ibid.*, pp. 173–85.
29. *ibid.*, pp. 186–203.
30. *ibid.*, pp. 207–19.
31. *ibid.*, pp. 209–10.
32. *ibid.*, p. 212.
33. *ibid.*, pp. 218–9.

Part Four

1. Family Obituaries, *CJ*, 16th January 1912 & *The Times*, 16th January 1912.
2. *Overstrand Church Parish Chronicle*, October 1904.
3. *The Ragged School Union became synonymous with the name of Lord Shaftsbury. Shaftsbury did not 'invent' the ragged school, but he threw over the movement the glamour of his great name. He was, however, president for forty years of the Ragged School Union which had been established first in London in 1844 by some Friends and Mr William Locke. Teachers engaged in Sunday School teaching found that many children were excluded from their schools in consequence of their dirty and ragged condition. The founders were anxious to have another class of schools and thought it an excellent plan to have a union so that they might assist each other in the gathering of the outcast and destitute. In many cases the children were admitted by personal application, in other cases by the teachers going round and seeking them out.

   When they were first taken into the schools most were in a very ignorant, destitute, neglected condition. Many were homeless, or entirely neglected by their parents; many were orphans, outcasts, street beggars and little hawkers of things about the streets. The schools also took in children of convicts who had been transported and those who had been imprisoned at home; children of the lowest tramps, of worthless drunken parents (of which they were many); children of stepfathers or stepmothers, often driven by neglect or cruelty to shift themselves; children of those who, although suitable for a workhouse, preferred to lead a vagrant life; children of parents who, though honest, were too poor to pay a penny a week for a school and could not clothe their children so as to obtain admission to better schools.

   In both day and evening schools the children not only received classes on the Scriptures, singing, reading, writing and arithmetic but in some schools industrial classes were held. Food was given – generally soup, occasionally meat, and good wholesome bread. Sometimes they received coffee or cocoa, and bread and cheese.

As a result of the Ragged Schools many children formerly of bad character were reformed.

4. Family Obituaries, *CJ*, 16th January 1912 and *The Times*, 16th January 1912.
5. *MM*, pp. 5–6.
6. *MM*, pp. 69–70.
7. *MM*, pp. 21–2.
8. *MM*, p. 23.
9. *MM*, p. 76.
10. *MM*, p. 102.
11. Brown, James Walter, *Round Carlisle Cross: old stories retold* [*3rd Series*] (Carlisle: C. Thurnam, 1923), pp. 46–7.
12. Johnston, Mary, *History of Rickerby House and Owners* (unpublished papers, held at Cumbria Archive)
13. Obituary, *CJ*, 1st October 1909.
14. *MM*, pp. 183 & 186–7.
15. MacInnes, Jean, *History of Rickerby* [pamphlet printed for Eden School].
16. Obituary, *CJ*, 6th March 1914.
17. *MM*, p. 173.
18. *ibid.*, pp. 153–4.
19. *ibid.*, pp. 169–170.
20. MacInnes, Jean, *History of Rickerby* [pamphlet printed for Eden School], p. 15.
21. Johnston, Priscilla, *Edward Johnston* (London: Faber & Faber, 1959)
22. *ibid.*, p. 235.
23. MacInnes, Jean, *History of Rickerby* [pamphlet printed for Eden School], p. 15.
24. *MM*, pp. 239–42.
25. Obituary, *CJ*, 1st October 1909.
26. *MM*, p. 249.
27. Obituary, *CJ*, 1st October 1909.
28. Thanks are due to Sir Thomas Beevor, Bt., and Lady Anne Carter for supplying information about Miss Beevor.
29. Obituary, *Cumberland News*, 16th February 1918.
30. Information supplied by Sir Thomas Beevor.
31. Obituary, *Cumberland News*, 16th February 1918.
32. *CJ*, 2nd July 1943, p. 3
33. Scott-Parker, Mary, *Forty Years On: Carlisle and County High School for Girls* (Carlisle: Bookcase, 1995)
34. Covert, James, A., *Victorian Marriage: Mandell and Louise Creighton* (London: Hambledon, 2000), pp. 269–70.
35. *ibid.*, p. 315.
36. Obituary, *CJ*, 30th November 1943.
37. Obituary, *CJ*, 3rd December 1943.
38. *CJ*, 23rd September 1927.
39. Fairholme, Edward G. and Pain, Wellesley, *A Century of Work for Animals: the history of the RSPCA, 1824–1924* (London: John Murray, 1924).

40. *CJ*, 7th November 1879.
41. Thank are due to Chris Reed, Records and Information Officer, RSPCA, West Sussex, for supplying this information.
42. *CJ*, 8th November 1889.
43. *ibid.*, 4th November 1892.
44. *ibid.*, 21st November 1993.
45. *ibid.*, 18th January 1912.
46. Murray, John, *A short history of nursing* (Carlisle: Carlisle Infirmary Education Centre), pp. 95–9.
47. *CJ*, 7th February 1880.
48. Thanks are due to the Carlisle Council for Voluntary Services for granting me permission to include extracts from their booklet, *100 Years of Service to the Community 1904–2004* compiled by CVS trustees who researched and collated the information, in particular Lawrence Fisher, John Barker and Joan Graham.
49. Burtram, Leslie, *The City General Hospital and its Poor Law* (Carlisle: Carlisle Infirmary Education Centre).
50. *CJ*, 16th January 1912.
51. *CJ*, 17th January 1912.
52. *ibid.*, 18th January 1912.
53. *ibid.*, 22nd January 1912.
54. *ibid.*, 1st March 1912.
55. *CJ*, 1st July 1913.

Epilogue

1. *Irby*, p. 221.
2. *ibid.*, p. 225.
3. *ibid.*, p. 230.
4. *ibid.*, p. 231.
5. *ibid.*, pp. 234–5.
6. *ibid.*, p. 234.
7. Johnston, Priscilla, *Edward Johnston* (London: Faber & Faber, 1959), pp. 30–1.
8. 'Portrait of Andrew Johnston', *Essex Review*, Vol. 12, 1903 & Vol. 31, 1922.
9. Johnston, Priscilla, *Edward Johnston* (London: Faber & Faber, 1959), pp. 31–2.
10. Gooch, Michael and Sheila, 'The People of a Suffolk Town – Halesworth, 1199–1900' in *Pears Cyclopaedia*, p. 130.
11. *MM*, pp. 26–4.
12. *ibid.*, p. 264.
13. *ibid.*, pp. 266–7.
14. *ibid.*, p. 268.
15. Obituary of Mrs MacInnes, *CJ*, 6th March 1914.
16. Obituary of Mrs MacInnes, *CJ*, 13th March 1914.
17. MacInnes, Jean, *History of Rickerby*.
18. Family Obituary, *The Times*, 3rd October 1900.
19. Obituary of Miss Amy Beevor, *Cumberland News*, 16th February 1918.

20. Records of the Dalston Road Cemetery Bereavement Services.
21. *CJ*, 23rd September 1927.
22. *ibid.*, 6th June 1944.
23. *ibid.*, 3rd December 1943.
24. Scott-Parker, Mary, *Forty Years On: Carlisle and County High School for Girls*, p. 2.
25. *CJ*, 23rd September 1927.
26. *ibid.*, 30th November 1943.
27. *ibid.*, 5th December 1943.
28. *ibid.*, 6th June 1944.
29. Scott-Parker, Mary, *Forty Years On: Carlisle and County High School for Girls*, p. 61.

Index of Families

Buxton Family
Charles (d. 1872) 60, 81, 124, 203
Chenda 124, 137, 141, 143–4
Edward 124, 137, 165
Ellen (b. 1848) 2, 127, 129, 134, 139, 147, 158, 163, 168, 170–1, 175, 179, 184, 195–7
Fowell ii 60, 124, 127, 137, 142, 168, 201, 204
Hannah Lady (*née* Gurney 1773–1872) 3, 4, 11, 21, 27, 31, 35, 38–9, 42–3, 47, 49, 52–5, 57–60, 62, 80, 124–5, 127, 129, 137–9, 141–2, 144, 155, 160, 162,165, 169, 194, 195, 200, 201, 203, 204–5
Hannah (d. 1820) 55–6
Harry 54, 77, 126–7, 152
Louisa (d. 1820) 54, 56
Priscilla (1808–1852) 5, 46–50, 59, 60, 62–3, 72, 73, 76–8, 82–4, 87, 91, 93
Rachel (d. 1820) 54–6
Sarah (1789–1839) 15, 16, 61, 78, 82
Suzannah (b. June 1811–d. Nov. 1811) 47
Sir Thomas Fowell (1786–1845) 2–4, 12–13, 15, 25, 27, 31, 34–5, 38–9, 40, 42, 44–5, 49, 52, 54, 58, 74, 76, 82, 85–87, 103, 107, 115, 122, 124, 126, 129, 150, 153, 281, 306, 311
Thomas Fowell (d. 1820) 52, 53, 56, 90–1

Creighton Family
Ellen R.C. 'Kisty' 127, 170–1, 196–7
James Robert (1844–1896) 302–3
Mandell (1843–1901) 302–3
Mary Ellen 'Polly' (1849–1944) 302–5, 349, 371–3

Robert (d. 1878) 302

Fry Family
Elizabeth 'Betsey' (*née* Gurney) 2, 3, 17–21, 27–8, 32, 54, 104–5, 112–13, 122–3, 125–6, 150, 205, 275, 328
Joseph 15, 150

Gurney Family
Catherine (*née* Bell d. 1792) 22, 31
Catharine 'Kitty' 22, 31–5, 38–40, 66, 129, 146
Daniel 12, 32, 150, 201–3
Elizabeth 'Betsey' (1780–1845) 2, 3, 17–20, 21, 27, 28, 32, 54, 80
Hannah (Lady Buxton 1783–1872) 3, 18, 26, 31, 34–5, 38–40, 42, 47, 49, 52–5, 57–60, 62, 80
John of Earlham (1749–1809) 3, 21–2, 27, 40
Joseph John 2, 12, 32, 34–5, 112, 126, 129, 138
Lame Anna (1795–1857) 12, 14, 16, 61, 88, 101, 113, 124, 129, 151, 153
Louisa 32–3,
Priscilla 32, 62
Richenda 18, 32–4, 55
Samuel 2, 12, 32, 129

Johnston Family
Ada 362, 364
Alice (*née* Douglas) 362–5
Andrew (1835–1922) 5, 98, 101, 111, 115, 124, 142, 146–7, 155, 168, 194, 200, 222, 231, 234, 244, 344, 359–64

Andrew (1878–1862) 5, 11, 80, 82–4, 86–7, 91–4, 100, 102–3, 107, 109, 111–12, 119, 121, 123, 125, 140, 144, 147, 159, 160, 166, 168, 190
Andrew (1897–1917) 365–6
Barbara (b. 1906) 362
Beatrice (d. 1862) 166, 168, 361
Bridget (b. 1903) 362
Catharine Isabel 'Isa' (1844–1915) 5, 111, 121, 125, 141, 146, 155, 168–9, 174,
Charlotte Anne (*née* Trevelyen) 147, 166, 168, 194, 200, 360–2
Edward (1872–1944) 362, 364–5, 367
Euphemia 'Effie' (1837–1914) 5, 6, 102, 111, 143, 146–7, 155, 168
Fowell Buxton (1839–1914) 5, 111, 115, 142, 146, 200, 359, 363, 365, 366
Julia (*née* Chalmers) 362–3
Miles 362–3
Olaf 365
Priscilla (*née* Buxton 1808–1852) 5, 11, 91, 93–4, 96, 99, 100, 103, 104, 106, 107, 111–16, 119–25, 139–44
Priscilla (b. 1912) 362–4
Priscilla Hannah 'Pris' (1842–1912) 1–7, 11, 25, 114–16, 119, 121–2, 125–6, 129–30, 141, 145–6, 150, 155, 159, 160, 162, 165, 169, 176, 178–9, 190–1, 194–6, 200–5, 211–16, 218–24, 226–7, 231–4, 236, 238, 244–6, 253, 254–8, 261–3, 270–1, 274, 279–80, 282, 295, 300, 302, 305, 320, 325–7, 329–30, 332–3, 337–9, 341–3, 345–7, 349–50, 357, 359, 370
Sarah Maria (b. 1840) 5, 111, 140–1, 146, 155, 164, 168–9, 174, 190, 203

MacInnes Family
Campbell (d. 1878) 283, 293, 295, 369
Dora (d. 1941) 283, 293, 295
Mrs E J MacInnes 2
Euphemia (*née* Johnston 1837–1914) 6, 156, 162, 168, 200, 202–3, 274, 279, 290–3, 295, 297, 298, 344, 360, 368–9
Eva (d. 1942) 283, 293
Grace (d. 1934) 170, 283, 292
Harry (d. 1884) 279, 283, 296, 369
Jean 2, 292, 296
John (d. 1925) 283, 296, 368–9
Miles (1830–1909) 2, 6–7, 155, 168, 200, 222, 279, 283, 285–91, 295–9, 364, 367–8
Neil (d. 1815) 283, 295, 297, 344
Rennie (d. 1931) 283, 293, 296, 369

Walker family
Arthur de Nóe Walker 200, 245, 370
Catharine Isabel 'Isa' (*née* Johnston) 200, 221–2, 231, 245, 370, 372

Wilson Family
Rev. Daniel F Wilson 190, 200
Sarah Maria (*née* Johnston) 200

Index of Others

Bardsley, Mrs 342
Bashi-Bazouks 227, 230, 235, 236,
Beevor, Amy 6, 7, 279, 300, 305, 349, 353, 370, 371
Blake, Dr Jex 366
Bowman, William 328
Broome, Revd. Arthur 310–3,
Burdett-Coutts, Baroness 320
Carlyle, Thomas 6, 213, 137
Dickens, Charles 335
Disraeli 221, 237
Evans, Arthur, of the *Manchester Gazette* 235, 236, 255, 258
Erskine, Lord 309
Fox, George 21, 22, 23
Gladstone 2, 213, 136–8
Garrow, Sir William 309,
Gompertz, Lewis 312–14

Head Head, George (b. 1799) 288–9
Irby, Adeline Paulina 2, 5, 206, 209–12, 214–16, 218–27, 231–4, 236–8, 244–6, 253–8, 261–3, 270, 274, 357–9
Jose, Professor 224, 234, 254
Laseron, Dr Michael 227
Macghan, J.A. of the *Daily News* 229, 231
Manby, Captain 152–4
Martin, Richard 309–12
May, Sophia 246
Monkhouse Head, Joseph (b. 1759) 156
Muir MacKenzie, Georgina 210–12, 216, 236
Nightingale, Florence 6, 211, 214–15, 223–6, 228, 245, 255, 261, 329

Paget, Verily Anderson 2, 130, 148, 151, 199
Pultney, Sir W. 308
Pusey, Edward Bouverie 328
Rathbone, William 328–9
Robinson, Mary 328
Romilly, Samuel 309
Sewell, Anna 1, 2
Saul, G.F. 282, 325, 344, 346, 352–3
Shore Smith, William 223–6, 256
Wakefield, Priscilla 4
Wilberforce 66, 308–9
Victoria, Queen 150, 171, 312, 315–16,

Index of Places

Bank House, Halesworth 5, 108–10, 114, 120, 140
Carlisle and County High School for Girls 6, 279, 300, 305, 371, 373
Carlisle and District State Management Scheme 372
Carlisle and District Women's League 372
City General Hospital, Carlisle 334, 336, 340
Corby Nr Carlisle 183–6
Earlham Hall 2, 22, 26, 28, 41, 42, 46, 79, 146
Easneye 197–8
Fusehill Union Workhouse, Carlisle 283, 334, 336
Holton Hall, Sussex 84, 147, 158, 166
Lanercost 191
Leytonstone 127, 142, 161, 163, 197
MacInnes Memorial Hall, Stanwix, Carlisle 353, 367
Mumps Hall, Glisland 186–90
Newgate Prison 12, 19

Northrepps Hall, Cromer 5, 15, 61, 80, 111, 114–16, 120–2, 125, 127, 130, 134, 137, 148, 158, 165, 174, 194, 196, 206, 293
Northrepps Cottage, Cromer 15, 61, 78, 112–13, 124, 129
Overstrand Church 124, 139, 144, 167–8, 203–5, 280–1, 353–4
10 Ovington Gardens, London 231–3, 245
Rennyhill, Fifeshire 5, 84–5, 94, 96, 98, 101–2, 104–6, 108
Rickerby 6, 7, 155–7, 179, 286–94, 296–8
St Martins College 334
St Mary's Church, Halesworth 116, 118, 167
St Michael's Church, Stanwix 367, 369
Stanwix Cemetery 341, 370–2
The Beeches, Rickerby 1, 6, 274, 279, 302, 341, 345, 349, 350, 370
Uffizi Art Gallery, Italy 370
Wetheral Nr Carlisle 180–3
Willis's Rooms, London 213, 237, 253,

Index of Places Abroad

Agram 224
Austria 233, 253–4, 258, 261–3, 274, 357
Balkans 206, 212–13, 216
Bosnia 5, 210–12, 218–19, 222–3, 232–3, 236–8, 253–4, 256, 258, 261–3, 357–9
Brod 217, 219
Bulgaria 2, 226–7, 229, 231–2, 342
Croatia 214, 232, 234, 254, 358
Dalmatia 214, 223, 234, 236, 255, 258, 358
Gradiska 219, 224
Herzegovina 2, 210, 218, 221, 223, 237–8, 256, 357

Hungary 233, 254, 257
Knin 233–6, 244, 253–5, 258, 262
Montenegro 223, 227, 256, 358
Ottoman Empire 228, 256
Pakrac 233, 244
Ragusa 226, 234
Sarajevo 5, 212, 216–20, 261–3, 274, 357, 358
Serbia 2, 222–3, 227, 232–3, 254, 263, 357, 358
Slavonia 212, 234, 237
Strimca 234
Zara 234

Index of Events

1862 Great Exhibition, Crystal Place Sydenham 171–173
1873 Wedding of Prince of Wales 174–179
Anti Slavery Campaign/Bill 67, 81–3, 86–7, 92, 95
Cross of Takova 262

Gladstone's speech (1877) 238–244
National Health Service 340
Poor Law Act 335, 336
Treaty of Stefano 213
The Eastern Question 212, 213

Index of Funds

The Bosnian and Herzogovina Fugitives Orphan Relief Fund 213–14, 222–3

The Eastern War Sick and Wounded Relief Fund 228
Turco-Serbian Relief Fund 228

Index of Societies

Carlisle Board of Guardians 2, 6, 282, 335
Carlisle Charitable Organisation 2, 6
Carlisle Charity Organisation Society 282, 301, 330, 332–3
Carlisle Council of Social Services 334
Carlisle County Voluntary Service 333
Carlisle District Nursing Association 2, 6
Cumberland & Westmorland Branch of the RSPCA 323–4
Dr Barnardos 362
Girls' Friendly Society 304
Metropolitan Drinking Fountain and Cattle Trough Association 350
Naples Society for the Protection of Animals 282, 325–7, 346
National Aid Society 228
NSPCC 2, 282, 320
Nursing Association 283, 342
Royal Society for the Prevention of Cruelty to Animals 2, 6, 11, 25, 282, 291, 301, 306, 322, 323, 325, 342, 344–6, 352
Society of Friends (Quakers) 12, 21–3, 25, 27, 246
Women's Temperance Association 342